# Seven Gothic Dramas

## 1789–1825

*Edited with an Introduction*
*by* JEFFREY N. COX

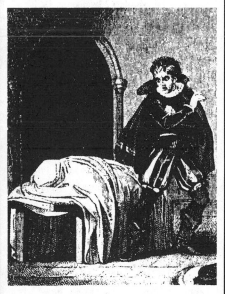

OHIO UNIVERSITY PRESS ATHENS

**Library of Congress Cataloging-in-Publication Data**

Seven Gothic Dramas, 1789–1825 / [edited by] Jeffrey N. Cox.
Includes bibliographical references.
Contents: The Kentish barons / by Francis North — Julia of
Louvain, or, Monkish cruelty / by John Cartwright Cross — The
castle spectre / by Matthew G. Lewis — The captive / by Matthew G.
Lewis — De Monfort / by Joanna Baillie — Bertram, or, The castle
of St. Aldobrand / by Charles Robert Maturin — Presumption, or, The
fate of Frankenstein / by Richard Brinsley Peake.
ISBN 0–8214–1015–6     ISBN 0–8214–1065–2 (pbk.)
1. Horror plays, English.   2. Gothic revival (Literature) — Great
Britain.   3. English drama — 19th century.   4. English drama — 18th
century.   I. Cox, Jeffrey N.
PR635.H67S48   1992
822'.05270806 — dc20   91–31262   CIP

Introduction copyright © 1992 by Jeffrey N. Cox
Printed in the United States of America
Ohio University Press books are printed
on acid-free paper ∞

97  96  95  94  93     5  4  3  2  1   (pbk.)
Library of Congress Cataloging in
Publication Data appears on the last
printed page of this book.

# Contents

# Introduction

On 14 December 1797, Matthew Gregory "Monk" Lewis's *The Castle Spectre* was played for the first time at the Theatre Royal, Drury Lane. Rarely did Drury Lane have such a success. Opening half-way through the season, *The Castle Spectre* was performed forty-seven more times before the theater closed for the summer in June, an extraordinary run at a repertory theater of the day. It was offered another nineteen times during the next season at Drury Lane; and, in eloquent testimony to the play's popularity, the rival Theatre Royal, Covent Garden, also presented the play on 30 April 1799 during a period when it was still being offered on almost a weekly basis at Drury Lane.

*The Castle Spectre* long continued as part of the repertoire, receiving regular performances until the 1820s and revivals in 1838 (Drury Lane), 1840 (Sadler's Wells), and 1880 (Gaiety). It opened in New York on the first of June 1798 and was still being performed there thirty-six years later, in 1834. Lewis's biographer and best critic, Louis F. Peck, records the comments on the Drury Lane playbills that testify to the audience's infatuation with the play: "The Fatigue attending the representation of some of the Characters renders it impossible to repeat the performance every night in the week" (18 December 1797); "Notwithstanding the great demand for places for the Castle-Spectre; the system of giving as much Novelty as possible at this Theatre necessarily prevents its repetition till Monday next, when it will be performed for the 22nd. time" (15 January 1798). John Waldie, D. Lit. and indefatigable theater enthusiast, might stand for many other avid theater-goers in his continued delight in the play, which lead him to see it at least four times at different theaters over a ten-year period.[1]

The *Biographia Dramatica* tells us that "Except, perhaps, *Pizarro* and *Blue Beard*, this piece was, we believe, more productive of *profit* to the theatre than any other for twenty years preceding it." Of course, the *Biographia Dramatica* goes on to relate an anecdote about a disagreement between Lewis and Sheridan: "about the end of the season, Sheridan and Lewis had some dispute in the green-room; when the latter offered, in confirmation of his arguments, to bet Sheridan all the money which the Castle Spectre had brought, that he was right—no, said Sheridan, I cannot afford to bet so much; but I'll tell you what I'll do—I'll bet you *all it is worth*!"[2]

Immense popularity and little critical respect—this might be the epitaph for the Gothic drama that filled the London stages in the decades around the turn from the eighteenth to the nineteenth century. We almost completely ignore these plays, that found such favor with audiences of the day, not yet finding in them the interest we have discovered in the Gothic romances which also sit at the margins of the "great tradition." It is ironic, given the obscurity of the Gothic drama, that the Gothic romance provides a key example of the new processes of canon reformation within the academy. A core of masterworks has been established, led by Radcliffe's *Italian*, Lewis's *The Monk*, Shelley's *Frankenstein*, and Maturin's *Melmoth the Wanderer* and backed up by many obscure popular novels that demonstrate the breadth of the Gothic's appeal. To demonstrate the importance of the Gothic to works within the traditional canon, scholars have located the Gothic impulse in as varied practitioners as Percy Shelley, Lawrence, Austen, and the Brontës. Criticism also reminds us of the Gothic presence still lurking within the horror movies and romances of contemporary culture. The Gothic novel is thus established as an important area of academic study, one valuable in its own right and having significance for the examination of the novelistic tradition as a whole and the exploration of our own culture.

But the Gothic drama has received no comprehensive attention since Bertrand Evans's *Gothic Drama from Walpole to Shelley* (1947). This neglect has persisted despite the fact that Lewis was at least as well known for his *Castle Spectre* as for *The Monk*, that Maturin was made famous by his tragedy *Bertram*, or that the popular image of *Frankenstein* probably owes more to a number of melodramas (and the films that grew out of them) than to the novel they purported to stage. We note the importance of the Gothic to the romantic poets but not the fact that Wordsworth and Coleridge, Shelley and Byron were more engaged in the Gothic drama than the novel. The Gothic drama has for the most part simply dropped out of our vision of the late eighteenth and early nineteenth centuries.

The Gothic drama's disappearance down a vampire trap of dramatic history is perhaps not so very surprising given the traditional scholarly treatment of late eighteenth- and early nineteenth-century drama. The history of the drama—particularly as it is embodied in anthologies and survey courses—leaps over the nineteenth century, or at least that part of it that precedes the advent of Ibsen, Strindberg, Checkov, and Shaw. However refined specific scholarly analyses of early nineteenth-century plays are, we teach a vastly simplified version of the history of the drama of which they are a part and, by doing so, perpetuate a devaluation of the past.

As Jerome McGann identifies a "romantic ideology" permeating the criticism of early nineteenth-century poetry which he believes has made it impossible for us to view this poetry objectively,[3] we might postulate a "dramatic ideology" found in the treatment of this period's drama which makes it nearly impossible for us to perceive it at all. We might define this "dramatic ideology" through two key features. First, there is what we might call the "peak phenomenon": a small number of great figures are seen as speaking to one another across the ages, from the rare mountain-tops of dramatic excellence—essentially Classical Athens, Renaissance and Baroque England, Spain, and France, and modern Europe from Ibsen to Brecht, Beckett, and Pinter. The rest of dramatic history is largely condemned to silence. The second underlying tenet might be termed the "culture gap": canonized plays are presented as having more in common with their great precursors and descendents than with the dramatic and theatrical cultures within which they were created. An account of dramatic history based on such precepts offers neither a synchronic grasp of the institution of drama during a particular period nor a diachronic sense of the drama's development. Such a "dramatic ideology" creates a deeply ahistorical conception of dramatic art, a "great man" account of the drama.

Of course, not all scholars of the drama or the theater have been captured by this "dramatic ideology"; we have many important studies that place plays within their context or that trace the slow evolution of dramatic features and forms. However, within this dominant critical perspective, the drama of the nineteenth century must always be a "valley" when compared to the celebrated "peaks" of dramatic history. Most anthologies, most survey courses, and even many histories of the drama skip from the late seventeenth century to the late nineteen-hundreds, with perhaps a glance at Sheridan, a glimpse of Diderot, or a nod at the great German drama of Goethe, Schiller, and Kleist. Even collections drawn specifically from nineteenth-century drama (such as those by Rowell and Corrigan) focus on Victorian plays and slight the earlier part of the century. The presence of the "culture gap" is even more striking in such selections of nineteenth-century plays, for these volumes tend to enforce the split between "high" and "low" culture that we are all told exists during the period. Thus, Kauvar and Sorenson's collection includes only verse dramas by major romantic and Victorian poets, from Wordsworth's *The Borderers* to Swinburne's *Atalanta in Calydon*, while Michael Booth's two volumes of nineteenth-century drama eschew the works of the poets for those of popular writers such as Pocock and Boucicault.[4]

This distorts our sense of the development of nineteenth-century drama. The concentration upon dramatic "peaks" results in a tendency to see nineteenth-century drama from the perspective of the great works of realism and naturalism that arise at the close of the era. The enforcement of the "culture gap" then artificially divides the drama of the period, relegating the works of the great writers of the day to the "closet" and finding in the popular works the preconditions for late nineteenth-century drama. The "peak" at the end of the century imposes a teleology on histories of the period: everything is presented as working towards the realistic drama—otherwise, it is dismissed as retrograde, mere "Elizabethanizing." The "gap" insures that our best dramatic and theatrical histories of the period provide a place for the Boadens, Kotzebues, and Pixérécourts, but not the Byrons, Schillers, and Hugos—let alone the Lewises, Baillies, and Maturins.

In order to have a fuller and more accurate history of nineteenth-century drama, we need to have before us the plays obscured by this "dramatic ideology." The Gothic drama provides one central set of texts that challenge the controlling preconceptions about nineteenth-century drama. These plays provide an opportunity to explore the complex interactions between authors, texts, genre, the literary institution of the theater, and larger cultural or ideological constructs during the late eighteenth and early nineteenth centuries. That is, they force us to move beyond an account of "great" dramatists and "key" texts to investigate the entire dramatic and theatrical scene as part of the even larger literary, cultural, and political landscape. The Gothic—as a meeting point between high and low culture negotiated by both popular writers such as James Boaden and J. C. Cross and canonized poets such as Byron and Shelley, as a mode that extends throughout much of the period's dramatic and nondramatic writing, and as a particular response to the literary, theatrical, and political pressures of the age of revolution—can tell us much about the drama and culture of its day. The story of the Gothic drama contradicts standard dramatic and theatrical histories, closing the gap between high and low forms, linking poetry and the novel to the theater, and establishing an alternative tradition to the movement towards late nineteenth-century realism.

This collection of Gothic dramas argues for a reconsideration of these all-but-lost plays. The volume includes works interesting in their own right and that also offer a framework for a history of the Gothic drama. While the Gothic arose as early as Walpole's *Mysterious Mother* (1768), the present collection begins with the explosion of Gothic works in the 1790s, offering the texts of Francis North's *Kentish Barons* (1791) and J. C. Cross's *Julia of Louvain; or, Monkish Cruelty* (1797). These plays can help us to define the Gothic drama during its first period of widespread success and to understand how it fit within the generic, institutional, and ideological structures of its day; more specifically, we will see that the Gothic becomes *the* dramatic form for the revolutionary years of the 1790s. Matthew Lewis's *The Castle Spectre* (1797), as I have already noted, stands as the greatest theatrical success of the Gothic drama, and it also serves as an exemplary model of Gothic dramatic techniques and tactics. Together with Lewis's *The Captive* (1807), *The Castle Spectre* enables us to explore the generic permutations of the Gothic, for these plays embody the two poles of dramatic practice at the turn of the century—the monodrama and the melodrama—and they suggest how Lewis, among others, would work to convert the Gothic into tragedy. We will also see how this move to transform the Gothic into "high" culture worked to limit its radical potential.

Joanna Baillie's *De Monfort* (1798) demonstrates that the Gothic was open to lines of development other than this conservative reformation. Like Lewis's plays, *De Monfort* comes at a point within the evolution of the Gothic that enables its author to reflect upon Gothic conventions, but Baillie does so not to render the Gothic ideologically tame but to raise potentially radical questions about its portrayal of women. The final two plays in the volume, Charles Robert Maturin's *Bertram; or, The Castle of St. Aldobrand* (1815) and Richard Brinsley Peake's *Presumption; or, The Fate of Frankenstein* (1823) provide a sketch of the second major phase of the Gothic drama, during the post-Napoleonic period. We find these plays continuing and extending Gothic conventions, but they do so within a changed literary and ideological moment. The Gothic drama after Waterloo is no longer the key theatrical resolution of the generic and political questions facing the dramatist; it is instead a protest against the dominant ideology of the day and against the rise of the new dominant popular form, the domestic melodrama. As a group, these plays outline a history of the Gothic drama and point to its importance to romantic literature, to subsequent drama, and to the transformations we identify with the age of democratic revolution.

## *1   Definitions of the Gothic*

Before examining the Gothic drama and theater in particular, we need a sense of what Gothicism has come to mean in general. Not surprisingly, our understanding of Gothic literature is derived almost solely from the study of the novel. There have been attempts (for example, Peter Thorslev's) to see the Gothic as representing a distinct vision of life within the culture of the romantic era, and some scholars have worked to sort out the relationship between the fiction and Gothic architecture. But, with the exception of Evans's ground-breaking study of the Gothic drama, the novel has dominated the discussion of the Gothic.[5] While these approaches to the Gothic through the novel will be useful in recovering the Gothic drama, we will only understand these plays and the literary history of which they are a part when we place them within their own particular generic and institutional context. Any discussion of the Gothic must begin with the ground-breaking work done on the romance, but any discussion of the Gothic *drama* must go beyond these studies.

Two main approaches to the Gothic novel have been pursued. The most prevalent strategy is to define the Gothic through its appurtenances—particularly the almost obligatory castle and its resident villain but also dungeons, monasteries, bands of robbers, gloomy forests, supernatural or monstrous creatures, rain-swept seacoasts, madwomen, suits of dusty armor, and mysterious strangers. Such definitions discover the Gothic in its settings, stock characters, and conventionalized situations; in the works of Montague Summers and Eino Railo, for example, we are offered massive compendia of Gothic devices. At its most limited such an approach can produce merely a list of atmospherics, but other studies, such as Eve Kosofsky Sedgwick's *The Coherence of Gothic Conventions*, emphasize the recurrence of motifs in order to understand the way they structure a comprehensible literary world, virtually a modern, popular myth. When these conventions are taken seriously for themselves, this approach offers a semiotics of the Gothic as a closed and self-coherent system of atmospheric signs.[6]

The second approach, which might be termed thematic rather than atmospheric, arises from the interpretation of this myth, when the focus shifts from these signs to what they signify. There have been three major attempts to thematize the Gothic. First, from Devendra Varma to Judith Wilt and R. D. Stock, the Gothic has been defined as a revelation of the holy, or numinous, whether it be defined as the providential, the demonic, or Dread. Another group of critics—William Patrick Day is one excellent example—explores the Gothic as a fantasy that uncovers the desires repressed by modern culture; this essentially psychological reading is particularly concerned with the ways in which the Gothic novel configures the self, gender, and sexuality. A third approach identifies the Gothic as a political myth, as a way of imagining the terrors of the French Revolution (Ronald Paulson, Peter Brooks), for example, or as a means to image the threatening rise of proletarian power (Chris Baldick).[7]

All of these are powerful approaches to the Gothic novel and ones that will be useful in understanding the Gothic drama. While they locate the meaning of the Gothic in different realms—the numinous, the psychological, the political—they share a common structure; for each of these approaches sees the Gothic as unveiling or recovering some unmediated absolute that stands outside the boundaries of the natural and social orders, whether it be the supernatural that miraculously disrupts these orders in *The Monk* or *Melmoth*, the psychologically repressed that returns in *Turn of the Screw* or *Frankenstein*, or the politically oppressed that threatens to erupt in *Caleb Williams* or, again, read differently, in *Frankenstein*. What this shared structure reveals is the extremism of the Gothic, its attempt to embody exactly those features of the psyche, the social order, or the cosmos that are least susceptible to representation and least liable to be controlled and assimilated. If the "great tradition" of the novel is concerned with minute particulars, with circumstancing characters and events within specifically defined social, psychic, and providential orders, then the Gothic novel seeks to explore the Absolute or the Chaos (depending upon one's vision) that can never be contained by those orders. It is not surprising that the masterworks of the Gothic arise at moments when the "great tradition" suffers ruptures in its development, with the key moment of the Gothic novel coming between the providential novels of the eighteenth century and the historically and socially grounded novels of the nineteenth and with later Gothic moments occurring in the rifts prior to the advent of both the modern and postmodern novel. The Gothic is an attempt to thematize exactly those features that resist containment within the various explanatory systems and contextualizations of the main novelistic tradition.

The Gothic drama shares with the novel the same appurtenances, and it embraces the same thematics of the extreme in its exploration of the supernatural, the psychological, and the political. However, the Gothic drama arises to resolve different problems than does the Gothic novel, for it takes its place in a different immediate institutional context—that of the theater—and its rather rapid rise and fall occur within a specific historical period defined by particular ideological pressures. More precisely, the Gothic drama—while it arises with Walpole and continues as a theatrical form throughout the nineteenth century—has two key historical moments, one during the 1790s and one around 1815. While it may seem too easy to link the Gothic to the two most symbolically charged events of the era—the fall of the Bastille and the fall of Napoleon—I contend that it is only during the period organized around these two events that the Gothic drama achieved its full power.

The first problem facing the dramatist inhered in the contemporary institution of theater: how to deal with a changing theatrical environment marked by both new and redesigned theatrical spaces. Second, the dramatist had to confront a perceived crisis in the hierarchy of dramatic forms, as tragedy and the comedy of manners, the traditional summits of the dramatist's art, no longer seemed to command large audiences or to be able to represent the issues of the day. Interwoven with these institutional and generic issues are the ideological struggles of the day. The Gothic, particularly in the drama and the theater, is a collective, historical construct, even if we may be more interested in either the Gothic's turn to the interior life or its interest in the atemporal supernatural. The ideological component of these plays reminds us that the drama more than any other literary form is a social product, an attempt to resolve social problems, here understood as involving ideological, generic or formal, and institutional components. In order to understand the development of the Gothic drama, we need first to have a firm sense of what these problems were. Neither the semiotics of Gothic atmosphere nor the thematics of Gothic structure will help us understand the Gothic drama until they are placed within the context that gave Gothic signs and structures their power.

## II  The Gothic Drama and the Theater

The immediate world of the Gothic drama was the physical space of the English stage. Both Drury Lane and Covent Garden, the two patent or "major" theaters in London, were enlarged during the 1790s. In 1792, Covent Garden was expanded to hold 3,013 people, about a fifty-percent increase over its size of 2,170 seats after its 1782 redesign. In 1794, Drury Lane was rebuilt. It had held 2,300, but it was reconstructed to hold at least 3,600 people and perhaps as many as 3,900.[8] As has often been noted, this change of scale had an immediate impact upon dramatic composition, acting, and staging techniques. Richard Cumberland's contemporary comments can be taken as typical:

Since the stages of Drury Lane and Covent Garden have been so enlarged in their dimensions to be henceforward theatres for spectators
rather than playhouses for hearers, it is hardly to be wondered at if
their managers and directors encourage those representations, to
which their structure is best adapted. The splendour of the scenes,
the ingenuity of the machinist and the rich display of dresses, aided
by the capitivating charms of music now in a great degree supercede
the labours of the poet. There can be nothing very gratifying in
watching the movements of an actor's lips, when we cannot hear the
words that proceed from them; but when the animating march
strikes up, and the stage lays open its recesses to the depth of a
hundred feet for the procession to advance, even the most distant
spectator can enjoy his shilling's-worth of show. What then is the
poet's chance?[9]

Cumberland laments the days of Garrick when what mattered was the
text and the actor's subtle interpretation of it. It was now impossible for an
actor or actress to rely upon small effects of voice or movement in such
cavernous halls. To give one indication of change, the 1794 Drury Lane
required the actor to project over 100 feet from the front of the stage while
the earlier theater had had a depth of only 60 feet. While some still felt
that the relatively small (1,500 seat) Haymarket theater offered a fine
showcase for the details of acting, Covent Garden and Drury Lane demanded new, larger gestures and effects.

Of course, the enlargement of theatrical space during the 1790s did not
occur only within Drury Lane and Covent Garden; it also occurred outside their walls and their will, through the opening of new theatres. The
two theatres royal had had patents granted to them in 1660, and their control of dramatic representation in London had been reinforced by the Licensing Act of 1737. The eighteenth century had seen the success of two
other theaters, but they were not direct threats: the "little theater" in the
Haymarket was licensed to perform plays during the summer when the
two "major" theaters were closed; and the King's Theatre became the
home to Italian opera. The cultural monopoly of the two main theaters
was still the central fact for the institution of the theater at the moment of
the Gothic drama's arrival, but there were increasingly important challenges to the patent houses as the century came to a close. In 1791, when
the King's Theatre opened to perform opera, the Sans Souci offered one-
man musicals; it was not the last time that the use of music would be essential to the survival of rivals to the theatres royal. Other theaters relied
upon alternative modes of entertainment. Astley's Royal Grove (one of
its many names) opened in 1777 as a site of equestrian shows that had

been given in the open air since 1768; it was outfitted with a stage as well as a circus ring in the 1780s and was reconstructed with perhaps the largest and finest stage in London in 1803. Its equestrian entertainments were matched by those of its main competitor, The Royal Circus, which opened in 1782. Sadler's Wells was offering nautical shows as early as 1765 and became under Charles Dibdin a major theatrical force at the very close of the century. These were so-called transpontine theaters, across the river from the city and the major theaters; but John Palmer tried a direct confrontation with the control of the "major" theaters in opening the Royalty Theatre offering plays at Wellclose Square in 1787. He hoped that a theater for Eastern London away from the Western theaters of Drury Lane, Covent Garden, and the Haymarket would be allowed, but the managers of the patent theaters forced his closure.[10]

Such new theaters—when they survived—did not just offer more seats to the ever growing population of London. They did not just compete with the "major" theaters for patrons. They offered a competing form of drama. Theaters specializing in naval spectaculars, equestrian shows, or pantomimes did not depend upon the spoken word. Of course, they were blocked by statute from offering the spoken drama, which was reserved for the patent theatres royal. Music, gesture, scenery, and spectacle thus became the basic theatrical tools for those "minor" houses. This form of the drama is best represented in the current volume by J. C. Cross's *Julia of Louvain; or, Monkish Cruelty* offered at The Royal Circus in 1797. The play is a pantomime that relies upon songs and sets for dramatic effect, though banners with simple messages are used at several key moments to make sure the audience understands a crux in the plot. Such plays and the non-verbal effects upon which they of necessity relied drew enthusiastic audiences. The enlarged theatres of Drury Lane and Covent Garden, the legally protected bastions of the spoken word, ironically came to rely upon these same new techniques not only because they were suitable to their cavernous auditoriums but also because the audiences increasingly demanded such fare. It is the new importance of sets, costumes, effects, and music that Cumberland laments, but these features provided the artists who collectively created dramatic events a whole new arsenal of theatrical techniques.

The nature of the new drama that arose in this expanded theatrical world can be suggested in a number of ways. One can point to the enormous advances in theatrical techniques, with the major innovations in lighting, scene painting, traps, and special effects being so important that one might want to find the true dramatic genius of the day not in the ranks of authors but in the company of such scenic artists as Philippe

Jacques de Loutherbourg, Thomas Greenwood, and William Capon. One might also note the shifts in acting styles. While the period is sometimes referred to as the Age of Kemble, it would make more sense to name it after his sister, Sarah Siddons, whose passionate and apparently overwhelming performances marked the new taste in acting that would also produce Edmund Kean. Again, one can note the dramatic types that come to dominate not only the "minor" stages but the "major" theaters as well. The melodrama became the key new form of the day, and as its name implies, music was essential to its success. The burletta, as Joseph Donohue has shown,[11] also began as a musical form, arising as it did from the comic opera; it became a device for the minor theaters to challenge the theatres royal, first by offering burletta versions of traditional plays such as *Macbeth* and then by slowly dropping the musical accompaniment to the spoken word. Pantomimes, spectaculars, and extravaganzas all filled the stage with non-verbal effects.[12]

There is, then, a "revolution" in the institution of the theater at the very concrete level of its material means of stage production—the structure of the theaters, the stage techniques, the acting styles. Such changes questioned the traditional theatrical means used to master theatrical space and to attract an audience. They also tended to undermine traditional generic distinctions. As the proliferation of new forms suggests, this transformation of theatrical techniques is matched by a shift in the hierarchy of dramatic types. John Genest's descriptions of plays of the period testify to the erosion of the traditional definitions of dramatic forms. We repeatedly find him making the complaint he lodges against Francis North's *Kentish Barons*, included in this volume, that a play is "a jumble of Tragedy, Comedy and Opera."[13] The collapse of the earlier hierarchy of dramatic types is testified to in the struggle between what comes to be termed the "legitimate" and the "illegitimate" drama. As Barry Sutcliffe among others has shown,[14] the "legitimate" drama—primarily tragedy and the comedy of manners—came to be seen not only as the legally protected form of the spoken drama controlled by the patent theaters but also as an embodiment of traditional moral, cultural, and social values. Questions about the "legitimate" drama were inevitably linked to questions of "legitimacy" in the political realm. The "illegitimate" drama was thus felt to be not only a threat to aesthetic quality—as pantomimes or equestrian spectacles edged Shakespeare or Congreve from the stage—but also as a challenge to the political and cultural order.

We should be very careful about paralleling "revolutions" in artistic styles with revolutions in the economic, social, and political orders. The troubled relations between the artistic avant-garde and radical politics in

our century teach us to be skeptical of easy links between artistic and political innovations; the French Revolution's reinvigoration of classicist motifs in an age we label romantic is another challenge to such connections.
Still, the 1790s do offer a moment when radical transformations in the
institution of the theater and in the hierarchy of dramatic forms are seen
as parallels to the revolutionary events of the day; or, perhaps more precisely, the changes within the theater and the drama offer an opportunity
for writers to work out in artistic terms the ideological struggles of the era
of Burke and Paine.

I want to make the rather surprising claim that the Gothic drama is the
most subtle theatrical attempt of the 1790s to resolve the ideological, generic, and institutional problems facing playwrights of the day. At least
for a moment, the Gothic drama offered a way to overcome the strains
placed upon theatrical representation—essentially through a new aesthetic of sensationalism. It seemed to resolve the tensions within the hierarchy of genres—essentially by discovering a new ground of high
tragedy in the tactics of popular drama. And the Gothic provided the
means to represent the ideological struggles of the day in a way that would
not arouse the wrath and thus the censorship of the Lord Chamberlain's
Examiner of Plays, John Larpent. The Gothic is *the* theatrical form in the
1790s because it could contain all of pressures placed upon the drama.

### III   The Birth of the Gothic Drama from the Spirit of Sensationalism

Of course, the Gothic drama did not arise with the Fall of the Bastille,
though it is only after 1789—the year not only of the Bastille but also of
Ann Radcliffe's first novel, *The Castles of Athlin and Dunbayne*—that the
Gothic drama becomes a real force in the theater.[15] Horace Walpole's *The
Mysterious Mother* (1768; printed privately and not performed) is usually
cited as the first Gothic drama. While plays such as Home's *Douglas* (Edinburgh, 1756; Covent Garden, 1757) are cited by Evans as examples of
even earlier works with Gothic tendencies and while one can trace elements within Gothic plays back to Otway, Southerne, and Lee, to the
heroic drama, and to Elizabethan and Jacobean works, *The Mysterious
Mother* marks a convenient point of origin, especially as it can then be
matched with Walpole's *Castle of Otranto* (1764), the first Gothic novel.
This "first" Gothic play already includes many of the surface features that
would continue to mark the Gothic drama, and its author already understood the innovations of the Gothic that would be empowered by the
charged atmosphere of the 1790s.

We find in Walpole's play much of the machinery that would comprise
the Gothic. The play opens upon a desolate castle, described as having

"antique towers / And vacant courts [that] dull the suspended soul, / Till expectation wears the cast of fear"(I, i).[16] The appropriately fearful atmosphere established, we are introduced to the reclusive countess, clearly consumed by guilt and remorse for some unnamed past crime. Her only neighbors are the friars of a nearby convent, one of whom—Friar Benedict—will seek revenge for her refusal to find comfort in confession and the Church. The climax of the play hinges upon the revelation of a series of past family relations—that the countess has, on the night of her husband's death and in order to prevent her son from consummating an affair, found her way to her son's bed and later borne him a child; and that the son—banished all these years—has secretly returned to marry, unknowingly, his sister/daughter. The countess goes mad with guilt upon revealing her secret, and the son exits to die in war after telling his wife/sister/daughter to enter a convent. The castle, the reclusive hero or heroine, the guilty past, the accumulation of appalling horrors and deaths—these would continue to be the hallmarks of the Gothic drama.

The most controversial feature of Walpole's play—and the one that marks its participation in the Gothic's thematics of the extreme—is the incest at the center of his plot. In recognizing in the postscript to his play that incest would serve primarily to disturb his audience ("The subject is more truly horrid than even that of Oedipus," he wrote), Walpole points to the link between thematic extremism and the key stylistic feature of the Gothic drama, its sensationalism, its status as a theater of shock, surprise, seduction, and terror:

> . . . I found it so truly tragic in the essential springs of terror and pity, that I could not resist the impulse of adapting it to the scene, though it could never be practicable to produce it there. I saw, too, that it would admit of great situation, of lofty characters, of those unforeseen strokes, which have a singular effect in operating a revolution in the passions, and in interesting the spectator: it was capable of furnishing not only a contrast of characters, but *a contrast of virtue and vice in the same character*; and *by laying the scene in what age and country I pleased pictures of manners might be drawn*, and many allusions to historic events introduced . . . .[17]

Walpole seems to find the Gothic to be a free-floating signifier that can be attached to "*what age and country I pleased*," the chosen time and place providing the appropriate historical allusions. What I will suggest is that the later Gothic drama becomes at least temporarily fixed after the taking of the Bastille, that its free-floating signifiers drift to the shore of revolutionary history. Walpole's analysis of his play as embodying a form that is clearly at odds with the ideological and aesthetic structures that underpin the notions of decorum and moral sentiment already suggests the reasons why the Gothic could serve playwrights confronting the aesthetic, institutional, and ideological problems of the 1790s.

At the center of Walpole's defense of his representation of incest is his claim for its sensationalist emotional appeal, its ability to create a "revolution in the passions." This sensationalism is different from both sentimentalism and sensibility, hallmarks of the earlier eighteenth-century drama. Janet Todd has defined a "sentiment" as "a moral reflection, a rational opinion usually about the rights and wrongs of human conduct . . . . a 'sentiment' is also a thought, often an elevated one, influenced by emotion, a combining of heart with head or an emotional impulse leading to an opinion or a principle." As Todd's definition suggests, the literature of sentiment evokes emotions as complements not opponents to the reason appealed to in other eighteenth-century works, for both reason and sentiment are providentially ordered paths to moral truths. Todd then argues that "sensibility" "came to denote the faculty of feeling, the capacity for extremely refined emotion and a quickness to display compassion for suffering."[18] While sensibility is often linked to the physical structure of the nervous system and while it can easily become excessive, it too is normatively seen as moral, as the exercise of refined emotions leading to compassion. Walpole's passage on *The Mysterious Mother* calls upon neither sentiment nor emotional sensibility but the passions— which are often seen as opposed to rather than working with reason; and it calls for a revolution in these passions, or a complete overthrow of the normal emotional order. Walpole is not offering a work that will link emotion to reason in a providential pattern issuing in a didactic moral lesson; his work is meant to shock, to overcome our conventional responses, to elicit passion outside of any providential or moral order.

This move beyond conventional moral response is also revealed in his account of the characters to be portrayed in his work, which he tells us will be morally mixed with "virtue and vice in the same character." This ambiguity surrounding the moral valence of the Gothic characters creates a tension between the sympathy and judgment that were in harmony in the literature of sentiment and sensibility. Walpole declares war here upon the decorous ideas of morally classified characters and of poetic justice. This creation of characters who escape the moral vision of the work that contains them was to be one of the most controversial features of the Gothic drama, decried by Coleridge and Scott among many others.

This sensationalist and perhaps amoral drama was seen as particularly dangerous, for—as Walpole's statement again suggests—the Gothic could be offered as a new form of tragedy: the "illegitimate" drama threatened to replace the central form of the "legitimate" drama. Within the charged context of the years following the French Revolution, the Gothic would arise as a new form of serious drama. In the hands of writers such as Baillie, Lewis, and Maturin—not to mention Shelley and Byron—it would for a moment seem to create a new, at times subversive form of tragedy. Walpole, then, already outlines a potentially revolutionary form that would challenge conventional aesthetics and launch an assault upon the tragic summit of the dramatic hierarchy. Within the context of the 1790s, this revolutionary form would be seen to move to the rhythms of the Revolution itself.

## IV  The Triumph of the Gothic Drama: The 1790s

Between Walpole's *Mysterious Mother* and 1789 a few plays appeared that clearly belong to the Gothic drama, most importantly works by Hannah More (*Percy;* Covent Garden, 1777) and Hannah Cowley (*Albina, Countess of Raimond;* Covent Garden, 1779). The Gothic was familiar enough by the late 1780s for James Cobb to offer his comic opera *The Haunted Tower* (Drury Lane, 1789) which burlesques Gothic motifs, and yet new enough for Miles Peter Andrews to call the supernatural effects of *The Enchanted Castle* (Covent Garden, 1786) an "experiment" that "hitherto . . . has not been made."[9] Still, it is in the 1790s that the Gothic drama truly comes to dominate the theater.

The drama of the 1790s is represented in this volume by Francis North's *The Kentish Barons,* offered at the Haymarket in June of 1791, J. C. Cross's *Julia of Louvain; or, Monkish Cruelty,* staged at the Royal Circus in 1797, and Lewis's *The Castle Spectre,* first played at Covent Garden in the same year. These dramas offer a sense of the Gothic across the decade and across the theatrical landscape, from the patent theatre royal at Covent Garden to the "little" theater in the Haymarket and the Royal Circus, a "minor" theater. While in formal terms, these plays range from a verse play with hints of tragedy (*The Kentish Barons*) to a pantomime (*Julia of Louvain*), they engage a strikingly similar set of dramatic conventions and tactics. Together they suggest the ways in which the Gothic drama of the 1790s served as a popular solution to a series of problems facing the dramatist.

As noted above, the first problem was simply that of winning an audience. North's *Kentish Barons* was, according to the *Biographia Dramatica,* "well written, and was favourably received"; the *Morning Chronicle* (26 June 1791) reported that the drama was performed "to a most crowded audience and received with very marked and rapturous applause." Genest tells us the play was performed ten times, a respectable run; it opened on 25 June and had its final performance a month later on 25 July. This is, of course, far short of the success of *The Castle Spectre* with its initial run of forty-seven performances and its continuing presence in the repertoire.[20]

In order to be successful, a play had to be able to command its theatrical space and compete with other theaters all trying to fill their halls with spectators. As I have already suggested, this challenge was largely met by creating a new theater of shock and sensation. As in the current horror or Gothic film, special effects could make or break a new Gothic drama. It was clearly the appearance of the ghost in *The Castle Spectre*, for example, that made Lewis's play such a success. Writing in 1825, Boaden could still say that this play "is too strongly impressed upon the memories of all my readers to require in this place any detail of its story." It is the ghost that particularly fills Boaden's memory:

> . . . I yet bring before me, with delight, the waving form of Mrs. Powell, advancing from the suddenly illuminated chapel, and bending over Angela (Mrs. Jordan) in maternal benediction; during which slow and solemn action, the band played a few bars, or rather the full *subject* at all events, of Jomelli's *Chaconne*, in his celebrated overture in three flats.[21]

It is important to remember how much of the effect of the Gothic drama (and its cinematic descendants) is generated through simply having something jump out at us unexpectedly. Whether it is North's Mortimer charging on stage to prevent the captured Elina from escaping in *The Kentish Barons* or the fight between the hero and villain as a storm erupts overhead in *Julia of Louvain* or the editing cut to a slashing knife in *Psycho*, the Gothic relies upon the jolts and joys of sensationalism. We are so used to such effects that I think we forget their radical departure from conventional stagecraft. Most drama is structured to fulfill our expectations; even dramatic irony is a reordering of our expectations, a move to force us to see that what we had been perceiving one way actually makes sense in another way. Thus, *Oedipus*, which in one way has as sensational a content as any Gothic drama, does not shock us through the unexpected, but instead offers us the awe-ful truth of the providentially ordered: what happens to Oedipus is exactly what has been expected and predicted by the oracle. *Macbeth*, for all its witches and supernatural aura, does not rely upon shock tactics. *Macbeth*, like all traditional tragedy, may evoke terror and pity, but it moves to purge them from the audience even as they are experienced within the play. The Gothic drama, however, even when it reaches for the tragic heights, provokes terror in the audience. Macbeth is terrified by the witches; *we* are terrorized by the spectres and madmen of the Gothic.

Critics and audiences found this sensationalism new and disturbing, and not merely for aesthetic reasons. As the attack upon the Gothic through the satiric *Rovers* (1798) in *The Anti-Jacobin* indicates, the new drama was linked to political innovation. The fictitious Jacobin author of *The Rovers* explains that what is called by *The Anti-Jacobin* the "German drama" requires a new "SYSTEM comprehending not Politics only, and Religion, but Morals and Manners, and generally whatever goes to the composition or holding together of Human Society; in all of which a total change and Revolution is absolutely necessary."[22] Wordsworth seems in agreement with *The Anti-Jacobin* when he attacks "frantic novels" and "sickly and stupid German Tragedies" in the "Preface" to *Lyrical Ballads* (1800); for this complaint about Gothic novels and dramas occurs in the midst of a discussion of the destruction of the public's ability to respond to life imaginatively, a reduction of the people to a "savage torpor" brought on by "the great national events which are daily taking place, and the encreasing accumulation of men in cities, where the uniformity of their occupations produces a craving for extraordinary incident."[23] Coleridge, too, would attack the Gothic for political as well as aesthetic reasons, recalling the *The Anti-Jacobin*'s assault in defining the Gothic as "the modern jacobinical drama":

> Eighteen years ago [in *Satyrane's Letters* of 1798] I observed, that the whole secret of the modern jacobinical drama, (which, and not the German, is its appropriate designation,) and of all its popularity, consists in the confusion and subversion of the natural order of things in their causes and effects: namely, in the excitement of surprise by representing the quality of liberality, refined feeling, and a nice sense of honour . . . in persons and in classes where experience teaches us least to expect them; and by rewarding with all the sympathies which are the due of virtue, those criminals whom law, reason, and religion have excommunicated from our esteem.[24]

We hear stated in this passage the central objection to the Gothic, that it confuses our judgment by offering sympathy to immoral characters; and this too is linked to sensationalism ("the excitement of surprise") and seen primarily in political and class terms. Scott would follow Coleridge and others of his generation in finding in the Gothic "a sort of intellectual jacobinism."[25] The claim that literary choices have ideological implications would not have surprised these writers.

Such comments suggest that, at the time, political and theatrical change were seen to mirror one another. James Boaden claimed that "The present was the age of revolutions. The most surprising events had occurred on the stage of real life, and the mimic world followed. . . ."[26] Boaden commented more specifically upon the theatrical representations of the taking of the Bastille: "The French Revolution had now opened upon the world in all its horrors; and the stage, 'which echoes but the public voice,' was now destined to rave about that cage of tyranny, the Bastile [sic], which, like Newgate in the year 1780, had been besieged by a virtuous populace, and all its dark secrets returned to the light of day and the blessings of freedom."[27] It is in the context of such close links between theatrical innovation and political change that Elizabeth Inchbald's statement on the O.P. or Old Price riots makes sense: "If the public force the managers to reduce their prices a revolution in England is effected."[28]

Or, to follow the analogy in the other direction, we might note some of the theatrical images used by Burke to describe revolutionary events: "the French revolution is the most astonishing that has hitherto happened in the world. . . . Every thing seems out of nature in this strange chaos of levity and ferocity, and all sorts of crimes jumbled together with all sorts of follies. In viewing this monstrous tragi-comic scene, the most opposite passions necessarily succeed, and sometimes mix with each other in the mind; alternate contempt and indignation; alternate laughter and tears; alternate scorn and horror." Burke sounds here like Genest protesting the mixture of genres in the contemporary drama. Again, Burke finds the demand for revolution itself to be parallel to the demand for novelty and effect in the theater: "Plots, massacres, assassinations, seem to some people a trivial price for obtaining a revolution. A cheap, bloodless reformation, a guiltless liberty, appear flat and vapid to their taste. There must be a great change of scene; there must be a magnificent stage effect; there must be a grand spectacle to rouze [sic] the imagination. . . ."[29] At this point, it is not clear whether the "mimic world" is mirroring the Revolution or whether the Revolution itself is a result of a "debased" taste most clearly seen in the theatrical fare of the day.

What I want to suggest is that, for a moment in the 1790s, the separable histories of the institution of the theater, of dramatic forms, and of ideological struggle follow the same course. More specifically, the essentials of the Gothic setting and plot—the castle, the villain, the heroine's capture and escape—could be read as embodying the rhythms of the Revolution and its liberation of enclosed spaces from the powers of the past.

The castle is seen as so conventional a feature of the Gothic as to rate little more than obligatory notice, but in the 1790s the castle takes on a particular significance. It certainly is the case that the castle—or some other enclosed space—is a virtual necessity in the Gothic drama. Of the plays included here, two works—*The Castle Spectre* and *Bertram; or, The Castle of St. Aldobrand*—announce the presence of castles in their titles; North opens *The Kentish Barons* with the hero and his confidant Bertram within an "Old Castle." *Julia of Louvain* offers a convent with a horrifying sepulchre, and Lewis's *The Captive* transpires within an asylum/prison. While Baillie's *De Monfort* is an important example of a play without a castle, it still places its murder on a "wild path in a wood, shaded with trees" and closes in a convent. Later, Peake's dramatization of *Frankenstein* also offers wild natural scenery but, as we will see, presents a new sinister Gothic locale, the laboratory.

We could obviously extend the list with references to such plays as James Cobb's *The Haunted Tower* (Drury Lane, 1789), Miles Peter Andrews's *The Mysteries of the Castle* (Covent Garden, 1795), or George Charles Carr's *The Towers of Urbandine* (York and Hull, 1805); other Gothic sites can be found in James Boaden's *Fontainville Forest* (Covent Garden, 1794), the anonymous *Mystic Cavern* (Norwich, 1803), and Lewis's *Venomi; or, The Novice of St. Mark's* (Drury Lane, 1808). Manfred's "Gothic Chamber," the Castle of Petralla in Shelley's *The Cenci,* and the Borderlands of Wordsworth's *The Borderers* are all conventional Gothic scenes.

The significance of the castle can be quickly seen if we consider for a moment the actual physical appearance of these ancient fortresses. The castle is presented as a feature of the past being represented on stage. However, as the ruined nature of many of these castles suggests, this is not a depiction of the past as it was, since that would require the castles to be new; what we have instead is an emblem of the past's influence in the present, the hold that the old world—even in decay—has upon the future. In his preface to *The Castle of Otranto,* Walpole jests about his moral being "that *the sins of the fathers are visited on their children to the third and fourth generation*";[30] but he here illuminates a key feature of the Gothic, the representation of the past's attempt to control the present and the future. It is no accident that the Gothic drama with its imposing castles becomes increasingly popular on the London stage after 1789 and the Fall of the Bastille. Like the ruined Gothic castle, the Bastille might no longer be an actual tool of an oppressive *ancien regime,* but it stood as the emblem of a past that needed to be overcome. And, in fact, in the early days of the Revolution before the censor John Larpent moved to prohibit plays dealing directly with revolutionary events, several works such as John Dent's *The Bastille* (Royal Circus, 1789) and John St. John's *The Island of St. Marguerite* (Drury Lane, 1789) about the Man in the Iron Mask adopted

Gothic formulas to enact recent history. When history appears to play-wrights to move to a Gothic plot, we are encouraged to read Gothic devices in historical terms.

The plays that deal directly with the Revolution share with the Gothic drama a basic pattern of movement, from an enclosed space—a prison, a castle, a convent—to an open one. This dramatic trajectory may have its roots in conventions of dramatic romance (one thinks of the movement to a "green world" in Shakespeare's romances and romantic comedies),[31] but during the 1790s the pattern would be read as moving from the closed world of the past into the open world of a free future. The historical ground of this pattern can be seen in *The Bastille*, in which the taking of the Bastille and its horrific (if purely fictional) torture chambers is followed by a celebration on the Place de Dauphin; the very sets embody a move from imprisonment to liberation. In its final celebratory scene, Dent's play attempts to reenact a specific moment of revolutionary history, a speech given by Moreau de St. Mery to the French troops; but more interestingly, this Gothic history play predicts in its rhythms the pattern of later festivals enacted in revolutionary France.

This pattern is perhaps even clearer in a play included here, *Julia of Louvain; or, Monkish Cruelty*, a pantomime taken, the published text tells us, "from a paragraph in a Newspaper during the French Revolution."[32] The plot of Cross's play is simple. Julia is engaged to Clifford, but also sought by the aristocratic Gothic villain, St. Pierre. When she pledges herself to Clifford, St. Pierre offers her the choice of marriage to him or a convent. She chooses the convent, where she discovers she is at the mercy of St. Pierre's accomplices, Father Bonesse and the Abbess. When she continues to refuse St. Pierre, the religious entomb her beneath the convent until she is found "under a noisome sack . . . pale, emaciated, almost expiring, and for a time bereft of reason . . ." (sc. x). She is freed, St. Pierre is killed, the Abbess and the friar are arrested by the Municipality, and the play ends upon a scene reminiscent of a revolutionary fête: "A splendid and Picturesque View, with the Altar of Hymen at a distance." The open view and the classical altar mark this as a revolutionary space, where the victory of the lovers and of "Peace and pleasure" over the machinations of the aristocracy and the Church can be celebrated (sc. xi).

Dent's prophetic turn to a revolutionary festival and Cross's evocation of the great fêtes of revolutionary France suggest the links between these Gothic plays and the actual festivals that took place in France. Mona Ozouf's treatment of space in these festivals is extremely suggestive for a map not only of directly political plays but of the Gothic drama as a whole:

. . . from the beginning of the Revolution a native connivance linked rediscovered liberty with reconquered space. The beating down of gates, the crossing of castle moats, walking at one's ease in places where one was once forbidden to enter: the appropriation of a certain space, which has to be opened and broken into, was the first delight of the Revolution.

. . . .

In seeking a location for the festival, the organizers never lost sight of this imperative: public enjoyment must be able to extend regularly and without obstacle. What was needed was a festive space that could contain an endless, irrepressible, and peaceful movement like the rise of tidal waters. In this, indeed, the space of the festival was the exact equivalent of the Revolutionary space itself, as described by Fichte in his *Considerations*: "While the luminous flood irresistibly spreads, the obscure islets grow smaller and break up, abandoned to the bats and owls."

. . . .

. . . the open air had the enormous advantage of being a space without memory and was therefore able to symbolize entry into a new world. . . . sometimes the location of the festival had to be established in a fractured space, and the participants had to travel from the altar of the fatherland along winding paths, through ramparts, past ruined towers, and across drawbridges. It may have been very unusual for the feudal settings to have such an insistent presence. But did it? The official accounts are eager to avoid the issue by reducing it to aesthetic curiosity: "One object contrasted even more with the prevailing atmosphere of the civic festival: this was the picturesque prospect of the crumbling ruins of an ancient castle."[33]

I quote at length from Ozouf because her brilliant analysis of revolutionary space is so suggestive for Gothic spaces. It is interesting how often in the quotations Ozouf uses and in her own account the language of the Gothic arises to describe by way of contrast the space of revolutionary festivals. The citation from Fichte contrasts the open flow of the Revolution with the bat and owl invested islets of the past. Ozouf sees the open spaces of the revolutionary festival contrasted with the twisting, enclosed spaces of a feudal, Gothic past. This movement from the cramped Gothic quarters of the city to an open revolutionary space parallels the movement of the Gothic, a parallel made explicit when the crumbling castle is brought into the view of the revolutionary celebrants. While there is an attempt to make the castle merely an aesthetic object—a picturesque prospect—this in itself is a political statement, a denial of the power of the past, which in its decayed state can only serve as a piquant contrast to the vibrant future. Of course, this displacement of the historical onto the aesthetic can never be complete. The ruined castle is an emblem of the victory of the Revolution; but it is also a reminder of the violence necessary to break with the past, a violence Ozouf argues the revolutionary festivals sought to repress in their celebrations of the future but of which the Gothic is constantly aware.

In Gothic play after play, we see the liberation of enclosed spaces: the storming of a convent in Boaden's adaptation of Lewis's *The Monk* as *Aurelia and Miranda* (Drury Lane, 1798) and in Cross's *Julia of Louvain; or, Monkish Cruelty*, the penetration of the villain's castle in North's *Kentish Barons*, the mob demanding the release of the Man in the Iron Mask in John St. John's *Island of St. Marguerite*, and the joint release of an imprisoned wife from her cliff prison and of a pursued maiden from a convent in Henry Siddons's *Sicilian Romance; or, The Apparition of the Cliff* (performed as *The Castle of Otranto*, Newcastle, 1793; as *Sicilian Romance*, Covent Garden, 1794). Lewis's *The Castle Spectre* offers several escapes, as the hero leaps from the window of the castle, several servants escape through secret passageways, and a long-imprisoned father is finally rescued from a subterranean dungeon; counterpoised to these various incarcerated figures are the peasants and troops accumulating in the forest's free space surrounding the castle. We have here and elsewhere the central movement from enclosure to liberation, with a castle, a dungeon, or a convent standing for the oppressive institutions of the play's world and a natural landscape—the home to the natural rights of peasants, heroic troops, or perhaps a noble robber band—often providing the site of uncovered and recovered identities.

This movement of liberation—from castle to open ground, from enclosed past to open future—provides the backbone of the plot, but it does not really define its shape. We might have a better sense of the total shape of the Gothic drama if we take more seriously Genest's constant comment about Gothic plays, that they are bad because they are a jumble of tragedy, comedy, and opera. Setting aside the aesthetic judgement, we should see that Genest is saying more than that these plays violate the decorous separation of genres. I think that he is getting at the mixed nature of the plots of these plays (his comments are largely plot summaries), which are in fact a combination of tragedy, comedy, and operatic romance (they are mixed media as well, which is part of his comment—there are songs, for example). These three strands will let us view three important aspects of these plays: the romance or quest structure that organizes the broadest outlines of the plot—the movement from confinement to liberation we have been discussing; the comic movement that unites the lovers and joins the thematics of love with those of liberty; and the potential tragedy of the villain-hero. This multiple plot structure also suggests that the ideology of the Gothic drama is not embodied in the simple movement from past to liberated future, that its reaction to revolutionary history is more complex, more deeply conflicted.

*The Kentish Barons*, for example, is, in the largest terms, organized around a comic movement towards the union of Elina and Clifford and a romance pattern necessitating the victory of Osbert/Auberville over Mortimer. Both these plots engage the movement between open and closed spaces so important to the Gothic, here oscillations between castles and various natural settings. Elina has been taken from her own castle and imprisoned in that of Mortimer. The play opens with Clifford, Elina's true love, discovering her absence and lamenting her loss as he broods in his own "Old Castle." His problem is to liberate Elina from Mortimer's castle so that he can marry her. If we follow Frye's recipe for comedy we can see Mortimer and his henchman as representing the "blocking" society that attempts to prevent the union of the young lovers, who of course defeat their elders and reorder society around their joyful marriage.[34] Clifford is seconded, appropriately enough given this comic pattern, by a blustering but warm-hearted *miles gloriosus* figure, Bertram, whose stage ancestors run back through eighteenth- and seventeenth-century drama to Benedict in *Much Ado About Nothing*.

Clifford and Osbert also receive aid from a comic drunk, Gam the gardener, who is only one of many such droll servants in Gothic drama; we need only look in the current volume to Motley in *The Castle Spectre* or to Fritz in *Presumption; or, The Fate of Frankenstein* to see the pervasive presence of this type. Much time in the first two acts is spent with Gam and his endless discourse on drinking, and such comic relief often seems as important to the Gothic as terror itself. When we find plays that exclude such comic figures—as in Baillie's *De Monfort* and Maturin's *Bertram*—we are involved in works that wish to convert the Gothic wholly to tragedy. These comic scenes—which usually shift verse plays to prose (as in *The Kentish Barons*) and which treat homely subjects such as eating, drinking, and the travails of marriage—offer a center of conventional domesticity to contrast with the horrors of the central Gothic action. The audience, even as it laughs at Gam with his drunkenness and his problems with his wife, can locate through him a set of everyday concerns that may be threatened by the intrusion of the Gothic universe but which continually reassert themselves. In such scenes, we find the values of the nascent domestic melodrama that would eventually preempt the Gothic drama in the theaters of London. There may also be a wise dramatic tactic at work here: Gothic drama goes for extreme effects in terror, which in themselves can provoke laughter if not handled correctly—there are few things as funny as a botched attempt to invoke horror. By providing laughter—and even at times directing that laughter at the Gothic itself—these playwrights may be insulating their creations from the jeers of the pit. Lewis in particular is the master of a "camp" style in the Gothic, laughing at the very conventions he evokes, having his dramatic confection and eating it too.

North's romance plot, revolving around Osbert's hidden heritage as the kidnapped son of Mortimer's enemy and thus Elina's brother, is introduced within the castle of Mortimer, where Osbert is kept as an oppressed servant. (These devices gave rise to such satiric turns in the *Anti-Jacobin*'s anti-Gothic *The Rovers* as the moment when a waiter is discovered to be "No waiter, but a Knight Templar."[35]) We know that the supposed servant Osbert will prove noble, for Elina feels some strange attraction for this boy who has "a mind / Above the meanness of his low condition . . . I cou'd recall some features I once lov'd / Which much resembled his" (I, iv). Osbert's heroic charisma is evidenced by the fact that everyone, even Mortimer, is drawn to him. When we hear of a birthmark that had stood out on the arm of Auberville's lost son (I, ii), we immediately know how Osbert will recover his identity.

After Osbert tries to aid Elina's escape, he is dismissed from the castle, but only—Mortimer thinks—to die in the harsh wilderness. He instead finds his way to the comic figure Gam, who is tending a garden in the midst of the forest. Gam recognizes the birthmark and takes Osbert to Clifford to reclaim his title. Here the comic move towards the union of the lovers and the romance quest for Osbert's true identity are joined, as our two heroes collaborate to defeat Mortimer, who intends to force Elina into bed with him, deceiving her through a false wedding involving a former priest now in his employ.

Fulfilling his role as a hero from operatic romance, Osbert/Auberville concocts a plan to enter Mortimer's castle with Clifford and his friend Bertram as minstrels and to communicate with Elina through song—a device found elsewhere in the Gothic drama, for example in an infamous scene in Lewis's *Castle Spectre* where Kemble playing the hero Percy is urged through song to escape the villain's castle by throwing himself out a window, an athletic feat from a harlequinade deemed by the *Morning Herald* (16 December 1797) to be beneath Kemble's dignity. In *The Kentish Barons*, it is through this device that the play's frequent songs (an aspect of the play protested by Genest) are linked to the action. The play closes on a final song celebrating love and music, and there is a sense in which the play enacts the structural victory of operatic romance over the potential tragedy of the villain-hero Mortimer: that is, not only is Mortimer defeated, but his vision of life as a tragic round of violence and revenge is defeated as the cast bursts into a joyful finale when the lovers are united and Osbert finds his rightful identity and place in society. Thus, while the play does not move out of the castle at its close, it does end on a celebration of love—replete with pagan images—that recalls the end of *Julia of Louvain* and its celebration of "Peace and pleasure" before the altar of Hymen:

> Let Cupid shake his sportive wings,
>   While round the loves and graces fly;
> Apollo touch the trembling strings,
>   And Hymen lift his torch on high.
>
> Our fears are gone, the tempest past,
>   Here adverse winds no more annoy;
> Our vessel, safely moor'd at last,
>   Casts anchor in the port of joy.
>   (III, i)

As is suggested by the close of Dent's *Bastille*—where the liberator of the prison is united with his love who has been sought by an aristocratic villain—and by the end of *Julia of Louvain*—where the lovers defeat the powers of both the aristocracy and the Church—erotic freedom is linked in plays such as *The Kentish Barons* to political freedom, a connection that would continue to have power within the British radical tradition, as Shelley's *Revolt of Islam* and *Prometheus Unbound* indicate.

This victory through song also suggests the involvement of the Gothic with the carnivalesque as explored in the eighteenth century by Terry Castle. The final moments of plays such as *The Kentish Barons* or *Julia of Louvain* with their festivals of love, their singing and dancing, their unmasking of villains, all seem to partake of the carnival and its utopian dream of liberation from convention. There is, one might suggest, an interesting parallel between the form of the Gothic drama with its "jumble" of various generic levels and the " 'strange Medley' of persons—a rough mix of high and low" that Castle finds in the masquerade.[36] It is in such carnivalesque moments, such hints of utopian enjoyment, such moves to incorporate on stage what had been social celebrations or were revolutionary festivals, that we see the Gothic drama reaching for a vision of liberation open to the resonances of the day. And in this victory of popular song over high tragedy, we may also see the Gothic's stand in the struggle to reorder the hierarchy of genres.

However, for us, the greatest interest in *Kentish Barons* is generated by the tragic possibilities surrounding the villain, Mortimer. As has often been noted since the point was made by Evans, the focus of the Gothic drama increasingly centered around the villain, who becomes a villain-hero and the precursor of the Byronic hero. As we will see in Maturin's *Bertram* and as could also be seen in plays such as Byron's *Manfred* and Shelley's *The Cenci*, the Gothic villain-hero could be placed at the center of the new brand of tragedy crafted by the romantics. In part, the villain's prominence can be traced to the weakness of the official hero, a weakness that results from his role in the rather conventional comic and romance plots. For example, in Lewis's *Castle Spectre*, the hero Percy is a romance aristocrat in disguise as a peasant, wooing and then seeking to rescue his beloved Angela; but he is singularly ineffectual in his attempts, finding himself repeatedly outwitted and finally relying upon Angela for the defeat of the villainous Osmond. Osmond, in contrast, is a dynamic and intriguing character, displaying real passion for Angela, proving himself heroic in his confrontations with his foes and even with what he takes to be a ghostly apparition, and undergoing anguished self-examination. North's Clifford is perhaps a stronger figure than Percy, but he would still be moping in his castle were it not for the efforts of Osbert, Bertram, and Gam; and he certainly lacks the powerful attractions of the villain Mortimer.

Evans cites Mortimer as one of the earliest and more interesting villain-heroes. Evans stresses Mortimer's moralizing strain, as the playwright forces his villain to recognize and denounce his own evil. However, what actually makes Mortimer interesting is his libertine embrace of pleasure and egotism. His opening speech sets the tone:

> How disappointment loves to plague the heart
> Of the poor idiot man! who vainly thinks
> His reason given to direct and guide him.
> The happy brutes, who follow instinct's laws,
> Enjoy the blessings of the present hour:
> Their daily task perform'd, they lay them down,
> And never dream that the approaching morn
> Shall wake them to new labours: Man alone
> Looks through a flattering and deceitful glass
> And vainly strives to view futurity:

> Nature has wisely hid it from his sight;
> But purblind Reason, curious and inquisitive,
> Just sees enough to dazzle and mislead him.
> But I'll reflect no more—
> (I, iii)

This assault upon reason and admiration for instinct could be found in the mouths of many heroes of Restoration sexual comedy and heroic drama. The Restoration libertine hero is one of the less noted precursors of the Gothic villain-hero. The Gothic figure inherits his ancestor's sexual drives, his egotism, and his anti-rationalist rhetoric. The direct line of inheritance probably comes through Richardson's Lovelace, who like the Gothic villain-hero has the energy necessary to reform a corrupt society but chooses to use it to support a decadent and declining regime. The Gothic villain-hero, thus, belongs with those late eighteenth-century libertines analyzed by Starobinski—Mozart's Don Juan, Laclos's Valmont, and Sade's philosophical hedonists—the brightest lights of a world about to go into eclipse.[37]

North establishes his villain as a skeptic who doubts reason's ability to guide man's actions or to conceive the consequences of his deeds. Given to gloomy reflection, Mortimer admires the innocent and immediate pleasures of the beasts. Mortimer doubts our ability to know the future and thus to calculate the outcomes of our actions or the judgment that will be made upon them. Turning from the future, he hopes to embrace present pleasure; but more importantly, his dismissal of the future leaves him ironically in the grip of the past. For all of his energy, he can only repeat past ways, not create a distinct future, and thus he is doomed to live out the patterns of traditional tragedy.

We learn that Mortimer is driven by revenge for what he has suffered in the past at the hands of Auberville, the father of the heroine Elina whom Mortimer has abducted. In fact, the tension within Mortimer is less a struggle between villainy and morality, as Evans suggests, than a contest between two drives—his present desire for Elina and his demand for revenge for deeds committed in the past:

> Think you that Love, that silly deity,
> Can bend my steady nature? Osbert, no.
> A brighter, grander passion now enflames me:
> One which takes root in noble minds alone;
> The soft and common soil of vulgar souls
> Could never rear it: 'tis a great Revenge.
> (I, iii)

Mortimer—like many subsequent Gothic and romantic figures from Lewis's Osmond to Maturin's Bertram, from Byron's Cain to Hugo's Hernani—is torn between love and violent hate. They are linked for Mortimer in his past, for we learn that the enmity between Mortimer and Elina's father arose over a woman, Alicia, with whom both were in love. Alicia chose Auberville, whom Mortimer then challenged in combat:

> Within two days of our intended duel,
> The king forbad the combat, and confin'd me
> Close pris'ner, Osbert, in these castle-walls,
> For nine long winters. Did he think to Conquer
> (O foolish Man) the Soul of Mortimer
> By Solitude and vile Imprisonment?
> 'Tis true my anger took a different turn
> And grew more deeply rooted by reflection
> But to cut short my tale, Alicia's death
> At length releas'd me.
> (I, iii)

In a sense, Mortimer has undergone the struggles of a Gothic hero: he has had his love taken from him and been imprisoned. North suggests that the villain arises from the Gothic hero when he is ultimately frustrated: Clifford can remain a hero for he can confront his enemy and win his love, but Mortimer, imprisoned by the king, finds no outlet for his love or his hate and instead finds his emotions "more deeply rooted by reflection," by the dangerous inward turn to self-consciousness that is found throughout the Gothic and romantic drama.

The psychological dynamics here might be glossed with Blake's "A Poison Tree": "I was angry with my friend; / I told my wrath, my wrath did end. / I was angry with my foe: / I told it not, my wrath did grow."[38] Such a dynamic is important, for it suggests that inwardness—a depth psychology itself—is the problem confronted, not celebrated, by the Gothic. The villain-hero interests us deeply, but that interest should not be confused with approval. Blake's poem outlines the pattern of Gothic psychology: the individual who tells his wrath—who externalizes his feelings and thus has no hidden inner life—provides the model for behavior, while he who internalizes his wrath—who creates an inner life from repressed desires and violent feelings—may be of greater interest but is clearly on the wrong path. Psychological readings of the Gothic often argue that these works are interested in exploring the byways of consciousness and the unconscious, but it would seem more accurate to say that having an interesting consciousness, being possessed by uncon-

scious desires, is a mark of villainy. Heroes and heroines tend to be un-
interesting in these works because they have no psychology; they are
completely outward directed, controlled by conventions of appropriate
heroic and moral behavior.

Whatever Mortimer's wrath, his energy is clearly sexual, and his pursuit of the pleasures of the flesh would have seemed extreme on the contemporary stage.

> No hated Priest shall join our hands together,
> Whose Hearts cou'd never pair. Yet I'll deceive her
> With a feign'd Marriage: good, it shall be so:—
> The live-long night I'll revel in her beauties,
> And in the morning tell her she's undone.
> (II, ii)

His desires and his hate are almost always thus intermixed:

> Why thinkest thou, Osbert, that I brought her hither?
> Thinkest thou 'twas only to enjoy her person?
> That were but poor revenge; yet I'll enjoy her
> And quickly too. No, I had rather blast
> The fame of that detested house, than take
> Venus array'd in all the fancy'd beauties
> With which the poets deck the fickle goddess,
> Kind, warm, and yielding to my ardent bosom.
> (I, iii)

Elina finally sees him as a sadist, delighting only in the sufferings of others: "Nature cou'd never form so harsh a fiend, / So barbarous and inhuman, whose delight, / Whose only pleasure centers in the Pain / He can
inflict on others" (II, ii). Erotic energy with a sadistic turn will mark
many Gothic figures, finding its preeminent dramatic representation in
Shelley's Count Cenci.

North, like most Gothic dramatists, sketches in the outlines of a tragedy surrounding his villain. These villains—so much closer than the official heroes to the Shakespearean figures most important to the late
eighteenth- and early nineteenth-century stage such as the Machiavellian
Richard III, the jealous Othello, the brooding Hamlet, or the murderous
Macbeth—have the energy, the charismatic presence, and the absolute
sense of their own selves that mark the tragic figure. North's hint that
Mortimer is a warped Clifford is one clue that within the treatment of the
villain-hero is a lament for lost heroic potential, for a titanic energy both
needed and feared. Mortimer commands his play, and there is a sense of

loss in his defeat. Mortimer also maintains his self-control, his firm sense of himself. While Evans is correct in noting that Mortimer at times reflects upon his villainy and even feels remorse for his crimes, he never comes to the renunciation of his ways, as would be the case in more conventionally melodramatic works.

Remorse is often seen as a key theme in these plays, and Coleridge's play by that title can then be read as a culminating work in the Gothic tradition. However, Coleridge's play is in fact written *against* one main (and more radical) line of development within the Gothic, and Mortimer finds his place within this alternative vision. At the close of the play, Mortimer seems to have defeated his heroic opponents, Osbert and Clifford, and is about to force Elina to marry him. He is prevented only by the sudden intervention of Clifford's friend Bertram, backed by a troop of soldiers. Mortimer recognizes he is defeated, but he does not repent as he speaks to Osbert:

> Ne'er till now
> Did I despair. Even malice now forsakes me.
> Oh! I did hope (fool that I was to spare thee),
> That thou at least wou'dst have felt all my vengeance.
> But if thy soul is noble, boy, revenge thee;
> Insult me not with words; be merciful,
> Be merciful, and kill me.
> (III, i)

He leaves the stage not expressing remorse but advising Osbert of the necessity of violent revenge: "I cou'dn't kill thee; / It was the only weakness I e'er felt . . . . Boy, be wise; / Seize on this glorious opportunity, / To rid thee of a foe, whom nought but death / Can render tranquil" (III, i). Mortimer remains true to himself and thus retains his dignity. He has some of the power and grand self-assertion that marks an Othello or a Macbeth.

The attractions granted to a villain-hero such as Mortimer and the drift of Gothic plays towards a tragedy of the aristocrat's destruction should suggest to us that these plays do not embrace an unambiguous attitude towards the revolutionary movements of the day. While I have suggested that the largest pattern organizing these plays is a movement from enclosure to liberation, which mimics that of revolutionary festivals, it is important to remember that these plays also contain this potential tragic lament for a lost past. The overarching movement of these plays is that of liberation from the castle, its aristocratic villain, and the old regime it embodies; but as we watch these plays, we are drawn to the villain, his mysterious milieu, and the power granted him by his position and his heroic hauteur. We are invited to admire these oppressors, for they embody the possibility of an individual revolt counter to the communal liberation celebrated in hymenal union and uncovered social identities. Shadowing the ideology of liberation is the ideology of the isolated rebel, the suggestion that true liberty lies not in the social rejuvenation captured by comedy and romance but in the isolated pursuit of the individual's fears and desires tracked by tragedy. In its own way, the Gothic stages the central ideological tension within revolutionary politics, that between liberty and equality, between the removal of all restrictions upon the individual and the assertion of communal bonds and thus limits. In a sense, the Gothic already stages the debate between Marat the egalitarian and Sade the aristocratic liberator of the self that Peter Weiss would offer in *Marat/Sade*.

Michel Foucault has suggested that the Gothic represents an "appropriation of criminality in acceptable forms," as the popular criminal represented in broadsheets and viewed in public executions is replaced by the aristocratic villain-hero of the Gothic novel and crime fiction:

> . . . a whole new literature of crime developed: a literature in which crime is glorified, because it is one of the fine arts, because it can be the work only of exceptional natures, because it reveals the monstrousness of the strong and powerful, because it reveals villainy is yet another mode of privilege: from the adventure story to de Quincey, or from the *Castle of Otranto* to Baudelaire, there is a whole aesthetic rewriting of crime, which is also the appropriation of criminality in acceptable forms. In appearance, it is the discovery of the beauty and greatness of crime; in fact, it is the affirmation that greatness too has a right to crime and that it even becomes the exclusive privilege of those who are really great. . . . The literature of crime transposes to another social class the spectacle that had surrounded the criminal. Meanwhile the newspapers took over the task of recounting the grey, unheroic details of everyday crime and punishment. The split was complete; the people was robbed of its old pride in its crimes; the great murders had become the quiet game of the well behaved.[39]

In Foucault's version, the Gothic is a tactic of containment, a way for hegemonic social and cultural forces to combat the popular appeal of crime. However, the Gothic drama does not seem so much an art of containment as that of display; its strange "jumble" of forms does not so much contain one ideological vision within another as place them within a generic struggle, offering a kind of Bakhtinian heteroglossia. It is perhaps because the Gothic drama is so aesthetically confused, so "unacceptable" or "illegitimate," that it does not clearly serve the ideological movement out-lined by Foucault where crime is rendered aesthetic and acceptable. It is true that both the libertine, libertarian strain of the villain-hero's tragedy and the egalitarian, erotic theme of the lovers' romance would ultimately be contained within the turn to domestic morality that would mark the melodrama—in a sense, the comic domesticity offered within the Gothic (by Gam and his wife in *The Kentish Barons*) finally wins out over both aristocatic tragedy and revolutionary romance. But within the Gothic drama of the 1790s, the aristocratic villain *and* his opponents seem set against the status quo, against convention, against hegemonic contain-ment. In deploying the iconography of the castle and its liberation, in en-gaging the various plot strands of its mixed form, the early Gothic drama explores private as well as social revolt. It was, as Coleridge saw in linking the Gothic's radicalism to its eroticism, the "modern jacobinical drama" because it offered models of both individual and collective revolt. Until its ultimate displacement by the domestic melodrama, the Gothic drama could be used to stage a protest—both aesthetic and ideological—against convention and containment, against generic and political hierarchy. The later history of the Gothic reveals its transformations as it was now bent to more conservative ends, as it now voiced radical concerns, and as now it wavered before the coming victory of the melodrama and the "realistic" drama.

### V  Gothic Supernaturalism

North's *Kentish Barons* introduces us to all of the standard features of the Gothic drama except the one we most expect: the use of the supernatural. At least initially the Gothic drama shied away from ghosts and demons. Walpole—who loads *The Castle of Otranto* with supernatural occur-rences—avoids putting them on stage in *The Mysterious Mother*. Jephson in revising Walpole's novel for the stage relegates its ghostly accoutrements to narrative passages. North follows this pattern in keeping *The Kentish Bar-ons* strictly within the bounds of the natural, if not the believable; *Julia of Louvain* also stays clear of the supernatural.

The presence of the ghost within a play did not necessarily guarantee a dramatic excursion into a supernatural realm. Henry Siddons's *The Si-cilian Romance; or, The Apparition of the Cliffs*, as its title indicates, is part of the shift in Gothic taste during the 1790s that would climax in the famous ghost of Lewis's *Castle Spectre*. Throughout Siddons's play, we hear of a ghost stalking the rocks outside a castle. However, Siddons eventually of-fers a commonplace explanation for his ghost—it is the villain's imprisoned wife walking her rock prison—indicating that he adheres to the conventions established by the novels of Ann Radcliffe in which spirits and spectres are rationalized. This link may explain his decision to re-name the play from *The Castle of Otranto* to *The Sicilian Romance*, as he tries to attach his play to first one and then the other of the most important Gothic novelists, to neither of whom is his play directly indebted.

We perhaps expect the supernatural in the Gothic drama because it plays such an important role in the Gothic novel from Walpole, Radcliffe, and Lewis to Stoker or James or Stephen King. However, the stage rep-resentation of the supernatural is a quite different thing from its presen-tation in a narrative, as was recognized by another imitator of Ann Radcliffe, James Boaden, whose *Fontainville Forest* (adapted from Rad-cliffe's *Romance of the Forest*) offered the most famous ghost scene before Lewis's *Castle Spectre*. Boaden was aware that the novelistic treatment of the supernatural would not work on stage:

> [I] admired, as every one else did, the singular address by which Mrs. Radcliffe contrived to impress the mind with all the terrors of the ideal world; and the sportive resolution of all that had ex-cited terror into very common natural appearances; indebted for their false aspect to circumstances and the overstrained feelings of the characters.
>
> But, even in romance, it may be doubtful, whether there be not something *ungenerous* in thus playing upon poor timid human nature, and agonizing it with false terrors. The disappointment is, I know, always resented, and the laboured explanation commonly deemed the flattest and most uninteresting part of the production. Perhaps when the attention is once secured and the reason yielded, the pas-sion for the marvellous had better remain unchecked; and an interest selected from the olden time be entirely subjected to its gothic ma-chinery. However this may be in respect of romance, when the doubtful of the narrative is to be exhibited in the *drama*, the decision is a matter of necessity. While *description* only fixes the inconclu-sive dreams of the fancy, she may partake the dubious character of her inspirer; but the pen of the dramatic poet must turn everything into shape, and bestow on these "airy nothings a local habitation and a name."[40]

Boaden confronts directly the status of the supernatural in the novel that has come to occupy so much attention in twentieth-century criticism of the Gothic: the self-conscious, finally psychological exploration of the su-pernatural, the numinous, the divine. Margaret L. Carter's comments can be taken as typical: "an important use of the supernatural in eighteenth- and nineteenth-century fiction is to provide space for speculation about nonmaterial dimensions of existence, without demanding a positive act of either acceptance or rejection. . . . these stories characteristically use mediated narrative and limited perspective to invite the reader to identify with the protagonist's uncertainty. Thus an agnostic position regarding the supernatural is valorized."[41] Carter joins with Todorov, Siebers, and others in focusing upon texts that neither assert the reality of the supernatural (Todorov's category of the marvelous) nor explain away all preternatural occurrences (Todorov's uncanny) but instead engage speculative doubt about the more than human (Todorov's fantastic). Within the Gothic tradition, Radcliffe stands as an example of the tactic of offering a rational explanation that dispels the supernatural terror that attends her narratives, while Lewis was perhaps the most infamous example of the direct and unquestioned presentation of the demonic; Maturin in *Melmoth the Wanderer*, Shelley in *Frankenstein*, and Hogg in *Confessions and Private Memoirs of a Justified Sinner* followed the more ambiguous strategy of offering multiple, limited narratives and thus multiple, mediated theories of the supernatural.

Boaden makes the central point that this final option is not available to the dramatist. If there are no atheists in foxholes, there are also no agnostics about the supernatural on the stage. While the novelist engages "the inconclusive dreams of the fancy" and may allow the consciousness and "overstrained emotions" of the characters to mediate between the reader and the supernatural events, the dramatist must decide either to embody the supernatural or to banish it from the stage altogether. Boaden himself followed both courses, literalizing Radcliffe's ghosts in *Fontainville Forest* but banishing Lewis's demons in his adaptation of *The Monk* into *Aurelio and Miranda*. Lewis himself would offer the most famous example of the direct presentation of the supernatural in the theater when he allowed his much-protested ghost to glide across the stage in *The Castle Spectre*.

We find the novel's ambiguous and psychological treatment of the supernatural or demonic—the Gothic version of natural supernaturalism— to be the most interesting, but the drama's turn to either rational explanation of the numinous or direct representation of the spiritual had a more radical potential in the theater of the day. There seems to have been a general critical perception that religion was too serious a matter for literary representation, as we can see in comments ranging from Johnson's claim that any attempt to embellish Biblical texts and stories is "frivolous and vain . . . not only useless, but in some degree profane" to the attacks

on Byron's *Cain* which, Truman Guy Steffan notes, were grounded on
the view that "literature should not deal with theological or controversial
matters, nor even with biblical subjects, and that *Cain* should never have
been written or published."[42] The problem would seem to have been the
greatest on the stage, as we can see from the censor's attempts to exclude
all religious language from the texts he licensed. We repeatedly find passages using references to the divine marked for change or omission in the
licensing manuscripts; in Lewis's *Castle Spectre*, for example, we find that
even the word "hallelujah" was offensive and had to be replaced by
"jubilate."[43] When expressions such as "The Almighty" made it past the
censor, then the slip was sure to be remarked upon by some reviewer. For
example, the *Monthly Mirror* had this to say about *The Castle Spectre*, in
complaining about the villain-hero's atheism and the "frequent appeals to
Heaven, with a levity unusual to our stage": "The licenser, if he had
known the intention of his office, would have *struck his pen* across such
expressions as '*Saviour of the world*,' '*God of Heaven*,' etc."[44] This wide
criticism of the use of religious language suggests that there was agreement that the divine was not to be represented—or even referred to—
upon stage.

We can see this attitude again behind the reactions to Boaden's transformation of *The Monk* into *Aurelia and Miranda*. The play's composer,
Kelly, reports that the play was objected to because "many thought it indecorous to represent a church on the stage." Kemble's impersonation of
the monk was found inappropriate because it was so believable; the Duke
of Leeds complained, for example, that "his *religious feelings* hardly allowed
him to tolerate the powerful effects, which he saw produced upon the
stage."[45] Shelley's *The Cenci* was found similarly offensive in its suggestion
that religion can coexist with sinful acts. *The British Review* fumed that
"There is something extremely shocking in finding the truths, the
threats, and the precepts of religion in the mouth of a wretch, at the very
moment that he is planning or perpetrating crimes at which nature shudders. In this intermixture of things, sacred and impure, Mr. Shelley is not
inconsistent if he believes that religion is in Protestant countries hypoc-
risy, and that it is in Roman Catholic countries 'adoration, faith, submission, penitence, blind admiration; not a rule for moral conduct, and that
it has no necessary connexion with any one virtue.'—(Preface, p. 13.) Mr.
Shelley is in an error . . . ."[46] If Byron in *Cain* reveals the radical potential
in reworking the Bible—and thus realizes the fears of the censor who
banned religious language—Shelley pushes the kind of indecorous representation of religious behavior that was objected to even in the mild form
of Kemble's performance of Boaden's Monk.

There is, then, always a hint of blasphemy in such representations of the spiritual or numinous. Theatrical managers tried to block the appearances of ghosts, even though they proved to be good theater. Boaden insisted upon his ghost in *Fontainville Forest*, even though the management objected to it; the ghost appeared but only in a scene edited down to meet the complaints. Again, Lewis stubbornly refused to edit out his castle spectre, even though everyone involved with the production opposed its inclusion. The managers were obviously aware of the trouble such scenes could cause with the censors or with censorious critics such as Genest who found that Boaden's ghost rendered the play "contemptible," the same comment he makes upon *The Castle Spectre:* "the plot is rendered contemptible by the introduction of the Ghost."[47]

We can begin to understand the ideological implications of the Gothic's representation of the religious and the numinous if we glance at their treatment of the clergy and of nunneries. Given the range of references, we might assume that the status of ecclesiastical orders and institutions was a central issue in England of the day. Siddons's hero in *The Sicilian Romance* has called for the abolition of monasteries. Boaden noted that the Gothic "history" play *The Island of St. Marguerite* contained an allusion "to the dissolution of nunneries [that] was loudly applauded by such as knew nothing but the abuses of such institutions."[48] The title character of *Julia of Louvain* is given a choice between marriage and the convent, the horrors of the latter being painted for her in a song about the trials of being a nun (sc. vii). Lewis's *Venomi* was an adaptation of the notoriously anti-clerical *Les Victimes Cloîtrées*, and his portrayal of Father Philip in *The Castle Spectre* led Genest to observe, "where a Friar was concerned, Lewis's mind was strangely warped."[49] One might read these as merely expressing popular anti-Catholic sentiment, but in the charged atmosphere of the 1790s it is likely they were seen as a more general assault upon religion. It is noteworthy that Boaden complains about the audience's quick approval of an attack upon convent life; and it is even more important that this incident immediately brings to his mind the performance in Paris of Chénier's *Charles IX*, the first important political play performed under the French Revolution and one which Boaden in this passage links directly to the ultimate decision to guillotine the king. If the portrayal of anti-monarchical sentiments could lead to the death of a king, then the representation of anti-clerical feelings could lead to assaults upon the established church.

Of course, the presence of the supernatural in the Gothic drama is not always so strictly tied to Christianity. Ghosts may or may not have a providential function, and such figures as Lewis's Wood Daemon presumably do not. This move beyond conventional religious images had its own radical potential, however, as Byron's *Manfred* suggests. His poetic drama is a syncretic attempt to invoke a whole series of alternative religious visions—what the *Literary Gazette* calls his "heterogeneous assemblage of mythology."[50] The very mixed nature of his play's supernatural framework suggests that no single religious system can encompass man and his life. We get a taste of Byron's tactics in the first scene, where four nature spirits appear, apparently representing air, earth, water, and fire; but Byron adds three more spirits to break the traditional pattern of the four elements. Throughout the play, he interrupts or disrupts traditional religious structures, and thus his play finally comes to define a human life outside of religion. Faced with such partial religious visions, Manfred rejects the lure of the supernatural—from the elemental spirits of the first act to Arimanes in the second act and the God of the Abbot in the last act.

That a supernatural play could thus be agnostic or even atheistical would not have surprised the conservative opponents of the Gothic drama. Criticisms like that in the *Monthly Mirror* about the *The Castle Spectre*'s turn to "German" atheism suggest that the protectors of traditional faith were wary of the intention behind the presentation of the supernatural on stage. Osmond, like Manfred or more directly like Don Giovanni, confronts what he believes to be a spirit (it is, in fact, the hero Percy in disguise), proclaiming, "Hell and fiends! I'll follow him, though lightnings blast me!" (II, i). Osmond can be seen to represent a dangerous inclination not to believe in the power of the supernatural; in fact, a great part of his appeal was his willingness to stand against even supernatural opponents. Coleridge well understood this appeal, while lamenting it, in his attack in the *Biographia Literaria* upon Maturin's *Bertram* as a play which offers a "supernatural effect without even a hint of any supernatural agency."[51]

These various treatments of the supernatural and the objections to them again suggest the ideological impact of the Gothic's sensationalist techniques. When these techniques were used to display spectacular effects without a supernatural explanation as in *Bertram*, there was a suggestion that life, even in its extraordinary moments, can be understood without recourse to religion. When sensationalism was used to depict the supernatural, there was a suggestion that the absolute itself—as revealed through spectres, and wood daemons, and figures like Byron's Arimanes—can not be comprehended by established religion, that the absolute defies all traditional visions and interpretations. The union of sensationalist techniques and religious or supernatural subject matter may not produce the subtle uncanny effects of self-reflexive narratives, but it did provide a potentially radical message in the days of the Revolution, when the disestablishment of the Church was as central an issue as the dismantling of the monarchy.

## VI Lewis and the Gothic Drama: Melodrama, Monodrama, and Tragedy

By the time Matthew Gregory "Monk" Lewis came to write for the stage in 1797, the Gothic was firmly established in London's theaters. Lewis's contribution to this thriving Gothic tradition was finally as important as was his *Monk*'s to the Gothic novel. Lewis was neither the most popular nor the most impressive playwright of his day, but he was the most popular who could also lay claim to being a "serious" or "literary" dramatist. His position at the threshold between "mass" and "high" culture grants his plays added significance, for he wrote at a key moment in the history of the relations between literary women and men and the theater.

Whatever we think of the drama of this period, it was clearly an era of intense activity in the popular theater, as the already noted shifts in acting styles, alterations in theatrical architecture, and innovations in dramatic form attest. However, Lewis's productive years as a dramatist, 1797 to 1812, also saw a concerted effort to capture the stage by the literary figures we attach to the romantic movement. Lewis's plays find their context not only within the history of the popular drama but also in a moment when the first generation of romantic writers felt that the stage offered their poetry a path to a larger audience. Wordsworth hoped to see his *Borderers* staged when he submitted it to Thomas Knight, an actor at Covent Garden, and then to Harris, the manager. The play was rejected, as was Coleridge's *Osorio*, though Coleridge would later revise his drama as the successful *Remorse* acted in 1813. Scott published a translation of Goethe's *Götz von Berlichingen* in 1799 and wrote a number of unacted plays around 1800. Lamb's *John Woodvil* was offered to Kemble in 1799, who refused it. Godwin, however, had two plays performed, *Antonio* at Drury Lane in 1800 and *Faulkener* again at Drury Lane in 1807. Joanna Baillie began publishing her *Series of Plays Upon the Passions* in 1798; her *De Monfort* was performed at Drury Lane in 1800 with Kemble and Siddons in the leads, and a number of her other plays reached the stage. Southey also wrote a number of dramatic works, as did such less known figures as John Tobin and William Sotheby. There was, then, a moment when key literary figures expended a great deal of effort on the stage, when they sought to establish themselves by penning tragedies. Lewis's corpus belongs with these works, for while he wrote a number of plays designed primarily to capture a large audience, other works draw upon the popular forms he mastered in an attempt to revitalize tragedy. In many ways, Lewis—at least before Maturin—was the writer who was most successful in finding a version of tragedy that could win a popular audience.

Lewis's contribution to the theater is considerable. As has been noted, his *Castle Spectre* was one of the most popular plays of the period; it was equally popular with the reading public, going through eleven editions by 1803. Lewis's *Alfonso, King of Castille* was given out ten times, making it the most popular new tragedy between 1777 when Hannah More's *Percy* received nineteen performances and 1813 when Coleridge's *Remorse* had twenty-two; his other tragedy, *Adelgitha; or, The Fruit of a Single Error*, appeared at Drury Lane in 1807. For over ten years, Lewis supplied the London theaters with play after play—original dramas, translations, and adaptations. He worked in a wide variety of genres, from farce and comic opera to melodrama and high tragedy. He drew not only upon native English traditions but also upon French and German sources; credited with sparking the English rage for German tales of terror, Lewis also translated Schiller and Kotzebue and adapted the intriguing French convent play, Monvel's *Les Victimes Cloîtrées*.

Outside of his comedies (*The Village Virtues*, *The Twins*, *The Domestic Tyrant*, and *The East Indian*, also revised as *Rich and Poor*), all his works demonstrate Gothic traits. *Adelmorn the Outlaw* (Drury Lane, 1801) survived for nine nights and was later adopted as an afterpiece; but despite its heavy load of spectacular effects—three appearances by a ghost, an elaborate dream sequence (based on Goethe's *Egmont*) which offered a chorus of spirits as well as a pantomime of a hidden murder, and a lightning bolt destroying the wall of a dungeon to free a figure who can reveal the play's secret—it did not please as had *The Castle Spectre*.

Lewis's next play, *Rugantino; or, The Bravo of Venice* (Covent Garden, 1805), was a success, having thirty performances. An adaptation of Zschokke's romance *Aballino der grosse Bandit* (1794), the play centers upon a double masking by the central character, who appears as both the romance hero Flodoardo and the villainous bravo Rugantino only to reveal himself at the end as the Duke of Milan. The sets are described by contemporary reviewers as being the most spectacular of the day, and the play closed with a grand masque of the "Triumph of Thetis." *The Wood Daemon; or, "The Clock has Struck,"* also revised as *One O'Clock; or, The Knight and The Wood Daemon*, was first offered at Drury Lane on 1 April 1807 and ran for thirty-four performances. It combined every trick from

Lewis's Gothic repertoire: grand processions, an extravagant dream sequence, ghostly portraits who step down from the wall, a bed that descends into a magic chamber where the villain worships the wood daemon, and a spectacular appearance of the wood daemon in a chariot drawn by dragons. This evoked ecstatic praise from the *Monthly Mirror:* "The confusion and apparent horror which ensued after the appearance of the spectre combined to form perhaps the most terrific and sublime scene ever beheld on the stage."[52] *Timour the Tartar,* which brought horses to Covent Garden in 1811 and ran for forty-four performances, had a vicious villain, extraordinary castle and fortress sets, and, of course, the extremely popular equestrian performers. Similar Gothic and sensationalist effects are found in Lewis's adaptations of Schiller (*The Minister*) and of Monvel (*Venomi*), the latter of which seems to be the source for much of Lewis's work, including *The Monk.*

Lewis is represented here by his greatest theatrical triumph—*The Castle Spectre*—and by his greatest failure, *The Captive,* a Mono-Drama or Tragic Scene, which closed at Covent Garden in 1807 after a single performance. Interesting examples of the Gothic drama in their own right, these two plays also represent the two poles of dramatic form that, as I have argued elsewhere, defined the generic tensions organizing late eighteenth- and early nineteenth-century theater. These poles are the melodrama and the monodrama, and it is a mark of Lewis's centrality that he engages both. Moreover, his tragedies represent an attempt to rewrite these forms in keeping with the traditional shape of tragedy. This move to convert the Gothic into the tragic also worked to control the radical potential of the Gothic, with the "legitimate" form reshaping the Gothic drama's "illegitimate" ideological content.

*The Castle Spectre* is, as I have already suggested, the quintessential Gothic drama. The play has all of the standard Gothic features, from the castle replete with dungeons and sliding panels to the famous spectre, from one of the most impressive villain-heroes to some of the least successful comic characters. It embraces the dual vision of the Revolution that I have been arguing marks the Gothic. That is, it offers both a celebration of the liberation of the heroine from the clutches of a lustful aristocrat to be united with her rightful mate and sympathy for the charismatic but evil Osmond. Its ghost was the most famous example of the supernatural on stage and part of an impressive array of spectacular theatrical effects. Despite the worries of the managers of Drury Lane, despite some censorship by Larpent (in particular, speeches attacking slavery were cut), *The Castle Spectre* announces the victory of the Gothic drama, for it demonstrated that the Gothic could draw vast audiences, that it could touch upon revolutionary themes while placating the government's censor, and that it could begin to bridge the gap between popular dramatic fare and "high" literature.

*The Castle Spectre* was also a victory for the rising melodrama, the most important new dramatic kind of the day. The melo- or music-drama was the culmination of the development of non-verbal, spectacular theatrical techniques throughout the eighteenth century. It reached its "classic" form in the works of the French dramatist René-Charles Guilbert de Pixérécourt, of the German dramatist August von Kotzebue, and of the British playwrights George Coleman and Thomas Morton. An amazingly adaptable theatrical type—it could incorporate Oriental, nautical, Gothic, or domestic elements—the melodrama is still marked by three distinctive traits: sensationalist theatrical technique, overwhelming and generally violent plots, and an overriding sense of morality.

Music, set design, special effects—these are what made a particular melodrama a hit; the melodramatists drew upon the same arsenal of sensationalist weaponry that the Gothic playwrights turned upon their audiences. These powerful stage techniques were used to enact the victory of virtue over vice, but what is interesting—as the best students of the melodrama from Charles Nodier to Peter Brooks have noted—is that this moral triumph is only achieved through the release of violence. In the melodrama, virtue and vice at first lie hidden. The evil characters are in disguise or masked behind power and position, while the good figures are somehow barred from language, being sometimes deaf and dumb characters, sometimes very young children, sometimes individuals barred by class or sex from entering their society's central discourse; at the most extreme, animals came to occupy the center of the plot. The violence and the play's sensationalism work to rip the masks from characters and to force the non-verbal into annunication.

Violent acts, spectacular natural forces, and extreme situations and choices force the characters to reveal their moral valence, and thus the melodrama passes from apparent order, an order undermined by the fact that it is ruled by evil men, through violent chaos to moral clarification and the formation of a renewed social order. Melodramatic society is, however, renewed and not new; for while the melodrama is clearly tied into the French Revolution—if only through the biography of the "father" of melodrama, Pixérécourt, who lived through it—and while, as Peter Brooks has argued, the melodrama evokes the movement of the Revolution, it finally is a conservative, even reactionary form, seeking the restitution of conventional order in the face of revolutionary change. As Hegel was the first to point out, the melodrama—no matter what its flirtations

with illicit behavior as in Kotzebue, with extreme violence and sensationalism as in Pixérécourt, or with the Gothic as in Coleman and Morton—
ultimately enacts the "triumph of ordinary morality."[53]

The Gothic drama, as we can see in *The Castle Spectre*, could draw upon
the tactics and rhythms of the early melodrama, but the Gothic and the
melodrama part company over the latter's commitment to "ordinary morality." The Gothic always explores the extraordinary, the extreme. The
melodrama displays the ordinary, the norm. When this commitment to
"ordinary morality" became wedded to the techniques of nineteenth-
century theatrical "realism," then the final break came between the
Gothic and the melodrama. Lewis could still write a Gothic melodrama
in *The Castle Spectre*; Maturin would write his Gothic tragedy *Bertram* in
opposition to the domestic melodrama.

Lewis's *The Captive* represents the other pole organizing the dramatic
field in this period, the monodrama. As Lewis's favorite composer,
Michael Kelly, tells us, the monodrama was "much in vogue at Vienna,
and indeed all over Germany . . . and . . . has since been occasionally
introduced upon the English stage. The person who performs it is accompanied between the different speeches by music, made to accord with
the different passages of the recitation."[54] The first monodrama was apparently Rousseau's *Pygmalion*, begun in 1762 as a play for one actor and
musical accompaniment and performed successfully in Paris in 1772. *Pygmalion* follows the pattern described by Kelly, for in it short speeches alternate with passages of pantomime accompanied by music that reinforces
the emotional impact of the text. The goal is to reveal immediately and
powerfully a range of extreme emotional states. Rousseau found a number
of imitators, including Goethe and Southey; as A. Dwight Culler has
shown, the form continued to exert an influence at least as late as Ten-
nyson's *Maud*, and we might add the continuing popularity of one-actor
plays that explore a character—usually an artist or key historical figure—
in the full range of his or her biographical experience.[55]

Lewis's monodramatic *Captive* was offered on 22 March 1803. Mrs.
Litchfield played the captive wife, imprisoned in an asylum by her cruel
husband who has falsely accused her of madness. Trapped out of the
reach of her friends, surrounded only by the insane and an unsympa-
thetic gaoler, she begins in fact to lose control of her faculties. She finally
goes insane when another lunatic attempts to enter her cell. The play
ends with a pantomime of her recovery—as her father, brother, and son
come to rescue her—but the impact of the play was clearly in the depiction of tyranny and the madness it brought. In fact, when Lewis pub-

lished the play in his *Poems*, he decided to end upon her madness and to drop the scene of reconciliation that he had obviously felt necessary in the theater.

However, even this happy resolution of the plot did not prevent the play from terrifying its audience. Contemporary reviews repeatedly comment upon the impact of this monodramatic scene: the *Monthly Mirror* found that the play was "too strong for the feelings of the audience. Two ladies fell into hysterics, the house was thrown into confusion"; the *Satirist or Monthly Meteor* attacked the "*maniac* interlude, written (we believe) by the horror-breeding Lewis, and potently portrayed for one night only by Mrs. Litchfield, but with such efficacy as to send five or six women—two ladies, and two beaux—out of the theatre in fits"; and the *Biographia Dramatica* notes that "the author had included in this single scene all the horrors of a madhouse; imprisonment, chains, starvation, fear, madness, &c.; and many ladies were thrown into fits by the forcible and affecting manner of the actress."[56] Lewis wrote to his mother that the play:

> proved too terrible for representation, and two people went into hysterics during the performance & two more after the curtain dropped. . . . In fact the subject (which was merely a picture of Madness) was so uniformly distressing to the feelings, that at last I felt my own a little painful; & as to Mrs Litchfield, she almost fainted away. I did not expect that it would succeed, and of course am not disappointed at its failure; the only chance was, whether Pity would make the audience weep; but instead of that, Terror threw them into fits; & of course there was the end of my Monodrama.[57]

While the *DNB* scoffs at these reactions, claiming the play "may be read with impunity,"[58] these accounts suggest the power that the monodrama could have in the theater.

One reason for this extreme response lies in the form of the monodrama, which presented the character without any mediating pattern of judgement embodied in plot. The character's emotions—highlighted through stirring music, powerful pantomime, and affecting sets—are allowed to engage the audience directly with the play providing nothing else to distance us from our sympathy for this single, central figure. That is, in the monodrama we have a species of emotional sensationalism. It is important to note that Lewis's monodrama—while presented at Covent Garden—uses all of the tactics of a piece such as *Julia of Louvain* offered at a "minor" theater. The *Monthly Mirror* makes an interesting attempt to link the monodrama to its complementary form, the melodrama, and particularly to Holcroft's *Tale of Mystery*, the first English melodrama so-called: "The Captive is a poem in rhyme, consisting of several stanzas, each terminating with a kind of burthen: The whole is accompanied by pantomimic action, with appropriate music, in a manner somewhat resembling the Melodrama of the *Tale of Mystery*." This formal choice, this turn to new, "illegitimate" forms, is part of the play's radical departure and part of its power.

But there is also an ideological charge to this play, also hinted at by the *Monthly Mirror* in linking the play to Wollstonecraft's *Maria:*

> Mr. Lewis may have borrowed the idea of his *monodrame* from Mrs. Wollstonecraft's *Wrongs of Woman*. *Maria* is precisely in the situation of his *Captive;* and though we admit that the subject is too nearly allied to *horror* for public exhibition, we do not conceive there is any thing monstrous or unnatural in the notion that the sense of injury, the bitterness of reflection, and the effect of surrounding objects, may hurry a woman very speedily into actual distraction.[59]

Lewis's monodrama is not the only play of its kind that depicts women in oppressive situations or through displays of excessive emotion. Georg Benda offered monodramas about *Ariadne auf Naxos* (1774, with Jean Christian Brandes) and *Medea* (1782), while Southey dramatized the plight of *Lucretia* and *Sappho*.[60] Even in plays that are not formally monodramas, there are many monodramatic moments, and in particular there are many scenes depicting the movement of a distressed female through the stages of madness, as can be seen in Shelley's *The Cenci*, Maturin's *Bertram*, Baillie's *Orra*, or the Reverend Henry Hart Milman's *Fazio*. While these mad scenes often strike modern readers as dramatically weak, they actually drew upon an established and powerful monodramatic tradition for the display of exaggerated emotion. The appeal of such scenes arises in part from the period's interest in psychological portraiture and the investigation of the inner life; but beyond that, the monodrama seems to tap a deep fear in the audience, a fear of extreme subjectivity, of the inward turn beyond the reach of social mores and religious codes. Here the monodrama connects with and contributes to the Gothic drama's exploration of the individual's liberation and simultaneous solitude, of the possibility that revolt does not lead to collective liberty but an oppressive male libertinage that preys upon the isolated female.

Such an analysis suggests the links between the Gothic drama and the exploration of psychological extremity that has been found at the center of the Gothic novel. However, the link between *The Captive* and Wollstonecraft's *Maria, or The Wrongs of Woman* highlights the fact that Lewis's play is not merely an investigation of an extreme individual psychological state, but an indictment of a gendered social condition. Wollstonecraft's novel opens with an evocation of the Gothic only to assert the harsher horrors of the real:

> Abodes of horror have frequently been described, and castles, filled with spectres and chimeras, conjured up by the magic spell of genius to harrow the soul, and absorb the wondering mind. But formed of such stuff as dreams are made of, what are they to the mansion of despair, in one corner of which Maria sat, endeavouring to recall her scattered thoughts![61]

Lewis's play, like Wollstonecraft's novel, draws upon Gothic situations, but drops the distancing effects of the Gothic—this is no tale of Italy in some dark age but a portrait of modern domestic oppression in what the published version calls a "Private Mad-House." Moira Ferguson has argued that the "wrongs of women" noted in the subtitle to Wollstonecraft's *Maria* "are the legally and socially permissable acts of injustice perpetrated against women in eighteenth-century Britain."[62] As the author's preface puts it, the story exhibits "the misery and oppression, peculiar to women, that arise out of the partial laws and customs of society."[63] Lewis's play needs to be read with *Maria* in order to see that it is not merely an exploration of an abnormal psychological state but an investigation of an all-too-normal social state. *The Captive* is, I would suggest, a completely unknown piece of feminist theater, an attempt to dramatize in the most sensationalist and affecting terms one possible plight of women under eighteenth-century marriage and the law. The extreme reaction of the audience—Lewis's first biographer contends that "Never did Covent Garden present such a picture of agitation and dismay"—is not explicable merely in theatrical terms, for Lewis offered more horrifying scenes in *Adelmorn* or *The Wood Daemon* without having this effect; the play clearly touched a chord in the audience, unlocking a great emotional release: "Ladies bathed in tears—others fainting—and some shrieking with terror—while such of the audience as were able to avoid demonstrations like these, sat aghast, with pale horror painted on their countenances."[64] It is, I would argue, the play's direct portrayal of the subjugation of women that was so shocking. Audiences that could view spectres, chariots drawn by dragons, and murderous Tartars unalarmed were overwhelmed by the revelation of the real violence done to women.

*The Captive*, then, reveals the radical potential of the Gothic drama. *The Castle Spectre* also carried a political charge, for Lewis tells us he published the play in order to combat the charge that his "language was originally extremely licentious" and his "sentiments were violently democratic" (223). Lewis, though a member of Lord Holland's circle and a proponent of various liberal positions including the abolition of slavery, was still concerned with the accusations that he was a rabid democrat. In the case of *The Captive*, he made some changes in the performance version to lessen the "feminist" message of the play. The printed text sets the scene in a "Private Mad-House," making clear the institutional link between money and patriarchal control. It also ends with the captive going mad, while the performance version preserved in the licensing manuscript goes on to have her healed by the appearance of her father and brother and, most importantly, her son. This trinity of male figures recall her to sanity, as she—we assume—discovers that all men are not like her husband or his stand-in, the gaoler. She finds herself again when she sees herself reflected in sympathetic male eyes, and particularly when she can return to her maternal role. The performance version thus returns the woman to a place in a patriarchal order, unlike the printed version where the conclusion is dropped and the wrongs of woman are allowed to stand in all their full horror.

This attempt to blunt the impact of the play by reinstating traditional order as a frame for the Gothic, radical content is carried even further when Lewis seeks to discover in the Gothic a new ground for tragedy, as he does in *Alfonso, King of Castille* and *Adelgitha; or, The Fruits of a Single Error*, which can be read as re-visions of *The Castle Spectre* and *The Captive*, respectively. *Alfonso* might at first appear as a standard Gothic melodrama. The play centers upon a revolt led by Caesario who believes that Alfonso's actions have led to the death of Caesario's father, Orsino (Alfonso had ordered the death of Orsino for alleged treason, but he had been falsely accused and the king's daughter has kept Orsino alive). Caesario, like Osmond in *The Castle Spectre*, has considerable heroic charisma as he proves both on the battlefield—he has defeated the Moorish opponents of Alfonso—and in the bedroom—he has won the love of both Amelrosa, the Queen's daughter whom he has married, and Otillia, the wife of Guzman whom he has seduced as part of his plot.

However, while Lewis seeks to evoke sympathy for Osmond despite his villainies, he works to alienate us from Caesario despite his heroic attributes. Caesario contends that he fights in honor of his image of his father whom he sees as a "hero / A demi-god" (III, ii),[65] but it is clear that it is the selfish goals of glory and power that motivate him, along with a healthy dose of hate and revenge. The corrupt nature of his efforts is most clearly revealed when his father refuses to join his revolt, calling him a traitor. In fact, in the original version of the play, Osorio killed Caesario in order to save the King, but this was judged too horrible for audiences and was changed in performance. Caesario shares with many Gothic villain-heroes and romantic heroes a conflict between love and hate, but in Caesario sadism and violence seem to win out. When he finds that his love for Amelrosa is at odds with his hate for Alfonso, it is his hatred that takes precedence, for "To cease to hate him, I must cease to breath!" (II, i). He admits that he "*may* be guilty, but I *must* be great" (III, ii). And after he kills his mistress Otillia, he enters to his band of conspirators to proclaim his kind of rule as they shout a welcome to him:

> Aye, shout, shout,
> And kneeling greet your blood-anointed king,
> This steel [he grasps a bloody dagger] his sceptre! Tremble,
>     dwarfs in guilt,
> And own your master! Thou art proof, Henriquez,
> 'Gainst pity; I once saw thee stab in battle
> A page who clasped thy knees: And Melchior there
> Made quick work with a brother whom he hated.
> But what did *I* this night? Hear, hear, and reverence!
> There was a breast, on which my head had rested
> A thousand times; a breast, which loved me fondly,
> As Heaven loves martyred saints; and yet this breast
> I stabbed, knaves, stabbed it to the heart! Wine! wine there!
> For my soul's joyous.
> (IV, iv)

Caesario announces himself here as an anti-authority, who gains power through blood and destruction, anointed, not by God nor by the blood-line of succession, but by the blood of murder: Caesario is a Terrorist. He has the personal abilities one might look for in a leader—the courage, the energy, the power to draw others to him; but Lewis's play insists that personal qualities are less important than traditional, inherited position.

It is important to remember that this play is named *Alfonso, King of Castille* and not for Caesario or Osorio, the two characters who have most interested readers and critics; even Lewis himself, in his preface to the play, concentrates upon the tensions in Osorio and Caesario. The father and son continue Lewis's exploration of morally mixed character that had lent power (and potentially radical provocation) to earlier creations such as Osmond. Lewis, however, now seems troubled by the appeal generated by heroic qualities in evil characters, and he thus seeks to neutralize that appeal. In a sense, Lewis renders the villain-hero into a more traditional villain in the character of Caesario and thus leaves room to reintroduce a legitimate figure of authority, Alfonso. It is given to Orsino, who has suffered greatly at Alfonso's hands, to voice the claims for the monarch whom he calls "Alfonso / The wise, the good." Orsino continues to assert that he has been wronged, but he does not see his private or personal grievance against the King as having any weight when measured against the public good and the monarch's power. In an interesting verbal twist, Orsino creates rights for the monarch in finding that the King has done wrong: "What are my wrongs against a monarch's rights? / What is my curse against a nation's blessings?" (III, ii). The moral wrongs committed against Orsino are nothing in the context of the political rights possessed by the monarch, and the old man's curse is lost in the general blessings heaped upon the good king. The Gothic drama's investigation of both individual and Gothic revolt is swallowed up in a recovery of true kingly power, a hierarchical authority that Lewis may have felt essential to tragedy.

*Adelgitha* goes perhaps even further in creating a figure of positive authority as it rewrites monodrama as tragedy. *Adelgitha* is similar to other plays, such as those of Baillie to which we will turn shortly and Coleridge's *Remorse*, that draw upon monodramatic techniques to trace the development of a single emotion as it comes to dominate the central character. Adelgitha, the apparently virtuous wife of Robert Guiscard, has as a young girl loved a wounded soldier who betrayed her after leaving her pregnant. Her guilt over this liaison and her subsequent attempts to preserve her honor despite it determine her acts throughout the play, as she finds herself ever more deeply involved in the plots she pursues to save her name. Lewis seeks tragic inevitability in what he sees as the relentless mechanism of sin and guilt (he uses his own lines, " 'Tis in man's choice never to sin at all, / But sinning once, to stop exceeds his power," as an epigram). Importantly, this inevitability does not derive from Fate or Providence but from the working out of the central character's guilty emotions. Tragedy is found in monodramatic psychology.

In many ways, then, *Adelgitha* is a five-act version of *The Captive*, for like the captive Adelgitha is pursued by an oppressive male, in her case Michael-Ducas, the deposed Emperor of Byzantium, who learns her secret and uses it in his attempts to seduce her; like the woman in *The Captive*, Adelgitha goes mad and finds in her son the only tie to hope and life. However, where *The Captive* (at least in the published version) offers a rather comprehensive attack upon patriarchal power, *Adelgitha* makes the woman the criminal and rediscovers in Robert Guiscard the model husband and ruler. Called the "new Cato" and a "Norman Brutus" even by his enemy Michael, Guiscard stands as a force of political and domestic authority. The justice and moderation of his rule is contrasted to the violence and turbulence in Byzantium. In a world marked by revolt, murder, mysterious parentage, and sexual indiscretion—in a Gothic world, that is—Guiscard stands as an island of calm order. *The Captive*, like the Gothic plays of the 1790s, raises questions about authority, hierarchy, patriarchy, but *Adelgitha*, like *Alfonso*, celebrates the familial and political patriarch and seeks hierarchical order beyond Gothic chaos.

The alterations that Lewis works upon the Gothic in these plays reflect the changing institutional, generic, and ideological pressures he faced. The censor was ever more attentive to potentially dangerous lines and provocative plays; and critics and audiences were largely in agreement in this disapproval of the troubling during an era of national troubles. The very decision to write a tragedy also had implications for the shape of the Gothic. While the romantics would rework tragedy to reveal its generic possibilities, its openness to new content, tragedy as a conventional genre bodied forth in the traditional repertoire was an inherently conservative form. More specifically, the kinds of authority figures that arise in *Adelgitha* and *Alfonso* may have struck Lewis as essential to tragedy; they have certainly seemed so to some of the best students of tragedy, including George Steiner who, in the *Death of Tragedy*, locates the decline of the tragic exactly in the kind of questioning of hierarchical and providential order that can be found in the Gothic but not in Lewis's tragedies.[66]

Finally, Lewis's plays provide evidence of his awareness of the ideological climate in which he wrote. The prologue to *Alfonso*, for example, explicitly places the play in the political context of 1802. Wondering why modern tragedy—even Baillie's *De Monfort*—has failed, the prologue suggests that the public did not want to view tragedies while the greater "tragedy" of the war against France was being pursued: "While ruthless War his thunders hurl'd around, / The *laugh* might *soothe*, the sigh, tho' just, might wound." *Alfonso*, it is suggested, can succeed for it arrives with the peace overtures of early 1802. This reference to contemporary events frames the discussion within the play of a just war and a peaceful monarch that occurs in Orsino's defense of Alfonso; a parallel is created between Alfonso's righteous war against the Moors and England's struggle with Napoleon's France. A similar parallel is found in *Adelgitha*. In his preface to that play Lewis disclaims any interest in writing a history play; but, while he may have no interest in Guiscard and the Byzantine Empire, his play can be read as displacing onto the past the ideological struggles of the present age of the French Revolution. The opposition between the order of Guiscard's rule and the upheavals that mark Byzantine history can be seen as paralleling the standard juxtaposition of peaceful, prosperous England and violent France. These parallels suggest another reason why these plays turn away from the charismatic individual who stood at the center of the standard Gothic play and embrace instead conventional figures of authority: the difficulties and desires of individuals count for little in Lewis's tragedies when set against the vital role of the monarchy as institution in the midst of national unrest and the importance of Castille/Guiscard/England's fight against the Moors/Michael-Ducas/Napoleon. Charismatic villain-heroes might seem a bit too Napoleonic.

Lewis is, in many ways, the most interesting of the Gothic dramatists: he writes across the full range of the Gothic drama, creating sensational entertainments and tragedies, melodramas and a monodrama, verse plays and equestrian spectaculars; he exemplifies the power of the Gothic at the box office and on the page; and he explores the boundaries of the Gothic—the borderland between popular and "high" literature, the generic limits placed on its radical message. His "serious" works finally stand with those of a number of other writers whose attempts to convert the Gothic to aesthetic respectability led them to contain it within a concomitant ideological conservatism. Coleridge—the enemy of the "jacobinical drama"—more self-consciously seeks to rework the Gothic, rewriting *Osorio* as the tamer *Remorse* and more interestingly seeking to contain Gothic tragedy within a conservative romance in *Zapolya*. Even in Byron we see a move away from Gothic roots in *Manfred* and *Werner* towards a more traditional form in his historical tragedies, the ideological charge of which Shelley certainly recognized.[67] However, in the two plays included in this volume, Lewis still engages the radical heart of the early Gothic. Despite increasing pressures on the drama, despite a changing cultural and ideological climate, other key Gothic dramatists—Joanna Baillie and Charles Robert Maturin—would continue to draw upon this radical potential, and they would do so even as they sought to create modern tragedies.

### VII   *Joanna Baillie: Gothic Women*

From 1798 to 1851—for over half a century—Joanna Baillie was the most respected and arguably the most important playwright in England. She wrote twenty-six plays. Her first volume of *A Series of Plays: In Which It is Attempted To Delineate The Stronger Passions of the Mind Each Passion Being The Subject of A Tragedy and a Comedy* (usually referred to as the *Plays on the Passions*) went through five editions in the first six years following its publication in 1798. Seven of her plays were staged during her lifetime, the most important of them—*De Monfort*—being offered in London, Edinburgh, and New York. In 1851, the year of her death, she issued *The Dramatic and Poetic Works of Joanna Baillie, Complete in One Volume*, her "great monster book," as she called it, running over 800 pages.[68]

Baillie's *Plays on the Passions* were in many ways at the heart of the romantic project to remake the drama, embodying the kind of study of the psychology of passion that Wordsworth attempted in the *Borderers* and Coleridge in *Remorse* and influencing the more successful dramatic efforts of Byron and Shelley. Baillie was sought out by the major writers of the day such as Scott, Byron, and Wordsworth; Kemble and Siddons, the virtual king and queen of the theatrical world, solicited her for plays. Her *Collection of Poems, Chiefly Manuscript and from Living Authors* included poems by Scott, Wordsworth, Felicia Hemans, Anna Laetitia Barbauld, Crabbe, and Rogers and had a long list of subscribers beginning with the royal family. Scott called Joanna Baillie "the best dramatic writer since the days of Shakespeare and Massinger"; Byron claimed that Baillie "is our only dramatist since Otway and Southerne." Reviewers generally praised her work, as in this comment from the *Poetical Register* in 1804: "Among the modern writers of Tragedy the most honourable place must indubitably be awarded to Miss Baillie."[69]

The widespread admiration Baillie received from her contemporaries has, rather than making her attractive to modern readers, tended to blind us to her innovations, to her place in the literary revolutions of her day: she is too often treated as an exemplum of a failed dramatic school. Her work certainly did partake of the literary movements of her day. The arguments that she sets forth in her theoretical preface to her plays about purifying literary diction and about grounding literature in universal human emotions link her to Wordsworth and his famous preface. We can connect her through her interest in Scottish materials, history, and legend with Sir Walter Scott. More important for current purposes, many of her plays owe a debt to the Gothic tradition out of which she arises but on which she turns a self-reflective gaze. Baillie is central to a discussion of the Gothic because her plays offer a self-conscious examination of some of the fundamental conventions of the Gothic and of their implications for the construction of the feminine.

Baillie's plays engage the standard Gothic settings. *The Dream* (1812) takes place largely in a monastery near a castle. *Romiero* (1836) offers another castle and a ruined chapel, *Ethwald* (1802) an abbey, and *Henriquez* (1836) yet another castle complete with "The burying-vault of the castle, with monuments of the dead; and near the front of the stage, a newly covered grave, seen by the light of a lamp placed on a neighboring tomb, the stage being otherwise dark."[70] These buildings are, of course, equipped with the necessary accoutrements—hidden doors, tolling bells, torturous stairways. Beyond such gloomy structures are the natural settings most often found in Gothic dramas: the forests of *Ethwald* and *Rayner* (1804), the rocky wasteland of *The Family Legend* (1810), and the moor of *Witchcraft* (1836). As the title of this last play suggests, the supernatural also has an important place in Baillie's work, though she is part of the rational, Radcliffean school and thus eschews actual appearances by ghosts and demons. Her central male figures are important examples of the Gothic villain-hero as he develops into the Byronic hero. *De Monfort*, her best known, most successful play and the one included here, has as its protagonist a gloomy idealist, a man who attracts the affection of everyone around him but who is driven by his secret hatred for a childhood antagonist. De Monfort is a key instance of the mixing of moral qualities in Gothic characters and of the confused response such divided characters evoke. He is an obsessive murderer, but we are invited to sympathize with him. Baillie works now to create him as a hero—allowing him to leave the play with a grand gesture—and now seeks to judge him—claiming in a note that Jane De Monfort's defense of her brother represents the character's and not the author's sentiments. In her preface to her plays she tried to resolve this tension in a formula: "it is the passion and not the man which is held up to our execration."[71] But her plays participate in the confusion of psychological analysis with moral judgement that led Coleridge to condemn the Gothic drama.

It is not, however, her use of Gothic settings or properties or even her portrayal of the male hero that is most interesting in her plays; it is her investigation of the depiction of women in the Gothic. When her plays were first published anonymously, most male reviewers, praising their power and stylistic simplicity, assumed they were written by a man. Women readers, however, immediately identified the writer as a woman. Mrs. Piozzi argued in her commonplace book that the *Plays on the Passions* were written by a woman "because both the heroines are *Dames Passées* and a man has no notion of mentioning a female after she is five and twenty."[72] Mary Berry also argued the plays had to be written by a woman "because . . . no man could or would draw such noble and dignified representations of the female mind as Countess Albini [in *Count Basil*] and Jane de Monfort. They [men] often make us clever, captivating, heroic, but never rationally superior."[73] Such comments suggest that female readers found in Baillie's plays images of women that stood against stereotypes. I would go further to suggest that her plays explore the power that literary representations—and particularly dramatic ones—have to fix women within a particular cultural gaze. Her plays do not merely offer alternative

images of women; they offer a critique of various conventiona
dramatizing women, particularly those modes we identify
Gothic. A play such as *De Monfort* stands with Lewis's *The Cap*
of their period's contribution to a tradition of feminist theater.

Baillie's *De Monfort* can be read as an investigation of "Siddons-mania,"
the nearly hysterical response to the performances of Sarah Siddons. The
key to Mrs. Siddons's success was her portrayal of highly charged emotional states. For example, John Waldie, in his manuscript theatrical journal, describes Siddons acting in Home's *Douglas:* "her figure and
countenance are particulary fitted to expressing the passions. . . . her acting was the very image of fear, hope, anxiety, maternal affection and every
passion which could be felt in that situation . . . ."[74] Siddons's passionate
performances evoked corresponding emotions in her audience as the playwright James Boaden attests in his biography: "I well remember (how is
it possible I should ever forget?) the sobs, the shrieks . . . . We then, indeed, knew all the luxury of grief; but the nerves of many a gentle being
gave way before the intensity of such appeals, and fainting fits long and
frequently alarmed the decorum of the house . . . ."[75] Siddons's performances offered the acting equivalent to Lewis's texts; for she did not
purge pity and fear but provoked tears and terror. She was the perfect
actress for the Gothic drama, for she was at her best in the two stances the
Gothic demanded of women: women were either terrorized and mad or
stoic and indomitable, but they were always passive.

Baillie clearly wished to draw upon the power of Siddons's performances in *De Monfort*, for she designed the character of Jane De Monfort
with Siddons in mind; but I would suggest that Baillie sought to disen-
chant the conventional image of woman as passive responder that Siddons
embodied. Siddons specialized in wronged or abandoned wives who did
not so much act as emote, including Lady Randolph in Home's *Douglas*,
Calista in Rowe's *The Fair Penitent*, Mrs. Beverley in Moore's *The Gamester*,
and Belvidera in Otway's *Venice Preserved*. Even when she played strong
female characters such as Lady Macbeth, she seems to have reconceived
them in relation to more powerful men; Siddons wrote in her notes on
Lady Macbeth that she is "most captivating to the other sex,—fair, feminine, nay, perhaps even fragile— . . . captivating in feminine loveliness . . . a charm of such potency as to fascinate the mind of a hero so
dauntless, a character so amiable, so honorable as Macbeth . . . ."[76] Lady
Macbeth's power over Macbeth is made here passive—she is a seductive
object, not a manipulator of the action. It is interesting that the most famous image of Mrs. Siddons is Reynolds's portrait of her as the tragic
muse, where she is not seen acting, doing something, but is instead

enthroned as a static object of contemplation. Boaden uses an intriguing phrase in recalling Reynolds watching Siddons perform: "I saw him on this occasion in the orchestra, with great pleasure, sitting 'all gaze, all wonder'."[77]

Such an account of Siddons's performances suggests that the theater she dominated already was marked by the split between spectacle and narrative that Laura Mulvey has found in the classic cinema. Mulvey argues that the pleasure in looking evoked by the cinema is split between an active/male gaze through which the spectator identifies with the controlling male protagonist and a passive/female figure who is an erotic object both for the characters within the film and for the audience. Men control the action, the narrative, while women exist for display, for spectacle.[78] While there are important differences between the media of film and stage, Siddons's performances already seem to enact such a split. Her characters exist to respond to the action of the men; the enormous emotional charge felt by those who watched her suggests the desire and fear projected upon her. Joanna Baillie, I would suggest, understood the nature of Mrs. Siddons's appeal and sought to expose it in *De Monfort*.

The plot of *De Monfort*, Baillie's tragedy on hatred, is simple. De Monfort flees his home to avoid the presence of Rezenvelt, a childhood competitor whom he has come to hate, only to find himself again in the same town with his rival. Once Jane De Monfort arrives and attracts the attentions of Rezenvelt, the situation is set. Convinced that an alliance is forming between his rival and his beloved sister, De Monfort's hatred grows until he murders Rezenvelt. He is arrested only to die of remorse.

*De Monfort* appears at first as a straight-forward Gothic psychological thriller. It uses Gothic settings (dark woods and a convent), characters (the inwardly troubled De Monfort, the villainous Conrad), and atmospherics (lightning flashes, screaming owls, tolling bells) to provide the backdrop for its close investigation of the passion of hatred. As I have already suggested, the play explores the tensions in De Monfort's mixed character, and it evokes a divided response in us. The play appears largely conventional if we focus on De Monfort and his story. However, the play has another central figure, De Monfort's sister, Jane. While it is always assumed that he is the protagonist of the play, that it is named for him, Jane is also a De Monfort and in many ways is the dominating presence in the play. Her role is far less conventional, and Baillie's treatment of her reveals the play's revisionary stance towards its Gothic tradition.

While Baillie has the first appearance of each of her three main characters—Jane, De Monfort, and Rezenvelt—prepared for us by secondary characters, there is a striking difference between what we hear about De

Monfort and Rezenvelt and what we are told about Jane. The men are defined through past actions; anecdotes are retold to reveal their characters. We are given only physical descriptions of Jane, seen through the eyes of men. It is as if we are being told how to view Jane, as if our gaze was being directed. Jane would seem to exist as an object of male contemplation and erotic fascination.

However, when she appears, she is not what we have been told to expect. Men describe her as a great beauty, but we find from a page that she is older, perhaps plainer than we have been led to believe. She is called queenly but appears in humble garb at a fashionable ball. The men seem captivated by her, but she is clearly uninterested in attracting them. Of course, these expectations are created by men. The three central male characters—De Monfort, Rezenvelt, and their mutual friend Count Freberg—are all obsessed with Jane. Freberg becomes so fixated on his image of Jane as a beautiful and tempting woman that he arouses the jealousy of his wife. Rezenvelt also is drawn to Jane. He ignores her obvious discomfort at his attentions and the agony they cause her brother and persists in a flirtation with her. His preconditioned vision of her as a possible erotic object is stronger than the evidence of her actual presence and responses. De Monfort himself, clearly emotionally involved with his sister at a depth the play does not explore, also comes to view her as a possible partner for Rezenvelt. De Monfort's jealousy is fed by the Iagoesque machinations of Conrad, until he ceases to see Jane for what she is, but, Othello-like, sees her through the eyes of others.

Baillie works to make her audience self-conscious about the way in which the male gaze seeks to capture Jane but fails to do so. The simple contradiction between what we are told of Jane and what we see already begins to undermine our confidence in the conventional roles men want Jane to play. Baillie goes further by drawing attention to the fact that it is Mrs. Siddons playing Jane De Monfort. Siddons's friend and biographer Thomas Campbell felt that the play's first full description of Jane was a "perfect picture of Mrs. Siddons."[79] Such a comment suggests that audiences were made aware of the actress behind the character, with all of the culturally coded responses Siddons, the actress, evoked. Such self-consciousness breaks the dramatic illusion and the power of dramatic stereotypes by making the audience think about Siddons and her conventional roles. The men in the play want Jane De Monfort to be a typical Siddons character: emotionally responsive, powerfully attractive, passive. They want her to be the spectacle at the center of their narrative, the object over which they fight—both in the social realm of flirtation and in actual combat. She, however, simply refuses to play that role. It is not she but the men who are dominated by their emotions. She is the calm one, the peace-maker, the one who exercises self-control.

In fact, with one exception, throughout Baillie's *Plays on the Passions* it is the men who are subject to the passions that are her central subject. Once Rezenvelt and her brother are dead, Jane takes control of the play. The other characters offer her their allegiance and allow her to direct their actions and thoughts. It is left to Jane to understand what has transpired and to interpret it for the other characters and the audience. Baillie imagines here a female character freed from the masculine gaze and beginning to define herself beyond the roles offered by a male-centered social system. And perhaps Siddons, made self-conscious about her own performance as Jane, understood what Baillie was doing, when she asked of the playwright, "Make for me more Jane De Monforts."[80]

Baillie did not recreate Jane De Monfort, but she did continue to explore how the Gothic drama structures the way women are perceived. In *Witchcraft*, she tackles the most obvious Gothic image of the female and seeks to historicize and psychologize it, to understand the conditions that would make women believe themselves to be witches. In *Basil*, her tragedy on love, she again examines the way in which women are constructed and constricted by the male gaze: the play opens upon a crowd in Mantua who are waiting for a glimpse of Victoria who is reputed to be "wondrous fair" and who captures the heart of Basil when he first gazes upon her; later Victoria debates with the two other female characters in the play about the power of female sexual attraction, with Victoria celebrating "the glances of her conquering eye" and the Countess Albini worrying that "she who only finds her self-esteem / In other's admiration, begs an alms . . . And is the very servant of her slaves."[81]

Perhaps most interestingly, *Orra*, Baillie's tragedy on fear, explores the impact of Gothic terror on women; not only does the play exhibit such hallmarks of the Gothic as a vaguely medieval setting, a haunted castle, and a band of robbers, but it also reflects upon the power of Gothic conventions over the mind of its female protagonist. In a sense, *Orra* is the tragic counterpart of Austen's *Northanger Abbey*. Orra is pursued by a range of male characters from the oafish Glottenbal and the villain Rudigere to the heroic Theobald, but she makes it clear that she does not want to marry anyone. She seems to replace sexual desire with a joy in fear. Baillie then explores the erotic charge underlying the dynamics of Gothic terror by having her plot hinge upon the varying uses the men make of terror in seeking to win Orra: Rudigere seeks to exploit her lively sense of fear by imprisoning her in a supposedly haunted castle; Theobald seeks to rescue her disguised as the ghost, but she believes him to be truly a supernatural apparition and goes mad.

Orra at first sees her delight in terror, which she shares with her maids in bouts of story-telling, as a mode of female emotional bonding free from the male domination so marked in the society of the play. But Baillie suggests that the Gothic heroine—insofar as she finds herself entranced and even titillated by the mysterious surroundings controlled by her male persecutors—is in fact a participant in the set of structures that oppress her. Orra's pleasurable terrors leave her to be manipulated by men—by both the villain and the nominal hero; she plays a role in their fantasies—one of domination, the other of rescue, but both fantasies in which the woman, helpless and paralyzed by fear, finally succumbs to the power of the male. Orra rejects marriage but fails to understand that her emotional responses—programmed by the patterns of the Gothic—still entrap her within a male plot. Unlike Jane De Monfort who breaks free at the end of her play to control both speech and action—the two components of dramatic presentation—Orra finds herself so completely subjected to male plots that she loses even the power of rational speech, as the play closes upon the pure emotional response of Orra's madness that would have provided Sarah Siddons with a great scene.

Baillie's accomplishment in *De Monfort* and in such less well known plays as *Orra* is considerable. These plays explore the ways in which accepted dramatic modes such as the Gothic and the acting style of Mrs. Siddons entrap women within conventional forms of emotional response. The Gothic, with its sensationalism and thematics of the extreme, clearly had the ability to explore radical positions, whether in the reflections upon revolution embodied in such plays as *Julia of Louvain* or in the examinations of gendered oppression in such plays as *The Captive*. Baillie uses Gothic techniques to reflect upon the Gothic itself and its underlying ideology, particularly its construction of the feminine. Her plays embody a sustained meditation upon the roles and plots that constrict women, a meditation not matched in her period by other dramatists or for that matter by the better known Gothic novelists. Her self-reflective turn upon the Gothic tradition represented one way of revitalizing the Gothic drama as the theatrical, cultural, and ideological world changed from that of the 1790s and the Gothic's triumph.

*VIII Transforming the Gothic Drama: From Heroes to Monsters*

For at least two anthologizers of nineteenth-century drama, Charles Robert Maturin's *Bertram; or, The Castle of St. Aldobrand* marks a "climax" in the history of the Gothic drama, though for one this was an ironic success since "the craze for Gothic drama . . . was to some extent sobered by the excesses of *Bertram*."[82] First offered on 9 May 1816 with Edmund

Kean in the lead, *Bertram* clearly spoke to its audience and to the reading public of the day, achieving twenty-two performances before the end of the season and going through seven editions during its first year of publication; but it is also testimony to changes in the Gothic that would eventually lead to its decline before the popularity of the domestic melodrama.

*Bertram* takes its place among the largest collection of important Gothic plays performed since the 1790s. In 1813, Coleridges's *Remorse* had a respectable run. Milman's *Fazio* (Surrey, 1816; Covent Garden, 1818) was another hit of the period with ties to the Gothic. Sheil had a success with *Evadne; or, The Statue* (Covent Garden, 1819). Byron wrote a series of plays that owed debts to the Gothic: *Manfred* (1817; performed at Covent Garden in 1834), *Cain, A Mystery* (1821), and *Werner* (1823; performed at Bath and Drury Lane, 1830). Shelley's *The Cenci* (1819; performed by the Shelley Society, 1886) is the best play of its period and one with Gothic roots. There are also important adaptations of Scott such as Daniel Terry's *Guy Mannering* (Covent Garden, 1816) and of Byron such as William Dimond's *The Bride of Abydos* (Drury Lane, 1818). It is, however, Maturin who is the most important figure in this second phase in the history of the Gothic drama; the Matthew Lewis of his day, he wrote Gothic novels, including his masterpiece *Melmoth the Wanderer*, and dramas, *Manuel* (Drury Lane, 1817), and *Fredolfo* (Covent Garden, 1819) in addition to *Bertram*.

Despite such successes, the Gothic drama was not the commanding force during Maturin's day that it had been in the 1790s. Increasingly, the domestic melodrama came to be the central popular form. One can see the Gothic and the domestic drama as variations of the larger form of the melodrama, but there is finally a significant difference between them, as I have suggested above. Their common ground can be seen in a play such as Thomas Holcroft's *A Tale of Mystery* (Covent Garden, 1802), adapted from Pixérécourt, and the first English play labeled as a "melodrama," or in a work like Isaac Pocock's *Miller and his Men* (Covent Garden, 1813); these dramas have many Gothic features—wild scenery, villains marked by past crimes and dominated by lust—but they move away from the Gothic's thematics of the extreme, reducing the complex amorality of the villain-hero to a moral stereotype, rejecting the Gothic's exploration of the supernatural for more everyday concerns, and turning from the display of collective or individual revolt to the celebration of domestic, familial, and patriotic virtue. While there is surely a Gothic presence in the theater throughout the nineteenth century, by 1820 and W. T. Moncrieff's *The Lear of Private Life; or, Father and Daughter* (Coburg), the domestic melodrama had displaced the Gothic, as Gilbert

Cross has argued.[83] We can trace the transformation of the Gothic drama during this period through two plays included in this volume, *Bertram* and Richard Brinsley Peake's adaptation of Mary Wollstonecraft Shelley's masterpiece, *Frankenstein*, as *Presumption; or, The Fate of Frankenstein* (English Opera House, 1823).

The Gothic drama of Maturin's day—that is, the post-Napoleonic period—appears less as a popular entertainment than as a form of protest drama, as a self-conscious return on the part of "avant-garde" artists such as Shelley and Byron to an earlier form with radical associations. It is significant that the greatest Gothic plays of the period—*Manfred* and *The Cenci*—were published but not performed, *Manfred* explicitly turning away from the stage and *The Cenci* being blocked from the theater because of its radical content. To adapt loosely Schiller's famous distinction, the early Gothic plays are naive works arising as an immediate response to generally perceived artistic, institutional, and ideological difficulties, while these later plays are sentimental ones that evoke the Gothic for more self-conscious, reflective purposes.

One key difference between the early Gothic plays of the 1790s and later ones is found in the treatment of revolt. Works such as *Julia of Louvain* or *The Kentish Barons* included not only the story of the isolated protest of the villain-hero but also images of mass movements and popular protests. Post-Napoleonic plays such as *Bertram*, while maintaining vestiges of the earlier portraits of broad-based protest (Maturin includes a Schillerian robber band that actually has little to do in the play), focus upon the single titanic or satanic individual. One could see the relation of plays such as Maturin's *Bertram* to the Gothic drama of the 1790s as similar to the stance of Osborne's *Look Back in Anger* towards the earlier tradition of protest drama or drama of ideas. While the drama of protest from Ibsen to Shaw and Brecht had a radical potential, Osborne invokes this tradition not as a means of imaging, say, the liberation of women or the power of mass political movements or the transformation of ideology and culture but as a way of staging the solitary stand of the isolated rebel, whether he be an "angry young man" crying out against post-war Britain or Luther unable to understand the peasant uprisings. Maturin's Bertram (or Byron's Manfred) also strikes one as an alienated rebel without a cause rather than a leader of popular protest. The hero of a popular spectacular such as *Julia of Louvain*, even an aristocratic villain-hero such as Lewis's Osmond, embodied the protest of the audience, but these later Gothic figures are, like Manfred, "not of thine order" and have "no sympathy with breathing flesh."[84] This is the age of Napoleon, not the masses, of Byron, not Paine.

It is not surprising that these dramas of the post-Napoleonic era should turn to the isolated, titanic figure. A play such as *Bertram* can be read as expressing the period's fascination with the grand figure of Napoleon— seen in Scott, Hazlitt, and Byron among many others. The tie to portraits of Napoleon can be made by comparing Maturin's Prior on Bertram with Byron on Napoleon:

> High-hearted man, sublime even in thy guilt,
> Whose passions are thy crimes, whose angel-sin
> Is pride that rivals the star-bright apostate's.—
> Wild admiration thrills me to behold
> An evil strength, so above earthly pitch—
> Descending angels only could reclaim thee—
> (III, i)

> There sunk the greatest, nor the worst of men
> Whose spirit, antithetically mixt,
> One moment of the mightiest, and again
> On little objects with like firmness fixt;
> Extreme in all things! hadst thou been betwixt,
> Thy throne had still been thine, or never been;
> For daring made thy rise as fall: thou seek'st
> Even now to re-assume the imperial mien,
> And shake again the world, the Thunderer of the scene![85]

Napoleon, like Bertram, is here the Gothic villain-hero, "antithetically mixt," who commands admiration and who can control everything but himself. Bertram, who has challenged his monarch in some unspecified way, who has led a robber/rebel band, and who now has turned to despair and misanthropy, is also linked to the image of the post-revolutionary Englishman as a depressed solitary—a figure who moves through the poetry of the day from Wordsworth's *Excursion* (1815) through Byron's *Childe Harold* (1812, 1816, 1818) to Keats's *Endymion* (1818). *Bertram* took on an immediate ideological charge in the company of such works, as can be seen in Coleridge's attack upon the play in the *Biographia*.

The *Biographia* takes its place as part of a reactionary cultural moment, an attempt to define the post-Napoleonic era in conservative terms and thus to offer a conservative reading of the French Revolution and the period's cultural revolutions as well. *The Excursion* is the great poetic work of this moment, and the *Biographia* the great critical piece; but it is Coleridge's *Lay Sermons (The Statesmen's Manual; or the Bible the Best Guide to Po-*

*litical Skill and Foresight,* 1816; *A Lay Sermon Addressed to the Higher and Middle Classes on the Existing Distresses and Discontents,* 1817) that perhaps most clearly reveal the program behind such texts, a program that was clear enough for Hazlitt to launch an attack upon the *Lay Sermons* through *The Examiner* even before they were published. The place in such ideological battles of the *Biographia,* too often read as a "pure" work of literary criticism, is made clear in its opening in which Coleridge says he is less interested in biography or even literature than in offering a "statement of my principles in Politics, Religion, and Philosophy . . . ."[86]

Coleridge's political reading of the poetic is perhaps clearest when Coleridge turns to the drama in "Satyrane's Letters" and in the review of *Bertram* in Chapter 23. In these sections, Coleridge takes up again the attack upon the Gothic drama launched by *The Anti-Jacobin* in 1798 (Coleridge's letters were originally written in 1798–99). As I have noted, Coleridge defines the Gothic drama as the jacobinical drama, a definition he offers twice, once in the letters and again, in shortened form, in the assault on *Bertram,* quoted above.

As in 1798 when Gifford and his journal attacked Gothic playwrights and adaptors of German plays as dangerous radicals, this 1816 accusation against Maturin as a purveyor of dramatic jacobinism could not be taken lightly. 1816 was a year of considerable unrest leading up to the Spa Field Riots at the end of the year; in fact, Coleridge wrote the *Lay Sermons* to address the "existing distresses and discontents," so he was quite aware of the tense political situation and the impact of attaching this particular ideological label to a work of art. And, of course, Coleridge was not alone in finding *Bertram* troubling (though we should note that the conservative Scott was Maturin's greatest supporter and the one who arranged for its performance through Byron). Maturin's ecclesiastic superiors were certainly not entertained by the play. As the editors of Maturin's correspondence with Scott put it, "The production of *Bertram* ended all chance of Maturin's advancement in the church, containing as it did sentiments regarded as suspicious by his superiors. There were even reports that the author would be suspended for holding such sentiments."[87]

Coleridge's objections to *Bertram* return to the point continually made about the Gothic, from Walpole's comments on his *Mysterious Mother* through the attacks in *The Anti-Jacobin:* that the Gothic subverts morality and "the natural order of things" by confusing sympathy and judgment, by finding "noble" qualities in lower class figures and by offering sympathy to rebels. Coleridge makes clear that what might appear as a violation of literary decorum was read as a turn to a dangerous ideology opposed to religious and political order. As Coleridge says in protesting the adulterous union between Bertram and Imogine, "The shocking spirit of jacobinism seemed no longer confined to politics."[88]

Coleridge might have been even more shocked had he read the original version of the play. When he saw the performance version, he objected to its handling of religious matters, both its presentation of religious ritual in the fifth act ("the profane representation of the high altar in a chapel, with all the vessels and other preparations for the holy sacrament. A hymn is actually sung on the stage by the chorister boys!") and, as we have seen earlier, its staging of extraordinary events without a providential framework.[89] What would he have said of the author's original determination to bring the devil himself into the theater? In fact, the original play seems roughly modeled on the Faust legend, perhaps Goethe's *Faust* in particular. Maturin's revisions—made at the suggestion of Scott, Byron, and George Lamb—move the play away from the Faust legend towards *Othello* or, as Coleridge suggests, towards the Don Juan legend.

We have a rather full record of the revisions made to the play. Maturin sent the original manuscript of the play to Scott as a gift, and it is still held in the library at Abbotsford. Maturin corresponded with Scott, Byron, and Lamb about the play, and they discuss at length the changes to be made. The licensing manuscript held in the Larpent collection gives us the version finally submitted to the Lord Chamberlain by the theater and thus approximates the performance version. Many of the proposed changes had to do with the length and pacing of the play (particularly with breaking up long speeches); Maturin made most of these alterations, but refused to remove the adultery between Imogine and Bertram or the death of Imogine's child, both of which had been objected to on moral grounds and which would later cause him difficulties with Coleridge and other reviewers. Maturin's insistence upon keeping these incidents within the play suggests his sense of the play's radical shock value. Two other sets of alterations are particularly significant here: the excision of the "Dark Knight of the Forest" and the alteration in Bertram's final fate.

The original version of *Bertram* included the titular hero's pact with the "Dark Knight," whom Scott identifies with the devil in describing his efforts to eliminate him from the play:

> [Maturin] had our old friend Satan (none of your sneaking St. John-street devils, but the arch-fiend himself) brought on the stage bodily; I believe I have exorcised the foul fiend—for, though in reading he was a most terrible fellow, I feared for his reception in public.[90]

The manuscript included several early comments about the Dark Knight, and then in what is now III, i and was II, ii, St. Aldobrand and his page have an exchange about the Dark Knight, in which Aldobrand scoffs at the stories of this devilish figure. The Prior and Bertram then talk of the Dark Knight, and Bertram makes known his decision to quest for the Knight's company. In lines cut from what is now IV, i and was III, i, Bertram, gazing upon Imogine's window and noting her desperate situation, exclaims, "Away—away—to the Dark Knight of the Forest / To hell from this."

In what was IV, i, Bertram returns from his encounter newly dedicated to revenge and destruction:

> I felt those unseen eyes were fix'd on mine,
> If eyes indeed were there—
> Forgotten thoughts of evil, still-born mischiefs,
> Foul fertile seeds of passion and of crime,
> That wither'd in my heart's abortive core,
> Rous'd their dark battle at his trumpet-peal:
> . . . .
> I am not what I was since I beheld him—
> I was the slave of passion's ebbing sway—
> All is condensed, collected, callous now—
> The groan, the burst, the fiery flash is o'er,
> Down pours the dense and darkening lava tide,
> Arresting life and stilling all beneath it.

Bertram goes on to murder Aldobrand at Imogine's feet, which drives her mad, her insanity leading her to murder her child. The final scene—and here we see the other set of changes discussed in the letters—would have had Imogine dying in remorse for having caused her child's death but still praying for a "blessed death": "When comes the fiend to bear my soul away— / Linked with my cherub-form, his prey will mock him." The Prior then rushes on stage to tell us that Bertram has fled with the devil: "It is too late to pray for Bertram's soul."

This ending—in which the woman accused of child-murder is possibly saved because she has loved, and where the villain-hero flees in the company of the devil—seems based on the ending of *Faust I*. I would argue that Maturin originally wrote a Faust play, in which Bertram acquires not infinite knowledge or power but instead self-certainty in which "All is condensed, collected, callous now." Bertram's problem—and it is the problem of all the figures of Gothic and romantic tragedy—is that he has no firm basis upon which to act, no clear providential signs such as an oracle, no clear hierarchical role—he is a rebel, not a king or prince. He lives in a world in which the solid ground offered to the traditional hero has been cut away, leaving merely self-assertion, self-creation. What he discovered in the original scenes was a sanction for his destructive revenge in a supernatural source—in the devil, if not in God. Maturin's play suggests that the uncertainty of modern, romantic subjectivity prefers the demonic to the abyss of self-consciousness and relativism; Bertram, wracked by guilt and uncertainty as he contemplates Imogine's fate and his blighted love for her, says, "To hell from this." Coleridge in the *Biographia* suggests that the demand of the Gothic and Don Juan figures is for self-confirmation: "it is among the mysteries, and abides in the dark ground-work of our nature, to crave an outward confirmation of that *something* within us, which is our *very self*, that something, not *made up* of our qualities and relations, but itself the supporter and substantial basis of all these."[91] Bertram finds his "outward confirmation" in the Dark Knight, and it enables him to become one of the few truly strong, commanding figures of the romantic and Gothic theater. Where so many figures of the Gothic and romantic drama (one thinks of De Monfort, Manfred, Musset's Lorenzaccio) owe a debt to Hamlet and his self-reflective doubt, Bertram is a dynamic figure who appropriately defines himself through the language of lightning and volcano, for he is a force capable of "Arresting life and stilling all beneath it."

In cutting the Faustian elements of *Bertram*, Maturin had to reground Bertram's sense of himself. As Coleridge is aware, Bertram now seeks "outward confirmation" through the complete devotion of another being. Coleridge continues the passage quoted above, "Love *me*, and not my qualities, may be a vicious and an insane wish, but it is not a wish wholly without a meaning."[92] Bertram must demand that Imogine commit adultery—in the episode that shocked Coleridge and others—because he needs her to affirm him absolutely, beyond all social limits and restrictions. Bertram's tragedy in this final version is that he cannot finally rely upon love as the basis of his identity. Love puts him under the control of another, leaves his identity fluctuating with the rise and fall of the Other's emotions. Hate, on the other hand, enables Bertram to control the situation, to control the Other. Bertram thus turns from his love for Imogine to his hatred for Aldobrand. And Maturin redefines Bertram, now not as Faust but as Othello. For like Othello, he finds he cannot believe in a woman's love and must instead turn to the violence by which he has led the rest of his life; losing erotic faith, he finds in destruction—and finally self-destruction—the proof of his identity and his power. Bertram dies as a romantic Othello, stabbing himself and proclaiming, "I died no felon death— / A warrior's weapon freed a warrior's soul—" (V, iii).

The alterations in the play can be understood from a number of perspectives. Scott's and Lamb's objections to the Dark Knight and the original climax seem both aesthetic and ideological; that is, beyond their point that this poetic play (like *De Monfort*, the constant touchstone for playwrights of the day) moved too slowly for an audience used to spectacle and action, they are concerned—as playwrights from Siddons and Boaden forward had been concerned—with whether the supernatural would work on the stage; and they are worried that this direct presentation of the supernatural would offend some in the audience and amongst the critics, as it had in plays such as *The Castle Spectre*.

In many ways, the version that was performed and published was less radical than the original play; Maturin complained to Scott that the play was "*un-Maturined* completely, they have broken my wand and drowned my Magic Book, and Prospero himself, without his storms, his Goblins, & his Grammary, sinks into a very insignificant sort of Personage—."[93] Looked at in another way, however, the play retains a radical thrust, though its radicalism now centers in its treatment of the erotic. This shift is part of a larger ideological moment shared with Byron, Shelley, and Keats. As Jerome McGann has suggested, Byron's *Don Juan* is probably a response to Coleridge's reactionary reading of the Don Juan tradition in the attack on *Bertram*.[94] I would suggest that Byron offers a total response to the situation of *Bertram* that helps locate Maturin's play in the ideological struggles of the day; for Byron—who had read *Bertram* in its original version—not only offers a radical Don Juanism over against Coleridge's attack but also recreates *Bertram*'s rejected Faustian version in *Manfred* (Goethe, for one, noted the reworking of the Faust material in Byron's play). Maturin's turn from the first version of his play (1813) to the performance version (1816) is not unlike Byron's move from *Manfred* to *Don Juan*. It suggests a move on the part of radical authors from the metaphysical revolt of a Faust to the sexual revolution of a Don Juan; this turn to the sexual as radical politics has been outlined by Marilyn Butler as what she calls the "cult of the south."[95] Maturin's embrace of the erotic in *Bertram* places his play alongside of Shelley's *Laon and Cythna* (1817), Keats's *Endymion* (1818), and Byron's *Don Juan* (beginning 1819). Coleridge's attack upon the play, then, is an act of recognition of an ideological opponent by a reactionary spokesman.

In a cancelled passage to the play, Maturin seems to acknowledge the dangerous appeal of erotic tales:

> Far less I deem of peril is in such [horror stories]
> Than in those tales women most love to list to,
> The tales of love—for they are all untrue—
> Yet do they bear in them a wicked charm
> That sweetly stirs the blood it turns to fire
> As the light fanning of the vampire's wing
> Lulls the protracted slumber into death—
> (Abbotsford I, v)

This passage is of interest, for it places Bertram not only in the tradition of Don Juan but also as a precursor to one of Gothic literature's greatest contributions to popular myth, Dracula, the rebel of erotic liberation. Of course, the final play in this collection brought to the stage the Gothic's other great iconic figure: Frankenstein's monster. However, in linking *Bertram* to the vampire myth and the future of Gothic literature and in turning to Peake's Frankenstein play, we need to make a clear distinction between Maturin's play, which comes as a culmination or perhaps a coda to a tradition of Gothic drama embedded in the struggles of the revolutionary period, and later horror plays (and movies), that were written in response to different eras and different issues.

The vampire reached the stage in 1820 in Planché's *The Vampyre* (English Opera House). Richard Brinsley Peake brought Frankenstein and "(. . . . .)," as the creature is called in playbills, to the theater in 1823, also at the English Opera House. It is interesting that these two powerful Gothic images rise so late in the tradition, but finally it is not that surprising. These plays were written when the tide had turned against the Gothic in the theater, when the domestic melodrama had come to dominate the London stage. In a sense, these plays—as was *Bertram*— are a protest against the aesthetics and the vision of the domestic melodrama. But in another way, they are an adjustment to it, for domestic values are at the heart of these plays. In fact, what they do is reconstitute the Gothic as a story of two new challenges to domestic bliss: the threat no longer comes from young terroristic rebels or libertine aristocrats, but instead from one's own psyche, on the one hand, and from science, on the other. These final Gothic plays represent a turn from the directly social or political vision of the early Gothic and even away from the individual rebellion of *Bertram*. Instead, we get collective fears over sexuality and science.

Mary Shelley went to see the dramatization of her work as *Presumption; or, The Fate of Frankenstein* and wrote about it to Leigh Hunt on 9 September 1823:

But lo and behold! I found myself famous!—Frankenstein had prodigious success as a drama and was about to be repeated the 23rd
night at the English Opera House. The play bill amused me extremely, for in the list of dramatis personae came, —— by Mr. T.
Cooke: this nameless mode of naming the unnameable is rather
good. . . . I was much amused, and it appeared to excite a breathless
eagerness in the audience.[96]

Shelley clearly enjoyed the play and the recognition it brought her, but
she was also aware of how changed the drama was from her novel. Mary
Shelley's novel is a complex work that engages technological or scientific threats, the construction of gender and sexual relations, and the political upheavals of her day. The dramatization of her work draws out
from it a particular strand—the one dealing with the dangers of scientific
experimentation unchecked by any connection with or concern for one's
fellow human beings. The play essentially pits the monster against domesticity, scientific advance against the calm, orderly life of the family.
The drama works to contain the threats to conventional order raised by
other Gothic plays.

First, the Gothic's encounter with the absolute is redefined here. As
Shelley notes in discussing the naming of the unnameable in her letter,
the Gothic has always sought to encounter the numinous that lies outside
the rules and conventions of society. But in *Presumption*, the threat does
not come from a supernatural source, a castle spectre or Dark Knight, but
from the creation of science. It is significant that in the key scene of the
creature's animation (I, iii) Frankenstein calls him "a huge automaton in
human form." We see here the beginnings of the transformation of the
creature from Shelley's articulate being who defines himself through Mil-
ton to the bolt-headed half-man, half-machine monster of the film tradition. It is no longer a creature from beyond that intrudes but a man-made
object, a piece of technology. This turn might be read as a rejection of
Gothic displacements and an encounter with the actual technological
monstrosities that were being created through the factory system; but it is
also the case that this turn from the supernatural is a retreat from the
Gothic's radical questioning of traditional religion, a further step down
the path taken in exorcising the Dark Knight from *Bertram*. Peake's monster might (though I doubt it) raise questions about technology run mad;
but the ghosts and ghouls of the earlier Gothic drama raised questions
about Providence itself.

The play also works to control the radical potential of the Gothic
villain-hero by the way in which it depicts Frankenstein. If *Manfred* or the

original *Bertram* drew upon the Faust myth to suggest a way of conceiving life outside of traditional providential order, *Presumption; or, The Fate of Frankenstein* alludes to the Faust legend in order to reinvoke the conventional moral pattern already signalled by its title. We are told in the first scene by the comic servant Fritz that "my shrewd guess, sir, is, that, like Dr. Faustus, my master is raising the Devil" (I, i). Frankenstein prefers to compare himself to another favorite figure of the romantics, Prometheus: "Like Prometheus of old, have I daringly attempted the formation—the animation of a Being!" (I, i). However, he too comes to see his actions as the violation of God's order: "What have I accomplished? the beauty of my dream has vanished! and breathless horror and disgust now fill my heart. For this I have deprived myself of rest and health, have worked my brain to madness; and when I looked to reap my great reward, a flash breaks in upon my darkened soul, and tells me my attempt was impious, and that its fruition will be fatal to my peace for ever" (I, iii). The reviewer in the *Theatrical Observer* certainly got the point, seeing the play as revealing "the profane use of excursive science, in attempting to exceed the limits of man's proscribed powers, by trespassing on the work of the universal creator."[97]

This moralizing use of the Faust myth renders any potential tragic aura surrounding Frankenstein harmless. Even if we come to sympathize with him and his endeavor, we finally see him as a self-confessed rebel against God's order. It is important that in the stage and movie versions of *Frankenstein* the interest shifts from Victor to his creature (as the popular confusion in which the monster comes to be known by his creator's name suggests). In the Gothic tradition we have been tracing, the focus has been upon a human hero or villain-hero, a titanic human figure seeking to shatter religious, political, psychological barriers; the terror of earlier Gothic plays came in contemplating a human being freed from cultural, social, even personal ties, in recognizing something of ourselves (as Coleridge understood) in this villain-hero's egomaniacal quest. In *Presumption*, the titan is made into a repentant sinner, the interest shifts to the non-human monster, and the terror lies not in the abyss of total human freedom but in a threat to domestic tranquility. With the villain-hero rendered into the morally typecast Victor, leaving the monster as the play's villain, *Presumption* reconfigures the Gothic as a melodrama that enacts the victory of domestic values embodied in a serious way by Clerval and Elizabeth, Safie and Felix, and in a comic manner by Fritz and Ninon.

The domestic emphasis of the play is made clear by the amount of space devoted to portraits of family ties. In scenes derived from the novel but owing more to the domestic melodrama, we repeatedly witness the celebration of the bonds within the De Lacey family and between Clerval and Elizabeth, who are engaged in the stage version, Frankenstein's affections having been given to Agatha De Lacey. Elizabeth lives at "Belrive" and the De Lacys in the "Valley of the Lake," both names suggesting secluded, protected environments, where family life can flourish. We hear speeches and songs about the joy of familial bonds, as in Felix and Agatha's Duet which tells us that "Of all the knots which Nature ties, / . . . None is more pure of earthly leaven, / More like the love of highest heaven, / Than that which binds in bonds how blest / A daughter to a father's breast" (II, ii). Beautiful nature provides an appropriate backdrop to this delight in the family. We get a sense that nature and the family provide a retreat from the troubles of a larger world, in the play represented by Frankenstein's scientific work and by the abstract oppression brought against the De Laceys by the government and the treachery of the father of Safie, Felix's love. The vision here is closer to Coleridge's conservative *Zapolya* or the domestic melodramas that played alongside *Presumption* than to *The Castle Spectre* or *Bertram*.

Even the story of Frankenstein's animation of the creature and then his struggle with it is firmly imbedded in a vision of domestic relations. We learn from both Elizabeth and Frankenstein himself that he has turned to his pursuit of science because he has been disappointed in his love for Agatha: "love—blighted love, drove him to solitude and abstruse research" (I, ii). Had he had a happy family life, he never would have entered on his quest. The first act essentially contrasts Frankenstein's pursuit of his goal with the attempts of Safie and Felix, Elizabeth and Clerval to come together in love. The central part of the play moves the conflict into the monster, as he is torn between his desire to become part of the family circle around old De Lacey and his anger at his treatment by the humans he encounters. Where the first act ends with the animation of the creature and his fight with Frankenstein, the second ends with the monster's failed attempt to enter the De Lacey household; repulsed by the humans, he sets fire to their cottage, destroying their domestic retreat. The final act presents the monster on a rampage against the family, killing first William, Frankenstein's little brother, and then Agatha, his betrothed. The play ends with Frankenstein and his creature perishing in an avalanche, but this of course leaves Felix and Safie, Clerval and Elizabeth (not to mention the comic Fritz and Ninon) safe to find domestic bliss. The monster's threat to domesticity is defeated.

The vampire tradition works a similar transformation on the Gothic drama. To begin with, the vampire is another instance of rendering monstrous what was heroic in the Gothic. Dracula is perhaps the clearest descendant of the Gothic villain-hero, but he no longer represents a feared human potential. He is the undead, the inhuman; and insofar as we sympathize with him it is because we understand that his power is also a trap, that his immortality is a reduction, not a liberation, of human life. Plays such as Planché's *Vampyre* also redefine the radical eroticism of the Gothic into a problem of personal psychology. The erotic is no longer seen as a means of liberation but as a key to enslavement. In a pivotal moment in Planché's play, the heroine meets Ruthven the vampire for the first time and says, "Heavens! how strange a thrill runs through my frame." The vampire says in an aside, "Then she's mine."[98] Her desire gives her over to the vampire. Eroticism is not a social force but a personal bondage. To defend oneself from the vampire, one must order one's sexuality within the confines of conventional domesticity.

The victory of domestic, private values over the social visions of the early Gothic occurs not only within plays such as *Presumption* and *The Vampyre*; it was taking place on the larger stage of the theatrical world itself as the domestic drama displaced the Gothic and the Gothic became the horror play and later the monster movie. It is thus with such plays that the particularized, historical tradition of the Gothic drama we have been tracing comes to an end. Previously the Gothic drama had challenged religious orthodoxy. Peake's play avoids the supernatural to engage the scientific. The Gothic had found in the erotic a power to be used against systems of oppression and repression. Planché's play enters the Victorian and Freudian world where the erotic becomes an internal problem, a dangerous inner force that needs to be contained by new techniques of supervision and control. While the early Gothic had dramatized both mass and individual revolt, Peake and Planché redefine those who threaten order as monsters and celebrate a return to traditional family values. The sensationalism and extremism of the Gothic would remain, but they would be used no longer to evoke extraordinary human potential or to gesture beyond conventional order but instead to evoke the monstrous and the inhuman, in the face of which we willingly embrace conventional order.

The victory of the domestic melodrama is usually hailed in dramatic and theatrical histories as a move towards the great realistic drama of the late nineteenth century and away from the extravagance, the extremism, and the Elizabethanizing of the romantic and Gothic drama. This victory is thus seen as an aesthetic matter, as a question of "better" stage practices winning out over a hackneyed dramaturgy. If the reconsideration of the Gothic drama does nothing else, it should raise questions about the innocence of this story of "good" plays coming to replace "bad" theater.

The victory of the domestic melodrama was in part a question of theatrical practice, and in part a matter of a shift in the hierarchy of genres; but it was also the result of ideological struggle, of a cultural reaction against the extremism and radicalism of the Gothic. As we have seen, from North to Maturin, from the pantomimic *Julia of Louvain* to the tragic *De Monfort*, the Gothic drama had explored revolt—political, sexual, and metaphysical. The domestic melodrama may have treated "everyday life," even that of the common people, more directly than the Gothic with its interest in the extraordinary and its penchant for aristocrats. The domestic melodrama may have offered a series of theatrical techniques that have come to seem "natural" as opposed to the grand, large gestures of the Gothic stage. But whatever its theatrical innovations or dramatic merit, the victory of the domestic melodrama was a defeat for the "modern jacobinical drama," for the vision and ideology of the Gothic drama. This collection of plays will have succeeded if it not only reintroduces readers to some intriguing plays but also raises questions about our accepted dramatic and theatrical histories.

## Notes

1. Louis F. Peck, *A Life of Matthew G. Lewis* (Cambridge: Harvard University Press, 1961), p. 76. John Waldie, Journals and Letters of John Waldie of Hendersyde Park, Kelso, Scotland, University of California at Los Angeles MSS. 169. The first performance Waldie records in his journals is on 26 January 1799 (vol. IV, 169/89, 2), an Edinburgh performance he compares to an earlier staging at Newcastle; he also records seeing the play on 2 September 1805 (vol. XI, 169/14, 331–33) and on 17 April 1809 (vol. XIX, 169/19, 92–93), and makes a reference to the play as late as 7 March 1820 (vol. tXLV, 169/32, 167). For performances in London, see *The London Stage 1660–1800*, ed. Emmett L Avery, Charles Beecher Hogan, Arthur H. Scouten, George Winchester Stone, Jr., and William Van Lennep, 5 parts, 11 vols. (Carbondale: University of Southern Illinois Press, 1960–68); for information on revivals, see *Victorian Plays: A Record of Significant Productions on the London Stage, 1837–1901*, ed. Donald Mullin (Westport, CT: Greenwood Press, 1987).

2. *Biographia Dramatica* (London: Longman, Hurst et al., 1812), 2:87.

3. Jerome J. McGann, *The Romantic Ideology: A Critical Investigation* (Chicago: University of Chicago Press, 1983).

4. George Rowell, ed., *Nineteenth Century Plays* (1953; 2nd ed. Oxford: Oxford University Press, 1972); the earliest play included is Jerrold's *Black-Ey'd Susan* (Surrey, 1829). Robert W. Corrigan, ed., *Laurel British Drama: The Nineteenth Century* (New York: Dell, 1967); the earliest play included is Boucicault's *London Assurance* (Covent Garden, 1841). Gerald B. Kauvar and Gerald C. Sorenson, eds., *Nineteenth-Century English Verse Drama* (Rutherford: Fairleigh Dickinson University Press, 1973). Michael R. Booth, ed., *English Plays of the Nineteenth Century*, vol. 1: Dramas 1800–1850, vol. 2: Dramas 1850–1900 (Oxford: Clarendon Press, 1969); Booth does contain verse plays by Knowles and Bulwer-Lytton but no plays by major

poets of the century. The most useful anthology for my approach is that of J. O. Bailey, *British Plays of the Nineteenth Century: An Anthology to Illustrate the Evolution of the Drama* (New York: Odyssey Press, 1966); while, as its subtitle indicates, it adopts an evolutionary scheme that necessarily subordinates the early part of the century to the later, the volume contains verse plays (including *Bertram*) and prose works, tragedies as well as melodramas, plays from the Romantic as well as the Victorian period. There has been one previous anthology of Gothic plays, Stephen Wischhusen's *The Hour of One: Six Gothic Melodramas* (London: Gordon Fraser, 1975), which contains facsimile reprints of earlier editions of Lewis's *The Castle Spectre*, Holcroft's *Tale of Mystery*, Planché's *Vampire*, Milner's *Frankenstein*, and Fitzball's *The Devil's Elixir* and *The Flying Dutchman*.

5. Peter L. Thorslev, Jr., *Romantic Contraries: Freedom Versus Destiny* (New Haven: Yale University Press, 1984). Bertrand Evans, *Gothic Drama From Walpole To Shelley* (Berkeley: University of California Press, 1947).

6. Montague Summers, *The Gothic Quest* (London: The Fortune Press, 1939). Eino Railo, *The Haunted Castle: A Study of the Elements of English Romanticism* (New York: E. P. Dutton, 1927). Eve Kosofsky Sedgwick, *The Coherence of Gothic Conventions* (1980; rpt. New York: Methuen, 1986).

7. Devendra P. Varma, *The Gothic Flame* (London: Arthur Barker, 1957). Judith Wilt, *Ghosts of the Gothic: Austen, Eliot, and Lawrence* (Princeton: Princeton University Press, 1980). R. D. Stock, *The Holy and the Daemonic from Sir Thomas Browne to William Blake* (Princeton: Princeton University Press, 1982). William Patrick Day, *In the Circles of Fear and Desire: A Study of Gothic Fantasy* (Chicago: University of Chicago Press, 1985). Ronald Paulson, *Representations of Revolution (1789–1820)* (New Haven: Yale University Press, 1983). Peter Brooks, "Virtue and Terror: *The Monk*," *ELH* 40 (1973): 249–63. Chris Baldick, *In Frankenstein's Shadow: Myth, Monstrosity, and Nineteenth-Century Writing* (Oxford: Clarendon Press, 1987). I am indebted to these and many other studies of the Gothic novel; to name only a few additional items: Robert Kiely, *The Romantic Novel In England* (Cambridge: Harvard University Press, 1972); Elizabeth McAndrews, *The Gothic Tradition in Fiction* (New York: Columbia University Press, 1979); David Punter, *The Literature of Terror* (London: Longman, 1980); and G. R. Thompson, ed., *The Gothic Imagination: Essays in Dark Romanticism* (Pullman, Washington: Washington State University Press, 1974).

8. See Joseph Donohue, *Theatre in the Age of Kean* (Totowa, NJ: Rowan & Littlefield, 1975); Greater London Council, *Survey of London*, vol. 35: *The Theatre Royal Drury Lane and the Royal Opera House Covent Garden* (London: Athlone Press, 1970); R. Leacroft, *The Development of the English Playhouse* (Ithaca: Cornell University Press, 1973); and *The Georgian Playhouse: Actors, Artists, and Architecture 1730–1830*, An Exhibition designed by Iain Mackintosh (London: Arts Council of Great Britain, 1975).

9. *Memoirs of Richard Cumberland Written by Himself* (London: Lackington, Allen, & Co., 1807), 2:384.

10. See Donohue, *Theatre in the Age of Kean*, pp. 8–14, 31–38; Dennis Arundell, *The Story of Sadler's Wells* (New York: Theatre Arts Books, 1965); and A. H. Saxon, *Enter Foot and Horse: A History of the Hippodrama in England and France* (New Haven: Yale University Press, 1968).

11. Donohue, *Theatre in the Age of Kean*, pp. 46–50; and his "Burletta and the Early Nineteenth-Century English Theatre," *Nineteenth Century Theatre Research* 1 (Spring 1973): 29–53.

12. See David Mayer, *Harlequin in His Element* (Cambridge: Harvard University Press, 1969); Saxon, *Enter Foot and Horse;* Michael Booth, *Prefaces to English Nineteenth-Century Theatre* (Manchester: Manchester University Press, 1980) and *Victorian Spectacular Theatre 1850–1910* (Boston: Routledge & Kegan Paul, 1981); and Marian Hannah Winter, *The Theatre of Marvels* (New York: Benjamin Blom, 1962).

13. John Genest, *Some Account of the English Stage from the Restoration in 1660 to 1830* (1832; rpt. New York: Burt Franklin, 1965), 7:38.

14. Barry Sutcliffe, "Introduction," Plays by *George Colman the Younger and Thomas Morton* (Cambridge: Cambridge University Press, 1983), esp. pp. 1–8.

15. See the list of plays in Evans, *Gothic Drama*, pp. 239–45.

16. Walpole, *Mysterious Mother*, in vol. 1 of *The Works of Horatio Walpole, Earl of Orford* (London: Robinson & Edwards, 1798).

17. Walpole, "Postscript," *Mysterious Mother*, in *Works*, 1:125.

18. Janet Todd, *Sensibility: An Introduction* (London: Methuen, 1986), pp. 6–9.

19. James Cobb, *The Haunted Tower* (Dublin: P. Burne, 1790; *Songs, Duets, Trios, and Chorusses, in the Haunted Tower* was published in London: J. Jarvis, 1789). Miles Peter Andrews, "Preface," *The Enchanted Castle*, 1786, unpublished (*The Songs, Recitatives, Airs, Duets, Trios, and Chorusses Introduced in the Pantomime Entertainment, of the Enchanted Castle* was published in London, 1786); the play is presumably, as Evans argues, the same as the Larpent Collection play, *The Castle of Wonders*, Larpent Collection of Licensing Manuscripts, Henry Huntington Library, San Marino, California, LA 536; quoted in Evans, *Gothic Drama*, p. 67.

20. *Biographia Dramatica*, 2:354. Genest, *English Stage*, 7:37. The *London Stage* is the best resource for information about runs at Covent Garden, Drury Lane, and the Haymarket.

21. James Boaden, *Memoirs of the Life of John Philip Kemble* (1825; rpt. New York: Benjamin Blom, 1969), 2:206.

22. *The Anti-Jacobin*, 4 June 1798 (rpt. New York: AMS Press, 1968), p. 236.

23. Wordsworth, "Preface to *Lyrical Ballads*" (1802), in *The Oxford Authors William Wordsworth*, ed. Stephen Gill (Oxford: Oxford University Press, 1984), p. 599.

24. Coleridge, *Biographia Literaria*, ed. by James Engell and W. Jackson Bate (Princeton: Princeton University Press, 1983), 2:221.

25. Sir Walter Scott, "Drama," *Supplement to . . . the Encyclopedia Britannica* (Edinburgh, 1824), 3:669; quoted in Martin Meisel, *Realizations: Narrative, Pictorial, and Theatrical Arts in Nineteenth-Century England* (Princeton: Princeton University Press, 1983), p. 148.

26. James Boaden, *Memoirs of Mrs. Siddons* (1827; rpt. Philadelphia: J. B. Lippincott, 1893), p. 435.

27. Boaden, *Kemble*, 2:11.

28. From a letter (1809), quoted in James Boaden, *Memoirs of Mrs. Inchbald* (London, 1833), 2:143.

29. Burke, *Reflections on the Revolution in France*, in vol. 1 of *Works* (New York: George Dearborn, 1836): 459, 483–84.

30. Walpole, *Castle of Otranto*, ed. W. S. Lewis (Oxford: Oxford University Press, 1982), p. 5.

31. See Northrop Frye, *Anatomy of Criticism* (Princeton: Princeton University Press, 1957), pp. 182–84.

32. Citations from plays included in this collection will be given in the text and will give either act and scene numbers or my page numbers; bibliographic data can be found in the headnote to the respective play.

33. Mona Ozouf, *Festivals and the French Revolution*, trans. Alan Sheridan (Cambridge: Harvard University Press, 1988), pp. 126–29.

34. Frye, *Anatomy*, pp. 163–71.

35. *Anti-Jacobin*, 11 June 1798, p. 245. Byron would, of course, use this line in the "Addition to the Preface" for *Childe Harold's Pilgrimage*, in vol. 2 of *The Complete Poetical Works*, ed. Jerome J. McGann (Oxford: Clarendon Press, 1980).

36. Terry Castle, *Masquerade and Civilization: The Carnivalesque in Eighteenth-Century English Culture and Fiction* (Stanford: Stanford University Press, 1986), p. 28.

37. Jean Starobinski, *1789: The Emblems of Reason*, trans. Barbara Bray (Charlottesville: University of Virginia Press, 1982), pp. 35–40. On Lovelace, see Anthony Winner, "Richardson's Lovelace: Character and Prediction," *Texas Studies in Language and Literature* 14 (1972): 45–60.

38. Blake, "A Poison Tree," 11. 1–8, in *The Complete Poetry and Prose of William Blake*, ed. David V. Erdman (1965; rev. ed., Berkeley: University of California Press, 1982).

39. Michel Foucault, *Discipline and Punish*, trans. Alan Sheridan (New York: Vintage Books, 1979), pp. 68–69.

40. Boaden, *Kemble*, 2:97.

41. Margaret L. Carter, *Spectre or Delusion? The Supernatural in Gothic Fiction*, Studies in Speculative Fiction, 15 (Ann Arbor: UMI Research Press, 1986), pp. 1, 3. See also Tobin Siebers, *The Romantic Fantastic* (Ithaca: Cornell University Press, 1984); and Tzvetan Todorov, *The Fantastic: A Structural Approach to a Literary Genre*, trans. Richard Howard (Ithaca: Cornell University Press, 1975).

42. Johnson, "Life of Cowley," in *Lives of the English Poets*, ed. G. B. Hill (Oxford: Clarendon Press, 1905), 1:49–50; Truman Guy Steffan, *Lord Byron's "Cain": Twelve Essays and a Text with Variants and Annotations* (Austin: University of Texas Press, 1968), p. 333.

43. Lewis, *Castle Spectre*, IV, ii, LA 1187; the manuscript has "Hallelujah" crossed out by Larpent.

44. *Monthly Mirror*, 1 December 1797: 355.

45. Michael Kelley, *Reminiscences*, ed. Roger Fiske (Oxford: Oxford University Press, 1975), p. 252. The Duke of Leeds is quoted in Boaden, *Kemble*, 2:230. Both comments are quoted by Steven Cohan, "Introduction," *The Plays of James Boaden* (New York: Garland, 1980), p. xxxix.

46. *British Review*, 17 June 1821: 380–89; in *Romantic Bards and British Reviewers*, ed. John O. Hayden (Lincoln: University of Nebraska Press, 1971), p. 393.

47. Genest, *English Stage*, 7:163, 333.

48. Boaden, *Kemble*, 2:11–12.

49. Genest, *English Stage*, 7:333.

50. *Literary Gazette*, 21 June 1817: 337–38; in *Romantic Bards*, p. 234.

51. Coleridge, *Biographia*, 2:222.

52. *Monthly Mirror*, 1 April 1807: 280.

53. Hegel, *On Tragedy*, ed. Anne and Henry Paolucci (1962; rpt., New York: Harper & Row, 1974), p. 92. See Charles Nodier, "Introduction," to Pixérécourt, *Théâtre Choisi* (Paris: Tresse, 1841); Peter Brooks, *The Melodramatic Imagination* (New Haven: Yale University Press, 1976); Michael Booth, *English Melodrama* (London: Herbert Jenkins, 1965); Frank Rahill, *World of Melodrama* (University Park, PA: Pennsylvania State University Press, 1967); and Alexis Pitou, "Les Origines du mélodrame français à la fin du XVIIIᵉ siècle," *Revue d'histoire littéraire de la France* 18 (1911): 256–96. On melodrama and monodrama as key forms of the day, see Cox, *In the Shadows of Romance: Romantic Tragic Drama in Germany, England, and France* (Athens, OH: Ohio University Press, 1987), pp. 38–51.

54. Kelly, *Reminiscences*, pp. 138–39.

55. On monodrama, see A. Dwight Culler, "Monodrama and the Dramatic Monologue," *PMLA* 90 (1975): 366–85; Jan van der Veen, *Le Mélodrame musical, de Rousseau au romantisme* (The Hague: M. Nijhoff, 1955); and Kirsten Gram Holstrom, *Monodrama, Attitudes, and Tableaux Vivants* (Stockholm: Almquist & Wiksell, 1967).

56. *Monthly Mirror*, 15 April 1803: 266. *Satirist*, 1 December 1812: 554. *Biographia Dramatica*, 2:81.

57. Letter, 23 March 1803, in Peck, *Lewis*, pp. 221–22.

58. *DNB* article on Lewis, p. 1073.

59. *Monthly Mirror*, 15 April 1803: 266–67.

60. While I have not found translations during the period of Benda's monodramas, Rousseau's *Pygmalion* appeared in Hunt's *Indicator*, 10 May 1820: 241–46; and Goethe's *Proserpina* was translated in William Taylor, *Historic Survey of German Poetry* (London: Treuttel and Wurtz, 1830), 3:312–16. Southey placed five of his monodramas in *The Poetical Works of Robert Southey Collected by Himself in Ten Volumes* (London: Orme, Brown, Green, and Longmans, 1837), 2:101–16.

61. Mary Wollstonecraft, *Maria, or The Wrongs of Woman* (New York: W. W. Norton, 1975), p. 23.

62. Moira Ferguson, "Introduction," to *Maria*, pp. 5–6.

63. "Author's Preface," to *Maria*, p. 21.

64. Mrs. Cornwall Baron-Wilson, *The Life and Correspondence of M. G. Lewis* (London: Heny Colburn, 1839), 1:231–35.

65. M. G. Lewis, *Alfonso, King of Castille* (London: Bell, 1802); act and scene numbers will be given in the text.

66. George Steiner, *The Death of Tragedy* (London: Faber & Faber, 1961).

67. See Shelley's analysis of Byron's plays in a letter to Mary Shelley, 7 August 1821, *The Letters of Percy Bysshe Shelley*, ed. Frederick Jones (London: Oxford University Press, 1964), 2:317; and the discussion by Charles E. Robinson, *Shelley and Byron: The Snake and Eagle Wreathed in Fight* (Baltimore: Johns Hopkins University Press, 1976), pp. 144–60. On Coleridge's plays, see John David Moore, "Coleridge and the 'Modern Jacobinical Drama':

*Osorio, Remorse,* and the Development of Coleridge's Critique of the Stage, 1797–1816," *Bulletin of Research in the Humanities* 85 (1982): 443–64; Cox, "The French Revolution in the English Theater," in *History and Myth: Essays on English Romantic Literature,* ed. Stephen C. Behrendt (Detroit: Wayne State University Press, 1990), p. 49; and Janet Tvetan, "Vision and Revision in Coleridge's Dramas," Master's Thesis, Texas A&M University, May 1987.

68. Quoted in Martha Somerville, *Personal Recollections from Early Life to Old Age of Mary Somerville* (Boston: Robert Brothers, 1874), p. 265.

69. Sir Walter Scott, *Familiar Letters,* ed. David Douglas (Edinburgh: Douglas, 1894), 1:99. *Byron's Letters and Journals,* ed. Leslie Marchand (London: John Murray, 1973–1979), 3:109.

70. Baillie, *Henriquez,* III, iii. All of Baillie's plays can be found in *The Dramatic and Poetical Works of Joanna Baillie* (London: Longman, Brown, Green, and Longmans, 1851).

71. Baillie, "Introductory Discourse," *Works,* p. 16.

72. *The Intimate Letters of Hester Piozzi and Penelope Pennington,* ed. O. G. Knapp (London: John Lane, 1914), p. 173.

73. *Extracts of the Journals and Correspondence of Mary Berry from the Year 1783 to 1852,* ed. Theresa Lewis (London: Longman, 1865), 2:90.

74. Waldie, UCLA MSS, vol. 4, 169/8, 4 July 1789, 54.

75. Boaden, *Siddons,* 195.

76. Quoted in Thomas Campbell, *Life of Mrs. Siddons* (London: Effingham Wilson, 1834), 2:11–12.

77. Boaden, *Siddons,* 315.

78. Laura Mulvey, "Visual Pleasure and Narrative Cinema," in *Visual and Other Pleasures* (Bloomington: Indiana University Press, 1989), pp. 14–26; the essay originally appeared in *Screen* (1975).

79. Campbell, *Siddons,* 1:251.

80. Quoted in the biographical preface to the second edition of Baillie's collected works (London: Longman, Brown, Green, and Longmans, 1853), xi.

81. Baillie, *Basil,* I, i; II, iv.

82. Bailey, "Introduction" to *Bertram, British Plays,* p. 41. Booth, *Nineteenth-Century Theatre,* p. 11.

83. Gilbert B. Cross, *Next Week—'East Lynn': Domestic Drama in Performance 1820–1874* (Lewisburg: Bucknell University Press, 1977).

84. Byron, *Manfred,* II, i, 38; II, ii, 57, in *Works,* vol. 6.

85. *Childe Harold's Pilgrimage,* III, xxxvi.

86. Coleridge, *Biographia,* 1:5.

87. "Headnote," George Lamb letter to Maturin, 15 June 1816, *The Correspondence of Sir Walter Scott and Charles Robert Maturin with a Few Other Allied Letters,* ed. Fannie E. Ratchford and Wm. H. McCarthy, Jr. (Austin: University of Texas Press, 1937), p. 58.

88. Coleridge, *Biographia,* 2:229.

89. Coleridge, *Biographia,* 2:231–32, 222.

90. Letter to Daniel Terry, 10 November 1814, *The Letters of Sir Walter Scott*, ed. H. J. C. Grierson (London: Constable, 1932), 3:515.

91. Coleridge, *Biographia*, 2:216–17.

92. Coleridge, *Biographia*, 2:217.

93. Letter to Walter Scott, 2 July 1816, *Correspondence*, p. 59.

94. McGann, "Commentary" to *Don Juan*, *Works*, 5:668.

95. Marilyn Butler, *Romantics, Rebels and Reactionaries: English Literature and its Background 1760–1830* (Oxford: Oxford University Press, 1982), pp. 113–37.

96. Letter to Leigh Hunt, 9 September 1823, *The Letters of Mary Wollstonecraft Shelley*, ed. Betty T. Bennett (Baltimore: Johns Hopkins University Press, 1980), 1:378.

97. *Theatrical Observer*, 29 July 1823.

98. *The Vampire*, I, iii, in *Plays by James Robinson Planché*, ed. Donald Roy (Cambridge: Cambridge University Press, 1986).

A Note
on the Text

When one is confronted with a body of work such as the Gothic drama that has largely been ignored since the time of its composition, the process of selecting individual pieces for inclusion in a collection becomes extremely difficult. One cannot decide to include only "masterworks," since no works are as yet recognized as such; nor can one follow an alternative path of expanding the canon by offering marginalized pieces, since there is no canon of Gothic drama. I have tried to choose plays that are interesting in their own right and that also serve to outline the major developments within the Gothic tradition. I was guided by only one hard rule: each play had to have been performed during the period under discussion, so plays such as Walpole's *Mysterious Mother*, Byron's *Manfred*, Shelley's *The Cenci*, or Beddoes's *Death's Jest Book* were ruled out.

The choice of some plays was easy. Lewis's *Castle Spectre* and Maturin's *Bertram* are as close to recognized "masterworks" as we find in the Gothic drama. As the most important playwright of the period involved in the Gothic, Joanna Baillie has to be represented, and her *De Monfort* is the logical choice; while the less well known *Orra* was a tempting option, it was never performed. Peake's *Presumption; or, The Fate of Frankenstein* provides an opportunity to make available the first of the many influential dramatizations of Mary Shelley's novel. Two of the other plays—Lewis's *Captive* and Cross's *Julia of Louvain*—were included because they expand our sense of the range of Gothic theater, offering examples of the monodrama and the pantomime, respectively. The greatest difficulty came in selecting a play to represent the standard features of the early, "classic" Gothic drama. One might have picked Jephson's *Count of Narbonne*, Boaden's *Fontainville Forest* or *Aurelia and Miranda*, or Coleman's *The Iron Chest*; this alternative list would have provided dramatizations of novels by Walpole, Radcliffe, Lewis, and Godwin. Beyond my desire to free the discussion of the Gothic drama from the weightier presence of the Gothic romance, I selected North's *Kentish Barons* because it represents the range of early Gothic techniques and tactics and because it is less easily available than works by Jephson, Boaden, or Coleman.[1]

My decision to include only plays that were performed forced me to confront the dual existence of any dramatic text: its life on stage and its life as a printed book. Perhaps more than any other set of literary texts, plays engage the difficulties in editing explored by Jerome McGann. First, plays exist in two different modes of literary production created for two (at least potentially) different audiences. McGann's questioning of authorial intention is thus relevant for dramatic texts about which the author, along with others involved in the creation of the literary work, has at least two intentions—that it succeed on the stage and that it be preserved in print. Second, the drama is perhaps the best place to see the truth of McGann's assertion that "literary works are fundamentally social rather than personal or psychological products."[2] Dramatic works—whether we think of their production on the stage or their production by editors, compositors, and so on—have a socially determined and historically contingent existence.

The late eighteenth- and early nineteenth-century dramatic text lived its double life within a particular set of institutional circumstances. Like all literary works that reach print, these plays are the product not of only authorial intentions but also the interventions, corrections, and errors of editors, compositors, printers. Moreover, most of these plays went through another process of creation prior to printing, for plays performed on the stage during this period were usually published only after their performance (though in the current collection Baillie's *De Monfort* is an exception to that rule). The published edition was usually based upon some version of the performance text. Of course, this performance text could not reflect some hypothetical authorial intention, because the text presented by the author to the theater would be subjected to cuts by the manager and actors as well as to censorship by the Lord Chamberlain's office. Few authorial manuscripts have survived for these Gothic plays. What we usually have are the first (and any subsequent) editions and the licensing manuscript submitted by the theater to the Lord Chamberlain; we sometimes also have prompt books for particular performances or "acting" editions drawn from these prompt books. The texts we have are thus complex social products, subject to pressures from authors, theaters, printing houses, the government, and, of course, the audience and reading public.

The attempts to confront these problems are perhaps best represented by Barry Sutcliffe's excellent edition of *Plays by George Colman the Younger and Thomas Morton.* Sutcliffe has sought to return from the performance text to the lost authorial version by taking the first edition and then adding any additional passages fround in the licensing copy but excised either by the Lord Chamberlain's censor or by the theater as the play was further refined for performance; in Sutcliffe's words, "The present editions represent an attempt to reconcile the full texts as originally written by Colman and Morton (preserved in the Larpent Collection of Licensing MSS in the Huntington Library, California) with the curtailed forms in which they were published."[3] Such a procedure poses a number of problems; not only does it assume that the licensing copy somehow reflects the author's intentions when it was in fact a version prepared for the theater and the censor by a theater's copyist, but it also seeks to replace the actual historical text as it existed in print or on the stage with a hypothetical original and authorized version.

Perhaps two examples from the current collection can outline these problems. For Maturin's *Bertram*, we have both source texts used in Sutcliffe's procedure, the first edition and the Larpent licensing copy. The differences between these two versions are largely in the accidentals, and one would be justified in using the first edition as the textual basis in such matters rather than the theater copyist's version submitted to Larpent where the issue was censorship of content not accuracy in punctuation. According to Sutcliffe's procedure, we should also include any passages found in the licensing manuscript but deleted from the printed version, since these cut passages are said to represent authorial intention. In the case of *Bertram*, however, the printed text is at times fuller than the licensing manuscript, particularly with regard to stage directions. This is not, however, because the printed version now represents Maturin's intentions over against a performance version prepared by other hands; Maturin did not oversee the first edition, and he complained of the printed version that it had been "un-Maturined completely."[4] We have the manuscript of *Bertram*, which Maturin sent to Scott and which has been preserved in the Abbotsford library. As I have noted in the introduction, this verison is significantly different from both the performance version and the printed text. If our goal were to recreate "authorial intention," then we could print this as the actual text, but this manuscript has little or no historical presence beyond its possible influence upon Scott, Byron, and a few other readers. The *Bertram* that was a smash hit for Edmund Kean and that was avidly read, the *Bertram* that Shelley read or Hazlitt saw, is better represented by the Larpent text or the first edition than by this manuscript. To reprint the manuscript over against these other versions would be to privilege the author and a few readers in the closet over against the text created by the institutions of the theater and the printing house for a vast audience and reading public.

Baillie's *De Monfort* presents a somewhat different set of problems. Baillie printed her play before it was performed, so it cannot reflect cuts insisted upon by the theater and the censor. If we were to set aside for the moment McGann's arguments against authorial intention, we might select the first edition as Baillie's version of the play over against the Larpent version that presumably reflects changes made to the play by John Philip Kemble and his sister Mrs. Siddons as well as any cuts made to avoid problems with the censor. We do not, however, have a simple tension between an authorial version intended for the closet and a performance version adapted by actors for the stage. First, Baillie tended to alter the play as she republished it over the years, often including changes made in performance. We could select the first edition as representing original intention or the last (her complete works of 1851) as embodying final intentions, but what we really have is a work in process, evolving throughout Baillie's life. Second, this evolution occurred not in opposition to but in dialogue with the performance versions. Baillie was in accord about the changes made to the play for performance; she would later agree to even more drastic revisions made by Edmund Kean for his staging of the play in 1821. In fact, it appears that Baillie first wrote the play with Siddons and Kemble in mind, that she always viewed the play as being shaped by the stage and its performers, and that she was completely comfortable with the collaborative nature of composition for the stage. Third, newspaper accounts of the performance differ significantly from both the first and later editions *and* from the licensing manuscript. They are closer, however, to another manuscript, this one in the hand of the poet Thomas Campbell copied out for Sarah Siddons and including some of the actress's marginal comments. We do not have an authorized version prepared by a single author; what we have is a series of texts that evolve within an artistic community and that are produced by the institutions of the theater and the publishing house.

Given these conditions, how does one present a *De Monfort* or a *Bertram* in a way that does not distort its existence in a particular historical, social reality? An authorial manuscript, where it exists as in the case of *Bertram*, does not provide the text read or seen during the period. A printed edition has the advantage of offering a text read by a large number of people, but it often, as in the case of *De Monfort*, fails to represent the play as it was performed. Any acting version might help us recreate a particular performance and the licensing manuscript gives us a close look at the first performance (though, as *De Monfort* shows, not always an accurate look), but it does not offer the text read by an audience larger than that of any single theater.

Perhaps the most satisfactory solution would be to publish facing texts, the first edition of each play and either the licensing manuscript or another performance version. Such a text would attempt to recreate the play in its two most important historical embodiments. A facing edition of plays neglected by academics, producers, and audiences alike is not, however, very likely. I have adopted a more practical compromise and one that has a certain historical sanction. The goal of this edition is to offer an easily read text that provides the fullest account of the play's historical life as both a printed work and a performed theatrical piece. In nineteenth-century editions of acted plays, editors tagged lines omitted in performance by placing them within quotation marks. Following this practice, I have placed in double quotation marks lines that were dropped in the Larpent acting version or that were marked in the published version to be deleted in performance. (Since stage directions were often drastically reduced in the Larpent version, where the issue was the content of the speeches, I have not marked these cuts; I have drawn upon both printed and manuscript versions to produce the fullest possible stage directions.) In addition, material found in the Larpent version but not in the published version—that is, material *added* in performance—is marked by square brackets. Double quotation marks or brackets precede a speaker when an entire speech was cut or added; they precede the lines of the speech but not the speaker when only a portion was cut or a variant speech was offered. Substantive variants from the printed version in the Larpent version are offered in the notes (changes in place and character names are usually noted only the first time). While the hope is that the combination of variants and marked cuts and additions will provide on the page a portrait of both the performance and printed versions, certain variations are not noted: variants in accidentals are not indicated, nor have I sought to correct the original spelling, punctuation, or capitalization of the printed text or the manuscripts, except where the extremely erratic punctuation of the copyists involved in creating the Larpent copies would interfere with comprehension; variations in line breaks that result from added or deleted material are not always noted; and the format of stage directions, act and scene designations, lists of characters, and character designations before speeches has been regularized. There are also cases where it was difficult to decide between marking a passage as cut or merely noting a variant, as for example when a five-line passage was replaced by a four-line passage that used much of the same language. In general, I have marked major variations that include considerable pruning as cuts with

the variant passage offered in the note. Where it is a question of a sub-
stitution without a cut, the variant is simply given in the note. The notes
also provide light annotation on the texts.

There are some slight variations in this practice as a result of the varying texts available. For *The Kentish Barons, The Castle Spectre, De Monfort*,
and *Bertram*, I have used the first edition as the basis for my text, drawing
upon other versions to give us a sense of the performance text. There is
no Larpent version for *Julia of Louvain*, so I have drawn upon only the
printed version; the same is true of Act III of *The Kentish Barons*, where
the Larpent version is missing. Lewis published *The Captive* in his *Poems*
without stage directions; I have used this version for the text and supplied
the stage directions from Mrs. Cornwall Baron-Wilson's biography of
Lewis, looking to the Larpent version for any variations in performance.
In the case of Peake, for which there is only the Larpent version and an
acting edition, I have used the Larpent version as my text turning to the
printed version for punctuation and spelling. In the case of *Bertram*, I have
supplied some key material from the Abbotsford manuscript in an appendix. A biographical and bibliographical note precedes each play. My hope
is that the reader will be given the means to reimagine the dramatic text's
two initial historical incarnations, as a performance to be viewed on the
stage and as a book, a literary artifact.

### Notes

1. The Garland Press Series, Eighteenth-Century English Drama, ed. Paula R. Back-
scheider, has made available facsimile editions of such playwrights as Jephson, Elizabeth
Inchbald, Boaden, and Frederick Reynolds. The Cambridge University Press Series, British
and American Playwrights 1750–1920, ed. Martin Banham and Peter Thomson, has
provided edited texts for such writers as George Colman the Younger, Thomas Morton,
and J. R. Planché. The introductions to the volumes in both series are extremely useful.
Steven Earl Forry's excellent *"Hideous Progeny: Dramatizations of "Frankenstein" from Mary Shelley to the Present* (Philadelphia: University of Pennsylvania Press, 1990), which contains the
texts of a series of Frankenstein plays including Peake's, arrived too late to influence my
work and after I had decided to include Peake's *Presumption*. In any event, Forry offers a
transcription of the published Dick's version, while my text seeks to integrate Dick's with
the Larpent version.

2. Jerome J. McGann, *A Critique of Modern Textual Criticism* (Chicago: University of Chicago
Press, 1983), p. 44.

3. Barry Sutcliffe, "Note on the Text," *Plays by Colman and Morton*, p. 51.

4. Cited above, n. 93.

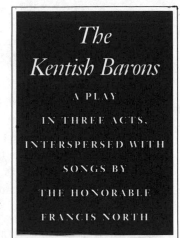

The
Kentish Barons

A PLAY
IN THREE ACTS,
INTERSPERSED WITH
SONGS BY
THE HONORABLE
FRANCIS NORTH

Francis North, fourth Earl of Guilford (1761–1817), was a patron of the stage, but he only wrote one play, *The Kentish Barons.* North was the second son of Anna and Frederick North, second Earl of Guilford (1732–1792), better known as Lord North, Prime Minister during the American Revolution. Francis North entered the army in 1777 but quit in 1794 after attaining the rank of lieutenant-colonel. The *Biographia Dramatica* tells us that he was also high steward of Banbury, patent comptroller of the customs, and an LL.D. He succeeded his brother, George Augustus North, third Earl of Guilford (1757–1802), on 20 April 1802. North came from a distinguished literary and political family. It boasted a poet in Dudley, fourth Lord North (1602–1677); and Roger, second Lord North (1531–1600), was the owner of the copy of Chaucer now known as the Ellesmere manuscript. It was also a powerful political family, particularly during the life of his father. While Francis North's own political beliefs are not clear, it is known that his brother, George Augustus, was a sympathizer with the Whigs and an advocate of the coalition between his father and Charles Fox.

The Kentish Barons was offered at the Theatre Royal, Haymarket on 25 June 1791 and enjoyed a run of ten nights. The *Biographia Dramatica* tells us the play was well received. The *Morning Chronicle* (27 June 1791) reports that the play was performed "to a most crowded audience and received with very marked and rapturous applause." There appears to have been some controversy over the play's costumes. The *Oracle* (27 June 1791) found, "The chief excellence of the play is the preservation of costume"; but the *Times* (27 June 1791) found that the shoes with peaked toes and chains, "though perfectly appropriate to the TIMES, had a rather ludicrous effect." On 28 June, the *Times* printed the following "Impromptu":

The Kentish men will surely rise
If antique spirit still remains—
No sight more sad can grieve their eyes
Than Kentish Beaux's bedecke'd with chains.

Both the *Morning Chronicle* and the *Times* indicate that the play was cut after the first performance, with alterations perhaps made by Sheridan. The *Chronicle* makes some interesting additional observations: "It is a drama of the most elevated species of opera. The tendency of despotic power to depravity both in tyrant and slave is sharply and happily delineated." The reference to the play as an opera suggests the confusion of genres that marked the period, and the comment about "despotic power" suggests that the play was perhaps read as having liberal or democratic tendencies.

The comments about the performance cuts and about the politics of the play are important, for they might help to explain why in the Larpent version of the play (LA 875) the third act is missing. This suggests to me that the third act was rejected by Larpent and returned for revisions, the corrected copy never having been filed with the original manuscript. If this theory is correct, then Larpent found something objectionable in the last act. The printed version (London: J. Ridgway, 1791) obviously includes the third act, but there is evidence that the printed version is a heavily pruned one. For example, several songs that are found in the Larpent copy's two acts are cut from the printed version. Most strikingly, the characters of Gam and Sue do not appear in the last act after a great deal of trouble has been taken in determining that they should accompany Clifford and Osbert on their voyage to Mortimer's castle. My text is based on the printed version of the play. Lines in the printed version but not in the Larpent text are marked by double quotation marks, while lines in the Larpent version but not in the printed text are marked by square brackets; variants are indicated in the notes.

### DRAMATIS PERSONAE
Theatre Royal, Haymarket, 25 June 1791[1]

| Clifford | Mr. Johnstone |
| Bertram | Mr. Aickin |

1. The Larpent manuscript indicates that the play was licensed to be performed 1 August 1790; it was not performed for almost a year because of a death in the family, according to *The History of the English Theatre* (1791).

| | |
|---|---|
| Gam | Mr. Bannister, Jun. |
| Osbert | Mrs. Goodall[2] |
| William | Mr. Chapman |
| Walter | Mr. Evatt |
| Mortimer | Mr. Bensley |
| Elina | Mrs. Kemble |
| Susan | Mrs. Webbe |
| Beatrice | Mrs. Taylor |

Servants, Soldieri, Priest[3] &c.
Music partly new by Gyrowetz, partly compiled by Miss Monck
from Paisiello, Sacchini, and Guglielmi.

## ACT I

SCENE I   *An Old Castle—Clifford and Bertram.*

CLIF. Is she then gone for ever? Oh, my Bertram,
My joys, which yesterday were fair and blooming,
Fresh as the lively verdure of the spring,
This morn some demon, envious of my happiness,
Has blighted.[4]
BER.          Say not so.
While jocund health and sprightly youth remain,
There's ample room for hope; nay, when old age
Slackens the sinews, and unnerves the mind,
In the last dregs of life, when memory fails,
Still flattering fancy, like the western sun,
Brightens the short remains of day-light left.
Extinguish hope!
CLIF.          [Prithee no more, my friend,
[You but inflame the wound you wish to heal—]
Bid me not hope:[5]—'twas hope alone destroy'd me.
The doubts, the fears I felt, were little pangs,[6]
Were light, were trivial, when compar'd to hope.
Hope! thou deceitful host! who but invit'st

---

2. Osbert was apparently a "breeches" part. 3. The priest is listed only in the Larpent version. 4. The Larpent version has "She's gone, forever gone!— / Just when I thought my happiness complete, / My Cares all over, Bertram, Envious Fate / Has dash'd my hopes in Pieces." 5. The Larpent version has "Why bid me hope?" 6. The Larpent version has "little things."

The soft credulity of man to taste
Thy specious banquet, poison'st all the dainties,
And when the soul is revelling in bliss,
Secure and thoughtless, easy, full of pleasure,
Wilt in a moment quit the chearful guest,
And yield thy empty seat to dark despair.
Talk'st thou to me of Hope, thou good old man!
Of Hope! O Heavens! when Elina is fled.
BER. Alas! Lord Clifford,
Thy griefs as yet are fresh, all council's harsh;
When time has stol'n the greenness from thy sorrow,
Reason and patience will effect thy cure.
'Tis somewhat strange that Elina, that she
Who seem'd so good, so modest, and so mild,—
She half seduc'd e'en me to think her honest—
No, 'tis not strange to those who know the sex:
Their whims, caprices, nonsense, affectation,
Which make them seem to loath what most they long for.
Yet, on the eve of her approaching nuptials,
To leave a gay young lover;—had it happen'd
After the marriage, ten, or twelve months hence,
Or e'en so many weeks, I should not then—
CLIF. Restrain thy peevish tongue:
And, by our mutual friendship, dearest Bertram!
Spare lovely Elina thy keen reproaches:
Her melting form is far too soft and tender
To bear the churlish blast of thy rough breath.
What, has the snow, just sprinkled o'er thy temples,
Congeal'd thy heart, and made it dead to beauty?
No, sure; a mind susceptible as thine,
So warm to friendship, once was warm to love!
BER. 'Tis true, indeed,[7] that age has somewhat cool'd
The hey-day of my blood; but in my youth
The little Urchin[8] took his aim at *me;*
And pierc'd my rugged bosom with his shaft;
But time, reflection, pleasure, wine, and war,
And Laura's falsehood, freed me from his bondage.
"And I'll free you:—"

7. The Larpent version has "'Tis but too true." 8. Cupid.

[SONG⁹

[No, Clifford, no, for six long Years
[I knew a Lover's hopes and fears;
[The raging frenzy now is past,
[Peace dawns upon my heart at last.

[Think not that I'd inconstant prove
[Where once I vow'd eternal Love.
[My breast had still felt all its flame
[And beauteous Laura's felt the same.

[Doom'd Absence lingering pangs to try
[I found a transport in each Sigh.
[My lot was happy though severe
[And pleasure mingled in each tear.

[In vain I tried each honest Art
[To stop her foolish fickle Heart
[But since she's gone, why let her go
[I'll sigh, no more, no, Clifford, no.

[CLIF. Come to my arms, my Bertram, nearer now
[Than ever to my heart, if thou hast felt
[The pangs, the Extacies which thou describ'st
[Thou sure must pity—
BER.                      [I'll do more, I'll cure you]
Let me be your physician, [trust me friend:]
You'll find my regimen not too austere.
With wine and wassel crown your festive board;
With mirth and music shake your castle walls;
[Cast off this Lethargy that hangs upon you.]
Spur the proud courser o'er your Kentish hills,
And chase this dull stagnation in your blood.
But O, beware the sex! in little minds
Where love a slender, doubtful empire holds,
Variety has prov'd an antidote;
But in a noble soul like yours, Lord Clifford,¹⁰
Where sentiment combines with fond desire,
Each deviation from the path of virtue

9. This is the first of several songs included in Larpent but missing from the first edition, perhaps reflecting performance cuts; the printed version jumps to Bertram's offer to be Clifford's "physician." 10. The Larpent version has "my Clifford."

May, for an instant, gratify the passions;
Yet dire remorse, with all her scorpion stings,[11]
Will lash the heart to madness.—
CLIF.                                    Fear me not.
Think'st thou while Elina reigns here, I ever
Could be inconstant to her, even in thought?
BER. When did you see her?
CLIF.                                    Not four days are past,
Since the false fair one coyly own'd she lov'd me.
O such a colour ran thro' all her veins,
As when Aurora[12] tips the mountain's top
And blushes day to an admiring world.
This very moment should have made me happy—
Last night, as if the tyrant had delay'd
My tortures, but to render them the fiercer,
She left her castle.
BER.                        How! was she alone?
CLIF. Her confidant, her favourite Beatrice,
She, whom I thought devoted to my service,
Who, when I woo'd her dear ungrateful mistress,
Feign'd such a tender interest in my passion,
Dispell'd my fears, and fed my heart with hope;
Who, next to Elina, and thee, my Bertram,
I thought my truest friend,—She, only she,
Was privy to her flight.
BER.                        It cannot be,
That one so gently bred, without some lover—
CLIF. [Oh! there's the Cause.]
Oh Bertram, Bertram! thou hast touch'd the string
Which quite untunes my soul. Another youth,
Less faithful, but more fortunate than I,
Has in a moment snatch'd the glorious prize
Which I so long was lab'ring to obtain.

11. North could be drawing upon the Biblical (1 Kings xii.11) and Miltonic (Paradise Lost II.701) image of a whip of knotted cords as a lash of scorpions. Byron used this image in The Siege of Corinth: "Scourge with a whip of scorpions, those / Whom vice and envy made my foes" (593–94). The link to remorse may, however, tie these lines to the claim that scorpions when surrounded by fire would sting themselves to death, a "fact" used to image remorse by Byron in The Giaour—"The Mind, that broods ov'r guilty woes, / Is like a Scorpion girt by fire" (422–23); Shelley also used the image in The Cenci—"And we are left, as scorpions ringed with fire. / What should we do but sting ourselves to death?" (II, ii, 70–71).
12. The goddess of dawn.

Oh! leave me, Bertram, I beseech thee leave me,—
Let me in solitude indulge my sorrows.—
[And give a loose to tears,] Oh Elina!¹³

AIR—CLIFFORD¹⁴
Equal to all the Gods is he
Who's favour'd by one smile from thee;
That accent sweet, that tender air,
Would vanquish death and calm despair.
Ah! now I feel the subtle flame,
Which shoots like light'ning thro' my frame,
And blasted by the heavenly fire,
Without one murmuring sigh expire.                    (*Exit*)

[BER. (*Solus.*) I'll follow;—'twere best leave him to himself.
[These Lovers feed on Air, thank Heaven my Stomach
[By temperance hath regain'd its proper tone
[And longs for more substantial food; within there!                    (*Exit*)]


SCENE II    *An Orchard.*¹⁵

*Gam discover'd working.*

AIR—GAM
Oh dear! dear! dear! I sure shall die,—
Poor Gam with sorrow is so dry;
Oh! how I'd weep if every tear
Wou'd turn from water into beer.
                    Oh dear, dear, dear!

Oh! I was once so blythe and merry,
I frisk'd and jump'd like uncork'd Perry:¹⁶
I'm now grown languid, dull, and dumb,
I've no more liquor left, but—Mum.¹⁷

*During the Song Sir Bertram enters behind Gam who starts at seeing him.*
GAM. May I never taste brandy again if it ben't Sir Bertram. Servant your
Honour, bless your noble Worship; terrible dry weather, your Honour; no

13. In the published version, Bertram exits here. 14. This song imitates the opening of
Catullus's imitation of Sappho, "*Ille mi par esse deo videtur*" (Catullus 51). 15. The Larpent
version has a garden. 16. Perry is a fermented beverage made from pears and resembling
cider. 17. Gam puns, as he both silences his song upon Bertram's entrance and signals that
he has some Mum, a Brunswick beer imported in the 17th and 18th centuries.

moisture, no, no, no. O dear, [O] dear, [O] dear, parch'd to a cinder. Heaven send us a little wet; bad season for the hops.

BER. Boy, bring the wine into the orchard here; see it be cool.

[GAM. Oh! Oh! Oh! To be sure, to be sure don't ye, don't ye shake [it. Master Serving Man, Oh lud! oh lud! oh lud!¹⁸ it will be all upon [the fret.¹⁹

[BER. Out of the way Puppy or you'll put me upon the fret.]

GAM. Oh! [lud,] sure; why don't your Honour know I? Oh! I'm terribly *fin'd* down since I seed your Honour last, no *body*²⁰ left your Worship.— Sure your Honour must remember poor, honest, sober Gam.

BER. Oh Master Gam, why thou art chang'd indeed, my honest fellow; what makes thee thus disguis'd in soberness, you drunken knave you?

GAM. Ah! there it is now! what does I get by being sober? nothing but reproaches for my drunkenness. Why when I'm sober in a morning, your Honour, my wife comes with her bitters.²¹ Oh! your Worship, O dear, I have scarce one *dram* of comfort left! O Sir Bertram, I'm quite an alter'd man; your Honour don't know how I loaths, hates, and detests a drunkard.—But the wine, your Honour, the wine!

BER. Egad well thought of—Step in and hurry them.      (*Exit Gam*)
I will indulge this fellow in his humour; it may perhaps divert the melancholy which preys upon my mind.

*Re-enter Gam with the Wine.*

GAM. Oh mercy.—Oh lud! [lud! lud!] your Honour!

BER. What's the matter with the fool? Put down the wine.

GAM. Oh, your worship, such a coil,²² such a spot of work! [lud! lud!] O dear, a sad change, a sad change! there's the butler's cheeks running down with water: I never seed the like afore. None of the serving men will eat or drink; they must be very sad, very sad, indeed. Dear, your Worship, pray what is the matter? They say poor Lord Clifford is quite broken hearted: what is the matter with him, your Honour?

BER. I don't know, Gam: there, drink, drink;—Why man, he has lost his wife: I don't know—Drink, Gam, drink.

GAM. Ha! ha! ha! ha! ha!

BER. Zounds,²³ what do you laugh at?

18. An exclamation; from "lord." 19. "Upon the fret" can refer both to secondary fermentation in liquors and to a state of agitation and ill-humor. 20. Liquor can be "fined down" or purified, clarified; something can also be "fined down" or dwindled away to the vanishing point. Wine and people have "body." 21. "Bitters" can refer either to "bitterness" or to a medicinal (usually alcoholic) drink. 22. Turmoil, a row. The Larpent version has "rumpus." 23. An oath; from "God's wounds."

GAM. Oh, dear your Honour, don't be angry; I can't help laughing, to think that a man should be sorrowful for the loss of his wife. Oh! Sue! Sue! I ha' never laughed till now, since my friends clap'd me on the shoulder, and told me I was a happy man.

BER. Ha! ha! ha! What made you marry her?

GAM. Oh, your Honour, there is no resisting, as our chaplain us'd to say, to predestination. When Lord Auberville turn'd, or rather kick'd me out of his service, I hadn't so much as a drop of drink to my throat.—Sue, for certain, was neither young, nor handsome, nor rich; but she kept an ale-house, your Honour.

BER. Ha! ha! ha!

GAM. Here's your Honour's good health. But what undid me, your Worship, was a cask of strong beer upon tap, which she promis'd to settle upon me. Oh, lud! lud! before the end of the honey-moon my fortune was all drunk out, and she reserved the key of the ale-cellar in her own hands.

BER. "That was" confounded hard, Gam.

GAM. Ah! wasn't it, your Honour? The poor liquor took it so to heart, that all died in a month. I did my duty by it: I bury'd all I could.— Well, your Worship, I determined to ask Lady Elina to pray the old Lord to take me again into his service; but he died suddenly; went off in an apoplexy.—Pop, your Honour, for all the world like the drawing of a cork.

BER. That was a pity; for Lady Elina was always her father's favourite, [and cou'd do anything with him.] I've heard, the Earl never lov'd his other children.

GAM. He never cou'd abide Lord William, because he lov'd music, and dancing, and poetry, and drank nothing but water, which, my old Lord us'd to say, wasn't fit for a man. Well, your Worship, he went into France with the Prince, where he died; with the Black Prince, your Honour, who first brought claret into England,[24] Heavens bless him! but my old master doated upon Lord Reginald, who was stolen at three years old, and hasn't

24. Edward the Black Prince (1330–1376) was the son of Edward III (1312–1377) who had several successful campaigns in France following the resumption of hostilities of the Hundred Years War in 1355. His victories in part led to the treaty of Bretigny or Calais in 1359. A later campaign into Spain may be the one referred to here, for illness struck the British troops including the Black Prince. Claret, now used in England to refer to red wines from Bordeaux, referred to any yellow or light red wine. The Black Prince did campaign in the region around Bordeaux and was governor of Aquitaine, so he may be thought of as introducing this region's French wines into England.

been heard of since. He was as like the Earl as two drops of sherries. I never saw him so crabbed as he was for half a year. Lud a mercy, your Honour, he was as sour as small beer after a thunder-storm.—Here is your Worship's good health.

BER. Thank you, Gam: but have there never been any tidings of Lord Reginald?

GAM. Never from that time; though Sue, who was his nurse, says she should know him among a thousand. He had a large mark on his left arm, for all the world like the stain of red wine on a table-cloth.

*Enter a Servant hastily.*

SER. Sir, my Lord entreats your presence.

BER. I'll attend him instantly.                                          (*Exit Servant*)

Here, fellow, there is a dollar²⁵ for you to buy raiment. Get home to your scolding wife and dead liquor.                                 (*Exit Bertram*)

GAM. (*Solus.*) Aye, if my wife was as dead as my liquor, he! he! he! Go home! what, with money in my pocket! No, no, Sir Bertram,—[I been [among the dead long enough, I'm now for the Land of the Living, ha! ha! [here's still some left.] (*Taking up the Bottle and Drinking.*) Buy Raiment a' faith! No, no. 'Back and side go bare, go bare.'²⁶ [(*Going out, Returns.*) I [thought I had forgot something—(*Takes the Bottle & drinks again.*)

[SONG—AIR

[What care I if my Wife should Scold
[When drunk I cannot hear her.
[When warm'd with Liquor I'm so bold
[Egad I never fear her.

[If Susan furious then shou'd rave
   [I Manfully abuse her
[Or if she should a favour crave
   [I Scornfully refuse her.
            [I know if I
            [Shou'd once comply
[Her tongue wou'd run the quicker.
            [What can subdue
            [So curs'd a Shrew?
[Why Liquor, Liquor, Liquor.                              (*Exit*)]

25. Bank of England dollars were not struck until 1797. "Dollar" was both the English name for the German "*thaler*" and slang for a five shilling piece, a crown. 26. The opening line of an English drinking song included in *Gammer Gurton's Needle* (1575) and alluded to here anachronistically. The scene in the published version ends here, with Ham singing as he exits.

SCENE III   *An Apartment in Mortimer-Castle.*

*Enter Mortimer.*[27]

MOR. How disappointment loves to plague the heart
Of that poor ideot man! who vainly thinks
His reason given to direct and guide him.
The happy brutes, who follow instinct's laws,
Enjoy the blessings of the present hour:
Their daily task perform'd, they lay them down,
And never dream that the approaching morn
Shall wake them to new labours. Man alone
Looks through a flattering and deceitful glass,
And vainly strives to view futurity:
Nature has wisely hid it from his sight;
But purblind Reason, curious and inquisitive,
Just sees enough to dazzle and mislead him.
[But I'll reflect no more—] Osbert!

*Enter Osbert.*

OSB. My Lord!

MOR. Well, you have seen this vain, imperious fair one,
This Phoenix[28] of her sex, whose polish'd form
Contains a heart of flint.—Clifford alone,

27. Mortimer may be named for Roger de Mortimer (1287–1330), 8th Baron of Wigmore, 1st Earl of March, who became the lover of Edward II's disaffected queen Isabella and helped overthrow the king; he was later imprisoned and executed by Edward III. This Mortimer would fit within the time period signalled by the references to the Black Prince, but his lands were in Wales not Kent, though there is a Mortimers manor in Kent. The play's title seems to evoke images of baronial struggles against the king. The barons were restless under Edward II. North's Mortimer later claims that the struggle between his family and the house of Auberville dates from the advent of the "Norman tyrants' conqu'ring arms." Auberville's name suggests a Norman connection, and the historical Mortimer's opponent, Edward II, was descended from William through his granddaughter Matilda and the Angevin line. North's Mortimer also speaks of his imprisonment by the king and Roger de Mortimer was imprisoned in the Tower by Edward II in 1322. One wonders whether North was drawing upon such connections to evoke images of baronial independence against kingly power, even "Saxon" liberty against "Norman" tyranny. In North's era of revolutions, "Saxon vs. Norman" had a political resonance; so, of course, did Kent due to its links to Wat Tyler's insurrection in 1380, fifty years after Roger de Mortimer's death. While the political valence of the play is now difficult to read, there is some evidence (such as the missing third act from the Larpent version) that the play ran into difficulties with the examiner. While the potential "rebel" Mortimer is clearly a villain, Larpent was loath to allow any allusion to revolutionary possibilities on stage. 28. A bird of Egyptian legend that consumes itself in fire and is then reborn from the ashes; but also a person or thing of peerless beauty or excellence, a paragon.

The gay young stripling Clifford; he, it seems,
Hath found the art to draw forth all its fire.
To *me* 'tis cold and hard. The haughty maid,
Stubborn and obstinate, remains unmov'd
Alike by prayers or threats.—"What think'st thou, Osbert?"
OSB. Might I presume, my Lord—
MOR. Well, boy, what then?[29]
OSB.                                     It were to use no force.
Her mind, though mild, is resolute; and sure,
Should you *succeed* by any means but love,
Slow and unwilling, she'd be dragg'd a victim,
Not lead a triumph to your couch.
MOR.                                     "Enough:"
Place her but there, a victim, or a triumph.[30]
Think you that Love, that silly diety,
Can bind my steady nature? Osbert, no.
A brighter, grander passion now inflames me:
One which takes root in noble minds alone;
The soft and common soil of vulgar souls
Could never rear it: 'tis a great Revenge.
What! thou turn'st pale, and tremblest at its name;
And well thou mayest, boy. Fifteen tedious years
It has laid[31] dormant, smothered in my bosom;
But now it wakes and blazes, nor shall sink
Till all my foes have perish'd in its flame.
OSB. Is't possible? Can she have ever wrong'd you?
MOR. All her House have wrong'd me.
The race of Auberville and Mortimer,
E'er since the Norman tyrants' conqu'ring arms
Reduc'd to slavery this warlike isle,
Have borne each other fierce and deadly hate.
Near thirty years are past, since the late Earl,
The father of this proud disdainful Elina,
Made overtures of peace. We then were both
In life's gay spring, and budding into manhood.
Our ages, passions, pleasures, were the same:—
Our enmity wore off, and ardent friendship
Succeeded to our dire hostilities.

29. The Larpent version has a different exchange: "OSB. Might I advise my Lord. *MOR.* Might you advise, / Well, Sir, what then." 30. The Larpent version has "Place her but there / A Victim, or a Triumph, how you talk." 31. The Larpent version has "lain."

But scarce twelve moons were wasted, when the fates,
Which doom'd our houses ever to be foes,
Kindled in both our breasts a fiercer discord,
A more inveterate malice.

OSB.                          What new fury,
What foe to peace and concord could dissolve
A league which seem'd so firm?

MOR.                              What fury think ye?
What fury, but a woman, could effect
So deep a mischief? 'twas a woman, Osbert.
Yes, yes, Alicia, thou shalt find me just.
The disappointment which thou mad'st me feel
Shall fall with tenfold vengeance on thy daughter.
My heart, yet unsubdu'd by love or beauty,
Became her captive: she disdain'd my offers,
And in a little month she gave her hand
To Auberville. Oh, hell is in the thought!
To him, my ancient foe! stung to the quick,
And grown too desperate for a cool revenge,
I challeng'd him to meet me in the lists.
Within two days of our intended duel,
The king forbad the combat, and confin'd me
Close pris'ner, Osbert, in these castle-walls,
For nine long winters. [Did he think to Conquer
[(O foolish Man) the Soul of Mortimer
[By Solitude and vile Imprisonment.
['Tis true my anger took a diffcrent turn
[And grew more deeply rooted by reflection]
But, to cut short my tale, Alicia's death
At length releas'd me.

OSB.                  Oh! my Lord, my Lord!
And does your anger still survive?

MOR.                                It does.
With well-dissembled tears I met my foe,
Deceiv'd the easy fool by feign'd contrition,
And ask'd forgiveness for my former fault.
His heart, then softened by a recent loss,
Took, like the melting wax, whate'er impression
I chose to stamp upon it. He believ'd me
As true a friend as I imagin'd him,
When his alluring form and specious words

Basely seduc'd the false Alicia from me.
Oh, happy Auberville, thy sorrow's past:—
While I am doom'd to drag a painful being,
And groan beneath this anxious load of thought,
Thou, my successful rival, sleep'st securely
Within the peaceful grave!
OSB.                              Oh! there, Sir, bury
Your anger, and your griefs. Oh good, my Lord!
Where love and friendship cease, envy and hate
May find repose.
MOR. No, never, Osbert, never:—
Never, while Elina remains; no never.
While there's one branch of that accursed tree
Alive and flourishing, my restless spirit
Shall, like a mildew, kill the wholesome blossom.
Why think'st thou, Osbert, that I brought her hither?
Think'st thou 'twas only to enjoy her person?
That were but poor revenge; [yet I'll enjoy her
[And quickly too.] No, I had rather blast
The fame of that detested house, than take
Venus array'd in all the fancy'd beauties
With which the poets deck the fickle goddess,
Kind, warm, and yielding to my ardent bosom.
'Tis fifteen[32] years—where does my passion drive me!
No, let me keep that secret bury'd here.
Yet fear not, boy, she shall escape me either.
What, think'st thou, that no threats can terrify,
No soft persuasion bend her to my wishes?
Art must be us'd then.—
OSB.                              Be assur'd, my Lord,
No threats can shake, no eloquence can move,
No art can undermine her steady virtue.
MOR. Come hither, boy.
Osbert, I know she likes thee. I've observed
That she esteems thee far above thy fellows;
Nor do I blame her for it.—Mark me well!
Behold this phial;[33] it contains a liquid
Which, soon as swallowed, 'numbs the faculties,
And seals the sense in oblivious sleep.

32. The Larpent version has "thirteen." 33. For "vial."

Within these two days, dost thou mark me well?—
Infuse it in her drink.—
OSB.                    Oh! pause a moment!
For heaven's sake pause, Sir. Sure so damn'd a deed,—
[One so replete with cruelty and horror,
[Ne'er shook the heart of Man, I cannot do it.]
MOR. Damnation, slave!
What dost thou say? Not do what I command!
What art thou mad? Speak such another word—
OSB. Oh, spare me, spare me.
Oh, Sir, relent, take pity on yourself.
When from this dreadful slumber she awakes,
Think how her frantic shriek will rend your heart.
Oh, heavens! [I see her dash her desperate head
[Against the flinty pavement.] Fiends of hell,
At such a sight [as this] would melt in tears,
Forget their pangs, and join in pitying her's.—
I will not do it.—
MOR.                    Quick, within there, hoa!
This moment is thy last.
OSB.                    Oh! mercy! mercy!
Give me the cursed phial; [Oh my nature
[Revolts at such an Act]—let me die;—
I will not do it. Stay a moment, stay.
Must I obey you?
MOR.                    Dar'st thou hesitate?
Within these two hours,[34] slave obey my orders,
And to the utmost point; or, by my soul,
The ling'ring rack shall tear thee limb from limb.
Within these two hours, Osbert,—Dost thou mark me?            (*Exit*)
OSB. (*Solus.*) Oh! ye soft spirits, who reside above,
And look with pity down on man's calamities,
Protect and guard me. Ah! what fault of mine,
What crime have I committed, that my fortune
Should urge me on to such a deed as this?
What can I do? O shameful! shameful Nature,
Why wilt thou plead for life, for guilty life,
Which proves a burthen to the wretch that bears it!
Yet who can, in the morning of his days,

34. Either Mortimer ups the stakes here, or North nods; for several speeches earlier he has
given Osbert two days to perform the deed.

Look without trembling on the night of death?
[Darkness eternal Darkness! O my soul!
[Recoils with horror at the dreary prospect,]
Ye powers, who take delight in innocence,
Direct me in the path I'm forc'd to tread;
Preserve my life, and save my youth from guilt!                    (*Exit*)


SCENE IV   *An Apartment in Mortimer-Castle.*

*Enter Elina and Beatrice.*

SONG—ELINA

Alas! alas! my faithful friend,
My sorrows, but with life can end.
Oh! Clifford! I would not complain,
Did I alone feel all the pain.

[Did grief this bosom rend alone
[My constant Heart wou'd Scorn to moan.
[Not for myself now flows the tear,
[It falls for one that's far more dear.]

Full well I know, thou gen'rous youth!
Thy honour, constancy, and truth;
My mind's from base suspicion free,
While thine is rack'd with jealousy.

[BEA. Why my dearest Lady
[Why waste the time in empty vain complaining?
ELI. [Ah! cease to persecute me Beatrice.
[What ray of hope—what Straw remains to catch at?]
Oh, Clifford! Clifford! would that I were laid
Deep in the silent grave:—that grief, my love,
Though bitter to thee, time at length might lessen.[35]
But, Oh! the thought, the sad heart-breaking thought,
Of Elina's, of my deceiving thee,
May force thee to a deed so dark and horrible,
That nature shudders at the bare suggestion.
BEA. Why will you raise imaginary terrors,

35. The Larpent version has "wou'd that I were laid / Deep in my Grave. Oh wou'd that
thou / Wer't now lamenting o'er the lifeless body / Of thy poor faithful Constant Elina. /
That Grief tho' bitter to thee, time might lessen."

Why weaken your sad mind, too much depress'd
With phantoms as delusive as they're dreadful?
There still is comfort left [where we expected
[To meet with none but Foes.] All pitying heaven
Has sent a friend, I dare be sworn, a true one,
In faithful Osbert.
ELI.                    Gentle youth, alas!
I feel for him; he seems to bear a mind
Above the meanness of his low condition.
And had not grief, and thy dear image, Clifford,
Effac'd all lesser objects from my memory,
I cou'd recall some features I once lov'd
Which much resembled his. It moves my wonder,
That one so mild and affable should please
So harsh a master.
BEA. There is a fascinating charm in gentleness
That wins the love of all men.—I have heard,
The hungry Lion will cast off his nature,
And lick an Infant's feet. The virgin's tear
Would melt the heart of any brute, but Mortimer;—
And even he, cou'd you descend to sooth him
And feign a kind compliance with his wishes.—
ELI. Feign a compliance!
No, Beatrice; my abject fortune never,
Never shall sink me in my own esteem.
[Girl, I cou'd almost hate thee for the thought.
[No more, no more.]
*Enter Osbert.*
OSB. Time wears apace, and every passing minute,
Drives me the nearer to the precipice,
Whence I must leap, and plunge in sin for ever.
My breast, which hitherto has been serene,
Calm, and unruffled as the summer sea,
Now heaves distracted with a murderer's thought.
[Oh Heavens! a Murderer! sure it cannot be.
[Too true alas! the blackest, basest Murderer
[Is a bright angel, when compared to me.
[They kill the body only, I more cruel—]
BEA. [Osbert,]
How fares it, Osbert? [trust me, you look pale.]
I fear you are not well.

OSB.                    Well, very well!
Oh torture! torture! torture! Oh, I cannot,
I dare not look upon her. Oh! one glance
From her bright eyes will penetrate my bosom,
And find the treachery which lies lurking there.
[I'll strive to speak to her, it will not be.]
Madam, my Lady Elina—
ELI.                    What say'st thou?
Thy tongue denies its office; a faint dew
Stands on thy brow; convulsions shake thy limbs:
What is it Osbert, labouring in thy soul?
Some horrid fancy.—[36]
OSB.                    [Oh! no, no, no,
[What did you say? Ah!] Have you then discover'd—
ELI. Discover'd what?
I'm truly griev'd your youthful bosom, Osbert,
Should harbour any thought that dreads discovery.
[Come give it vent; I'll be your Confessor.
[A frank avowal of your fault shall gain you
[My absolution.][37] Do not sigh so piteously.
His looks strike terror to me. [Ah! some plot
[Some curs'd plot, some deep infernal Mischief
[Thus shakes his frame.] Oh! [Beatrice,] I fear,
I fear this faithful friend—should he prove false,
We are indeed undone.—I cannot bear it.—
Oh my head turns—a sudden horror chills me.
Sure 'tis the hand of death.
OSB. (*Aside.*)                    Oh! would it were
[And do I live to say so, Monster, Monster:
[Inhuman, Savage Monster—. She recovers!
[Would for *her* sake, she died—I am resolv'd,
[Now will I do the—Oh!—how are you, Madam?
[BEA. Give her a little air, 'twill shortly pass.
[Be not alarm'd. Repose will soon restore her.
[Rally your Spirits, be assur'd this lowness
[Proceeds from want of rest.]
OSB. (*Aside.*) Now, now is the time,—

36. The Larpent version has "What dreadful fancy which thou fearest to utter? / Surely no horrid crime." 37. This cut made between the Larpent version and the published version may indicate a desire to eliminate potentially troublesome religious references; Larpent often insisted on such cuts.

[The time for What? Oh! mercy—but I'll on;]
Madam,—how can I say it—I've a liquid
Of sovereign remedy.—[I pray you take it.] (*Offers the Phial.*)[38]
[Ah! now 'tis done, 'tis done.—
[ELI.                                Good youth, I thank thee.
[I surely wrong'd thee by my hard Suspicions.
[Thou Osbert seem'st thyself to need a Cordial.
[I'll not deprive thee of it.
[OSB.                        Oh! do take it
[Madam, I'm well, I've another Vial.
[Here in my Chamber, I entreat you take it.
[ELI. (*Taking the vial.*) Well, give it me;
[Osbert declares 'twill cure me, and I think
[He'd not deceive me. (*Putting the Vial to her lips.*)
[OSB. Stop! Oh Stop! Oh! Oh! Oh! (*Faints.*)
[ELI. Gracious Heaven, he faints.
[Call for some help—Stay Beatrice—he moves.
[Oh! it was kind, it was generous in the Boy
[To give that Aid to me, he so much wanted.
[OSB. Where am I, sure in Hell. Oh all ye Devils
[Invent new Tortures for me, I have done
[A deed which Hell itself shall tremble at.
[Ah! is *she* there, O save me, save me, save me.
[ELI. (*Taking his hand.*) Be tranquil Osbert.
[I come no fiend to Torture, but an Angel
[To breathe soft peace and comfort to your Soul.
[Do you not know me.—
[OSB.                        Aye, too well, too well.
[For I have murder'd thee, the cursed Vial!
[ELI. I have not tasted it.
[OSB. Not tasted it, not tasted it! Oh heavens

38. After Osbert offers the vial, the printed version has a short exchange before Mortimer enters:
ELI. I take thy cordial:—
From any other hand, I might distrust:
But thee, good youth, I will not wrong
By hard suspicion.
OSB. O give me back the fatal remedy.
Your noble confidence has sav'd my soul
And thee; accept, O heaven, my penitence!
And thou, my guardian angel, from this hour,
Let me devote my life, my all, to serve you.

[Not tasted it. No, no, you surely mock me.

[Oh do not, do not, it is cruel in you—

[ELI. Convince thy Eyes. See where upon the floor

[The vial with the Liquor it contain'd

[Still lies untouch'd.

[OSB. Tis true, tis true. Oh! all ye heavenly Powers

[And thou my Guardian Angel, let me kneel,

[Devote my life, my Soul, my all to serve you.]

*Enter Mortimer, William, Walter, and Servants.*

MOR. Horror! confusion! what is't I see:

Slave thou hast dar'd to disobey my orders.

OSB. Do not frown, Sir,

For I have served you nobly; kneel with me,

And worship here, my Lord. [She has preserv'd us

[From utter irrecoverable Ruin—

[Oh she has sav'd that which Remains of Life

[To both of us, from Agonies too bitter

[For mortals to sustain. And for our Souls

[Our everlasting Souls, she—]

MOR.                      How's this, you villain![39]

Dare you to bandy words with me; what means

This crest erect, this haughty bold deportment?

Is this the wretch who, not two hours ago,

Crept at my feet, and howl'd aloud for pity!

OSB. I will confess, my Lord, before I knew

The honest pride, the dignity of virtue,

My coward heart shrunk at the thought of death.

But for a thousand, thousand years of life,

I'd not have done that deed, which Providence

So happily prevented.—Now, my Lord,

Now act your pleasure; for, escaped from guilt,

I do not fear to die.

MOR.                  Dost thou brave me boy?

Bring forth the rack. [Thou silly pious fool,

[That which remains of life to thee *shall* pass

[In Agonies; bring forth the Rack I say.]

ELI. (*Kneeling.*) Oh, Sir, behold me prostrate at your feet:—

Me, whom your threats could never yet dismay.

I'd scorn to kneel thus humbly for myself:

39. The Larpent version has "Ha! you villain."

If ever gentle pity touch'd your soul,
O spare that youth.
MOR.                    [Madam, I'm not us'd
[To grant my favours without some return.]
You, Lady, know the means to save his life:
Do you be merciful and spare him.
ELI.                              Oh!
My heart! my bursting heart!—Hear me, my Lord,
I swear within these three days, if no help,
No friendly aid, should free me, to be yours.
MOR. Release the slave.—
Strip off the gaudy trappings he now bears,
And, in a habit sordid as his mind,
Turn forth the wretch to starve. You'll keep your word.          (*Exit*)
OSB. Why wou'd you make so hard, so rash a vow.
Oh it were better far that I were dead
Than that my sweet deliverer—
ELI. Osbert, Osbert,
A word in private—can it be contriv'd?
OSB. My fellow servants we have liv'd together
Like friends and brothers—let me intreat ye,
Before we part for ever, but to grant me
One small request.
WIL. What wou'd you Osbert?
OSB.                         [Oh! my honest William
[I've ever found thee tender and Compassionate.
[Leave me then] William, I beseech thee,
Leave me one moment with this Lady.
WIL. Ah! [I fear] (*Pauses.*)
'Tis at the utmost hazard of my life:—
But still I can't refuse you: yet, remember
Your confidence must be short.
                    (*Exeunt William and Walter, Beatrice following*)
ELI.                         [Stay Beatrice,
[Sure there is nothing passes in my Heart
[I wou'd conceal from thee.] A glimmering ray
Begins to dawn upon my darken'd soul.
Hie thee, good Osbert, with thy utmost speed,
To Clifford Castle; it lies west from hence
Some half day's journey; tell my faithful love
The fate of his poor Mistress; bid him haste

(But he'll not want bidding) to her rescue.
This purse will furnish thee with means; farewel,
My worthy Osbert!
OSB.                Noble, noble Lady!
I feel myself so honour'd in your service,
I cannot speak! Accept these heartfelt tears.—
Adieu! and doubt not of success.[40]

[DUETT

[OSB.          Weep not dear Lady, now I go
              [To bring you comfort in distress.
[ELI.          To Snatch me from this place of Woe
              [And end my Miseries by Success.
[ALL THREE.   To snatch me/thee from this place of woe
              [And end my/thy miseries by success.
[OSB.          Dispell these mournful shades of Grief.
[BEA.          Let Joy, her brighter beams impart.
[ELI.          To-morrow's Sun may bring relief.
[OSB.          And Clifford press thee to his heart.

[ALL THREE.   To-morrow's sun may bring relief
              [And Clifford press thee/me to his heart.]
                              (*Exeunt generally*)

#### END OF ACT I

## ACT II

SCENE I   *Inside of an Ale House.*

*Susan enters. Gam is lying on a Bed, the whole Room in
disorder, Pots, Pans &c lying about.*
SUE. Mercy! mercy! what a hog-stye! Where's Gam? What a bed still!
[I'll give him a cold Pig,[41] I warrant ye. What Gam I say, you drunken
[Sot.] Why Gam! Gam! Gam!
GAM. (*Waking.*) Who's there? What Sue, my dear? [how kind this is in
[ye,] you needn't make a noise; I'm broad awake; you'll not disturb me.
(*Snores.*)
SUE. This is too much: But he shan't sleep, I'm determin'd. If he gives
me no pleasure, I'll give him no rest. Why drunkard, villain, sot! Gam!
Gam! Gam! I say.

40. In the published version, the act ends here with "Exeunt generally."  41. A "cold pig"
or "cold pie" is a colloquial expression for a dousing with cold water to wake someone.

GAM. I understood you before, my charmer. [That's right, that's right.] O dear, dear; now if you knew how much pleasure this gives me—that's a good wench; why, he! he! he! he! you make as much noise as the devil in the wine Cellar, [as the saying is, lud! lud! you are for all the World.]

SUE. Do you laugh at me, you rogue? devil, and wine cellar indeed! Ah! Gam! Gam! your head is always running in the wine cellar.

GAM. (*Half asleep.*) You lie, you lie, it's the wine cellar that's always running in my head.

SUE. (*Weeping.*) Was there ever faithful, constant young woman thus used; O you base man; what did you marry me for?

GAM. (*Half asleep.*) For the strong beer upon tap.

SUE. O villain! villain! Is it out then?

GAM. Heigho! O dear! dear! it has been out this eleven years.

SUE. Gam! you vile Gam! will you hear me?

GAM. [Not if I cou'd help it. Only you are louder than the Cannons [which the Old Lord us'd to fire when he drank the King's Health.] Hear ye [Sue]! why I've heard nothing else since we've been married.—On you go, always in the same tone, rattle, rattle, ding, ding, for all the world like shot at the bottom of a bottle.

SUE. Don't talk to me, don't talk to me, you perjur'd wretch, of your rattles[42] and your shots. You terrify me out my senses; a poor weak woman, a woman in my situation.—

GAM. (*Starting.*) Hey! what's that? what's that?—what situation?

SUE. Hem! hem! why married to an idle, drunken, infamous—

GAM. O lud! O lud! O lud! is that all? (*Snores.*)

SUE. Is that all! aye, and enough too. You tiger—You wolf—You butcher, you, you, you'll break my spirit.—You will—[you will]—you will—you will. (*Stamps and roars violently.*)

GAM. He! he! he! that's good 'faith—[well said Sue, that will never do, [that will never do, lud a mercy, lud a mercy.] thy Spirit! "Lud a "mercy"—I verily believe thou hast more than the old tierce[43] of brandy at the Benedictine convent hard by.

SUE. Do you mock me; am I become your laughing-stock? but I'll bear it no longer, with my nails I'll—

GAM. (*Getting out of bed.*) Paws off, Sue!—Paws off.—Offer to scratch—and may I never get drunk again, if I don't [Hoop your Barrel.[44] (*Offers to [strike her.*)

[SUE. O you insolent revengeful, I don't know what to call you, no [name's bad enough for you, no none.

42. The Larpent version has "Cannons." 43. A "tierce" is a measure of liquid equal to ⅓ pipe, or 42 gallons. 44. "To Hoop the barrel" is to beat soundly.

[GAM. That's hard! devilish hard, I've already the worst in the Parish.
[Come Sue, come my chicken.

[SUE. Stand away. Stand away, you Barbarian. Come not near, pho! how
[you smell. Am I a Barrel to be Hoop'd am I—

[GAM. (*Drunk & Staggering.*) No, Sue, no such luck, no such luck, I wish
[you were. O Sue, Sue, how happy I should be if you were a Barrel.

[SUE. A Barrel, Fellow.

[GAM. Aye, a Barrel, Sue. Oh! how we should Kiss; our Lips wou'd be
[never asunder. (*Sings.*) Liquor, liquor! liquor!]

SUE. Oh Gamel, Gamel! is this usuage for me who refused so many noble offers for you; who gave you my heart, beast, when I was in my
prime.

GAM. Don't lie, Sue, don't lie. You know it was your second vintage. Old
Humphry, your late husband, might, for what I know, have you neat as
imported; but you were adulterated when you came to me; adulterated
with the damnable spirit of contradiction.

SUE. Adulterated indeed! by the mass I defy thee. Thou shalt stand in
the church in a white sheet for this; this is downright reformation, you
villain.

GAM. In a white sheet! with all my heart, I ha'nt been in a white sheet
these six months; and as for reformation, damn me I never had a thought
of it.[45] Wounds, Sue, the wine I drank last night—Yes, wine you
wench—has made me confounded thirsty. Do now, my love—do my
dearest, pretty, young, little, dainty Sue, do now, one cup, one cup of ale.
Sir Bertram gave me a dollar,[46] and I've brought all home to you my dear.

SUE. Ah! good Gam, dear Gam, where is it? You shall have the ale directly; where is it? [where is it, my sweet Gam.]

GAM. (*Striking his head.*) Where is it! why here to be sure, where the devil
shou'd it be.

SUE. Oh you drunkard, you drunkard, you vile abominable man! not a
drop, not a drop, [tho your whole inside—]

GAM. Don't be in a passion, Sue; consider your youth, my love; indeed,
for one of your tender years, the care of the ale cellar is too weighty, too
laborious a charge; it's fitter for a person advanced in life, one who's ex-
perienc'd in them matters—One who is grown mellow (*Hiccups.*) by age.

45. One stood in a white sheet during the mass as part of the ancient penance for incontinence. It came to designate the utmost penitence, such as might be felt for being part of
a heretical "reformation," a word Sue and Gam pun on, though Sue's use is anachronistic.
"Wounds" in the next sentence is apparently for the oath "zwounds" or "God's wounds."
46. The Larpent version has "a mark," which would indicate an old English weight of silver, worth 13s 4d.

SUE. No, no, I'll keep my fortune in my own hands; I'm no such chicken neither, [I'd have you to know, Master Gam.]

GAM. Well then be mov'd, be mov'd, my dear old hen.

SUE. Old hen! old hen, indeed!

GAM. Why the devil's in you, Sue; can nothing please you? why you'll neither be old nor young: will you be middle-aged then?

SUE. Middle-aged, Mr. Gamel!

GAM. Lud! Lud! if you an't more obstinate than Peter Botchaway, the cobler, who'd neither drink strong beer, nor mix'd beer, nor small beer. (*Kneeling to her.*) One cup, one cup of ale, it shall be the last, Sue.

SONG—GAM[47]

Twelve years ago I went to woo,
The comfort of my life, my Sue;
I then was twenty-eight,[48] and you,
My pretty chick—were forty-two.　　(*Piano*)
　　　　　　　　forty-two,　　(*Pianissimo*)
　　　　　　　　forty-two;　　(*Pianissimo*)
My pretty chick—were twenty-two.　(*Forte*)

Runs time as glibly as of yore,
You must be verging on threescore;
But women now grow old no more,
And Susan blooms at fifty-four;　　(*Piano*)
And Susan blooms at fifty-four,
　　　　　　　fifty-four;—　　(*Pianissimo*) [49]
And Susan blooms at thirty-four.　(*Forte*)

['Tis strange as some wise folks wou'd say
[That one so Old should be so gay.
['Tis Stranger far as I grow Grey
[My wife grows greener every day—
[My wife grows greener every day—
[My wife grows greener every day.]

47. The text of this song is only a plausible reconstruction. The published version lacks the final stanza and the volume designations. The Larpent version has volume designations for the first two stanzas, but they and the references to Sue's age seem inconsistent. A version offered in the *Morning Chronicle* for 27 June 1791 helps with some punctuation problems and with one of the age references. 48. In the Larpent version he is thirty-eight. 49. The Larpent and published versions have "thirty-four, fifty-four," but the *Chronicle's* version seems more plausible; but perhaps Gam speaks the lower one loudly, the other softly. The Larpent version closes the stanza with her being fifty-four (*pianissino*).

SUE. Oh Gam! you wheedling rogue, you!

OSB. (*Without*.) Holloa! within there! be quick, be quick; what do you mean, good people, to keep me in the rain all day?

GAM. Mercy on us, who's that? Oh Sue! Sue! I wish it mayn't be the peace officer come with a warrant against us for the hare! Oh, Sue! you'll be whipp'd, Sue; and I shall be—

SUE. Never mind that, [I'm all in a Muck with—]⁵⁰

OSB. (*Without*.) What, are you all asleep? Holloa! holloa! come instantly, I say; I'll break the door down.

GAM. It must be an officer by his manners; Lud! Lud! [Lud!] what is to be done; where shall we hide us? Can't we creep into the empty cask there?

SUE. Aye, aye; Oh fackins,⁵¹ there is only room for one.

GAM. Give me the key to the ale cellar; I'll hide in the butt below.

SUE. It's full, it's full; you'll be drowned.

GAM. Quick, quick, give me the keys. I warrant you I'll drink myself into my depth—In good Sue, in, in.

OSB. I'll delay no longer. (*Breaking open the door.*) What, are you dead? (*Entering.*)

GAM. (*Bowing very low.*) No, please your worship, nor drunk neither.

OSB. Prithee, my good fellow, bring me a chair:—I'm worn almost to death.

GAM. (*To Sue.*) I don't believe he is an officer, he is so condescending: best be civil though.

SUE. Please your worship, I hope your worship will take compassion upon us; though we are poor, we are honest; we have many enemies, your worship: my husband, an' please your reverence, is a sober, hard working man; and I a quiet, laborious woman, your honour. Hopes for the matter of the hare, which he chanc'd to pick up in the high road, as your honour is an officer—

OSB. Ha! ha! [ha!] dismiss your fears, I'm no officer.

SUE. Not an officer! how dare you then break down poor people's doors in this here manner? Get out you impudent, vile, good-for-nothing vagabound.

*Osbert turns to her.*

SUE. (*Screams*.) Mercy! mercy!—It is!—It is!—It is!

GAM. Is it? Oh Sue! Sue!—An' please your worship—

SUE. A ghost!—A ghost!—A ghost!—It is, I can take my bible oath on't, it is my old master.

---

50. To be "in a muck" is to smothered in dirt, literally or figuratively.   51. In truth, verily.

GAM. Mercy on us! it is as like him as ever it can stare: (*Falls on his knees.*) Bless your lordship. [Oh dear your Lordship, forgive me, forgive me, [Heaven is my Witness, my Lord I never robb'd you of nothing but sheer [Drink. As for the Silver Spoon, as I hope for mercy it was all a Lie [trump'd up by Robert the Butler.] Lud a mercy, I am so glad to see your lordship! Your lordship never look'd so well in your born days, as since your death.

OSB. [What are you mad, or do you mean to mock me with this [distracted Folly.] I your master! you fools, I'm little better than yourselves; was born some dozen miles from hence, and never was here before.

SUE. Oh! don't be angry, your lordship. I'm sure you are the young Lord Reginald, who was stolen—I'm confident it is he. O my child! my dear child. (*Throws her arms around his neck and kisses him.*)

OSB. Woman stand off.—[No more of this. Remember you're in my [power.] No more, or you shall smart for this impertinence.

SUE. (*Weeping.*) My lord! my lord! answer me one question; do my dear, dear lord—"Doesn't your lordship bear upon your arm—"[52]

GAM. [Aye,] a mark, your lordship, a large red mark on your lordship's left arm.

OSB. (*Starting violently.*) Gracious Heaven! is't possible!
E'er since my birth, I've borne upon my arm
A mark, and such a one as he describes.
Come hither both of you: see this spot?

SUE. (*Almost fainting.*) Oh! 'tis the same, 'tis the same; I'll take my corporal oath[53] on't, before any justice of the peace in England.

GAM. Oh! 'tis the same, 'tis the same! Huzza! huzza! I'll swear to it, tho' I never saw it in my life. My young Lord is found again: Oh! such rejoicings, such bonfires, such luminations, such roasted oxen, such hogsheads of ale! I'll never be sober again in my life. Huzza! huzza!

OSB. My friends [as you esteem my happiness
[I pray] restrain this wild excess of joy.
You seem to know the mystery of my birth;
Unfold it.

GAM AND SUE. Yes, yes, yes, my Lord.

SUE. Hold your peace, that clack[54] of your's will be eternally running. Sure I must know the most of the master; I who suckled his lordship.—

---

52. The Larpent version has "Have you a mark." Osbert replies, "(*Starting.*) A Mark! what mean you?" 53. An oath ratified by touching a sacred object such as the bible or a relic. 54. From the clack of a water-mill, meaning a tongue.

Well then, my Lord, almost fifteen[55] years ago—I can't for the life of me recollect the day.—

GAM. It was on the third of January, my Lord's birth-day; he was three years old that very day. My Lord, your old father, my late master, Lord Auberville, as was—

OSB. Lord Auberville! good Heavens! Proceed! proceed!

GAM. My Lord, as I was a saying, my Lord Auberville gave a great dinner that day. I shall never forget it, we were all in our best liveries.

OSB. Damn your liveries—I'm on the rack man.

GAM. (*Aside.*) My old master to a hair.

SUE. Lud, Gam, what signifies the liveries?

GAM. Why yes, it does signify; my Lord, your boots must be wet, and your throat must be dry.—Run, Sue, and make a fire in the kitchen. Sure, my Lord, you must be tired.—If your Lordship will descend so far as to walk into the kitchen, over a cup of ale, I'll tell you the whole tote[56] of the matter in as concise and circumstantial a manner as possible.

OSB. Well, be it so.

I'm much fatigu'd, and wish for some refreshment.

Come, man, come quickly.

(*Exeunt Gam and Sue squabbling*)

SCENE II    *An Apartment in Mortimer-Castle.*

*Enter Mortimer and William.*

MOR. Well, did he whine and wail, and beat his breast?
Nurs'd here in ease, and bred in luxury,
He'll find the pangs of hunger insupportable;
Too slight a punishment for slaves and vassals,
Who dare to presume to think and disobey
The mandates of their master. [—Did he howl.
WIL. [No, my Lord,] I never
Beheld in such a youth so firm a spirit.
He press'd me by the hand, and smiling, said,
Farewel, good William. With my eyes I follow'd him,
And saw him bound, fleet as the mountain roe,
Over the hill, which to the westward lies
Some hundred paces.
MOR.                    Ah! what did he smile?

55. The Larpent version has "13 years." 56. A pleonastic phrase, since "tote" means the total amount.

Smile, say you? Did he smile?—I like not that.
[Stay! let me pause a Minute. O fool! fool!]
He has seen Elina. I have remark'd,
Instead of weeping for her favourite's absence,
A sullen kind of triumph seems to sit
Upon her brow, which menaces some evil.
What can I fear? [O rather let me think
[What I have not to fear.] Observe me, William, "tell me,"
Tell me, and as your life will answer it,
Did the base traitor, e'er he left the castle,
See Elina alone?

WIL. (*Frightened.*) My Lord, my Lord.—

MOR. You seem surpris'd. I'll take another method. (*Aside.*)
Nay, fear not, William; tho' I did not wish
That he shou'd see her, yet I'm not so cruel,
As to blame thee, good fellow: did he see her?

WIL. [(*Aside.*) I dare not trust you—] No, my Lord, he did not.

MOR. Art sure of't, William? Come, come, tell the truth.
For shame, man, do not lie; I am not angry.
Damnation do you mutter? Speak the truth,
Or I will—Speak the truth, my honest William.[57]

WIL. [I assure you]
My Lord, he did not see her.

MOR. All's safe, I hope, then:—yet I do not like
That smile of Osbert's. Why did he escape me?
Wou'd I had made him sure when in my power.
If ever soft compassion, or that weakness
Call'd Pity,[58] touch'd my heart, it was that boy,
That Osbert, that ungrateful timid Osbert,
Found out the frailty. I'm almost asham'd
To own, e'en to myself, how much I lov'd him.
No more of that. Within these three days Elina[59]
Has promis'd, should no friendly aid arrive,
To wed me.—[O infatuated Girl,
[Who baits the Hook, when he has caught the fish.
[Unless some friendly Aid—Psha! 'tis impossible.
[Hence you vain dreams, you foolish fancies hence.
[I will be happy spite of all your strugglings.

57. The Larpent version has "Or I will tear thy Soul out. / Come tell the truth good
William, I'm your slave." 58. The Larpent version has "Friendship." 59. The Larpent
version has "Within three days this Elina."

[No, I will not be cruel, I'll not drag you
[Unwilling to the Altar, no, no Priest]
No hated priest shall join our hands together,
Whose hearts cou'd never pair. Yet I'll deceive her
With a feign'd marriage: good, it shall be so:—
The live-long night I'll revel in her beauties,
And in the morning tell her she's undone.
Ha! William, why, you knave, you grow so pursy,[60]
So indolent, so fond of ease and pleasure,
[Thou lik'st a Wench, I see it in thy face,]
Sure nature form'd thee, fellow, for a friar.
WIL. I'm glad to see your Lordship grown so merry.
I *was* a churchman once, Sir.
MOR.                                Wert thou, William?
Thou shalt be so again ere long.—Go in:
Go in, Most Reverend Father; count thy beads,
And mumble o'er thy prayers.                          (*Exit William*)
                          Merry! Merry!
O thou poor fellow, little dost thou know
What passes here. How wretched is the man
Who builds upon deceit! though fraud and artifice
May for a while support the tottering fabric,[61]
Tho' it seem fair and beauteous to the eye,
Yet all is grief and wretchedness within;
And tho' by nature bold, he feels a horror,
A dread of something which he strives in vain
To banish from his mind; that spoils the harmony,
And mars the heavenly music of the soul.
[But the plain honest man fears no detection.
[Secure he ventures on life's open Sea
[And Steers directly to his destin'd Port.
[Tho' hostile Winds may shatter his Stout Bark
[He keeps his Steady Course, and ne'er can founder
[While the main timbers of his Heart are Sound.
[*Enter Beatrice.*
[Ah! Beatrice, come hither Beatrice.
[How fares your lovely Mistress?
[BEA.                                Oh, my Lord
[How can you ask the question.

60. To be "pursy" is to be short of breath as a result of being overweight. 61. A building.

[MOR. Hey! why not?

[BEA. Sure your own feelings might inform your Lordship

[How my poor Mistress fares, drag'd from her friends

[Torn from the Man she loves, and now betroth'd

[To him, whom most on earth—

[MOR.                              She Execrates.

[Nay, never mince the matter. What art sad?

[What is it Beatrice, not melancholy

[To see thy Mistress Wed before the Wench.

[Do not despair, I'll find thee out a Husband

[You pretty witty Wench.

[BEA.                    Oh no, my Lord.

[Cou'd I but see my Mistress once more happy

[I wouldn't wish to Change my State, O no!

[SONG—BEATRICE

['Twou'd surely argue want of wit

[Shou'd I my Lord a Courting go.

[Shall I my much lov'd Mistress quit

[And seek a tyrant Husband—No.

[O Cupid do not vengeful prove

[Ah! spare me from thy fatal bow.

[Alas! I've known too much of Love

[To wish to taste its joys—O no!

[If e'er I give my heart to man

[My passions from Esteem shall flow

[But still I'll keep it if I can

[Nor risk my peace of mind—no no—]

Enter *Elina*.[62]

MOR. Oh! what a pleasure wou'd your presence give me,

[My heart wou'd bound with transport at your sight,

[Shake off this load of grief and dance with joy,]

Did sportive smiles adorn that heavenly face.

Oh! do not weep: I cannot, "cannot" bear it.

Unhappy Mortimer, art thou the cause?

[The Cause of Misery to her whom most—]

ELI. Forbear, my Lord, forbear, and do not add

Insult and mockery to the injuries

62. In the printed version, Beatrice enters here as well.

Which you've already done me. Can you ask,
If you're the cause? My Lord, you know too well,
You are alone the cause of all my woe.
MOR. Oh, do not be unjust: I'm but the agent;
Love is the mighty cause. I own my weakness;
Nor should you blame a fault, fair Elina,
Which love has forc'd me to commit. [Your bosom
[Pure and unsullied as the driven Snow
[Has felt the force of love!]
ELI.                          For shame! [for Shame!]
Do not profane its sacred name, my Lord:
O do not call a wild licentious passion,
A base, a brutal inclination, Love.
Love softens nature, elevates the mind,
Creates a feeling in the hardest breast.
MOR. What breast more hard than mine, till gentle love
And your all-powerful charms subdu'd my heart.
My rigid temper ne'er relax'd till now—
Till now I never—
ELI.              Dost thou then relent?
O heaven be prais'd! Yes, I forgive thee, Mortimer:
Forgive and pity thee.
MOR.                   Oh! 'tis too much.
And do you pity me? Why then delay
Our marriage, for so long?—to-night.—
ELI. What mean you?
MOR. Do not revoke your pity, 'twere unkind.
[And sure wou'd break the heart you've made so blest.]
To-night—my love—to-night.
ELI.                         Base tyrant, no.
My word is pledg'd, 'tis true, but not to-night.
I swear no force shall drag me.
MOR.                            Do not frown.
Kill me not with your anger. Well, my angel,
I will consent then to postpone my bliss:
But don't forget your promise; two days hence,
My Elina, my goddess, will be mine.
I see you pity me; I'll leave your Lady:
Indulge the generous feeling of your soul.
Farewel, my Elina!                            (*Exit*)

ELI. Nature cou'd never form so harsh a fiend,[63]
So barbarous and inhuman, whose delight,
Whose only pleasure centers in the pain
He can inflict on others.—['Tis but just
[That he himself should feel the bitter pangs
[With which he wishes to torment Mankind.]
Sure, e'er this good Osbert is arriv'd.—
[And Clifford hastens to our rescue.] Yes, "Beatrice"
Still I will fondly hope.
BEA.                        Your hopes, e'er night
Has thrown her dusky mantle o'er yon hill,
Shall all be chang'd to certainties.
ELI. Oh! Beatrice!

SONG—ELINA

Ah, why! Ah, why! ye heavenly pow'rs,
    Why in my life's more early day,
Strew'd ye my easy path with flowers,
    To make more sharp this thorny way!

Yet still, will I invoke thy aid,
    Still lift to you my fervent prayer.
Take pity on a helpless maid,
    And turn her footsteps from despair.

(*Exeunt*)

SCENE III   *Outside of Clifford-Castle.*

*Enter Osbert.*

OSB. Where is this loitering fellow? [how provoking
[When I am mad with hurry.] Holloa, Gam!—
How wond'rous strange this mystery of my birth.—
[Above twelve Years a Slave, and now almost
[A Prince. Oh do not Expectation
[Lift up my hopes too high. For the next tide
[Of fortune on a sudden may destroy
[The Building she has rais'd. Where can he be?]
Where is this Gam?—She—Elina my sister,[64]

63. The Larpent version has "a fiend like this." 64. The Larpent version has "Oh! Elina, my Sister. She my Sister."

Whom I so lately—Heavens, how I tremble,
To think upon the danger I've escap'd!
[Oh Mortimer, what Hell is bad enough—]
*Enter Gam.*
Oh! you are there? You've been a pretty guide.

GAM. Yes, your Lordship, [yes, yes,] yes. To be sure, for the first quarter of a mile [from our House,] the path winds like a corkscrew; but when you are once in the road, it is as streight as the neck of a bottle.

OSB. What you've been tippling in some ale-house, now.

GAM. Tippling! I never tipples, as folks say. I sometimes drinks as much as does me good. I do not go for to deny it; but I scorns to tipple. Ale house, your honourable Lordship, it was no ale-house: it was a house where you goes, and gets your liquor, and pays your money. No, upon my soul, it was no ale-house.

OSB. Have a care; you have been talking, Gam. [But come, make haste, [make haste.]

GAM. Who! I talk! no, my Lord, I never talks. [I never says no more [words than is necessary.] No, no, i'fackins, I have been too long used to drink, to be leaky in my cups; besides, d'ye see, My Lord, I claps this pipe into my mouth, d'ye see, by way of a spigot, for fear any thing shou'd run out.

OSB. Enough! enough!—Well, are we near the castle?

GAM. The castle! the castle! the castle! Oh! ho! ho! Lord bless you, no, we be seven miles from it.

OSB. What do you mean? Why, but just now, you said we were not twenty paces.

GAM. Did I?—I was drunk then. Auberville-Castle—

OSB. Auberville-Castle; pshaw! No, give me patience, [what a con-[founded fool,] no, Clifford-Castle.—

GAM. Oh, lud! lud! lud! why it's hard by; you may be there in the drinking of a dram. Lord'a'mercy, how main passionate you great people be— Passion, as our chaplain us'd to say, is for all the world like—

OSB. Never mind the chaplain. Is that the house?

GAM. Oh! my old! my old master! he never cou'd abide the chaplain. Le's see, "let's see;" yes, yes, yes, that's the house, sure enough.—No [it ben't;] I don't see the smoke coming out of the kitchen-chimney.—Damme, what makes the trees so merry?—Why they dance "like"—[yes, yes, yes, that's the House, that's the house, Holloa! Hip [holloa, Master Butler.]

OSB. [Be quiet Gam.—] "Pshaw,"—is this the door?

GAM. Why, to be sure it is: why, you must be tipsey.—Don't you know a door when you see it? He! he! he! [Master Butler, holloa, holloa! Mas-[ter Butler.]

[*Enter a Servant.*

[SER. Who's there that calls so loud. Oh, it is you.

[Go get you hence you drunkard.

[OSB. I do beseech you, Sir; pay no attention

[To that same Fellow there, stay but one instant.

[SER. Sir. Well, what do you want?

[OSB. Sir, I have business

[And of the utmost moment with Lord Clifford.

[Inform him instantly a Gentleman

[Entreats to speak with him.

[SER. Gentleman. Quotha.[65]

[GAM. Tell him, Lord Regi—

[OSB. (*Shaking him gently.*) For Heaven's sake

[Now my good fellow, Gam; pray, pray be quiet—

[And get you home, Dear Gam; indeed you know not

[Whom you refuse, Sir:—Let me in this minute,

[Fellow I tell thee, I'm a Messenger

[Of Comfort to your Lord—I will come in. (*Lays his hand upon his Sword.*)

[SER. Oh! you're for that Sport are you?

[I'll send you one, my pretty *Gentleman*,

[Shall talk to you and in a different way.

[(*Exit and Locks the Door*)

[GAM. (*Going up to the Door.*) Hey! Oh Lud! lud, why he has lock'd the [Door, close fast as the Ale Cellar; is this Usage for a Lord, you knave.]

OSB. (*Seizing him by the collar and striking him.*) Curse on you, booby! Gam! take care, take care; I am not in the mood to trifle, Gam. Get home this moment, or I'll [strike thee harder.]

GAM. My old Lord [again]!—No, no, no, that's not like my old Lord. He always struck as hard as he cou'd first, and threaten'd afterwards.— Damme, I believe he is but a bye-blow.[66]

OSB. What shall I do with him? (*Aside.*)

Go to the ale-house, Gam; do, my good Gam.

[I ask your pardon for the blow I gave you.

[GAM. Oh my Lord, my Lord—

65. An expression of surprise or contempt.   66. A bastard.

[OSB. (*Kicking him.*) Again, Confound you;—Get home or I'll—]

GAM. My Lord!—I'll go to the ale-house, or I'll go any where, but home.
Oh, Lord! Lord! it goes against my stomach, "my Lord." [It's for all the
[world like beginning at the Bottom of a bottle and Drinking to the Top.
[Damme he is but a bye blow. Well my Lord,] I'll go to the ale-house.

[OSB. Go to the Devil, any where.

[GAM. With all my Heart, any where but home.

[OSB. (*Offering to Strike him.*) Will you be gone.

[GAM. Yes, yes, yes, Oh Lud; he is main passionate; no, no, he is no bye
[blow—I'm a going, I'm a going. Hold! Hold—Don't you see I'm a going.
[My Old Master, My Old master; he is no bye blow.]          (*Exit Gam*)

OSB. Oh I cou'd weep from anger and vexation. (*Knocks hard.*)
Will no one hear? I'll enter, tho' I die for't.[67]
I will! I will come in. (*Knocks very hard at the door.*)
*Enter Bertram.*

BER. Why, what's all this!
You will come in! why, who are you? hey, sirrah!
Why, what means all this noise? your haughty words
Agree not with your habit. Who are you?

OSB. One, Sir, not us'd to such a rough behavior.
Delay no time now; every moment's precious.
[Upon my Knees] I beg you let me enter.

BER. (*Aside.*) By the Rood,[68] a pretty boy! [I should be loth to hurt him.
[And see he weeps,] it grieves me to refuse him.
Lord Clifford can't be seen, let that content you.

OSB. Hear me! hear me!
I bring him tidings will rejoice his soul.
[Will raise him from the Grief that weighs him down.
[And call him back to happiness and Love!
[Do not deny me, I entreat you do not.
[I see Compassion glistening in your Eye.
[Oh let it fall upon me.]

BER. What are your tidings?

[OSB. Oh, Sir; Excuse me; they are of a nature
[I cannot reveal with honour.

[BER. Not reveal them.
[Why then you cannot Enter here, why boy
[I am Lord Clifford's Friend, his Counsellor,
[One who knows all his Secrets. Tell me youth

---

67. The Larpent version has "I'll not be so put off, no, tho' I die for't." 68. By the Cross.

[What are the news you bring.
[OSB. Good Sir, I must not
[Tho' you're Lord Clifford's friend, I dare not do it.]
Sir, my injunctions are to speak with him;
I cannot trust another.
BER. Cannot trust me—
Well keep thy secret to thyself. Good-morrow. (*Going into the house.*)
OSB. Oh! stay and hear me.
Why shou'd I come here, wherefore shou'd I suffer
Such base indignities? I pray you think
Why I should wish to see Lord Clifford, Sir?
I know him not, I've nought to ask from him.
[I am no Thief, or if I were a Thief
[What cou'd he fear from a poor Youth like me.
[Oh. If your pity grant not my request
[Consult your reason; sure you won't refuse me.]
Oh! if you are his friend,
[BER. If I'm his friend. Dare but to doubt it.
OSB. [Good Sir, be appeas'd.]
Oh let me in, in truth you'll not repent it.
BER. (*Aside.*) The boy speaks well—
[He wou'd not trust me tho'. Ah! let me see.]
Where can he come from? Stay, a thought occurs.
[I'll not betray myself. Tell me the truth.]
Come you not from a woman? Ha! you blush.
Come, come, I know you do.—
OSB. I can't deny it.
BER. You can't deny it; well then, what's her name?
OSB. The question's somewhat blunt.
He who's intrusted with a lady's secret,
Should keep a padlock fix'd upon his lips,
And throw away the key. We trifle time—
I pray conduct me.
BER. Who! what! I conduct you!
Boy! do you take me for a serving man,
A lacquey, one who runs on messages?
I am a soldier, boy; a rough old soldier;
A very testy, touchy, crabbed fellow.
Can you deny that?
OSB.              He were prone indeed
To argument, and fond of controversy,

Who wou'd dispute a fact so clear and palpable.

BER. Ha! ha! ha!

Give me your hand, my boy; I like your frankness:

Give me your hand.—Well, you shall see Lord Clifford.

But prithee tell me now, who sent thee hither?

Was it the rich old widow Margaret,

Or dame Elizabeth, with her wanton cousin?

[OSB. I entreat your pardon.

[Though not inclin'd to Mirth as Heaven can Witness

[I can't refrain from smiling—

BER.                                        [—What at me?

[Laugh on and welcome;] then there's one Elina, a flaunting hussey,

A flaring jilt, a—⁶⁹

OSB. Hold! [Damnation]

'Tis false as hell; her sweet ingenuous face

Is but the index of her purer mind.

Thou say'st not well, old man.

BER. I am glad to hear it:

Let me embrace thee, rogue. Com'st thou from her?

I see thou dost, and with good tidings, hey!

Is she then safe and honest?

OSB. Yes, sir, yes.

Conduct me instantly.—I ask your pardon.

BER. Conduct you? by my holy dame, I will.

I'm in good humour now: but you young fellows

Waste such a cursed deal of time in talking;—

You run from one extreme into the other;

You're either sharp, and sour as a crab,⁷⁰

Or sweet and luscious as a sugar plumb;

You fret and laugh, and swear, and kiss, and scold,

And then are friends again, and always chattering:

You never go directly to the point,

And lose the hour for action in debate;

And then you're so confus'd—What was I saying?

OSB. Oh never heed it now, come, good Sir, come.⁷¹

BER. Thou art a pretty boy, but too loquacious,

While you are prating here, the time slips by.

Come let us in; what, wou'd you talk all day?

For shame, let's in, I say.

OSB.                                 Thank heaven, at last!           (*Exeunt*)

69. The Larpent version has "there is one Elina / A flaunting, fleering jilt—a—" 70. Crab apple. 71. The Larpent version has "now come, do, Sir, come."

SCENE IV  *Gam's House.*

*Enter Sue.*

SUE. Why Gam's a main long time a coming from the Castle. He pro-mis'd, so he did, to return directly; but he never keeps his word, [a vile [perfidious—] Heigho! well, now my Lord is come back, I hope he'll do some what for me and my poor babes; if I am made a Lady, I'll be parted from Gam, and look out for a mild, quiet, sober husband, of a temper and disposition like my own. Oh! Gam! Gam! Gam! I cou'd tear your eyes out, so I cou'd.

[SONG—SUE
[What a terrible Life
[Has a Drunken Man's Wife.
[I'd rather be tied to a Log.
[When Drunk he'll so beat her
[And cruelly treat her
[When Sober he's sick as a dog.

[He comes home at night
[In so hideous a plight
[Poor wife must go sleep all alone.
[Oh then how he burns
[But when Morning returns
[Alas! he's as cold as a Stone, a Stone.
[Alas! he's as cold as a Stone.]

*Enter Gam.*

GAM. Hip! hip! holloa! Sue! my comfort, my plague, my vexation, my darling, my torment; [pack up, pack up, we are off, you Jade.] Pack up, pack up, don't forget the ale, Sue. Oh! [lud, Oh lud! I am Damnably [Sick! Oh!] I shall die, Sue; I shall die. Have you got a drop of nothing good in the house? I shall die, I shall die.

SUE. Ah! you always says so: you do it on purpose to plague and disap-point me. How are you, you villain: how do you do? [how do you do?] (*Loud as possible.*)

GAM. Very ill. I thank you, Sue, I hope you are the same with all my soul. Pack up, Sue, pack up.

[SUE. Why you Monster, you inhuman Monster, you have left me nothing [to pack up. What shall I pack Up? What do you say, what do you say, [you—

[GAM. Nothing.

[SUE. Nothing! Oh you unfeeling Wretch. Nothing! not a word of comfort [for your Poor Wife. Oh! Oh! Oh! Nothing, I can't bear it, I can't bear it.

[GAM. Why what is the matter now?

[SUE. Nothing! Oh! do I live to see the day. Am I to be treated in this
[Contemptible, Barbarous manner––I'll complain to my Lord, I will! Oh!
[Oh!

[GAM. Why, what will you complain of.

[SUE. Nothing. You Abominable, Shocking, Nothing! Nothing! (*Sobbing
[violently.*)

[GAM. Oh! Ho! ho! ho! What you are going to set up your Pipes. Well
[with all my heart. But Sue! Sue! Sue! Now if you *wou'd* be quiet, since
[nothing Offends you so cursedly, I'll tell you *Something*.

[SUE. (*Stamping.*) Quiet! Quiet! why an't I always quiet. Did you ever
[hear me any thing but quiet.

[GAM. Why if you were quiet I shou'd never hear you at all: we are to
[become great Folks, Sue.

[SUE. Great Folks, as how, Gam, as how?

GAM. [Why] we are to travel.

SUE. Travel!

GAM. Aye! why don't all your great folks travel? we are to have a horse,
Sue, you shall ride before: you shall hold the reins, egad, you are us'd to
that, and I'll ride like a bottle at your back; you must not look behind you,
Sue, now we are in the road to fortune, you must look forward! Oh lud!
lud! lud! How I will feague[72] the ale! (*Aside.*)

SUE. Is not this all a lie now, sirrah?

GAM. True. Sue; true, as two pints make a quart. [We be to go to Lord,
[there, I forgot his Name's Castle. All in the Night time but don't ye be
[afraid. Sue, I never was a feard of *Spirits* in all my life, but] you won't
like it, Sue: for you must not talk.

SUE. Not talk; but I will talk—that's what I will.

GAM. Why so said I—says I, Sue will talk.

SUE. Did you? why then you said a lie, for I won't talk, I'll not be forc'd
to talk, nothing shall make me talk, I won't, I won't: but Gam, Gam, how
did you hear all this?

GAM. Why Sue, if you wou'd but talk, I'd tell you; but while you are silent, I can't get in a word.—Why from the butler, who was order'd to
keep it a secret, so as soon as he know'd it, he runs down to the alehouse,
and taps the whole of the matter. Come Sue, let's go.

SUE. [Lud a mercy,] I *won't* go.

---

72. The OED offers "to whip" for "to feague." The 1811 *Dictionary of the Vulgar Tongue* has
this entry: "To feague a horse; to put ginger up a horse's fundament, and formerly, as it is
said, a live eel, to make him lively and carry his tail well. . . . Feague is used, figuratively,
for encouraging or spiriting one up."

GAM. Won't you, my dear, dear Sue! (*Runs and kisses her.*)

SUE. Yes, but I will go, and you shan't hinder me.[73] I'll go myself.

GAM. Yes; for you shan't go with me.

SUE. But I will not go alone. You shan't go without me.

GAM. Will you? Why then take my arm when you can catch it. You are well made for running.                    (*Exeunt, running*)


SCENE V   *An Apartment in Clifford Castle.*

*Enter Clifford, Osbert, and Bertram.*

[CLIF. Oh my Deliverer, let me, let me Clasp thee.

[Oh Osbert, thou hast sav'd me more than life

[Than fame, or Honour, may my gratitude—]

OSB. Talk not to me of gratitude, my Lord.—

[This kindness, if I may presume to call it so,

[Is as a drop of Water in the Ocean

[Compar'd with the immeasurable favour

[Which lovely Elina's conferr'd on me.

[CLIF. Oh she was born to bless the Human Race,

[To make mankind as happy as she's fair,

[The tender hand of pity fram'd her heart

[Where every generous Virtue loves to dwell,

[Angelic Mansion, Happy, happy Clifford!]

OSB. It grieves me much to interrupt your transports;

Think where she is, and scarce a day remains

[To gain the treasure which your heart so pants for.][74]

BER. Well, we must set forward

Some half hour hence; all is prepar'd, my Lord,

---

73. The Larpent version ends the scene differently. Sue continues: "I'll tell my Lord you wanted to prevent me; I'll complain to the Vicar, I'll indite you for stealing the Hare, I'll, I'll, I'll—" Then Sue and Gam sing a duet:

GAM. What means now all this noise and Strife.

SUE. 'Tis you that loves to Bicker.

GAM. You're the torment of my Life.
  Zooks I've a mind to Kick her.

SUE. I'll not endure it by this light.
  I'll run and tell the Vicar.
  What makes you get drunk every night?

GAM. Why *Liquor, Liquor! Liquor!*—
  *Sue runs out, Gam follows her three or four paces then turns about and runs out the other way.*

74. In the Larpent version, Bertram enters here, and Osbert says, "Here comes Sir Bertram."

Except our plan: the last thing which you boys
E'er think of. [Oh! 'tis lucky you've a head
[Not full of Youth and Love, but cool and temperate,
[Eh! you rogue Osbert.
CLIF.                    [Well, my honest Soldier]
Shall we by force attack the tyrant's castle,
And drag him from his den?
[BER.                          Ay, ay, by force
[If that should fail, but pshaw! it cannot fail,
[Why milder methods may be us'd.]
OSB. Oh lay aside all thoughts of force, my Lord:
The Castle's strong, the Baron's brave and vigilant.
If we succeed, yet still the helpless Elina
Remains the victim of his brutal passion.[75]
It sure were best by art to gain admittance,
[To take him unsuspecting; should he then
[Dare to oppose us, force may do the rest.
[CLIF. Thou Counsel'st well, but say, What Strategem
[What Art can lull asleep the Watchful Dragon
[That we may Seize the golden fruit and bear it
[Far from his reach for ever.[76]
OSB.                         [I've bethought me.]
I know each path, and by-way to the castle.
Do you, Sir Bertram, place our little band
In a deep glen due east; myself will lead them
Thro' the thick covert of a lofty wood,
Whose foliage will conceal them from the sight
Of any passengers. We, my good Lord,
Must think of some disguise.
BER. Disguise! I hate it.
CLIF.                      Bertram, be advis'd.
Let the wretch blush that puts it on for malice:
But he who wears it in a cause like ours,
To punish villainy and rescue virtue,
When he casts off his cloud, shews, like the sun,
More radiant from his late obscurity.
OSB. We shall arrive upon the every eve
Of his projected marriage; all his servants
Will be preparing for the festival.

75. The Larpent version has "May fall a Victim to his brutal passion." 76. In classical myth, a dragon guards the golden apples in the Garden of the Hesperides.

The Baron, tho' his heart is fierce and arrogant,
Has yet a soul for harmony; when passion
Would, like a whirlwind, tear his frantic bosom,
Oft have I sooth'd him to a sullen calm,
By touching of my lute; he'd sit [for] hours,
And heave such sighs; nay, down his rugged cheek
A silent tear wou'd steal against his will;
Which he'd dash from him with a haughty air,
And curse his weakness; then he'd sink in thought,
And meditate new mischiefs, even in music.
[Yourself, my Lord, are skilled in the Art.]
Let us like minstrels, at the close of day,
Approach the outward gate, and crave admittance.
CLIF. 'Tis well conceiv'd:[77] what think you, Bertram?
BER.                                                      Sir,
To say the honest truth, I like it not.
Make me a minstrel! tie a hurdy-gurdy[78]
About my neck!—[I'd rather tie a Rope there.
[CLIF. Nay check this peevish humour I beseech thee.
[Either adopt this Plan, or form some other
[More likely to succeed—
BER.                              [No, Sir; not I.
[I have no taste for tricks,] but to serve you
I will consent for once to play the fool.
Besides, my boys, 'tis possible this frolick
May end in broken heads: on second thoughts,
I don't so much dislike it. [Gentle Osbert
[Excuse my Freedom.
[OSB.                        Oh, Sir, say no more.
[He has but a sickly superficial Eye
[That can't discern a Dimond thro' its roughness.
[BER. I marvel, Osbert, one so young as you
[Shou'd be so wise, and yet I wonder more
[That one so wise shou'd act so foolishly.
[Why will you take that tipling Rascal Gam
[And the curs'd witch his wife. Your foliage, friend,
[May well conceal our Men from curious Eyes
[But if she's there, and every Passenger

77. The Larpent version has "The Plot / Is well conceiv'd." 78. Not the barrel-organ we think of, but a stringed instrument like a lute; a rosined wheel is rubbed against the strings which are stopped by means of keys.

[Shou'dn't be deaf, their Ears will find us out.
[CLIF. Good Osbert, take them not.
[OSB. My lord, indulge me.
[I have such reasons, but the tale is long
[And will beguile our Journey.]⁷⁹
CLIF. "Come, let's away! my soul is all on fire!"⁸⁰
BER. Sir, by your leave, tho' I am little read,
I well remember that the ancient Greeks,
Before they went to battle, fortified
Their stomachs with rich food, and good old wine.
I have prepar'd a bowl—boy, bring it in.⁸¹
*"Enter Boy with a bowl of wine.*
"Ho, there! where are these knaves! what, no one stir!
"Are none afoot to shew their zeal, and service,
"To their good lord at his departure?
*"Enter Vassals.*

"What!

"You're come at last, rogues! swell your rusty throats,
"And, while we quaff success to this same enterprise,
"Rouse up our spirits with a mellow strain,
"And join us in our chorus. Sing, and lustily!"

QUINTETTO AND CHORUS
'Tis love that now my bosom fires,
'Tis wine which now the soul inspires,
Friendship and gratitude shall prove
At least a match for wine and love:
Then let us hail the league divine,
Of love, of friendship, and of wine.

Fortune our virtuous schemes shall bless,
'Twere cowardly to doubt success;
    Where friendship leads,
    Where wine inspires,
    And ardent love the bosom fires,

79. In fact, Gam and Sue never appear again. These lines suggest that we should hear of them again, so perhaps they were in the version of the third act that I speculate was returned by Larpent. 80. The Larpent version has "To Horse, to Horse." 81. The Larpent version ends here with a trio, identical in wording to the published version's quintet. Clifford is given lines 1, 7, and 11; Bertram has lines 2, 8, and 10; Osbert sings lines 3, 4, and 9; and all three sing lines 5, 6, 12 and 13.

Then let us hail the league divine
Of love, of friendship, and of wine.

END OF ACT II

## ACT III

SCENE I  *An Apartment in Mortimer Castle.*

*Enter Mortimer.*

MOR. Two days are past, the third declines apace:
I now am near the summit of my wishes.
My soul will soon be glutted with the luxury
It has so long been thirsting for, Revenge.
But yet I am not happy: why base Nature,
Why did'st thou fix so deeply in my breast
The bitter root of envy? from thee, spring
Pride, falsehood, hatred; all the noxious weeds
Which choak and over-run the idle soil
Where pity, love, and truth, are thinly scatter'd.
But wherefore Nature, wherefore blame I thee?
Oh! had I listen'd to thy gentle voice,
Had I not stifl'd all thy infant strugglings,
I ne'er had felt the pangs I now endure.
But I've perverted thee, have chang'd thy course,
Poison'd the genial springs which feed the heart,
And turn'd thy wholesome waters into gall.
*Enter Elina and Beatrice.*
To come thus unsolicited, my angel,
Is kind indeed. Oh! may my future life—
ELI. Be different from the past: I truly wish it.
Nay, for your sake I wish it: why, my Lord,
Why will you force me to this hated marriage?
I frankly own that I can never love you.
MOR. Love me, or love me not, you must be mine:
You now are in my power: you may subdue me,
And bind me to your will; but oh! beware,
Beware, rash maid, how you excite my anger.
ELI. Full well, my Lord, I know your cruel temper;
The unrelenting fierceness of your nature.

Yet, Mortimer, I swear, by heaven I swear,
I'd rather meet your anger than your love.
MOR. Well, Madam, I'll be cool. Why will you Lady,
Why will you, since you know my mind's infirmity,
Instead of quenching, by a mild demeanor,
The vivid spark that burns within my breast,
Why will you blow it to a flame, whose fury
Once kindled may consume us both? O think,
Since you must wed me, Madam; it were better
To wed me as your slave than as your tyrant.
ELI. I should despise you equally as either.
Blush and remember how you brought me hither.
When I receiv'd you as a favour'd guest,
My castle gates, which wou'd have mock'd your fury,
Were open'd, as I vainly, vainly, thought,
To a dear friend; one, who profess'd himself
My father's friend, a friend to all our house.
In the dead hour of night, the fittest season
To perpetrate a deed so dark and villainous;
When all but fiends and guilty spirits seek
The blessing of repose; this mighty Mortimer,
This proud imperious Baron, deign'd to bribe
My hinds and vassals, to betray their mistress.
MOR. Rail on, rail on; in love and war, dear Lady,
All stratagems are honest, he's no soldier
Who uses force where art can more avail him.

CLIFFORD (*Sings Without.*)
Then vaulted on his milk-white steed,
The thrice renowned Palamede.[82]

ELI. Oh Beatrice, 'tis he! 'tis Clifford's voice.
BEA. Be not so earnest, Madam.

CLIFFORD (*Without.*)
Fitzosborne's lance he burst in twain,
Which had the proud Fitzallan slain.[83]

82. In Arthurian romance, Sir Palamedes is a Saracen knight in love with Ysolde; he is defeated and converted by Tristram. 83. There was a William Fitzosbern, Earl of Hereford, who died in 1071. He was a Norman nobleman and a friend to William the Conqueror with whom he served at the battle of Hastings. There are several Fitzallans who were soldiers, but none that fits the rough time scheme of the play.

MOR. Madam, this musick seems to give you pleasure;
Hint but your wishes, shall they play the while
We sit at table?
ELI. Give them instant entrance.
MOR. Ha! I'm rejoic'd
To find within this Castle's horrid walls,
There's something can beguile you of your grief.
*Enter William.*
WIL. Please you, Sir, three minstrels,
Worn with fatigue and toil, entreat admittance.
MOR. Prepare the banquet, William: let them enter.
*Enter Clifford, Bertram, and Osbert, disguised as minstrels.*
MOR. Give 'em a bowl of wine: ye seem fatigued.
CLIF. My Lord, we have journey'd far.
ELI. It is his voice, it is, it is my Clifford! (*Aside.*)
MOR. Sing me a love song;
And let it be impassioned, such a one
As may befit a sprightly bridegroom.
CLIF. If I could find a female voice—
MOR. My love.—
CLIF. His love! I can't endure it—I shall burst—(*Aside.*)
BER. For shame, for shame, my Lord;
Controul this passion. (*Aside.*)
MOR. Well fellow!
CLIF. 'Tis, my Lord, a simply ditty,
Which speaks the language of a heart in love:
It was compos'd long since; a Nobleman
Woo'd a fair maiden, whose fond heart he won:
But her stern parent never wou'd consent:
The love-sick youth, sunk into deep despair;
At length he rous'd him; in a mean attire
He sought the Castle, where the beauteous Emma
Was held a captive.
ELI.              Sing, minstrel, sing!

### DUET—CLIFFORD AND ELINA

CLIF.   Say, lovely Emma, do your eyes
Discover me through this disguise;
Or does my voice inform your ear,
Your love, your fond deliverer's near?
ELI.   Yes, gallant youth, I know thee well;

But tell, my love, O prithee tell,
How from this Castle I may fly,
With Edward live, with Edward die!
BOTH.　The hopes which swell my anxious breast,
In accents true, though faint suggest,
That from this Castle I may fly,
With Emma live, with Emma die.

MOR. Break off the song I say:—
'Tis late, 'tis late, retire my Elina.

(Exeunt Mortimer, Beatrice, and Elina)

WIL. Well, my good Masters, shall we drink a round?
No—why to bed then—that way lies your chamber.

(Exeunt Clifford and Bertram)

I'faith I'm tir'd, and must refresh awhile.
When there's good cheer I'm little prone to sleeping.
Ha! stay'st thou boy? well, sit thee down and welcome.
OSB. William, I say.
WIL. (*Starting.*) Ha!
OSB. William, do you know me?
WIL. Oh, I am undone, I am ruin'd; should the Baron—
I'll raise the Castle—why were you so rash—
But since it is so, you must suffer—Walter,
Edmund, hoa! Francis!
OSB. Peace, I say this instant.
Speak not above thy breath; ah! then thou diest. (*Pulling out a dagger.*)
WIL. Defend me, mercy!
You wou'd not kill me, Osbert, wou'd you kill
Your old and faithful William?
Oh! good Osbert, put up the dagger.
OSB. Not yet William—say—
Know you this Lady whom the cruel Baron
Holds herein custody?—Thou'rt safe, man; speak.
WIL. I know her name is Elina, and ne'er
Beheld so fair a creature: don't become me
To pry into the secrets of my master;
But I suspect foul play.
OSB.　　　　　　　Suspect it! oh
You know it but too well. Yourself were privy
To the damn'd treachery that brought her here.
Thou'rt kind by nature, and 'twas fear alone,

Fear of that cursed fiend, who aw'd us all,
Forc'd thee to do—
WIL.                    Indeed 'tis true, good Osbert;
Indeed I've pity'd the poor helpless Lady,
And wish'd 'twere in my power—
OSB.                         To release her,
Would'st thou then William?
WIL. What, release her—no,
I'd not betray my master!
OSB.                    Betray thy master,
But I will not blame thee.
Yet think'st what thou betray'st, humanity,
Truth, honour, virtue and benevolence.
Ah William! can'st thou pity so much goodness,
And yet, when now the means are in thy power,
Refuse assistance to the radiant angel
Thou can'st not help adoring. Ha, thou weep'st!
Be not asham'd; the tear which trickles down
The good man's cheek should not be wip'd away
Like vulgar drops.—But wilt thou only weep?
No—thou wilt do more.
WIL. You move me strangely, Osbert.
Alas! what means have I?
OSB. What means hast thou! Who keeps the Castle keys?
WIL. Oh! I dare not,
I dare not, Osbert: should the furious Baron
Suspect me, he would doom my wretched body
To linger on the rack: or if by flight,
I should escape his anger, I must starve.
OSB. Starve! fear not that, good William;
I'll find thee out a better, kinder master.
WIL. How can I serve you?
I'll do't, though death itself—
OSB. Come to my heart! and now I sheath my dagger.
No force shall drive thee, William, to do good.
We have been faulty, but it was through fear.
Whilst we were base, we both were cowards, William;
But virtue now directs us. Walk secure,
We cannot fall in her plain open road.
Let us thank Heaven then, William, though we've stumbled;
Yet e'er our strength was gone, our better fate

Has push'd us backward from the dreadful gulph,
Which yawn'd to swallow us. Within, there, Richard.
*Enter Bertram.*
BER. What would you, brother Arthur?
OSB. We are all friends.
Now stand we on the very wheel of fortune;
And every minute leads us on to happiness,
Or draws us to despair. William is with us:
You'll find him honest.
(*To William.*)          Go with that Gentleman.
Success attend you. Clifford and myself
Will stay here in the Castle. Should our plot
Miscarry, we are enow to fall the victims
To Mortimer's fell rage; and by some signal
May either hasten you to succour us,
Or warn you to retreat. Farewel to both.          (*Retires*)
          (*Exeunt William and Bertram*)

*Enter Elina and Beatrice.*
ELI. Ah! canst thou, cruel!
Deny me, after six days painful absence,
To see my Clifford? Oh, good Beatrice,
For the last time, perhaps.—Who's there?
Ha! Osbert!—He'll not refuse me.—
Prythee, gentle Osbert, indulge a woman's weakness,
And conduct me where I may view—
OSB. Beware.—We are undone,
Shou'd any of the servants of the Castle
See where you are.—But e'er we part, permit me
To ease my loaded bosom; Oh, too full
For words to give it vent.
ELI. What say you?
OSB. Oh, let my tears,
Let those instruct my Elina,
That Osbert is—I hear a step:—By hell,
'Tis Mortimer!          (*Exeunt*)
*Enter Mortimer.*
MOR. I cannot sleep.—And dost thou, foolish heart,
Dost thou then faint, so near thy journey's end?
No, thou shalt on, tho' all thy strings shou'd crack.
How weak, how vain is man! why wilt thou fancy,
Why wilt thou conjure up these airy phantoms,

Which shake me like an ague?—William, hoa!
*Enter Walter.*
Where's William, Sirrah?
WAL. Good, my Lord, I know not.
I'll seek him instantly.
MOR.                    Stay, stay a while.
Is Anthony arriv'd? Is he prepar'd,
With all the holy trumpery of the Church?
Say, is he come?
WAL.            My Lord, he is within.
Please ye that I should send him to you?
MOR.                                    Aye.—
No.—Stay, it is no matter. Let me think.—
Yes, yes, 'tis better so: she has oft seen William:
Besides, I have remark'd that fellow
Is of yielding temper. Ha! what's that?
Didst thou not hear a noise? Hark! it advances.
Stand back, stand back.
*They retire.*
*Enter Clifford.*
CLIF. I can delay no longer: tho' an age
Of happiness should be the bright reward,
I cou'd'nt now resist the sweet temptation
Which leads me on. No, I must speak to her.
MOR. (*Aside.*) Speak to her! ha!
CLIF. This is the door, I think.—My love, my life!
Dost thou not hear me? Oh! my Elina,
Arise! arise! it is thy Clifford calls thee.
MOR. (*Aside.*) Clifford! confusion! devils!
*Enter Elina.*
ELI. Who's there? my Clifford? Oh! my faithful Clifford!
Why wou'd you venture?
CLIF.                  Do not fear, my love:
All's hush'd as death. The unsuspecting tyrant
Securely sleeps, and dreams upon to-morrow.
He little thinks what danger now surrounds him;
That the right hand of his avenging Diety
Is rais'd to strike him.
MOR. Here, Walter, William, Edmund!
*Enter Servants.*
                        Seize the traitor;

Drag him to instant death.

ELI.                              Oh! hear me! hear me!
He never injur'd you. Spare, spare his life.
I will be your's.

MOR. You will be mine, indeed; 'tis kind in you,
*Now* to comply. *Now* the avenging Deity
Raises his hand to strike me. Now no longer
You're in my power: the gallant Clifford *now*
Has freed you from my thraldom. Be content;
He shan't die yet; no, he shall live to see
The unsuspecting tyrant, he who sleeps,
And dreams upon to-morrow, now, this moment,
Married to his dear constant Elina.
Drag forth the other slaves:

*Enter Osbert, guarded.*

                              bring the priest here:
Here let him join us.

*Bertram and Soldiers burst in behind.*

BER.              Hold! break off, I say;
Unhand your pris'ners.

MOR. Ha! betray'd! how, am I fallen, then!

OSB. To sink thee lower,
Know, tyrant, that the hand which weights thee down
Is AUBERVILLE's.

MOR.              Damnation! Reginald!

ELI. Ha, Reginald! my brother! heavens!

MOR. Distraction! Oh! let me pluck my heart out. N'er till now
Did I despair. Even malice now forsakes me.
Oh! I did hope (fool that I was to spare thee),
That thou at least wou'dst have felt all my vengeance.
But if thy soul is noble, boy, revenge thee;
Insult me not with words; be merciful,
Be merciful, and kill me.

OSB.              Mortimer,
I will not tarnish this day's happiness
By any drop of blood. Live, and repent thee.
When I was in thy power, thou sparedst my life;
Take thine, then, in return.

MOR.              Rash, foolish youth,
Thou weak young man, will no experience teach thee?
I spared thy life; behold the consequence.

Oh! had I crush'd thee, all this damned mischief
Had been prevented. When thou wert an infant,
I stole thee from thy father's, brought thee here,
And bred thee up a slave. I cou'dn't kill thee;
It was the only weakness I e'er felt;
And I'm severely punish'd.—Boy, be wise;
Seize on this glorious opportunity,
To rid thee of a foe, whom nought but death
Can render tranquil.                    (*Exeunt Mortimer and guards*)
CLIF.              Oh! Auberville.
My friend, my brother; now, my dearest Elina,
Art thou then mine at last?
ELI. For ever, Clifford.
BER.                Osbert, Auberville,
What is your name, Sir? If a soldier's friendship,
An honest one's, tho' I am bold to say so,
Is worth your taking,—why, accept of mine.
AUB. Now all are blest,
Save *him* who caus'd our misery.—My friends,
We will not think on vengeance; let us leave him
To his own mind, to disappointed malice;
That will inflict a far severer torture
Than man can use to man: revenge is sweet
To little minds alone. The noble soul
Pities the fallen foe, and finds a source
Of purest pleasure in a brave forgiveness.

### FINALE

Let Cupid shake his sportive wings,
    While round the loves and graces fly;
Apollo touch the trembling strings,
    And Hymen lift his torch on high.

### ELINA AND CLIFFORD

Our fears are gone, the tempest past,
    Here adverse winds no more annoy;
Our vessel, safely moor'd at last,
    Calls anchor in the port of joy.

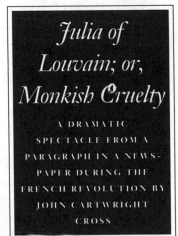

**Julia of Louvain; or, Monkish Cruelty**

A DRAMATIC SPECTACLE FROM A PARAGRAPH IN A NEWSPAPER DURING THE FRENCH REVOLUTION BY JOHN CARTWRIGHT CROSS

J. C. Cross (d. 1809) is one of many men and women who were vital to the late-eighteenth- and early nineteenth-century theater and who are all but forgotten today. An actor, a dramatist, and a theater manager, he was a master of the forms that arose within the "minor" theaters of the day.

Little is known about Cross's personal life except that he was married twice—to the singer Mrs. Cross who died and to Sarah Sophia Jones, whom he married on 23 August 1798—and that he died on either 1 or 14 December 1809 at either Manchester or Liverpool while on tour with Elliston. Cross's life in the theater began as an actor. He is first mentioned in a Covent Garden playbill for *The Provocation* on 4 October 1790. For the next several years, he continued to play at Covent Garden during the regular season and at the Theatre Royal, Haymarket in the summers.

Cross began to write for the theater in 1793 when his *A Divertissement* was offered on 23 November at Covent Garden; this musical interlude with music by Charles Dibdin was the first of his successes, being offered 23 times that season and remaining in the repertoire for years. Other early successes include his musical drama *The Purse; or, The Benevolent Tar* which had 16 performances at the Haymarket in 1794, and his pantomime *Harlequin and Quixote; or, The Magic Arm* which delighted holiday audiences for 30 performances during the 1797–1798 season.

In 1796, the license for the Royal Circus Theatre in St. George's Fields, Southwark became available. The Royal Circus had been built by subscription in 1782 by Dibdin and Charles Hughes to join together the pleasures of the stage and the circus ring and to offer equestrian performances, ballets of action, burlettas, and pantomimes. George Jones, an equestrian, succeeded Hughes as part proprietor and arranged to bring Cross to the Royal Circus as a dramatist. Cross became a co-proprietor in

1798, but called himself manager of the stage department in a management that also involved Robert Wright Hodgson, the clown Follet, the actor Thomas Haymes, and the imitator Rees. The theater, in decline during the early 1790s, prospered under Cross and his colleagues until it burned to the ground on 5 August 1805. The building was insured for only a fourth of its value, but the proprietors constructed what was at the time perhaps the best stage in London. The new theater did not do well, and it was thus leased to Robert Elliston in 1809, who reorganized it as the Surrey.

The full extent of Cross's dramatic writing for the Royal Circus may never be known, but about fifty interludes, melodramas, pantomimes, dramatic spectacles, and ballets can be ascribed to him. He published two collections of his works, *Parnassian Bagatelles: being a Miscellaneous Collection of Poetical Attempts* (1796) and *Circusiana, or A Collection of the most favourite Ballets, Spectacles, Melodramas, &c. performed at the Royal Circus, St. George's Fields* (London: Lackington, Allen, and Co., 1809; rpt. as *The Dramatic Works of J. C. Cross*, 1812). Dedicated to the Earl of Craven, with a subscription list that includes Cross's rival John Astley, Betty the Young Roscius, Dibdin, Grimaldi, and many actors, *Circusiana* announces itself in its preface as a collection of "Minor Dramas" which had been successful on the stage but might not "boast much attention in the Closet."

I have taken the text of *Julia of Louvain* from *Circusiana;* there is no Larpent version. Cross has received virtually no critical attention. For biographical information, see *A Biographical Dictionary of Actors, Actresses, Musicians, Dancers, Managers & Other Stage Personnel in London, 1660–1800,* by Philip H. Highfill, Jr., Kalman A. Burnim, and Edward A. Langhans (Carbondale, IL, 1975); see also, the "Short Sketch of the Royal Circus" in *Circusiana* and A. H. Saxon, *Enter Foot and Horse: A History of Hippodrama in England and France* (New Haven, 1968).

DRAMATIS PERSONAE
Royal Circus, 15 May 1797

| | |
|---|---|
| Victor St. Pierre | Mr. Helme |
| D'Arcourt (Brother to Julia) | Mr. Crossman |
| President of the Municipality | Mr. Smith |
| Abbe Bonesse | Mr. D'Egville |
| Ambrose (The Abbey Porter) | Mr. Bologna, Sen. |
| Louis | Mr. Pilbrow |
| Municipal Officers | Messrs. Herbert, |
| | Allan, &c. |

| | |
|---|---|
| Friars | Messrs. Jenkinson and Jeffries |
| Clifford | Mr. Bologna, Jun. |
| The Abbess La Ramee | Miss Valois |
| Nuns | Mrs. Herbert, Mrs. Jeffries, Mrs. Bologna, Miss Hall, Mrs. Jenkinson, &c. |
| Theresa | Mrs. Iliff |
| Julia | Mrs. Parker |

The Music composed and selected by Mr. Cross and Mr. Saunderson. The Scenery by Mr. Greenwood, Jun. and the Machinery by Mr. Underwood.

SCENE I  *A View in Louvain*

*The residence of D'Arcourt—Vineyards at a distance—Villagers discovered decorating a tree with garlands, on which they have placed this inscription:*

"THE NUPTIALS OF CLIFFORD AND JULIA ARE TO BE SOLEMNIZED THIS DAY."[1]

*Enter other Villagers dancing.*

CHORUS

Sol's chearing ray
Bespangles day,
Mild breathes the wooing air;
The purple grape
In clusters heap,
To the Vintage girls repair.
And as you lightly trip to labour,
Measure each step to the tap of the tabor.[2]

*They go off to replenish their baskets with fruit as presents to the bride.—Clifford enters, with D'Arcourt, highly delighted at their attention—is informed by a Servant that Julia is not prepared for his reception—retires for music to serenade her.—Louis enters followed by Villagers.*

1. Scrolls, signs, and placards were used to convey verbal messages in pantomimes, since "minor" theaters such as the Royal Circus were forbidden by law from presenting the spoken drama. 2. A small drum with one head of calfskin, usually accompanied by the pipe.

SONG—LOUIS

From Paris come, I have bring de news,
   Will tickle de heart so sweet, ma foi![3]
Mon Maitre beauty fondly views,
   And will soon trow himself at her feet, ah, ah!
Wid him sa, sa, sa, he de world command,
Le fille vid[4] ha! ha! ha!
     So ve dance, sing, and laugh,
     Vive la marriage quaff,
Et la fortune de la Guerre;[5]
Wid a tin, tin, tin, and a tan, tan, tan, tan,
   And a tin, tin, tintamarre,
     We dance, sing, and laugh,
     Vive la marriage quaff,
Et la fortune de la Guerre.

Let him have his way and his temper's mild,
   As good humour ever bred, ma foi!
But contradict and vid anger wild,
   Be gar[6] but he soon frown you dead, ah, ah!
Wid him sa, sa, sa, sa, he de world command,
Le fille vid ha! ha! ha!
     So ve dance, sing, and laugh,
     Vive la marriage quaff,
Et la fortune de la Guerre;
Wid a tin, tin, tin, and a tan, tan, tan, tan,
   And a tin, tin, tintamarre,
     We dance, sing, and laugh,
     Vive la marriage quaff,
Et la fortune de la Guerre.

*After song Villagers retire, and D'Arcourt re-enters, to whom Louis intimates that his master, St. Pierre, demands her hand—Barges cross the water with music, in which are supposed to be St. Pierre and his Attendants singing the following*

CHORUS

Wafted by the wooing breeze,
Swift we cut the silver seas:
Keeping time as gay we row,
To the merry, merry Bargeman's yeo, yeo, yeo!

---

3. "My faith"; "Mon Maitre" in the next line is "my master." Louis's song is a mix of French phrases and "dialect." 4. "The woman weds" (?). 5. "Vive the marriage quaff / And the fortunes of war." A "quaff" is a deep drink. 6. "By gad."

*They land in procession—his attendants are commanded to withdraw—St. Pierre expresses his wishes—D'Arcourt intimates she is betrothed to Clifford, which enrages him, and he threatens to deprive him of his possessions and the place he holds if he refuses consent—dreading his power, he reluctantly complies, and receives him into his mansion—Clifford enters with a Guittar, on which he plays a short air— Julia appears at the balcony, and requests him to be gone, his stay being pregnant with danger, and closing her window retires.—He raps at the door, from which a Servant enters, who expresses the same alarm—grown desperate, he draws his sword, and rushes past him into the house, the Servant following.*

SCENE II  *A Romantic View.*

*Villagers cross the stage with presents for the bride.*

SCENE III  *A Chamber in D'Arcourt's Mansion.*

*Julia enters, followed by villagers with presents, which she receives, and dismisses them—appears much distressed at her situation—Clifford rushes on, they plight mutual vows of constancy, she producing this scroll,*

"DEATH WHEN I PROVE FALSE."

*—In the moment of protestation St. Pierre and D'Arcourt enter.—St. Pierre draws his sword, rushes on Clifford, and disarms him—he escapes—Julia faints in her brother's arms, and is hurried off by St. Pierre to the altar.*

SCENE IV  *A Street.*

*Enter Clifford despondent—Father Bonesse and Friars approach, to whom Louis enters, requiring their attendance at St. Pierre's marriage, to be celebrated at midnight—Clifford, overhearing this, resolves to be a spectator—they exeunt.*

SCENE V  *Inside of Chapel with Altar-Piece, &c. and Monument.*

*Enter Clifford—bell strikes the appointed hour—he hides behind the monument— procession of Friars, Nuns, &c. to the altar by torch-light—at the period the ceremony is about to take place Clifford stalks from the monument with his sword drawn, to which is attached the scroll of*

"DEATH WHEN I PROVE FALSE,"

*and holding another in the other hand with this inscription,*

"REMEMBER YOUR VOW."

*—Julia fixes her eyes on and follows him to the wing; where, overpowered by her feelings, she faints.—St. Pierre drags her back to the altar.—She refuses her acquiescence, rushes from him, and is borne off almost distracted.*

SCENE VI    *Outside of Convent.*

*Enter Abbey Porter with provisions—Lady Abbess and Nuns go into the convent—St. Pierre, D'Arcourt, and Julia enter, preceded by Father Bonesse—Julia is offered this alternative—*

"ST. PIERRE OR A CONVENT"

*—the latter she readily embraces, and is given up to the care of the Abbess La Ramee.—St. Pierre, irritated at her resolution, and finding her still hang about his heart,[7] determines on another interview, and follows her into the convent—Clifford, who observes this, determines on the same, but is refused admittance by the Porter, 'till, by obtaining a Grey Friar's[8] habit, he by means of that disguise is admitted.*

SCENE VII    *An Interior View of the Convent.*

*Nuns discovered in attitudes of devotion—the Lady Abbess introduces Julia, who shudders at the melancholy picture before her, but resolves on taking the veil, though strongly dissuaded from it by Sister Theresa in the following*

PATHETIC BALLAD

Hark! yon solemn awful bell
  Commands you bid the world adieu;
With lonely solitude to dwell,
  No ray of hope, no change in view!

Sad victim! Prisoner forlorn!
  By the taper's dying light,
The Nun's sad bosom pants for morn,
  While grief prolongs her tedious night.

Hard penance rigid zeal must prove,
  Pale poverty her steps attend;
Religion quench the flame of love,
  And death alone appear a friend.

7. This is the reading of the printed text; the sense requires "hanging."    8. A Grey Friar is a Franciscan.

*However, at her request, she for the present becomes a novice—on withdrawing to exchange her dress for that purpose, St. Pierre enters with Father Bonesse, whom he bribes to destroy her or make her his, at the same time agreeing for the concurrence of the abbess.*

BRAVURA—ST. PIERRE

The tempest rages here! in vain
   I bid the storm depart;
Ambition racks my tortur'd brain,
   And tyrant love my heart.

Give to my arms the scornful maid,
   Tho' hatred be her dower;
Or on the cold earth see her laid,
   The victim of my power!

Thus, should the timid hare essay,
   T'escape the watchful tyger's eyes,
He eager fastens on his prey,
   It faintly struggles, groans, and dies.

*Abbess appears leading on Julia in the habit of a novice—Father Bonesse and St. Pierre meeting them, Julia shudders at again beholding her persecutor, who renews his hateful addresses—she spurns him as the last alternative, Father Bonesse presents her the following scroll:*

"DEATH OR ST. PIERRE."

*—St. Pierre, &c. retire, leaving her to reflect, and speedily determine—she resolves on the former, kissing the word "DEATH" on the scroll—at which period Clifford, disguised as a friar, approaches her.—She wildly screams on his discovering himself, and St. Pierre, &c. rushing on, he is overpowered and hurried off by the brotherhood—St. Pierre once more proffers her his hand, which she again resolutely refusing, as he goes off, he commands Father Bonesse to do his duty, who throws open the folding doors in the centre of the scene, leading to a gloomy sepulchre, in which she is forced (in vain appealing to the abbess) to pine away existence, as the melancholy companion of decayed mortality.*

SCENE VIII   *A Garden Belonging to the Convent.*

*Enter Clifford, struggling with Friars, from whom he disengages himself and draws his sword—St. Pierre interrupts him in his endeavour to escape—they fight, and the monster falls, carried off in the agonies of death by the brotherhood— a storm commences—the Abbey Porter enters; and to secure himself from the inclemency of the weather, puts on the Grey Friar's habit—the Brotherhood return, and conceiving him one in the plot, seize and hurry him off.*

### SCENE IX  *Outside of a Convent.*

*Ambrose, the porter, is turned out by Bonesse and Friars, on whom he vows revenge.—The Municipality enter, as taking their rounds, and Ambrose accuses Bonesse and the Abbess of cruelty, which is seconded by the appeal of Clifford and D'Arcourt, who burst open and enter the convent gates; the Municipality follow them; and after a short period return and (having seized) hurry off the Abbess; Ambrose, with marks of the strongest indignation, hauling Father Bonesse after her.*

### SCENE X  *An Interior View of the Convent.*

*Noise of clanking of chains is heard without—Clifford rushes into the Convent, but is astonished to find it lonely and deserted!—Traverses the place distracted, 'till perceiving an entrance door to the sepulchre, he bursts it open, but is disappointed still in the object of his search, 'till a groan evinces that some human being is near; after considerable search, under a noisome sack, he discovers the object of his choice, pale, emaciated, almost expiring, and for a time bereft of reason; on the return of which she gratefully thanks heaven and her deliverer—several Nuns and her Brother entering, the whole form an interesting group—and the scene is closed to slow music.\**

### SCENE XI  *A Street.*

*The Abbess is brought on by the Municipality, and delivered into the hands of justice, as is Father Bonesse by Ambrose the Porter.*

### SCENE XII  *A Splendid and Picturesque View, with the Altar of Hymen[9] at a distance.*

*Julia receives the hand of her Lover, and the piece concludes with an*

**APPROPRIATE DANCE,**

*and the following*

**FINALE**

\*N. B. *In general the piece concludes here.* (Cross's note) 9. The god of marriage.

**THERESA**

In the journey of life, ah! how varied the scene,
  The prospect now dark and now bright;
Disappointment's dark cloud will too oft intervene,
  And eclipse the fair face of delight.

**2D. NUN**

But to grief bid adieu, to all anguish and care,
  Peace and pleasure inhabit each breast;
To love now has yielded the monster despair,
  And beauty and virtue are blest.

Chorus.—*But to grief, &c.*

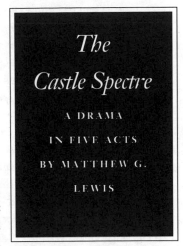

The
Castle Spectre
A DRAMA
IN FIVE ACTS
BY MATTHEW G.
LEWIS

Lewis (1775–1818) is the best known and perhaps the most important of the Gothic dramatists. Born on 9 July 1775 in London to Matthew (a deputy secretary of war) and Frances Lewis, he attended Marylebone Seminary, Westminster School, and Christ Church, Oxford, from which he graduated in 1794. He served on the embassy staff to the Hague in 1794, and entered the House of Commons as the member from Hindon, Wiltshire from 1796 until 1802. His parents had separated when he was in school, and he broke with his father over the elder Lewis's connection with Mrs. Ricketts; he remained close to his mother, and his correspondence to her is a valuable source of information about his life and career. His father died in 1812, leaving the whole of his large holdings in Jamaica to Lewis. Lewis arrived in Jamaica in January 1816, paying particular attention to the care of his slaves. He returned to England in March and went on to Europe where he visited with Byron and Shelley at the Villa Diodati. He returned to Jamaica in 1818 and died of yellow fever on the return voyage, 14 May 1818.

The central moment in Lewis's literary life came with the anonymous publication of *The Monk* in 1796. The book was an immediate sensation, attracting a large readership and violent attacks upon its moral character. He found himself a literary celebrity at twenty, gaining entry into high society; his status as a writer would earn him the friendship of Scott, with whom he collected *Tales of Wonder* (1801), and Byron among other literary figures. His non-dramatic works include his *Poems* (1812) and his *Journal of a West India Proprietor* published posthumously in 1834.

*The Castle Spectre* was the first of Lewis's dramas to reach the stage; it opened on 14 December 1797 and had an initial run of forty-seven nights, remaining in the repertoire for a good part of the nineteenth century. His other plays include *Adelmorn the Outlaw* (Drury Lane, 1801), *Alfonso, King of Castille* (Covent Garden, 1802), *The Captive* (Covent Garden, 1803; see below), *Rugantino; or, The Bravo of Venice* (Covent Garden, 1805), *The Wood*

*Daemon* (Drury Lane, 1806), *Adelgitha; or, The Fruits of A Single Error* (Drury Lane, 1807); *Venomi; or, The Novice of St Mark's* (Drury Lane, 1808; from Monvel's *Les Victimes Cloîtrées*), and *Timour the Tartar* (Covent Garden, 1811). The range and popularity of his work mark him as the most successful writer of serious drama at the turn of the century.

My text of *The Castle Spectre* is based on the first edition, published in London by J. Bell in 1798; there is a Larpent version (LA 1187). Material in the printed version but excluded from the Larpent performance version is marked with double quotation marks; material in the Larpent version but missing from the published version is marked by square brackets. Variants are indicated in the notes. In a postscript to the play, included here, Lewis indicates that he published the play "almost verbatim, as originally written" in order to combat assertions "that the language was originally extremely licentious" and "that the sentiments were violently democratic." In fact, the published version still deletes some controversial material. That the play touched some sensitive cultural and political nerves is indicated not only by the reviews but also by Larpent's requested deletions in the manuscript, indicated in my notes.

*The Life and Correspondence of M. G. Lewis* by Mrs. Cornwell Baron-Wilson (London, 1839) is an essential source of information, providing in addition some pieces not published anywhere else. Louis F. Peck's *A Life of Matthew G. Lewis* (Cambridge, MA, 1961) is the best work on Lewis. See also Bertrand Evans, *Gothic Drama from Walpole to Shelley* (Berkeley, 1947), and Joseph J. Irwin, *M. G. "Monk" Lewis* (Boston, 1976).

## DRAMATIS PERSONAE
### Drury Lane, 14 December 1797

| | |
|---|---|
| Osmond | Mr. Barrymore |
| Reginald | Mr. Wroughton |
| Percy | Mr. Kemble |
| Father Philip | Mr. Palmer |
| Motley | Mr. Bannister, Jun. |
| Kenric | Mr. Aickin |
| Saib | Mr. Truman |
| Hassan | Mr. Dowton |
| Muley | Mr. Davis |
| Alaric | Mr. Wentworth |
| Allan | Mr. Packer |
| Edric | Mr. Wathen |
| Harold | Mr. Gibbon |

| Angela | Mrs. Jordan |
| Alice | Mrs. Walcot |
| Evelina | Mrs. Powell |

The Music Composed by Mr. Kelly, with one selection from Jomelli.
Scenery by Mr. Greenwood, executed by his son, Pugh, and others.

## PROLOGUE
### Spoken by Mr. Wroughton

Far from the haunts of men, of vice the foe,
The moon-struck child of genius and of woe,
Versed in each magic spell, and dear to fame,
A fair enchantress dwells, Romance her name.
She loathes the sun, or blazing taper's light:
The moon-beam'd landscape and tempestuous night
Alone she loves; and oft, with glimmering lamp,
Near graves new-open'd, or 'midst dungeons damp,
Drear forest, ruin'd aisles, and haunted towers,
Forlorn she roves, and raves away the hours!
Anon, when storms howl loud and lash the deep,
Desperate she climbs the sea-rock's beetling[1] steep;
There wildly strikes her harp's fantastic strings,
Tells to the moon how grief her bosom wrings,
And while her strange song chaunts fictitious ills,
In wounded hearts Oblivion's balm distills.
    A youth, who yet has lived enough to know
That life has thorns, and taste the cup of woe,
As late near Conway's time-bowed towers he stray'd,
Invok'd this bright enthusiast's magic aid.
His prayer was heard. With arms and bosom bare,
Eyes flashing fire, loose robes, and streaming hair,
Her heart all anguish, and her soul all flame,
Swift as her thoughts, the lovely maniac came!
High heav'd her breasts, which struggling passions rent,
As prest to give some fear-fraught mystery vent:
And oft, with anxious glance and alter'd face,
Trembling with terror, she relaxed her pace,
And stopt! and listened! Then with hurried tread
Onwards again she rush'd, yet backwards bent her head,

1. Projecting, overhanging.

As if from murderous swords or following fiends she fled!
　　Soon as near Conway's walls her footsteps drew,
She bade the youth their ancient state renew:
Eager he sped the fallen towers to rear:
'Twas done, and fancy bore the fabric[2] here.
Next choosing from Shakespeare's comic school,
The gossip crone, gross friar, and gibing fool—[3]
These, with a virgin fair and lover brave,
To our young author's care the enchantress gave;
But charged him, ere he bless'd the brave and fair,
To lay th'exulting villain's bosom bare,
And by the torments of his conscience show,
That prosperous vice is but triumphant woe!
　　The pleasing talk, congenial to his soul,
Oft from his own sad thoughts our author stole:
Blest be his labours, if with like success
They soothe their sorrows whom I now address.
Beneath this dome, should some afflicted breast
Mourn slighted talents, or desert opprest,
False friendship, hopeless love, or faith betray'd;
Our author will esteem each toil o'er paid,
If, while his muse exerts her livelier vein,
Or tells imagined woes in plaintive strain,
Her flights and fancies make one smile appear
On the pale cheek, where trickled late a tear;
Or if *her* fabled sorrows steal one groan,
Which else her hearers would have given their own.

## ACT I

SCENE I　*A Grove.*

*Enter Father Philip and Motley.*

F. PHIL. Never tell me!—I repeat it, you are a fellow of a very scandalous course of life!

MOTL. And I repeat it, I'm a perfect image of the purest virtue, compared to whom, for sobriety and continence, Cato was a drunkard, and Lucretia little better than she should be.[4]

2. Structure, building. 3. See Lewis's "To The Reader" following the play. 4. Cato is the Roman senator renowned for his stoic and sober behavior; Lucretia, who committed suicide after being raped, is an emblem of modesty.

F. PHIL. Oh! hardened in impudence!—Can you deny being a pilferer, a lyar, a glutton—

MOTL. Can I?—Heaven be thanked, I've courage enough to deny any thing!

F. PHIL Doesn't all the world cry out upon you?

MOTL. Certainly my transcendent merit has procured me some enemies, and, in common with many other great men, my virtue at present labours under something of a cloud. But understand me right, Father: Though I don't assent to the sum-total of your accusation, possibly I may acknowledge some of the items; the best actions frequently appear culpable, merely because their motives are unexplained. Therefore produce your charges,[5] "let me justify my conduct, and I doubt not I shall retrieve my "reputation from your hands as immaculate and pure as a new sheet of "foolscap.[6]

F. PHIL. "To begin then with your pilfering"—Did you, or did you not, break open the pantry-door, and steal out the great goose-pye?

MOTL. Begging your pardon, Father, that was no fault of mine.

F. PHIL. Whose then?

MOTL. The cook's undoubtedly; for if he hadn't locked the pantry-door, 'tis an hundred to one I shouldn't have taken the trouble to break it open. [Then, as to my taking the Pye—I did it from motives of pure Christian [Charity: a poor helpless creature, born dumb and very hungry, intreated [me so pitcously to give her a morsel just to keep her from starving.

[F. PHIL. A poor Creature born dumb you say?

[MOTL. 'Tis very true Father! if you had but seen the old Tabby Cat come [to me with tears in her eyes—

F. PHIL. [Psha! don't talk to me of the Cat!] "Nonsense! Nonsense!—" I tell you, you've been guilty of stealing, which is a monstrous crime! And what did you steal? Had you taken any thing else I might have forgiven you: but to lay irreverent hands upon the goose-pye!—As I'm a Christian, the identical goose-pye[7] which I intended for my own supper!—But this is not my only objection to your conduct.

"MOTL. No?"

F. PHIL. What principally offends me is, that you pervert the minds of the maids, and keep kissing and smuggling[8] all the pretty girls you meet. Oh! fye! fye!

MOTL. I kiss and smuggle them? St. Francis forbid! Lord love you, Father, 'tis they who kiss and smuggle me. I protest I do what I can to

---

5. The Larpent version has "appear culpable, till their motives are known—Produce your charges." 6. Foolscap is a size of paper, typically 16×13 inches, named for the watermark of a fool's cap traditionally applied to the paper. 7. The Larpent version has "identical morsel." 8. Fondling or caressing.

preserve my modesty; and I wish that Archbishop Dunstan[9] had heard the lecture upon chastity which I read last night to the dairy-maid in the dark! "he'd have been quite edified." But yet what does talking signify? [It's all to no purpose.] The eloquence of my lips is counteracted by the lustre of my eyes; and really the little devils are so tender, and so troublesome, that I'm half angry with nature for having made me so very bewitching.

F. PHIL. Nonsense! Nonsense!

MOTL. Why it was but yesterday that Cicely and Luce went to fisty-cuffs, quarrelling which looked neatest—my red leg, or my yellow one.[10] Then they are so fond and so coaxing. They hang about one so lovingly! And one says, 'Kind Mr. Motley!' and t'other, 'Sweet Mr. Motley!'—Ah! Father Philip! Father Philip! How is a poor little bit of flesh and blood, like me, to resist such temptation?—Put yourself in my place: Suppose that a sweet smiling rogue, just sixteen, with rosy cheeks, sparkling eyes, pouting lips, &c.

F.PHIL. Oh! fye! "fye! fye!"—To hear such licentious discourse brings the tears into my eyes!

MOTL. I believe you, Father; for I see the water is running over at your mouth.[11] "However, this shews you—

"F. PHIL. It shews me that you are a reprobate, and that my advice is "thrown away upon you: In future I shall keep those counsels to myself, "which I offered you from motives of pure Christian charity.

"MOTL. Charity, my good Father, should always begin at home: Now, "instead of giving yourself so much trouble to mend me, what if you "thought a little of correcting yourself?

"F. PHIL. I?—I have nothing to correct.

"MOTL. No, to be sure!

"F. PHIL. The odour of my sanctity perfumes the whole kingdom.

"MOTL. It has a powerful smell about it, I own, not unlike carrion; you "may wind it a mile off.

"F. PHIL. All malice!

MOTL. "Not exactly:"[12] I could mention some little points which might be altered in you "still better than in myself;" such as intemperance, gluttony—

F. PHIL. Gluttony?—Oh! abominable falsehood!

9. Dunstan (925?–988), a monastic reformer, was made Archbishop of Canterbury in 961. 10. A reference to his motley clothes; Oxenberry's acting edition indicates that the actor playing Motley wears "Touchstone's dress." 11. That is, he's drooling. 12. The Larpent version has "But now, good Father."

MOTL. Plain matter of fact!—Why will any man pretend to say that you came honestly by that enormous belly, that tremendous tomb of fish, flesh, and fowl? "I protest I'm grateful to Heaven that among the unclean "Beasts who accompanied Noah, there went not into the ark a pair of fat "monks: they must infallibly have created a famine, and then the world "would never have been re-peopled."[13]—Next, for incontinence, you must allow yourself that you are unequalled.

F. PHIL. I? I?

MOTL. You, you.—May I ask what was your business in the beech-grove the other evening, when I caught you with buxom Margery the miller's pretty wife? Was it quite necessary to lay your heads together so close?

F. PHIL. Perfectly necessary: I was whispering in her ear wholesome advice.

MOTL. "Indeed? Faith then she took your advice as kindly as it was "given, and exactly in the same way too:"[14] you gave it with your lips, and she took it with hers!—Well done, Father Philip!

F. PHIL. Son, Son, you give your tongue too great a licence.

MOTL. Nay, Father, be not angry: Fools, you know, are privileged persons.

F. PHIL. I know they are very useless ones; "and" in short, Master Motley, to be plain with you, of all fools I think you the worst; and for fools of all kinds I've an insuperable aversion.

MOTL. Really? Then you have one good quality at least, and I cannot but admire such a total want of self-love![15]

*An horn sounds without.*

But hark! 'tis the dinner-horn. Away to table, Father—[for] depend upon't, the servants will rather eat part of their dinner unblessed, than stay till your stomach comes like Jonas's whale, and swallows up the whole.[16]

F. PHIL. Well, well, fool, I am going: but first let me explain to you, that my bulk proceeds from no indulgence of voracious appetite. No, son, no: Little sustenance do I take; but St. Cuthbert's[17] blessing is upon me, and

---

13. The reference to Noah, cut in the Larpent version, is the kind of religious joke that would annoy the examiner. The Larpent version substitutes "and" for "next" in the next sentence. 14. The Larpent version has the father say of his advice, "and she took it as I gave it." Motley responds, "So she did, faith, Father. You . . . ." 15. The Larpent version has the friar say, "and for fools of all kinds I've an insuperable aversion, and that you'll own at least is a virtue." To which Motley replies, "It is indeed, Father, it is a total want of self love!" 16. The Larpent version has "than stay till grace announces that your stomach is come like Jonah's whale." 17. Cuthbert (d. 687) was an English monk and saint. He was Prior of Melrose (661–664) and Bishop of Lindisfarne (685–687).

that little prospers with me most marvellously. Verily, the Saint has given me rather too plentiful an increase, and my legs are scarce able to support the weight of his bounties.                                                                    (*Exit*)

MOTL. (*Alone.*) He looks like an over-grown turtle, waddling upon its hind fins!—Yet at bottom 'tis a good fellow enough, warm-hearted, benevolent, friendly, and sincere; but no more intended by nature to be a monk, than I to be "a" maid of honour to the queen of Sheba.[18] (*Going.*)
*Enter Percy.*

PERCY. I cannot be mistaken: "in spite of his dress, his features are too "well known to me!" Hist! Gilbert! Gilbert!

MOTL. Gilbert? Oh Lord, that's I!—Who calls?

PERCY. Have you forgotten me?

MOTL. Truly, sir, that would be no easy matter; I never forgot in my life what I never knew.

PERCY. Have ten years altered me so much that you "cannot"—

MOTL. Hey!—Can it be—Pardon, my dear master, pardon!—In truth, you may well forgive my having forgotten *your* name, for at first I didn't "very well" remember my own. However, to prevent further mistakes, I must inform you, that he who in your father's service was Gilbert the knave, is [now] Motley the fool in the service of Earl Osmond.

PERCY. Of Earl Osmond? This is fortunate. Gilbert, you may be of use to me; and if the attachment which "as a boy" you [formerly] professed for me still exists—

MOTL. It does with ardour unabated, "for" I'm not so unjust as to attribute to you my expulsion from Alnwic Castle:[19] in fact[20] I deserved it, for I cannot deny but that at twenty I was as [idle and as] good-for-nothing a knave as ever existed; consequently old Earl Percy dismissed me from his service, "but I know that it was sorely against your inclination. You "were then scarce fourteen, and I had been your companion and play-"fellow from your childhood." I remember well your grief at parting with me, and that you slipped into my hand the purse which contained the whole of your little treasure. That act of kindness struck to my heart: I swore at that moment to love you through life, and if ever I forget my "oath, damn me!"[21]

PERCY. My honest Gilbert!—And what made you assume this habit?

MOTL. Ah, my Lord! what could I do?—In spite of my knavery and tricks I was constantly upon the point of starving, and having once con-

---

18. Sheba is an ancient Arabic kingdom. 19. Still standing, Alnwick Castle was the seat of the Percys. 20. The Larpent version has "in faith." 21. The Larpent version has "and it will prove my Life's bliss to prove my sincerity."

tracted an idle habit of eating, I never could bring myself to leave it off. After living five years by my wits, want drove me almost out of them: I knew not what course to take, when I heard [accidently] that Earl Osmond's jester had fled the country. I exerted my knavery for the last time in stealing the fugitive's cast coat, was accepted in his place by the Earl, and now gain an honest livelihood by persuading my neighbours that I'm a greater fool than themselves.

PERCY. And your change is for the better?

MOTL. Infinitely; indeed your fool is universally preferred to your knave—and for this reason; your fool is cheated, your knave cheats: Now every-body had rather cheat, than be cheated.

"PERCY. Some truth in that."

MOTL. And now, sir, may I ask, what brings you to Wales?

PERCY. A woman, whom I adore.

MOTL. Yes, I guessed that the business was about a petticoat. And this woman is—

PERCY. The orphan ward of a villager, without friends, without family, without fortune.

MOTL. Great points in her favour, I must confess. And which of these excellent qualities won your heart?

PERCY. I hope I had better reasons for bestowing it on her. No, Gilbert; I loved her for a person beautiful without art, and graceful without affectation—for an heart tender without weakness, and noble without pride. I saw her at once beloved and reverenced by her village companions: they looked on her as a being of superior order;[22] and I felt, that she who gave such dignity to the cottage-maid, must needs add[23] new lustre to the coronet of the Percies.

MOTL. From which I am to understand that you mean to marry this rustic.

PERCY. Could I mean otherwise, I should blush for myself.

MOTL. Yet surely the baseness of her origin—

PERCY. Can to me be no objection: in giving her my hand I raise her to my station, not debase myself to hers; nor ever, while gazing on the beauty of a rose, did I think it less fair because planted by a peasant.[24]

MOTL. Bravo!—And what says your good grumbling father to this?

PERCY. Alas! he has long slept in the grave!

22. The Larpent version has "I saw that her village companions looked upon her as a being of a superior order." 23. The Larpent version has "could not but add." 24. The Larpent version has "who ever thought a rose less beautiful because planted by a peasant."

MOTL. Then he's quiet at last! Well, God grant him that peace in heaven, which he suffered nobody to enjoy on earth![25]—But, "his death hav-"ing left you master of your actions," what obstacle "now" prevents your marriage?

PERCY. You shall hear.—Fearful lest my rank should influence this lovely girl's affections, "and induce her to bestow her hand on the noble, while "she refused her heart to the man," I assumed a peasant's habit, "and pre-"sented myself as Edwy the low-born and the poor." In this character I gained her heart, and resolved to hail, as Countess of Northumberland, "the betrothed of Edwy" the low-born and the poor!

"MOTL. I warrant the pretty soul wasn't displeased with the discovery!

PERCY. "That discovery is still unmade." Judge [then] how great must have been my disappointment, when, on entering her guardian's cottage with this design, he informed me, that the unknown, who sixteen years before had confided her to his care, had reclaimed her on that very morning, and conveyed her no one knew whither.[26]

MOTL. That was unlucky.

"PERCY. Was it not?—Ah! had I declared myself one day sooner, ere this "she would have been my wife.

"MOTL. True; and being your wife, if a stranger then had conveyed her "no one knew whither, you might have thought yourself mightily obliged "to him."

PERCY. However, in spite of his precautions, I have traced the stranger's course, and find him to be Kenric, a dependent upon Earl Osmond.

MOTL. Surely 'tis not Lady Angela, who—

PERCY. The very same! Speak, my good fellow! do you know her?

MOTL. Not by your description; for here she's understood to be the daughter of Sir Malcolm Mowbray,[27] my master's deceased friend. And what is your present intention?

PERCY. To demand her[28] of the Earl in marriage.

MOTL. "Oh!—" that will never do:—"for" in the first place you'll not be able to get a sight of him. I've now lived with him five long years,

25. The Larpent version has "Well, Heaven grant him that peace above which he suffered nobody to enjoy below." The more careful religious language is a response to complaints such as that of the *Monthly Mirror* (December 1797) which attacked Lewis's "frequent appeals to heaven, with a levity unusual to our stage"; "The licencer, if he had known the intention of his office, would have *struck his pen* across such expressions . . . . " 26. The Larpent version has "had that very morning reclaimed and conveyed her away no one knew whither." 27. Lewis may be thinking here of Robert de Mowbray (d. c.1125) who killed Malcolm of Scotland in 1093 at Alnwick, the site of Percy castle in the play. He was deprived of his earldom for supporting Count Stephen of Aumale. 28. The Larpent version has "I will demand her."

and, till [Lady] Angela's arrival, never witnessed a guest in the Castle.— Oh! 'tis the most melancholy mansion! And as to its master,²⁹ he's the very antidote to mirth: He always walks with his arms folded, his brows bent, his eyes louring on you with a gloomy scowl: He never smiles; and to laugh in his presence would be high treason. He looks at no one— speaks to no one. None dare approach him, except Kenric and his four blacks—all others are ordered to avoid him; and whenever he quits his room, ding! dong! goes a great bell, and away run the servants like so many scared rabbits.

PERCY. Strange!—and *what* reasons can he have for—

MOTL. "Oh! reason in plenty." You must know there's an ugly story respecting the last owners of this Castle—Osmond's brother, his wife, and infant child, were murdered by banditti, as it was said: unluckily the only servant who escaped the slaughter, deposed, that he recognized among the assassins a black still in the service of Earl Osmond.³⁰ The truth of this assertion was never known, for the servant was found dead in his bed the next morning.

PERCY. Good heavens!

MOTL. Since that time no sound of joy has been heard in Conway Castle. [Earl] Osmond instantly became gloomy and ferocious; he now never utters a sound except a sigh, has broken every tye of society, and keeps his gates barred unceasingly against the stranger.

PERCY. Yet Angela is admitted:—But, no doubt, affection for her father—

MOTL. Why, no; I rather think that affection for her father's child—

PERCY. How?

MOTL. If I've any knowledge in love, the Earl feels it for his fair ward: But the Lady will tell you more of this, if I can procure for you an interview.

PERCY. That³¹ very request which—

MOTL. 'Tis no easy matter, I promise you; but I'll do my best. In the meanwhile wait for me in yonder fishing hut—its owner's name is Edric;—tell him that I sent you, and he will give you a retreat.

PERCY. Farewell, then, and remember that whatever reward—

MOTL. Dear master, to mention a reward insults me. You have already shown me kindness; and when 'tis in my power to be of use to you,³² to need the inducement of a second favour would prove me a scoundrel undeserving of the first.                                              (*Exit*)

---

29. The Larpent version has "as to the Earl himself." 30. The Larpent version has "the present Earl." 31. The Larpent version has "The." 32. The Larpent version has "when I can be of use to you."

PERCY. How warm is this good fellow's attachment! Yet our Barons complain that the great can have no friends! If they have none, let their "own" pride bear the blame. Instead of looking with scorn on those whom a smile would attract, and a favour bind for ever, how many firm friends might our nobles gain, if they would but reflect[33] that their vassals are men as they are, and have hearts whose feelings can be grateful as their own.　　　　　　　　　　　　　　　　　　　　　　　　(*Exit*)

SCENE II　*The Castle-Hall.*

*Saib and Hassan meeting.*

SAIB. Now, Hassan, what success?

HASS. My search has been fruitless. In vain have I paced the river's banks, and pierced the grove's deepest recesses. Nor glen nor thicket have I passed unexplored, yet found no stranger to whom Kenric's description could apply.[34]

SAIB. Saw you no one?

HASS. A troop of horsemen passed me as I left the wood.

SAIB. Horsemen, say you?—Then Kenric may be right. Earl Percy has discovered Angela's abode, and lurks near the Castle in hopes of carrying her off.

HASS. His hopes then will be vain. Osmond's vigilance will not easily be eluded—sharpened by those powerful motives, love and fear.

SAIB. His love, I know; but should he lose Angela, what has he to fear?

HASS. If Percy gains her, every thing! Supported by such wealth and power, dangerous would be her claim to these domains should her birth be discovered. Of this our Lord is aware; nor did he sooner hear that Northumberland loved her, than he hastened to remove her from Allan's care. "At first I doubt his purpose was a foul one: her resemblance to her "mother induced him to change it. He now is resolved to make her his "bride, and restore to her those rights of which himself deprived her."

SAIB. Think you the Lady perceives that our Master loves her?

HASS. I know she does not. Absorbed in her own passion for Percy, on Osmond's she bestows no thought, and, while roving through these pompous halls and chambers, sighs for the Cheviot Hills,[35] and Allan's humble cottage.

---

33. The Larpent version has "did they not forget." 34. The Larpent version has "My search has been vain: Not a Glen did I leave unexplored, but found no stranger to whom Kenric's description could apply." 35. The Cheviot Hills run along the English-Scottish border.

SAIB. But as she still believes Percy to be a low-born swain, when Osmond lays his coronet at her feet, will she reject his rank and splendour?

HASS. If she loves well, she will. Saib, I too have loved! I have known how painful it was to leave her on whom my heart hung; "how incapable "was all else to supply her loss!" I have exchanged want for plenty, fatigue for rest, a wretched hut for a splendid palace. But am I happier? Oh! no! Still do I regret my native land, and the partners of my poverty. Then toil was sweet to me, for I laboured for Samba; then repose ever blest my bed of leaves, for there by my side lay Samba sleeping.

SAIB. This from you, Hassan?—Did love ever find a place in your flinty bosom?

HASS.[36] Did it? Oh Saib! my heart once was gentle, once was good! But sorrows have broken it, insults have made it hard! I have been dragged from my native land, from a wife who was every thing to me, to whom I was every thing! Twenty years have elapsed since these Christians tore me away: they trampled upon my heart, mocked my despair, and, when in frantic terms I raved of Samba,[37] [they] laughed, and wondered how a negro's soul could feel! In that moment when the last point of Africa faded from my view, when as I stood on the vessel's deck I felt that all [on [earth] I loved was to me lost for ever, in that bitter moment did I banish humanity from my breast. I tore from my arm the bracelet of Samba's hair, I gave to the sea the precious token, and, while the high waves swift bore it from me, vowed aloud endless hatred to mankind.[38] "I have kept "my oath, I *will* keep it!"

SAIB. Ill-starred Hassan! your wrongs have indeed been great.

HASS. To remember them unmans me—Farewell! I must to Kenric. Hold! Look, where he comes from Osmond's chamber!

SAIB. And seemingly in wrath.

HASS. His conferences with the Earl of late have had no other end. The period of his favour is arrived.[39]

SAIB. Not of his favour merely, Hassan.

HASS. How? Mean you that . . . .

SAIB. "His anxiety for independence, his wish to withdraw himself from "Wales—yet more, certain mysterious words and threats for some time "past have made our Lord uneasy. By him was I this morning commis- "sioned. . . . " Silence! He's here! you shall know more anon.

36. In the Larpent version, this speech is marked for deletion in the margin, presumably by the examiner. Contemporary allusions were found troublesome: a review of the printed text by the *Monthly Mirror* (December 1797) questioned the "propriety of any allusion to the *Slave Trade.*" 37. The Larpent version has "of my beloved." 38. The Larpent version has "hatred to the peace of man." 39. The Larpent version has "The day of his favour is past."

*Enter Kenric.*

KENR. "His promise ever evaded! My request still heard with impa-
"tience, and treated with neglect.—Osmond, I will bear your ingratitude
"no longer.—"⁴⁰ [How] now, Hassan, found you the man described?

HASS. Nor any that resembled him.

KENR. Yet, that I saw Percy, I am convinced. "As I crossed him in the
"wood, his eye met mine. He started as had he seen a basilisk,⁴¹ and fled
"with rapidity. Be on your guard, my friends! Doubtless he will attempt
"to gain admission to the Castle.

"HASS. Can we be otherwise than watchful, when we see how well the
"Earl rewards his followers?

"SAIB. Of that, Kenric, you are an example. Have you obtained that rec-
"ompence so long promised? Do you enjoy that independence which. . . .

KENR. "Saib, the Earl's ingratitude cuts me to the heart! Attached to
"him from his infancy, I have long been his friend, long fancied him
"mine. The illusion is now over. He sees that I can serve him no further—
"knows that I can harm him much; therefore he fears, and, fearing, hates
"me! But I will submit no longer to this painful dependence. To-morrow,
"for the last time, will I summon him to perform his promise: If he re-
"fuses, I will bid him farewell for ever, and, by my absence, free him
"from a restraint equally irksome to myself and him."⁴²

SAIB. Will you so, Kenric?—Be speedy then, or you will be too late.

KENR. Too late! And wherefore?

SAIB. You will soon receive the reward of your services.

KENR. Ha! Know you what that reward will be?

SAIB. I guess, but may not tell.

KENR. Is it a secret?

SAIB. Can you keep one?

KENR. Faithfully!

SAIB. As faithfully can I. Come, Hassan.                    (*Exeunt*)

KENR. (*Alone.*) What meant the slave? Those doubtful expressions. . . .
Ha! should the Earl intend me false. . . . Kenric! Kenric! how is thy nature changed! There was time "when fear was a stranger to my bosom—"
when, guiltless myself, I dreaded not art in others. Now, where'er I turn
me, danger appears to lurk; and I suspect treachery in every breast, because my own heart hides it.                               (*Exit*)

---

40. The Larpent version has "Ungrateful Osmond! No, with to-morrow's dawn—" 41. A
legendary reptile with fatal glance and breath. 42. The Larpent version has Kenric say,
"But no matter, Osmond's interests are no longer mine: I will away from the Castle and free
him by absence from the sight of one he hates."

*Enter Father Philip, followed by Alice.*

F. PHIL. Nonsense!—You silly woman, what you say is not possible.

ALICE. I never said it was possible. I only said it was true; and that if ever I heard music, I heard it last night.

F. PHIL. Perhaps the fool was singing to the servants.

ALICE. The fool indeed? Oh! fye! fye! How dare you call my Lady's ghost a fool?

F. PHIL. Your Lady's ghost!—You silly old woman!

ALICE. Yes, Father, yes: I repeat it, I heard the guitar lying upon the Oratory table play the very air which the Lady Evelina used to sing while rocking her little daughter's cradle. She warbled it so sweetly, and ever at the close it went (*Singing.*)

'Lullaby! Lullaby! hush thee, my dear!

'Thy father is coming, and soon will be here!'

F. PHIL. Nonsense! "nonsense!"—Why, pr'ythee, Alice, do you think that your Lady's ghost would get up at night only to sing Lullaby for your amusement?—Besides, how should a spirit, which is nothing but air, play upon an instrument of material wood and cat gut?

ALICE. How can I tell?—Why, I know very well that men are made; but if you desired me to make a man, I vow and protest I shouldn't know how to set about it. I can only say, that last night I heard the ghost of my murdered Lady. . . .

F. PHIL. Playing upon the spirit of a cracked guitar!—Alice! Alice! "these fears are ridiculous!" The idea of ghosts is "a" vulgar prejudice; and they who are timid and absurd enough to encourage it, prove themselves the most contemptible—

ALICE. (*Screaming.*) Oh! Lord bless us!

F. PHIL. What?—Hey!—Oh! dear!

ALICE. Look! look!—A figure in white!—It comes from the haunted room!

F. PHIL. (*Dropping on his knees.*) Blessed St. Patrick!—Who has got my beads? Where's my prayer-book?

ALICE. It comes!—it comes!—Now! now!—Lack-a-day,[43] it's only Lady Angela!

F. PHIL. (*Rising.*) Lack-a-day! I'm glad of it with all my heart!

ALICE. Truly so am I.—But what say you now, Father, to the fear of spectres?

43. For "alack the day," originally meaning "Shame or reproach to the day!" but coming to be an expression of surprise.

F. PHIL. In good faith, Alice, that my theory was better than my practice. However, the next time that you are afraid of a ghost, remember and make use of the receipt which I shall now give you;[44] instead of calling for a priest to lay the spirits of other people in the red sea, call for a bottle of red wine to raise your own. *Probatum est.*[45]                    (*Exit*)

ALICE. (*Alone.*) Wine indeed! "—I believe he thinks I like drinking as "well as himself." No, no! Let the old toping friar take his bottle of wine; I shall confine myself to plain cherry-brandy.

*Enter Angela.*

ANG. I am weary of wandering from room to room; in vain do I change the scene, discontent is every where. There was a time when music could delight my ear, and nature could charm my eye:—when, as the dawn unveiled the landscape, each object it disclosed to me looked pleasant and fair; and while the last sun-beams[46] yet lingered on the western sky, I could pour forth a prayer of gratitude, and thank my good angels for a day unclouded by sorrow!—Now all is gone,[47] all lost, all faded!

ALICE. Lady!

ANG. Perhaps at this moment he thinks upon me! Perhaps he wanders on those mountains where we so oft have strayed, [or] reclines on that bank where we so oft have sat, "or listens sadly to the starling which he taught "to repeat my name." Perhaps then he sighs, and murmurs to himself, 'The flowers, the rivulets, the birds, every object reminds me of my well-beloved; but what shall remind her of Edwy?'—Oh! that will my heart, Edwy; I need no other remembrancer!

ALICE. Lady! Lady Angela!! She minds me no more than a post!

ANG. Oh! are you there, good Alice? What would you with me?

ALICE. Only ask, how your Ladyship rested?

ANG. Ill! very ill!

ALICE. Lack-a-day! and yet you sleep in the best bed!

ANG. True, good Alice; but my heart's anguish strewed thorns upon my couch of down.

ALICE. Marry,[48] I'm not surprised that you rested ill in the Cedar-room. Those noises so near you—

ANG. What noises? I heard none.

ALICE. How?—When the clock struck one, heard you no music?

44. The Larpent version has "however, to preserve you in future from the terror of Ghosts—" 45. "It is good." 46. The Larpent version has "last beam of the sun." 47. The Larpent version has "changed." 48. An ejaculatory invocation meaning "simply, to be sure."

ANG. Music!—"None.

"ALICE. And never have heard any while in the Cedar-room?

"ANG. Not that I—Stay! now I remember that while I sat alone in my "chamber this morning—

"ALICE. Well, Lady, well!

"ANG. Methought I heard some one singing; it seemed as if the words ran "thus—(*Singing.*)—

" 'Lullaby! Lullaby! Hush thee, my dear!'

"ALICE. (*Screaming.*) The very words!—It was the ghost, Lady! it was "the ghost!

"ANG. The ghost, Alice!—I protest I thought it had been you.

"ALICE. Me, Lady!—Lord, when did you hear this singing?

"ANG. Not five minutes ago, while you were talking with Father Philip.

"ALICE. The Lord be thanked!—Then it was not the ghost. It was I, "Lady! It was I!—And have you heard no other singing since you came to "the castle?"

ANG. None. But why that question?

ALICE. Because, Lady—But perhaps you may be frightened?

ANG. No, No!—Proceed, I entreat you!

ALICE. Why, then, they do say, that the chamber in which you sleep is haunted. You may have observed two folding-doors, which are kept locked: they lead to the Oratory, in which "the" Lady Evelina passed most of her time, while my Lord was engaged in the Scottish wars.[49] "She would sit there, good soul! hour after hour, playing on the lute, and "singing airs so sweet, so sad, that many a time and oft have I wept to "hear her." Ah! when I kissed her hand at the Castle-gate, little did I suspect that her fate would have been so wretched!

ANG. And what was her fate?

ALICE. A sad one, Lady! Impatient to embrace her Lord, after a year's absence, the Countess set out to met him on his return from Scotland, accompanied by a few domestics and her infant-daughter, then scarce a twelvemonth old. But, as she returned with her husband, robbers surprised the party scarce a mile form the Castle; and since that time no news has been received of the Earl, of the Countess, the servants, or the child.

ANG. Dreadful! Were not their corses[50] found?

49. Lewis fails to make clear the era of his play, but the earlier mention of Dunstan would place it in the late tenth century. There were then key struggles between the Scottish kingdom and Northumbria, including in the next century the defeat of Macbeth by Northumbria's Earl in 1054 and the death of Malcolm III at the hands of Robert de Mowbray, discussed above. 50. The Larpent version has "bodies."

ALICE. Never! The only domestic who escaped pointed out the scene of action; and as it proved to be on the river's banks, doubtless the assassins plunged the bodies into the stream.

ANG. Strange! And did Earl Osmond then become owner of this Castle?—Alice! was he ever suspected of—

ALICE. Speak lower, Lady! It was said so, I own: but for my own part I never believed it. To my certain knowledge Osmond loved "the" Lady Evelina too well to hurt her; and when he heard of her death, he wept, and sobbed as if his heart were breaking. Nay, 'tis certain that he proposed to her before marriage, and would have made her his wife, only that she liked his brother better. "Well she might indeed, for Earl "Reginald was a sweeter gentleman by half."

ANG. And in that Oratory, you say—Good Alice, you have the key of it: Let me see that Oratory to-night.

ALICE. To-night, Lady? Heaven preserve me! I wouldn't enter it after dark for the world!

ANG. But before dark, Alice?

ALICE.[51] Before dark? Why that indeed—Well, well, we'll see, Lady. But I hope you're not alarmed by what I mentioned of the Cedar-room?

ANG. No, truly, Alice; from good spirits I have nothing to fear, and heaven and my innocence will protect me against bad.

ALICE. My very sentiments, I protest! But Heaven forgive me, while I stand gossiping here I warrant all goes wrong in the kitchen! Your pardon, Lady: I must away! I must away!                                    (Exit)

ANG. (Musing.) Osmond "was" his brother's heir. His strange demeanour!—Yes, in that gloomy brow is written a volume of villainy!— "Heavenly powers! an assassin then is master of my fate!—An assassin "too who—I dare not bend my thoughts that way!—" Oh! would I had never entered these Castle-walls!—had never exchanged for fearful pomp the security of my pleasures—the tranquillity of my soul!

51. The Larpent version handles this passage to Alice's exit differently:

ALICE. Before dark? Why that indeed—Well, well, we'll see, Lady. But while I stand gossipping here, I warrant all goes wrong in the kitchen: I must away!—But I hope, Lady Angela, you're not alarmed by what I mentioned in the Cedar-room?

ANG. No, truly, Alice; from good spirits I have nothing to fear; and heaven and my innocence will protect me against bad.

ALICE. My very sentiments, I protest! But some people are so foolish and troublesome about ghosts. Would you believe it, Lady?—Father Philip just now taking you for a spectre was in such a trembleation, that had your Ladyship only seen him, I warrant your Ladyship would have cracked your Ladyship's sides with laughing.—His fat melted away like so much butter; and though he came into the room with a bushel of belly—Lackaday, he went out of it, as slim as a farthing candle.                                    (Exit)

Return, return, sweet Peace! and o'er my breast
Spread thy bright wings, distill thy balmy rest,
And teach my steps thy realms among to rove;
Wealth and the world resign'd, nought mine but love!
Ah! cease thy suit, fond girl! thy prayer is vain,
For thus did Love his tyrant law ordain.
—'Peace still must[52] fly that heart where *I* still reign.'     (*Exit*)

END OF ACT I


## ACT II


SCENE I  *The Armoury.—Suits of Armour are arranged on both Sides upon Pedestals, with the Names of their Possessors written under each.*
*Enter Motley, peeping in.*
MOTL. The coast is clear!—Hist! Hist!—You may enter.
*Enter Percy.*
PERCY. Loiter not here!—Quick, my good fellow!—Conduct me to Angela!
MOTL. Softly, softly! "A little caution is needful; and" I promise you just now I'm not upon roses.—"You remember the servant who hinted that "Earl Osmond had an hand in his brother's murder?—Should I be sus-"pected of admitting you to the Castle, his fate might be mine; and what-"ever you may think of it, my Lord, I shouldn't be at all pleased at wak-"ing to-morrow morning, to find myself dead in my bed.
PERCY. "If such are your fears," why[53] not lead me at once to Angela? "Are we not more exposed in this open hall?"
MOTL. Be contented, and leave all to me: I will contrive matters so that Osmond shall have you before his eyes, and be no jot[54] the wiser.— Here!—(*Taking down a suit of armour.*)—Put on this coat of mail: you must make up your mind to play a statue for an hour or two.
PERCY. How?
MOTL. Nay, 'tis absolutely necessary—Quick! quick! ere the servants quit the hall, where they are now at dinner.—Here's the helmet!—the gauntlet!—the shield!—So now take this truncheon in your hand; and there we have you armed cap-a-pee![55]
PERCY. And now be good enough to explain what purpose this masquerade is to answer.

---

52. The Larpent version has "shall." 53. The Larpent version has "But why." 54. The Larpent version has "not a jot." 55. From head to foot.

MOTL. Willingly. "You are to know, that since" the late Earl's "death the "Castle is thought to be haunted: the" servants are fully persuaded that his ghost wanders every night through the long galleries, "and parades the "old towers and dreary halls" which abound in this melancholy mansion. He is supposed to be drest in compleat armour; and that which you wear at present was formerly his. Now hear my plan. The Earl prepares to hold a conference with Lady Angela; even now I heard her summoned to attend him in the Armoury. Placed upon this pedestal you may listen to their discourse unobserved, and thus form a proper judgment both of your mistress and her guardian. As soon as it grows dark I will conduct you to Angela's apartments: the obscurity will then shelter you from discovery; and even should you be observed, you will pass for Earl Reginald's spectre.

PERCY. I do not dislike your plan: but tell me, Gilbert, do you believe this tale of the apparition?

MOTL. Oh! Heaven forbid! Not a word of it. Had I minded all the strange things related of this Castle, I should have died of fright in the first half-hour. Why, they say that Earl Hubert rides every night round the Castle on a white horse; that the ghost of Lady Bertha haunts the west pinnacle of the Chapel-Tower; and that Lord Hildebrand, who was condemned for treason some sixty years ago, may be seen in the Great Hall, regularly at midnight, playing at foot-ball with his own head![56] Above all, they say that the spirit of the late Countess sits nightly in her Oratory, and sings her baby to sleep! However, if it be so—

*A bell sounds thrice, loud and solemn.*

—Hark! 'tis the Earl!—Quick to your post!—

*Percy ascends the pedestal.*

—Farewell! I must get out of his way; but as soon as he quits this chamber I'll rejoin you.

PERCY. Do so; and farewell.                    (*Exit Motley*)

*The folding-doors are thrown open: Saib, Hassan, Muley, and Alaric enter, preceding Earl Osmond, who walks with his arms folded, and his eyes bent upon the ground. Saib advances a sopha, into which, after making a few turns through the room, Osmond throws himself. He motions to his attendants, and they withdraw. He appears lost in thought; then suddenly rises, and again traverses the room with disordered steps.*

OSM. I will not sacrifice my happiness to hers! "For sixteen long years "have I thirsted; and now when the cup of joy again stands full before me, "shall I dash it from my lip?" No, Angela, you ask of me too much. Since

---

56. The Larpent version has "regularly at midnight may be seen in the Great hall walking without his Head!"

the moment when "I pierced her heart, deprived of whom life became "odious; since" my soul was[57] stained with his blood who loved me, with hers whom I loved, no form has been grateful to my eye, no voice spoken pleasure to my soul, save Angela's, "save only Angela's! Doting "upon one whom death has long clasped in his arms; tortured by desires "which I never hoped to satisfy, many a mournful year has my heart "known no throb but of anguish, no guest but remorse at committing a "fruitless crime. Hope, that stranger, once more revisits my bosom: the "fiend, who led me through passion's mazes to the heights of my guilt, "owns that a crime so great well merits a reward. He bids the monument's "jaws unclose: Evelina revives in her daughter, and soon shall the fires "which consume me be quenched in Angela's arms." What though her heart be Percy's?[58] "What though she prefers a basilisk's kiss to mine? "Because my short-lived joy may cause her eternal sorrow, shall I reject "those pleasures sought so long, desired so earnestly?" That will I not, by Heaven! "Mine she is, and" mine she shall be, though Reginald's bleeding ghost flit before me, and thunder in my ear—'Hold! Hold!'—Peace, stormy heart! She comes!

*Enter Angela.*

osm. (*In a softened voice.*) Come hither, Angela. Wherefore so sad? That downcast eye, that listless air, neither suit your age or fortunes. "Raised "from obscurity to rank and splendour, can this change call no smile upon "your cheek?" Where-e're you turn, respect and adoration wait you; "a "thousand servants move obedient to your nod." The treasures of India are lavished to adorn your person; yet still do I see you, forgetting what you are, look back with regret to what you were!

ang. Oh! my good Lord, esteem me not ungrateful! I acknowledge your bounties, but they have not made me happy. I still linger in thought near those scenes where I passed the blessed period of infancy; I still thirst for those simple pleasures which habit has made to me most dear. The birds which my own hands reared, and the flowers which my own hands planted; the banks on which I rested when fatigued, the wild tangled wood which supplied me with strawberries, and the village church where I prayed to be virtuous, while I yet knew of vice and virtue but the name, all have acquired rights to my memory and my love!

osm. What! these costly dresses, these scenes of pomp and greatness—

ang. Dazzle my eyes, but leave my heart unsatisfied. What I would meet with is affection, not respect; I had rather be obliged than obeyed; and all

---

57. The Larpent version has "became." 58. The Larpent version moves the second sentence of this speech here.

these glittering gems are far less dear to me, than one flower of a wreath which Edwy's hand have woven.

"osm. Confusion!

"ANG. While I saw you, Cheviot Hills, I was happy, Oh! how happy! "While I listened to your artless accents, friends of my childhood, how "swelled my fond heart with gratitude and pleasure. At morn when I left "my bed, light were my spirits, and gay as the zephyrs[59] of summer; and "when at night my head again pressed my pillow, I whispered to myself, " 'Happy has been to-day, and to-morrow will be as happy!' Then sweet "was my sleep; and my dreams were of those whom I loved dearest."

osm. Romantic enthusiast! These thoughts did well for the village maid, but disgrace the daughter of Sir Malcolm Mowbray: "Let them be "changed for others, better suited to your birth, to the fortune which "awaits you." Hear me, Angela; an English baron loves you, a nobleman than whom our island boasts few more potent. 'Tis to him that your hand is destined, 'tis on him that your heart must be bestowed.

ANG. I cannot dispose of that which has long been another's—My heart is Edwy's.

osm. Edwy's? A peasant's?

ANG. For the obscurity of his birth chance must be blamed; the merit of his virtues belongs wholly to himself.

osm. By Heaven, you seem to think that poverty is a virtue!

ANG. Sir, I think 'tis a misfortune, not a crime: And when in spite of nature's injustice, "and the frowns of a prejudiced and illiberal world," I see some low-born but illustrious spirit prove itself superior to the station which it fills, I hail it with pleasure, with admiration, with respect! Such a spirit I found in Edwy, and, finding, loved!

osm. My blood boils with passion!

ANG. "You say, that by these sentiments I disgrace my rank: I say, that to "break my given word would disgrace it more." Edwy has my plighted faith: He received it on the last evening which I passed in Northumberland, as we sat on a low bench before old Allan's cottage. It was an heavenly night, sweet and tranquil as the loves of angels: A gentle breeze whispered among the honeysuckles which bloomed above us, "and the full moon tinged "with her silver light the distant towers of Alnwic." It was then "that for "the first time" I gave him my hand, "and I swore that I never would give "it but to him!" It was then "that for the first time" he pressed his lips to mine, and I swore that my lips should never by pressed by another!

osm. Girl! girl! you drive me to distraction!

59. Winds from the west, from *Zephyros*, Greek god of the west wind.

ANG. You alarm me, my Lord! Permit me to retire.—(*Going, Osmond detains her violently by the arm.*)

OSM. Stay!—(*In a softer tone.*) Angela! I love you!

ANG. (*Starting.*) My Lord!

OSM. (*Passionately.*) Love you to madness!—"My bosom is a gulph of de-"vouring flames! I must quench them in your arms, or perish!"—Nay, strive not to escape: Remain, and hear me! I offer you my hand: If you accept it, mistress of these fair and rich domains, your days shall glide away in happiness and honour; but if you refuse and scorn my offer, force shall this instant—

ANG. Force? Oh! No!—You dare not be so base!

OSM. Reflect on your situation, Angela; you are in my power—"remem-"ber it, and be wise!"

ANG. If you have a generous mind, that will be my surest safeguard. Be it my plea, Osmond, when thus I sue to you for mercy, for protection! "Look on me with pity, Osmond!" 'Tis the daughter of the man you loved, 'tis a creature, friendless, wretched, and forlorn, who kneels before you, who flies to you for refuge! True, I am in your power: Then save me, respect me, treat me not cruelly; for—I am in your power!

OSM. I will hear no more. Will you accept my offer?

ANG. Osmond, I conjure you—

OSM. Answer my question!

ANG. Mercy! Mercy!

OSM. Will you be mine?—Speak! Speak!

ANG. (*After a moment's pause, rises, and pronounces with firmness.*) Never, so help me Heaven!

OSM. (*Seizing her.*) Your fate then is decided!

*Angela shrieks.*

PERCY. (*In a hollow voice.*)—Hold!

OSM. (*Starts, but still grasps Angela's arm.*)—Ha! What was that?

ANG. (*Struggling to escape.*) "Hark!" Hark!—Heard you not a voice?

OSM. (*Gazing upon Percy.*)—It came from hence!—From Reginald!—Was it not a delusion—Did indeed his spirit—(*Relapsing into his former passion.*) Well, be it so! Though his ghost should rush between us, thus would I clasp her—Horror! What sight is this!—

*At the moment that he again seizes Angela, Percy extends his truncheon with a menacing gesture, and descends from the pedestal. Osmond releases Angela, who immediately rushes from the chamber, while Percy advances a few steps, and remains gazing on the Earl stedfastly.*

—I know that shield!—that helmet!—Speak to me, dreadful vision!— "Tax me with my crimes!"—Tell me, that you come—"Stay! Speak!—"

*Following Percy, who, when he reaches the door, through which Angela escaped, turns, and signs to him with his hand. Osmond starts back in terror.*

—He forbids my following!—He leaves me!—The door closes—(*In a sudden burst of passion, and drawing his sword.*)—Hell, and fiends! I'll follow him, though lightnings blast me!—

(*He rushes distractedly from the chamber.*)*

SCENE II   *The Castle-Hall.*

*Enter Alice.*

ALICE. Here's rudeness! Here's ill-breeding! On my conscience, this house grows worse and worse every day!

*Enter Motley.*

MOTL. What can he have done with himself? "Perhaps weary of waiting "for me in the Armoury, he has found his way alone to Angela. How" now, dame Alice, "what has happened to you?" You look angry.

ALICE. By my troth,[60] fool, I've little reason to look pleased. To be frightened out of my wits by night, and thumped and pumped about by day, is not likely to put one in the best humour.

MOTL. Poor soul! And who has been thumping and bumping you?

ALICE. "Who has? You should rather ask who has not."—Why only hear:—As I was just now going along the narrow passage which leads to the Armoury—"singing to myself, and thinking of nothing," I met Lady Angela flying away as if for dear life!—So I dropp'd her a curtsey—but might as well have spared my pains. Without minding me "any more than "if I had been a dog or a cat"—she pushed me on one side; and before I could recover my balance, somebody else, who came bouncing by me, gave me t'other thump—and there I lay sprawling upon the floor. However, I tumbled with all possible decency, "and took great care that my "petticoats should cover my legs."

MOTL. Somebody else! What somebody else?

ALICE. I know not—but he seemed to be in armour.

MOTL. In armour? Pray, Alice, looked he like a ghost?

---

*When I wrote the foregoing scene, I really believed the invention to be entirely my own: But the situations of Angela, Osmond and Percy, so closely resemble those of Isabella, Manfred, and the animated portrait in The Castle of Otranto, that I am convinced the idea must have been suggested to me by that beautiful Romance.—Wherever I can trace any plagiarisms, whether wilful or involuntary, I shall continue to point them out to the reader without reserve. (Lewis's note)

60. One's pledged word.

ALICE. What he looked like, I cannot say;—but I'm sure he didn't feel like one: However, you've not heard the worst. While I was sprawling upon the ground, my Lord comes tearing along the passage[61]—The first thing he did was to stumble against me—away went his heels—over he came—and in the twinkling of an eye there lay his Lordship! As soon as he got up again—"Mercy!" how he stormed!—He snatched me up—called me[62] an ugly old witch—shook the breath out of my body—then clapped me on the ground again, and bounced away after the other two!

MOTL. My mind misgives me!—But what can this mean, Alice?

ALICE. The meaning I neither know, or care about;—but this I know—I'll stay no longer in an house where I'm treated so disrespectfully. " 'My "Lady'—says I—'Out of my way!'—says she, and pushes me on one "side.—'My Lord,'—says I—'You be damned!'—says he, and pushes me "on t'other!"—I protest I never was so ill used, even when I was a young woman! *(Exit)*

MOTL. This account alarms me!—Should Percy be discovered—The very thought gives me a creak[63] in my neck!—At any rate I had better inquire whether—*(Going.)*

*Enter Father Philip hastily.*

F. PHIL. *(Stopping him.)* Get out of the house!—That's your way!

MOTL. Why, what's the meaning—

F. PHIL. Don't stand prating here, but do as I bid you!

MOTL. But first tell me—

F. PHIL. [I can't.] I can only tell you to get out of the house. Kenric has discovered Earl Percy—You are known to have introduced him—The Africans are in search of you—If you are found, you will be hung "out of "hand." Fly then to Edric's cottage—hide yourself there!—Hark!—Some one comes! Away, "away," ere it is too late!—*(Pushing him out.)*

MOTL. *(Confused.)* But Earl Percy—But Angela—

F. PHIL. Leave them to me! You shall hear from me soon. Only take care of yourself, and fly with all diligence!—Away! *(Exit Motley)*

F. PHIL. *(Alone.)* So, so, he's off, and now I've time to take breath. I've not moved so nimbly for the last twenty years; "and, in truth, I'm at "present but ill calculated for velocity of motion." However, my exertions have not been thrown away: I've saved this poor knave from Osmond's vengeance—and should my plan for the Lady's release succeed—Poor little soul!—To see how she took on, when Percy was torn from her! Well, well, she shall be rescued from her tyrant. The moveable pannels—the

---

61. The Larpent version has "tearing along like a mad bull." 62. The Larpent version has "cursed me for." 63. For "crick," a spasmodic stiffness of the muscles.

subterraneous passages—the secret springs well-known to me—Oh! I cannot fail of success; But in order to secure it, I'll finally arrange my ideas in the Buttery. Whenever I've any great design in hand, I always ask advice of a flaggon of ale, and mature[64] my plan over a cold venison-pastry. "Oh! what an excellent genius must that man have had, who first "invented eating and drinking!"                                    (*Exit*)


SCENE III   *A spacious Chamber: On one Side is a Couch: on the other a Table, which is placed under an arched and lofty Window. Enter Osmond, followed by Saib, Hassan, Muley and Alaric, who conduct Percy disarmed.*

OSM. This, Sir, is your prison; but, doubtless, your confinement will not continue long. The moment which gives me Angela's hand shall restore you to liberty; and, till that moment arrives, farewell.

PERCY. Stay, Sir, and hear me!—By what authority presume you to call me captive!—Have you forgotten that you speak to Northumberland's Earl?

OSM. Well may I forget him, who could so far forget himself. Was it worthy of Northumberland's Earl to steal disguised into my Castle, and plot with my servant to rob me of my most precious treasure?

PERCY. Mine was that treasure—"You deprived me of it basely," and I was justified in striving to regain my own.

OSM. Earl, nothing can justify unworthy means. If you were wronged, why sought you not your right with your sword's point? I then should have esteemed you a noble foe, and as such would have treated you: But you have stooped to paltry artifice, and attacked me like some midnight ruffian, privately, and in disguise. "By this am I authorized to forget your "station, and make your penance as degrading as your offence was base."

PERCY. If such are indeed your sentiments, prove them now. Restore my sword, unsheathe your own, and be Angela the conqueror's reward!

OSM. No, "Earl" Percy!—I am not so rash a gamester as to suffer that cast to be recalled, by which the stake is mine already. "Angela is in my "power: The only man who could wrest her from my arms, has wilfully "made himself my captive: Such he is, and such he shall remain."

PERCY. Insulting tyrant![65] "Your cowardice in refusing my challenge "proves sufficiently—"

OSM. Be calm, Earl Percy!—You forget yourself. That I am no coward, my sword has proved in the fields[66] of Scotland.—My sword shall again

64. The Larpent version has "digest." 65. The Larpent version has "Insulting coward."
66. The Larpent version has "plains."

prove it, if, when you are restored to liberty, you still question[67] the courage of my heart! Angela once mine, repeat your defiance, nor doubt my answering.

PERCY. Angela thine?—That she shall never be! There are angels above who favour virtue, and the hour of retribution must one day arrive!— (*Throws himself upon the couch.*)

OSM. "But long ere the arrival of that hour shall Angela have been my "bride; and now farewell, Lord Percy!"[68]—Muley and Saib!

BOTH. My Lord!

OSM. To your charge I commit the Earl; quit not this apartment, nor suffer him for one moment from your sight.

SAIB AND MULEY. My Lord, we shall obey you.

OSM. (*Aside.*) If she refuse me still, the death of this, her favourite—his death! Oh! through what bloody paths do I wander in pursuit of happiness! "Yes, I am guilty!—Heaven! how guilty!" Yet lies the fault with me? "Did my own pleasure plant in my bosom these tempestuous passions?" No! "they were given me at my birth; they were sucked in with my ex-"istence!" Nature formed me the slave of wild desires; and Fate, as she frowned upon my cradle, exclaimed, 'I doom this babe to be a villain and a wretch!' *

(*Exit, followed by Hassan and Alaric, who lock the door after them*)

SAIB. Look, Muley, how bitterly he frowns!

MULEY. "Now he starts from the sopha!"—'Faith, he's in a monstrous fury!

SAIB. That may well be.— When you mean to take in other people, it certainly is provoking to be taken in yourself.

PERCY. (*After walking a few turns with a disordered air, suddenly stops.*) He is gone to Angela! Gone, perhaps, to renew that outrage whose completion my presence alone prevented! "Helpless and unprotected, with no "friend but innocence—no advocates save tears—how will she now repel "his violence?"

MULEY. Now he's in a deep study:—Marry,[69] if he studies himself out of this Tower, he's a cleverer fellow than I take him for.

---

*Having had good opportunities of knowing how wonderful are the talents for misinterpretation possessed by certain persons, I think it necessary to observe to my readers, that the foregoing speech is not meant to contain a moral sentiment, but to display the false reasoning of a guilty conscience.—If I were not to make this explanation, I should expect to see it asserted that the whole Play was meant to inculcate the doctrine of Fatality. (Lewis's note) Such disclaimers indicate Lewis's concern over charges that his play, like other Gothic dramas, adopted radical ideas.

67. The Larpent version has "you shall dare to question." 68. The Larpent version has "Be that your hope—till then farewell—."

69. An expression of surprise, from the Virgin Mary.

PERCY. Were I not Osmond's captive, all might yet be well. Summoning my vassals, who by this time must be near at hand, forcing the Castle, and tearing Angela from the arms of her tyrant—Alas! my captivity has rendered this plan impracticable! "Eternal curses upon Gilbert, who per-"suaded me to adopt this artifice!—Curses on my own rash folly, which "has thrown me thus defenceless in the power of my foe!—

"MULEY. That's right!—Another stamp or two, and the Tower comes rat-"tling about our ears."

PERCY. And are there then no hopes of liberty?

SAIB. He fixes his eyes on us.

PERCY. Might not these fellows—I can but try.—Now stand my friend, thou master-key to human hearts!—Aid me, thou potent devil, gold!—Hear me, my worthy friends!—Come nearer!

"SAIB. His worthy friends! Are we such, Muley?

"MULEY. Yes, truly we are—for friends in need are friends indeed:—"Marry, if he were not in need, he would call us his mortal foes."

PERCY. My good fellows, you are charged with a disagreeable office, and to obey a tyrant's mandates cannot be pleasant to you; there is something in your looks which has prejudiced me too much in your favour to believe it possible.

SAIB. Nay, there certainly is something in our appearance highly prepossessing.

MULEY. And I knew that you must admire the delicacy of our complexions!

PERCY. The tincture of your skin, my good fellow, is of little consequence: Many a worthy heart beats within a dusky bosom, and I am convinced that such an heart inhabits yours; for your looks tell me that you feel for, and are anxious to relieve, my sufferings.—See you this purse, my friends?

MULEY. It's too far off, and I'm short-sighted.—If you'll put it a little nearer—

PERCY. Restore me to liberty!—and not this purse alone, but ten times its value shall be yours.

SAIB. To liberty?

MULEY. That purse?

SAIB. Muley!

MULEY. Saib!

PERCY. (*Aside.*) By all my hopes, they hesitate!—You well know, that my wealth and power are equal, not to say superior, to Earl Osmond's: Release me from my dungeon, and share that power and wealth!—"On the "events of to-day depends my life's future happiness, nay perhaps my life

"itself: Judge then, if you assist me, how great will be the service ren-
"dered me, and believe that your reward shall equal my obligation.

"SAIB. I know not what to answer."

MULEY. In truth, my Lord, your offers are so generous, and that purse is
so tempting—Saib, what say you?—(*Winking to him.*)

SAIB. The Earl speaks so well, and promises so largely, that I own I'm
strangely tempted—

MULEY. Look you, Saib; will you stand by me?

SAIB. (*After a moment's thought.*) I will!

MULEY. There's my hand then!—My Lord, we are your servants!

PERCY. "This is beyond my hopes!"—A thousand thanks, my worthy
fellows!—Be assured that the performance of *my* promises shall soon follow the execution of yours.

SAIB. Of that we make no doubt.

PERCY. You agree then to release me?

MULEY. 'Tis impossible to do otherwise; for I feel that pity, generosity,
and every moral feeling command me to trouble your Lordship for that
purse.

PERCY. There it is!—And now unlock the door!

MULEY. (*Chinking the purse.*) *Here* it is!—And now I'm [much] obliged to
you. As for your promises, my Lord, pray don't trouble yourself to remember them, as I sha'n't trouble myself to remember mine.

PERCY. (*Starting.*) Ha!—What mean you?

SAIB. (*Firmly.*) Earl, that we are faithful!

"MULEY. I wonder you didn't read that too in our amiable looks!"

PERCY. What! Will you not keep your word?

MULEY. In good truth, No; we mean to keep nothing—except the purse.

"PERCY. Perfidious villains!"

"SAIB. You mistake us, Sir;—we cannot be villains, for I, you know, am
"your Lordship's 'worthy friend!'"

"MULEY. And I your Lordship's unworthy pensioner!"

PERCY. Confusion!—To be made the jest of such rascals!

SAIB. Earl Percy, we are none!—"but we should have been, could your
"gold have bribed us to betray our master." We have but done our duty—
you have but gained your just reward; for they who seek to deceive others,
should ever be deceived themselves.[70]

PERCY. Silence, fellow![71]—Leave me to my thoughts!—(*Throwing himself
passionately upon the couch.*)

MULEY. Oh! with all our hearts! We ask no better.

70. The Larpent version has "betray / betrayed" for "deceive / deceived." 71. The Larpent
version has "traitor."

SAIB. Muley, we share that purse?

MULEY. Undoubtedly: Sit down, and examine its contents—

*They seat themselves on the floor in the front of the stage.*

PERCY. How unfortunate, that the only merit of these villains should be fidelity!—"No hope now is left! Angela is lost, and with her my "happiness!"

CHORUS OF VOICES (*Singing without.*)
Sing Megen-oh! Oh! Megen-Ee!

MULEY. Hark!—What's that?

SAIB. I'll see. (*Mounting upon the table.*)—This window is so high—

MULEY. Here, "here!" Take this chair.—

*Saib places the chair upon the table, and thus lifts himself to a level with the window, which he opens.*

SONG AND CHORUS.

| | |
|---|---|
| MOTLEY (*Singing without.*) | Sleep you, or wake you, Lady bright? |
| CHORUS (*Without.*) — | Sing Megen-oh! Oh! Megen-Ee! |
| MOTLEY — — — | Now is the fittest time for flight. |
| CHORUS — — — | Sing Megen-oh! Oh! Megen-Ee! |
| MOTLEY — — — | Know, from your tyrant father's power |
| | Beneath the window of your tower |
| | A boat now waits to set you free: |
| CHORUS — — — | Sing Megen-oh! Oh! Megen-Ee! |
| | Sing Megen-oh! Oh! Megen-Ee! |

PERCY. (*Who has half-raised himself from the couch during the latter part of the Song, and listened attentively.*)—Surely I know that voice!

MULEY. Now, what's the matter?

SAIB. A boat lies at the foot of the tower, and the fisherman sing while they draw their nets.

PERCY. I could not be mistaken:—it was Gilbert!

SAIB. Hark! They begin again!—

SECOND STANZA.

| | |
|---|---|
| MOTLEY— | Though deep the stream, though high the wall, |
| CHORUS— | Sing Megen-oh! Oh! Megen-Ee! |
| MOTLEY— | The danger, trust me, Love, is small: |
| CHORUS— | Sing Megen-oh! Oh! Megen-Ee! |
| MOTLEY— | To spring below then never dread; |
| | My arms to catch you shall be spread; |

And far from hence you soon shall be,
CHORUS— Sing Megen-oh! Oh! Megen-Ee!
Sing Megen-oh! Oh! Megen-Ee!

PERCY. I understand him!—He bids me—Yet the danger—What course shall I pursue?

MULEY. Pr'ythee, come down, Saib; "I long to divide the purse—

SAIB. "Stay a moment:" one more stanza, and I'm with you. Now, silence!

### THIRD STANZA.

MOTLEY—Fair Emma hushed her heart's alarms:
CHORUS— Sing Megen-oh! Oh! Megen-Ee!
MOTLEY—She sprang into her Lover's arms;
CHORUS— Sing Megen-oh! Oh! Megen-Ee!
MOTLEY—Unhurt she fell; then swift its way
The boat pursued without delay,
While Emma placed on Edgar's knee
Sang 'Megen-oh! Oh! Megen-Ee!'
CHORUS— Sing Megen-oh! Oh! Megen-Ee!

MULEY. Will you never quit that window?

SAIB. (*Shutting it, and descending.*) Here I am, and now for the purse!— *They resume their seats upon the ground; Saib opens the purse, and begins to reckon the gold.*

PERCY. Yes, I must brave the danger—I will feign to sleep; and when my gaolers are off their guard, then aid me, blest Providence!—(*Extending himself upon the couch.*)

SAIB. Hold, Muley!—What if, instead of sharing the purse, we throw for its contents? Here are dice.

MULEY. With all my heart:—And look! to pass our time better, here's a bottle of the best sack[72] in the Earl's cellar.

SAIB. Good! Good!—And now, be this angel[73] for stake!—But, first, what is our prisoner doing?

MULEY. Oh! He sleeps: "Mind him not."—Come, come—Throw!

SAIB. Here goes—Nine!——Now to you.

MULEY. Nine too!—Double the stake.

SAIB. Agreed! and the throw is mine.—Hark! What noise?—

---

72. A dry white wine imported to England from Southern Europe. 73. A gold coin, more properly the angel-noble; first coined in 1465 by Edward IV, it had an image of the archangel Michael piercing a dragon. The date of this coin conflicts with other references that would seem to place the play ca. 1000.

*During this dialogue, Percy has approached the table in silence; at the moment that he prepares to mount it, Saib looks round, and Percy hastily throws himself back upon the couch.*

MULEY. "Oh!"—Nothing, nothing!

"SAIB. Methought I heard the Earl—

MULEY. "Mere fancy!—You see he is sleeping soundly. Come, come"—Throw!

SAIB. There then—Eleven!

MULEY. That's bad—Huzza!—Sixes!

SAIB. Plague on your fortune!—Come, Double or quits!

MULEY. Be it so, and I throw.—Zounds! Only Five!

SAIB. Then I think this hit must be mine.—Aces, by heavens!

MULEY. Ha! Ha! Ha! Your health, friend!

PERCY. (*Who has again reached the table, mounted the chair, and, opening the window, now stands on it, and signs to the men below.*)—They see me, and extend a cloth beneath the window!—'Tis a fearful height!

SAIB. Do you mean to empty the bottle!—Come, come—Give it me.

MULEY. Take it, blunder-head!—

*Saib drinks.*

PERCY. They encourage me to venture!—Now then, or never!—(*Aloud.*) Angels of bliss,[74] protect me!—(*He throws himself from the window.*)*

MULEY AND SAIB. (*Starting at the noise.*)—Hell and Furies!

SAIB. (*Dashes down the bottle, and climbs to the window hastily, while Muley remains below in an attitude of surprize.*)—Escaped! Escaped!

PERCY, MOTLEY, &C. (*Without.*)—Huzza! huzza! huzza!

### END OF ACT II

*This incident has been cried out against by many people, as being improbable; and some have gone so far as to term it impossible. To this I can only answer, with Alice in the First Act—'I never said it was possible, I only say it's true!'—This incident was furnished me by the German History, in which it appears, that a certain Landgrave of Thuringia, being condemned to death, made his escape by taking so desperate a leap from a window of his prison, that he was afterwards known throughout Germany by the name of 'Ludwig the Springer.'—There is a German Play on this subject, whence I borrowed the idea of making the gaolers play at dice; and Motley's Song bears some resemblance to an incident in Richard Coeur-de-Lion. (Lewis's note) The incident was thought not only improbable but also undignified; it was felt to be beneath Kemble to leap out a window; the *Times* (15 January 1798) felt it made a harlequin of Kemble. Ludwig der Springer (1076–1123), Landgrave of Thuringia, escaped by leaping from his prison onto his horse; the play Lewis refers to would appear to be *Ludwig der Strenge: ein Vaterlandishes Trauerspiel* (1782) by Ludwig Wilhelm von Langenau. Sedaine's *Richard Coeur de Lion* was translated by Leonard MacNally (Covent Garden, 1786) and Lieutenant General John Burgoyne (Drury Lane, 1786).

74. The Larpent version has "saviour of mankind."

# ACT III

SCENE I   *A View of the River Conway, with a Fisherman's Hut.—Sun-set.*

*Enter Allan and Edric.*

ALLAN. Still they come not!—Dear, dear, still they come not!—Ah!
these tumults are too much for my old body to bear.

EDRIC. Then you should have kept your old body at home. 'Tis a fine
thing truly for a man of your age to be galloping about the country after
a girl, who, by your own account, is neither your chick nor child!

ALLAN. Ah! She was more to me! She was my all, Edric, my all!—"How
"could I bear my home when it no longer was the home of Angela? How
"could I rest in my cottage at night when her sweet lips had not kissed
"me—and murmured, 'Father, sleep well!'—She is so good! so gentle!"—
I was sick once, "sick" almost to death! Angela was then my nurse and
comforter: She watched me when I slept, and cheered me when I woke:
She rejoiced when I grew better; and when I grew worse, no medicine
gave me ease like the tears of pity which fell on my burning cheeks from
the eyes of my darling!

EDRIC. Tears of pity indeed! A little rhubarb would have done you more
good by half.—But our people stay a long time: Perhaps Motley has been
discovered and seized; if so, he will lose his life, the Earl his freedom,
Angela her lover, and, what's worst of all, I shall lose my boat! I wish I
hadn't lent it, for I doubt that Motley's scheme has failed.

ALLAN. I hope not—Oh! I hope not!—Should Percy remain a captive,
Angela will be left unprotected in your wicked Lord's power—Oh! that
will break my poor old wife's heart for certain!

EDRIC. And if it should break it, a mighty misfortune truly!—Zounds,[75]
Master Allan, any wife is at best[76] a bad thing; a poor one makes matters
get worse; but when she's old, Lord! 'tis the very devil!

ALLAN. Hark! Hark! Do you hear!—'Tis the sound of oars!—They are
our friends!—Oh! Heaven be thanked! the Earl is with them.

*A boat appears with Percy, Motley, and Soldiers disguised as fishermen. They
land.*

PERCY. (*Springing on shore.*)—Once more then I breathe the air of liberty!—Worthy Gilbert, what words can suffice to thank you?

MOTLEY.   None—therefore do not waste your breath in the attempt. You
are safe, thanks to St. Peter and the Blanket! and your Lady's deliverance
now demands all your thoughts.—Ha! who is that with Edric?

75. An exclamation, an abbreviation of "God's wounds." 76. The Larpent version has
"least."

PERCY. Allan, by all my hopes!—Welcome, welcome, good old man!—
Say, came my vassals with you?

ALLAN. Three hundred chosen men are within the sound of your bugle.
"They scarce gave me time to signify your orders ere they sat in their
"saddles; and as I would needs come with them, Heaven forgive them for
"it! they put me on an hard-trotting horse!—Marry, he shook me rarely!
"he has almost broken my old bones:—But that matters little; my heart
"would have been broken had I staid behind."—But now,[77] my Lord, tell
me of Angela. Is she well? Did you speak to her? and speaks she sometimes of me?

PERCY. She is well, my old friend, and I have spoken to her—though but
for a moment. Scarce had I time to confess to her my rank, when Kenric,
whose suspicious eye had penetrated my disguise, forced me from her
presence.[78] But be comforted, good Allan! Should other means fail, I will
this very night attack the Castle, and compel Osmond to resign his prey.

ALLAN. Heaven grant that you may succeed!—Let me but once see Angela your bride! "Let me but once hear her say the sweet words, 'Allan,
"I am happy!' then I and my old wife will seek our graves, lay us down,
"and die with pleasure!"[79]

MOTL. Die with pleasure, you silly old man! you shall do nothing so ridiculous: You shall live a great many years; and, instead of lying down in
your grave, we'll tuck you up warm with your old wife in the best down-
bed of Alnwic Castle.—But now let us talk of our affairs, which, if I mistake not, are in the high road to success.

PERCY. How? Has any intelligence reached you of your ally, the Friar?

MOTL. You have guessed it. As it passed beneath his window, the pious
porpus[80] contrived to drop this letter into the boat. Its contents must
needs be of consequence; for I assure you it comes from one of the greatest men in England. Pray examine it, my Lord! I never can read when the
wind's easterly.

"PERCY. I believe, Gilbert, were it northerly you would be no jot the
"wiser: I remember that many a sound stick did our preceptor break upon
"your back in vain; and before you had learned to spell, your schooling
"had cost my father a forest.

"MOTL. (*While Percy reads.*) Nay, if learning could have been beaten into
"me, by this time I should be a prodigious scholar!—To do him justice,

---

77. The Larpent version has "But tell me." 78. The Larpent version has "Scarce had I time
to confess to her my rank, and vow to her eternal fidelity, ere Kenric pierced my disguise,
tore me from her in spite of struggling long." 79. The Larpent version has "then I can lay
me down and die with pleasure." 80. For "porpoise." The Larpent version has "father."

"Father Benjamin had a most instructive jirk[81] with his arm, and fre-
"quently used arguments so forcible when pointing out my faults, that
"many a time and oft has he brought tears into my eyes: Then I generally
"felt so penitent, and so low, that I was obliged to steal his brandy-bottle
"in order to recover my spirits.—Well, Sir, what says the letter?"

PERCY. Listen.—'I have recognised you in spite of your disguise, and
seize the opportunity to advise your exerting yourself solely to obtain Earl
Percy's liberty. Heed not Angela: I have sure and easy means for procur-
ing her escape; and before the clock strikes two, you may expect me with
her at the fisherman's hut. Farewell, and rely upon Father Philip.'—Now,
Gilbert, what say you? May the monk's fidelity be trusted?

MOTL. His fidelity may undoubtedly; but whether his success will equal
his good intentions is a point which time alone can decide. Should
it not—

PERCY. Then with my faithful vassals will I storm the Castle to-morrow.

"ALLAN. What, storm the Castle!—Oh! no, no! My darling never saw
"a bird die but she wept; then how will she bear to look on when men
"perish?

PERCY. "Be assured, old man, that nothing save invincible necessity
"shall induce me to bathe my hands in the blood of my fellow-
"creatures.—" But where are my followers.

ALLAN. Fearing lest their numbers should excite suspicion, I left them
concealed in yonder wood.

PERCY. Guide me to them, Edric, "for this night" I must [again] request
the shelter of your hut.

EDRIC. Willingly, my Lord! But my cottage is so humble, your treatment
so wretched—

PERCY. Silence, my good fellow! The hut, where good-will resides, is to
me more welcome than a palace, and no food can be so sweet as that
which is seasoned with smiles—You give me your best; a monarch could
give no more, and it happens not often that men ever give so much.[82]
Now farewell for an hour—Allan, lead on!     (*Exeunt Percy, Allan, &c.*)
*Manent Motley and Edric.*

MOTL. And in the mean-while, friend Edric, I'll lend you an hand in preparing supper.

EDRIC. Truly the task won't give you much trouble, for times have
gone hard with me of late. Our present Lord sees no company, gives no
entertainments, and thus I sell no fish. Things went better while Earl
Reginald lived!

81. Jerk. 82. The Larpent version has "and few Men, Alas!—ever give so much."

MOTL. What! you remember him!

EDRIC. Never shall I forget him, or his sweet Lady! Why, I verily believe, they possessed all the cardinal virtues!—So pious, so generous, so "mild!" so kind to the poor, and so fond of fish!

MOTL. Fond of fish!—One of the cardinal virtues, of which I never heard before!

EDRIC. But these thoughts make me sad. Come, Master Motley; your Lord's supper still swims in the river:—if you'll help to catch it, why do so, and thank you heartily. Can you fish?

MOTL. Can I! Who in this world cannot?—I'll assure you, friend Edric, there is no profession more universal than yours; we all spread our nets to catch something or other—and alas! when obtained, it seldom proves worth the trouble of taking. The Coquette fishes for hearts which are worthless; the Courtier, for titles which are absurd;* and the Poet, for compliments which are empty.—Oh! happy are they in this world of dis-appointments, who throw out no nets save fishing ones.          (*Exeunt*)

SCENE II   *The Castle-Hall.*

*Enter Kenric.*

KENR. Yonder he stalks, and seems buried in himself!—Now then to at-tach him while my late service is still fresh upon his memory. Should he reject my petition positively, he shall have good cause to repent his in-gratitude. Percy is in the neighbourhood; and "that secret, known only to "myself, will surely"—But, silence!—Look where he comes!
*Enter Osmond.*

OSM. It shall not be! Away with these foreboding terrors, which weigh down my heart!—"Does not all smile upon my fortunes? My rival wears "my chains; he cannot wrest her from me, and with to-morrow's dawn "Angela shall be mine. Bound then high, my heart! Pleasure, sweet "guest, so long a stranger, Oh! to my bosom welcome once more!"—I will forget the past, I will enjoy the present, and make those raptures again [be] mine, which—Ah! no, "no," no!—Conscience, that serpent, winds her folds round the cup of my bliss, and, ere my lips can reach it, her venom is mingled with the draught.

---

*On the strength of this single sentence, it was boldly asserted on the morning after the first performance, that the whole Play was written to support the Cause of Equality; and that I said in it, all distinctions of rank ought to be abolished, and thought it extremely wrong for any persons to accept titles! To make the thing complete, the assertors should have added, that I thought it extremely wrong for any persons to pay compliments, or possess hearts! (Lewis's note)

KENR. "How profound the gloom which obscures his brow!—" How fixed, how hopeless glares his dark eye-ball!—Oh! dreadful is the villains's look, when he ponders on committed crimes!

OSM. Evening approaches fast—(*Drawing near and opening the window.*) Already the air breathes cooler, and the beams of the setting sun sparkle on the waters of Conway. How fair, how tranquil all without! How dark, how comfortless all within!—Hark! the sound of music!—The peasants are returning from labour: they move with gay[83] and careless steps, carolling as they go some rustic ditty; and will pass the night in rest, for they have passed the day in innocence!

CHORUS (*Without*)
Pleased the toils of day to leave,
Home we haste with foot-steps light:
Oh! how gay the cotter's[84] eve!
Oh! how calm the cotter's night!

OSM. (*Closing the window with violence.*) Curses upon them—I will look, I will listen no more! I sicken at the sight of happiness, which I never more must enjoy; I hate the possessors of hearts untainted—hate, for I envy!— "Oh! fly from my eyes, bright Day! Speed thy pace, Darkness! thou art "my Love! Haste to unfold thy sable mantle, and robe the world in the "colour of my soul!

"KENR. Now then to accost him—Yet I tremble!

OSM. "Anguish! endless, hopeless anguish!—Day or night, no moment of "rest—When I sleep, dreams of strange horror still fright me from my "couch! When I wake, I find in every object some cause for distrust— "read the dread charge in every eye, 'Thou art a murderer!'—and tremble "lest the agents of my guilt should work its punishment."—And see where he walks, the chief object of my fears![85]—"He shall not be so "long!—His anxiety to leave me, his later mysterious threats—No, no! I "will not live in fear.—Soft!—he advances!"

KENR. So melancholy, my Lord?

OSM. Aye, Kenric, and must be so,[86] till Angela is mine. Know that even now she extorted from me a promise, that till to-morrow I would leave her unmolested.

KENR. But till to-morrow?

OSM. But till to-morrow?—Oh! in that little space a lover's eye views myriads of dangers!—Yet think not, good Kenric, that your late services

---

83. The Larpent version has "light." 84. A peasant who occupies a cottage attached to a farm where he must work. 85. The Larpent version has "Ah! see where advances the chief object of my fears." 86. The Larpent version has "And still must be so Kenrick."

are undervalued by me, or that I have forgotten those for which I have been long your debtor. When, bewildered by hatred of Reginald, and grief for Evelina's loss, my dagger was placed on the throat of their infant, your hand arrested the blow—Judge then how grateful I must feel when I behold in Angela her mother's living counterpart—"behold her such as "when, shielding with her body her fallen husband, Evelina received that "dagger in her breast which I aimed at the heart of Reginald!"—Worthy Kenric, how can I repay your services!

KENR. These you may easily.—"But what, Earl Osmond, what can repay "me for the sacrifice of my innocence?—I was virtuous till you bade me "be guilty—my hands were pure till you taught me to stain them with "blood—you painted in strong colours the shame of servitude—you "promised freedom, riches, independence—you vanquished the resis- "tance of my better Angel, and never since have I known one moment "of rest!

"OSM. Good Kenric—"

KENR. All here reminds me of my guilt—every object recalls to me Reginald and his murdered Lady![87]—Let me then claim that indepen- dence so long promised, and seek for peace in some other climate, since[88] memory forbids me to taste "it" in this.

OSM. Kenric, ere named, your wish was granted. In a far distant country a retreat is already prepared for you: there may you hush those clamours of conscience, which must reach me, I fear, e'en in the arms of Angela.— "Yet do not leave me till she is my bride—Stay yet a week in Conway "Castle; and then, though 'twill cost me many a pang, Kenric, you shall "bid it a long adieu."—Are you contented?

KENR. (*Affected.*) My Lord!—Gratitude—Amazement—And I doubted— I suspected—Oh! my good Lord, how have I wronged your kindness!

OSM. No more—I must not hear you!—(*Aside.*)—Shame! shame! that ever my soul should stoop to dissembling with my slave!—"Kenric, fare- "well!—Till Angela is mine, keep a strict eye on Percy; and then—" *Saib enters, and advances with apprehension.*

OSM. How now?—Why this confusion?—Why do you tremble?—Speak!

SAIB. My Lord!—the prisoner—

OSM. The prisoner?—Go on! go on!

SAIB. (*Kneeling.*) Pardon, my Lord, pardon! Our prisoner has escaped!

OSM. Villain!—

*Wild with rage he draws his dagger, and rushes upon Saib—Kenric holds his arm.*

87. The Larpent version has "wife." 88. The Larpent version has "which."

KENR. Hold! hold!—What would you do?

OSM. (*Struggling.*) Unhand me, or by Heaven—

KENR. Away! away!—Fly fellow, fly and save yourself!          (*Exit Saib*)

KENR. (*Releasing Osmond.*) Consider, my Lord—haply[89] 'twas not by his keeper's fault that—

OSM. (*Furiously.*) What is't to me by whose?—Is not my rival fled?—Soon will Northumberland's guards encircle my walls, and force from me—Yet that by Heaven they shall not! No! Rather then resign her, my own hand shall give this Castle a prey to flames: then plunging with Angela into the blazing gulph, I'll leave this ruins to tell posterity how desperate was my love, and how dreadful my revenge!—(*Going, he stops, and turns to Kenric.*)—And you, who dared to rush between me and my resentment—you who could so well succeed in saving others—now look to yourself!                                                      (*Exit*)

KENR. Ha! that look—that threat—Yet he seemed so kind, so grateful!—He smiled too!—Oh! there is ever danger when a villain smiles.

*Saib enters softly, looking round him with caution.*

SAIB. (*In a low voice.*) Hist!—Kenric!

KENR. How now?—What brings—

SAIB. Silence, and hear me!—[a good action ever meets with its [reward]—You have saved my life, nor will I be ungrateful—Look at this phial!

KENR. Ha! did the Earl—

SAIB. Even so: a few drops of this liquor should to-night have flavoured your wine—you would never have drank again! Mark me then—When I offer you a goblet at supper, drop it as by accident. For this night I give you life: use it to quit the Castle; for no longer than till to-morrow dare I disobey our Lord's commands. Farewell, and fly from Conway—You bear with you my thanks!                                                      (*Exit*)

KENR. Can it be possible? Is not all this a dream?—Villain! villain!—Yes, yes, I must away!—But tremble, traitor!—"A bolt, of which you little "think, hangs over, and shall crush you!"—The keys are still in my possession—Angela shall be the partner of my flight.—My prisoner too—Yet hold! May not resentment—may not Reginald's sixteen years captivity—Oh! no! Angela shall be my advocate; and, grateful for her own, for her parent's life preserved, she can, she will obtain my pardon—Yet, should she fail, at least I shall drag down Osmond in my fall, and sweeten death's bitter cup with vengeance!                                    (*Exit*)

89. By chance.

SCENE III  *The Cedar-room, with folding Doors in the middle, and a large an-*
*tique Bed; on one Side is the Portrait of a Lady, on the other that of a Warrior*
*armed. Both are at full length.—After a pause the Female Portrait slides back and*
*Father Philip, after looking in, advances cautiously.*

F. PHIL. (*Closing the pannel.*) Thus far I have proceeded without danger,
though not without difficulty. Yon narrow passage is by no means calculated for persons of my habit of body. By my Holidame,[90] I begin to suspect that the fool is in the right! I certainly am growing corpulent.—And
now, how shall I employ myself?—Sinner that I am, why did I forget the
bottle of sack?—The time will pass tediously till Angela comes.—And, to
complete the business, yonder is the haunted Oratory. What if the ghost
should pop out on me?[91] Blessed St. Bridget, there would be a tête-à-
tête!—Yet this is a foolish fear:—'Tis yet scarce eight o'clock, and your
ghosts always keep late hours; yet I don't like the idea of our being such
near neighbours. If Alice says true, the apparition just now lives next
door to me; but the Lord forbid that we should ever be visiting acquain-
tance!—Would I had something to drive her out of my head! A good book
now, or a bottle of sack, St. Augustine, or a cold venison pasty, would be
worth its weight in gold: but in the chambers of these young girls one
finds nothing good either to read, drink, or eat. Now my last patroness,
the Baroness O'Drench—Ah! to hear the catalogue of her crimes was
quite a pleasure, for she always confessed them over a sir-loin of beef,
and, instead of telling a bead, swallowed a bumper!—Oh! she was a worthy soul!—But hark!—Angela comes.
OSM. (*Without.*) What, Alice!—Alice, I say!
F. PHIL. By St. David, 'tis the Earl! I'll away as fast as I can!—(*Trying to*
*open the door.*)—I can't find the spring!—Lord forgive me my sins!—
Where can I hide myself!—Ha! the bed!—'Tis the very thing.—(*Throws*
*himself into the bed, and conceals himself under the clothes.*)—Heaven grant that
it mayn't break down with me; for, Oh! what a fall would be there, my
countrymen!—They come!—
*The door is unlocked. Enter Osmond, Angela, and Alice.*
OSM. (*Entering.*) You have heard my will, Lady. Till your hand is mine,
you quit not this chamber.

90. A variant of "halidome," created, apparently, in keeping with the popular etymology
that would derive the word from a plea to Mary; the word means a holy thing or relic used
in oaths. 91. From this point on, this speech is marked for deletion, presumably by the
examiner. Genest wrote of this speech, "how any person not destitute of sense could write
such stuff, is wonderful—but where a Friar was concerned, Lewis' mind was strangely
warped" (VII:333).

ANG. If then it must be so, welcome my eternal prison!—Yet eternal it shall not be!—My hero, "my guardian-angel" is at liberty! Soon shall his horn make these hateful towers tremble, and your fetters be exchanged for the arms of Percy!

OSM. Beware, beware, Angela!—Dare not before me—

ANG. Before you! before the world!—Is my attachment a disgrace? No! 'tis my pride; for its object is deserving. Long ere I knew him, Percy's fame was dear to me. While I still believed him the peasant Edwy, often, in his hearing, have I dwelt upon Northumberland's praise, and chid him that he spoke of our Lord so coldly! "Ah! little did I think that the man "then seated beside me was he whom I envied for his power of doing "good, whom I loved for exerting that power so largely!"—Judge then, Earl Osmond, on my arrival here how strongly I must have felt the contrast!—What person names you his benefactor? What beggar has been comforted by your bounty? what sick man preserved by your care?—Your breast is unmoved by woe, "your ear is deaf to complaint," your doors are barred against the poor and wretched. Not so are the gates of Alnwic Castle; they are open as their owner's heart.

ALICE. My hair stands on end to hear her!

"OSM. Insulting girl!—This to my face?

"ANG. Nay, never bend your brows!—Shall I tremble, because you "frown? Shall my eye sink, because anger flashes from yours?—No! that "would ill become the bride of Northumberland."

OSM. Amazement!—Can this be the gentle, timid Angela?

ANG. Wonder you that the worm should turn when you trample it so cruelly!—Oh! wonder no more: Ere he was torn from me, I clasped Percy to my breast, and my heart caught a spark of that fire which flames in his unceasingly!

ALICE. Caught fire, Lady!—"Bless me, I hope you didn't burn your-"self?"

OSM. Silence, old crone!—I have heard you calmly, Angela; now then hear me. Twelve hours shall be allowed you to reflect upon your situation: till that period is elapsed, this chamber shall be your prison, and Alice, on whose fidelity I can depend, your sole attendant. This term expired, should you still reject my hand, force shall obtain for me what love denies. Speak not: I will hear nothing!—I swear that to-morrow sees you mine, or undone![92] "and, Skies, rain curses on me if I keep not my oath!"—Mark that, proud girl! "mark it," and tremble!                              (*Exit*)

F. PHIL. Heaven be praised, he's gone!

92. The Larpent version has "Tomorrow either sees you my Bride or my Prostitute."

ANG. Tremble, did he say?—Alas! how quickly is my boasted courage vanished!—Yet I will not despair: there is a Power[93] in heaven, there is a Percy on earth; on them will I rely to save me.

ALICE. The first may, Lady; but as to the second, he'll be of no use, depend on't. Now might I advise, you'd accept my Lord's offer: "What "matters it whether the man's name be Osmond or Percy?" An Earl's an Earl after all; and though one may be something richer than t'other—

ANG. Oh! silence, Alice!—nor aid my tyrant's designs: rather "instruct "me how to counteract them. You have influence in the Castle;" assist me to escape, and be assured that Percy's gratitude and generosity—

ALICE. I help you to escape! Not for the best gown in your Ladyship's wardrobe! I tremble at the very idea of my Lord's rage; and, besides, had I the will, I've not the power. Kenric keeps the keys; we could not possibly quit the Castle without his knowledge; and if the Earl threatens to use force with you—Oh Gemini! what would he use with me, Lady?

ANG. Threatens, Alice!—I despise his threats! Ere it pillows Osmond's head will I plunge this poniard in my bosom.

ALICE. Holy fathers!—A dagger!

ANG. Even now, as I wandered through the Armoury, my eye was attracted by its glittering handle.—Look, Alice! it bears Osmond's name; and the point—

ALICE. Is rusty with blood!—Take it away, Lady!—Take it away!—I never see blood without fainting!

ANG. (*Putting up the dagger.*) This weapon may render me good service.—But, ah! what service has it rendered Osmond!—Haply 'twas this very poniard which drank his brother's blood—or which pierced the fair breast of Evelina!—Said you not, Alice, that this was her portrait?

ALICE. I did, Lady; and the likeness was counted excellent.

ANG. How fair!—How heavenly!—"What sweetness, yet what dignity, "in her blue, speaking eyes!"

ALICE. No wonder that you admire her, Lady; she was as like you [in ev-[erything, save height][94] as one pea to another. But this morning you know I promised to show you her Oratory, and here I've brought the key.—Shall I unlock the door?

ANG. Do so, good Alice!—Haply for a moment it may abstract my thoughts from my own sorrows.

*Alice unlocks the door and discovers the Oratory.*

F. PHIL. (*While Alice unlocks the door.*) Will the old woman never be gone?—"I dare not discover myself in her presence."

---

93. The Larpent version has "God."  94. This detail is added in the Larpent acting version, perhaps to signal an actual difference between the two actresses involved.

ALICE. (*Having opened the folding doors, an Oratory is seen, richly ornamented with carving and painted glass: Angela and Alice enter it.*) This room has not been opened since my Lady's death, and every thing remains as she left it. Look, here is her veil—her prayer-book too, in which she was reading on the very night before she quitted the Castle, never to return!

"F. PHIL. I'm out of all patience.

"ALICE. And that guitar!—How often have I heard her play upon that "guitar! She would sit in yonder window for hours, and still she played "airs so sad, so sweet—To be sure, she had the finest voice that ever—

"*During this speech Angela, who at first looks round with curiosity, throws the "veil carelessly over her face, and, taking the guitar from the table, strikes a few "wild and melancholy notes. Alice, whose back is towards her, turns hastily round, "screams, and rushes from the Oratory. Angela casts the veil and guitar upon the "table, and follows her.*

"ANG. What alarms you?

"ALICE. Is it you, Lady? Let me die, if I didn't take you for the ghost!— "Your air, your look, your attitude, all were so like the deceased Countess, "that—Well, well! I'll not enter that room again in an hurry! I protest, my "hand trembles so, that I can hardly turn the key!

"ANG. How contagious is terror! This silly woman's apprehensions have "spread to my bosom, and scarce can I look round without alarm. The "stillness too of evening—The wavering and mysterious light which "streams through these painted windows—And, hark! 'Twas the shriek of "the screech-owl, which nests in the tower above!"

ALICE. (*Having locked the folding doors.*) Ah! 'twas a sad day for me, when I heard of the dear Lady's loss! Look at that bed, Lady:—That very bed was hers.[95]

"F. PHIL. Was it so? Oh! ho!

ALICE. "How often have I seen her sleeping in that bed—and, oh! how "like an angel she looked when sleeping!" I remember, that just after Earl Reginald—Oh! Lord! didn't somebody shake the curtain?

ANG. Absurd! It was the wind.

ALICE. I declare it made me tremble! Well, as I was saying, I remember, "just after Earl Reginald had set out for the Scottish wars," going into her room one morning, and hearing her sob most bitterly.—So advancing to the bed-side, as it might be thus—'My Lady!' says I, with a low curtsey, 'Isn't your Ladyship well!'—So, with that, she raised her head slowly above the quilt, and, giving me a mournful look—

95. The Larpent version has "In that very Bed was she delivered of the young Lady Julia."

*Here, unseen by Angela, who is contemplating Reginald's portrait, Father Philip lifts up his head, and gives a deep groan.*

ALICE. Jesu Maria! the devil! the devil! the devil!* *(Exit)*

ANG. *(Turning round.)* How now? *(Father Philip rising from the bed—it breaks under him, and he rolls at Angela's feet.)*—Good heavens! a man concealed!— *(Attempting to pass him, he detains her by her robe.)*

F. PHIL. Stay, daughter, stay! If you run, I can never overtake you!

ANG. Amazement! Father Philip!

F. PHIL. The very same, and at present the best friend that you have in the world. Daughter, I came to save you.

ANG. To save me? Speak! Proceed!

F. PHIL. Observe this picture; it conceals a spring, whose secret is unknown to all in the Castle except myself. Upon touching it, the pannel slides back, and a winding passage opens into the marble hall. Thence we must proceed to the vaulted vestibule; a door is there concealed, similar to this; and, after threading the mazes of a subterranean labyrinth, we shall find ourselves in safety on the outside of the Castle-walls.

ANG. Oh! worthy, "worthy" Father! quick let us hasten! Let us not lose one moment!

F. PHIL. Hold! hold! Not so fast. You forget, that between the hall and vestibule we must traverse many chambers much frequented at this early hour. "Wait till the Castle's inhabitants are asleep." Expect me, without fail, at one; keep up your spirits, and doubt not of success. Now then I must away, lest the Earl should perceive my absence.[96]

ANG. Stay yet one moment. Tell me, does Percy—

F. PHIL. I have apprised him, that this night will restore you to liberty, and he expects you at the fisherman's cottage. Now, then, farewell, fair daughter.

ANG. Good Friar, till one, farewell!

*(Exit Father Philip through the sliding pannel, closing it after him.)*

ANG. "This is thy doing, God of Justice! Receive my thanks."[97]—Yes, Percy, we shall meet once more—shall meet never again to separate! "Those dreams shall be realized—those smiling golden dreams which "floated before us in Allan's happy cottage. Hand in hand shall we wan- "der together through life—partners in pleasure—partners in woe—and

---

*This incident is borrowed from "The Mysteries of Udolpho," but employed very differently. In the Romance it brings forward a terrific scene. In the Play it is intended to produce an effect entirely ludicrous. (Lewis's note)

96. The Larpent version has: "But I must away, lest the Earl should perceive my absence. And expect me without fail at one, keep up your spirits, and doubt not of success." 97. The Larpent version has "How impatiently shall I wait his return!"

"when the night of our existence arrives, one spot shall receive our bod-
"ies—one stone shall cover our grave.—Allan too, and the worthy
"Maud!—my parents—my more than parents!—to smooth the pillow of
"their age—to gild their last hours with sun-shine!" That thought is
heaven. So glorious are my prospects, that they dazzle me to look on, and
scarce can I believe them really to exist.—Oh! gracious God![98] should
my brain be bewildered by fancy—should I be now the sport of some
deceitful dream, seal up my eyes for ever, never let me wake again!—"I
"must not expect the Friar before one.—Till that hour arrives, will I kneel
"at the feet of yonder Saint, there tell my beads, and pray for morning!"[99]

**END OF ACT III**

## ACT IV

SCENE I  *The Castle-Hall: The Lamps are lighted.*

*Enter Father Philip.*

F. PHIL. 'Tis near midnight, and the Earl is already retired to rest. What
if I ventured now to the Lady's chamber? Hark! I hear the sound of footsteps!

*Enter Alice.*

F. PHIL. How, Alice, is it you?

ALICE. "So! So!"—Have I found you at last Father?—[Why] I have been
in search of you these four hours!—Oh! I've been so frightened since I
saw you, that I wonder I keep my senses!

F. PHIL. So do I; for I'm sure they're not worth the trouble. And, pray,
what has alarmed you thus? I warrant you've taken an old cloak pinned
against the wall for a spectre, or discovered the devil in the shape of a
tabby-cat.

ALICE. (*Looking round in terror.*) For the love of Heaven, Father, don't name
the devil! or, if you must speak of him, pray mention the good gentleman
with proper politeness. I'm sure, for my own part, I had always a great
respect for him, and if he hears me, I dare say he'll own as much.

F. PHIL. Respect for the devil, you wicked woman!—for that perfidious
serpent—that crafty seducer—

ALICE. Hush!—Hush!—Father, you make my teeth chatter with fright.
For aught I know he's within hearing, for he certainly haunts this Castle
in the form of my "late" Lady.

98. The Larpent version has "heaven." 99. The Larpent version does not have her pray;
instead she "throws herself on sopha."

F. PHIL. Form of a fiddlestick!—Don't tell me of your—

ALICE. Father, on the word of a virgin, I saw him this very evening in Lady Angela's bed!

F. PHIL. In Lady Angela's—On my conscience, the devil has an excellent taste! But, Alice!—"Alice!"—how dare you trot about the house at this time of night, propagating such abominable falsehoods?—One comfort is, that nobody will believe you. Lady Angela's virtue is too well known, and I'm persuaded she wouldn't suffer the devil to put a single claw into her bed for the universe!

ALICE. How you run on!—Lord bless me, she wasn't in bed herself.

F. PHIL. Oh!—Was she not?

ALICE. No, to be sure: But you shall hear how it happened. We were in the Cedar-room together; and while we were talking of this and that, Lady Angela suddenly gave a great scream. I looked round, and what should I see but a tall figure all in white extended upon the bed! At the same time I heard a voice, which I knew to be the Countess Evelina's, pronounce in a hollow tone—'Alice!—Alice!—Alice!'—three times. You may be certain that I was frightened enough. I instantly took to my heels; and just as I got without side of the door, I heard a loud clap of thunder, and the whole chamber shook as if tumbling into a thousand pieces!

F. PHIL. Well done, Alice!—A very good story, upon my word: It has but one fault—'Tis not true.

ALICE. Ods[100] my life, Father, how can you tell any thing about it? Sure I should know best; for I was there, and you were not. "I repeat it"—I heard the voice as plain as I hear yours: Do you think I've no ears?

F. PHIL. Oh! far from it: I think you've uncommonly good ones; for you not only hear what has been said, but what has not. Hark!—the clock strikes twelve:—'Tis late, and I'm sleepy, so shall bid you farewell for the present. As to this wonderful story of yours, Alice, I don't believe one word of it: I'll be sworn "that the voice was no more like your Lady's "than like mine; and" that the devil was no more in the bed than I was. Therefore, take my advice, set your heart at rest, and go quietly to your chamber, as I am now going to mine.—Good-night.

ALICE. Good-night?—Surely you'll not have the heart to leave me in this terrible situation!—Suppose Satan should appear to me when I'm alone!—Sinner that I am, I should certainly die of the fright!—"Good Fa-"ther, you are a priest, and an holy man; your habit frightens the evil spir-"its, and they dare not come near you:"—Oh! if you will but suffer me to pass the night in your company—[101]

100. For "God's," an oath as in "Ods bodkin." 101. The Larpent version has "chamber."

F. PHIL. Oh! monstrous!—Oh! impudence unparalleled!—You naughty, naughty woman, what could put such thoughts in your head?

ALICE. What's the matter now?

F. PHIL. Does not my sacred habit inspire you with awe?—Does not the exemplary chastity of my past life warn you to conceal such licentious desires?—Pass the night with me[102] indeed?—I'm shocked at the very thought!

ALICE. "The man's mad!"—Father, as I hope to be saved—

F. PHIL. Nay!—Come not near me!—Offer not to embrace me!

ALICE. I embrace you!—Lord! Fellow, I wouldn't touch you for the universe.[103]

F. PHIL. Was it for this that you still flattered my person, and declared that nothing became a man more than a big belly?—Was it for this that you strove to win my heart through the medium of my stomach; that you used to come languishing every day with some liquorish dish; and, while you squeezed my left-hand tenderly, placed a sack-posset[104] in the right?—Heavens! how deep-laid were your plans of seduction!—But mark me, tempter: "In vain has the soup been salted, the ragout "seasoned, and the pepper-box shaken with unsparing hand!" My virtue is proof against all your culinary spells; the fairness of my innocence[105] is still unblemished; and in spite of your luscious stews and savoury hashes, I retire like a second St. Anthony, victorious from Temptation's lists![106]                    (*Exit*)

ALICE. There, he's gone!—Dear heart! "Dear heart!" what shall I do now?—'Tis past twelve o'clock, and stay by myself I dare not. [Who [knows but the Devil may find me out, rush into my Chamber when I'm [alone, and—mercy on me what must be done.]—I'll e'en wake the laundry-maid, make her sit up in my room all night; and 'tis hard if two women a'n't a match for the best devil in Christendom.[107]       (*Exit*)

*Enter Saib and Hassan.*

SAIB. The Earl then has forgiven me!—A moment longer, and his pardon would have come too late. Had not Kenric held his hand, by this time I should be at supper with St. Peter.

HASS. Your folly well deserved such a reward. Knowing the Earl's hasty nature, you should have shunned him till the first storm of passion was

---

102. The Larpent version has "in my chambers." 103. The Larpent version has "I wouldn't touch you with a pair of tongs." 104. A posset is a drink composed of milk curdled with ale, wine, or other liquor, often with sugar or spices; here made with sack, a white wine. 105. The Larpent version has "chastity." 106. Saint Anthony (ca. 250–350) was an Egyptian monk and a founder of Christian monasticism; he is renowned for his temptations in the desert. 107. The Larpent version has "for the Devil himself."

past,[108] and circumstances had again made your ministry needful. "An-"ger then would have armed his hand in vain;" for interest, the white-man's God,[109] would have blunted the point of his dagger.

SAIB. I trusted that his gratitude for my past services—

HASS. European gratitude?—Seek constancy in the winds—fire in ice—darkness in the blaze of sun-shine!—But seek not gratitude in the breast of an European!

SAIB. Then, why so attached to Osmond? For what do you value him?

HASS. Not for his virtues, but for his vices, Saib: Can there for me be a great cause to love him?—Am I not branded with scorn?—Am I not marked out for dishonour?—Was I not free, and am I not a slave?—Was I not once beloved, and am I not now despised?—What man, did I tender my service, would accept the negro's friendship?—What woman, did I talk of affection, would not turn from the negro with disgust?—Yet, in my own dear land, my friendship was courted, my love was returned.—I had parents, children, wife!—"Bitter thought—in one moment all were "lost to me!"—Can I remember this, and not hate these white men?— "Can I think how cruelly they have wronged me, and not rejoice when "I see them suffer?"—Attached to Osmond, say you? Saib, I hate him! Yet viewing him as an avenging Fiend sent hither to torment his fellows, it glads me that he fills his office so well! Oh! 'tis a thought which I would not barter for empires, to know that in this world he makes others suffer, and will suffer himself for their tortures in the next!

SAIB. But say, you be one of those whom he causes to suffer, how then?—Hassan, I will sleep no more in the Lion's den!—My resolve is taken—I will away from the Castle, and seek in some other service that security—[110]

OSM. (*Within.*)—What—Hoa—Help!—Lights there!—Lights!—

HASS. Hark!—Surely 'twas the Earl!

*Osmond rushes in wildly.*

OSM. Save me! Save me!—They are at hand!—Oh! let them not enter!— (*Sinks into the arms of Saib.*)

SAIB. What can this mean?—See how his eyes roll!—"How violently he "trembles!"

HASS. Speak, my lord!—Do you not know us?

OSM. (*Recovering himself.*)—Ha! Whose voice?—Hassan's—And Saib too here?—Oh! Was it then but a dream?—Did I not hear those dreadful, those damning words?—Still, still they ring in my ears. [Oh!] Hassan!

---

108. The Larpent version has "over." 109. The Larpent version has "the Christian's God"; this entire passage, to Saib's speech before Osmond's entrance, is marked for deletion, presumably by the examiner. 110. The Larpent version has "tranquility."

Hassan! Death must be bliss, in flames or on the rack, compared to what I have this night suffered!

HASS. Compose yourself, my Lord: Can a mere dream unman you thus?

OSM. A mere dream, say'st thou? Hassan, 'twas a dream of such horror! "Did such dreams haunt my bitterest foe, I should wish him no severer "punishment." Mark you not, how the ague of fear still makes my limbs tremble? Rolls not my eye, as if still gazing on the Spectre? Are not my lips convulsed, as were they yet prest by the kiss of corruption? "Oh! " 'twas a sight, that might have bleached joy's rosy cheek for ever, and "strowed the snows of age upon youth's auburn ringlets!" Yet, away with these terrors!—Hassan, thou saidst, 'twas but a dream: I was deceived by fancy. Hassan, thou saidst true; there is not, there cannot be, a world to come.

HASS. My Lord!—

OSM. Answer me not!—Let me not hear the damning truth!—"Tell "me not, that flames await me!—that for moments of bliss I must endure "long ages of torture!"—Plunge me rather in the thickest gloom of Atheism!'''—"Say, that with my body must perish my soul!"—For, oh! should my fearful dream be prophetic!—Hark, fellows!—"Instruments of "my guilt, listen to my punishment!"—Methought I wandered through the low-browed caverns, where repose the reliques of my ancestors!— "My eye dwelt with awe on their tombs, with disgust on Mortality's sur- "rounding emblems!"—Suddenly a female form glided along the vault: It was Angela!—She smiled upon me, and beckoned me to advance. I flew towards her; my arms were already unclosed to clasp her—when suddenly her figure changed, her face grew pale, a stream of blood gushed from her bosom!—Hassan, 'twas Evelina!

SAIB AND HASS. Evelina!

OSM. Such as when she sank at my feet expiring, while my hand grasped the dagger still crimsoned with her blood!—'We meet again this night!' murmured her hollow voice! 'Now rush to my arms, but first see''' what you have made me!—Embrace me, my bridegroom! We must never part again!'—While speaking, her form withered away: the flesh fell from her bones; her eyes burst from their sockets: a skeleton, loathsome and meagre, clasped me in her mouldering arms!—

SAIB. Most horrible!

OSM. Her infected breath was mingled with mine; her rotting fingers pressed my hand, and my face was covered with her kisses!—"Oh! then,

111. The *Monthly Mirror* (December 1797) objected to "The *dream of Osmond*, his *Atheism*" as part of the play's suspicious "German" tendencies. 112. The Larpent version has "behold."

"then how I trembled with disgust!"—And now blue dismal flames gleamed along the walls; "the tombs were rent asunder;" bands of fierce spectres rushed round me in frantic dance!—Furiously they gnashed their teeth while they gazed upon me, and shrieked in loud yell—'Welcome, thou fratricide!—Welcome, thou lost for ever!'—Horror burst the bands of sleep; distracted I flew hither:—But my feelings—words are too weak, too powerless to express them.

SAIB. My Lord, my Lord, this was no idle dream!—" 'Twas a celestial "warning;"—'twas your better Angel that whispered—'Osmond, repent your former crimes!—Commit not new ones!'—Remember, that this night should Kenric—

OSM. Kenric?—Oh! speak! Drank he the poison?

SAIB. Obedient to your orders, I presented it at supper; but ere the cup reached his lips, his favourite dog sprang upon his arm, and the liquor fell to the ground untasted.

OSM. Praised be Heaven!—Then my soul is lighter by a crime!—Kenric shall live, good Saib. What though he quit me, and betray my secrets? Proofs he cannot bring against me, and bare assertions will not be believed. At worst, should his tale be credited, long ere Percy can wrest her from me, shall Angela be mine. "Angela!—Oh! At that name all again is "calm in my bosom. Hushed by her image my tumultuous passions sink "to rest, and my terrors subside into that single fear, her loss!—I forget "that I have waded to her arms through blood; forget all save my affection "and her beauty!

"SAIB. You forget too that her heart is another's? Oh! my Lord, reflect "on your conduct while it is yet time; restore the poor Angela to liberty; "resign her to her favoured lover—

OSM. "Sooner will I resign my life!—Fellow, you know not what you say: "My heart strings are twisted round the maid; ere I resign her, those "strings must break." If I exist to-morrow night, I will pass it in her arms—If I exist?—Ha! Whence the doubt? 'We meet again this night!'— So said the Spectre!—Dreadful words, be ye blotted from my mind for ever.—Hassan, to your vigilance I leave the care of my beloved. Fly to me that instant, should any unbidden foot-step approach yon chamber-door. I'll to my couch again. Follow me, Saib, and watch me while I sleep. Then, if you see my limbs convulsed, my teeth clenched, "my hair bris- "tling," and cold dews trembling on my brow, seize me!—Rouse me!— Snatch me from my bed!—I must not dream again.—Oh! faithless Sleep, why are thou too leagued with my foes? There was a time, "when thy "presence brought oblivion to my sorrows;" when thy poppy-crown was mingled with roses!—Now, Fear and Remorse thy sad companions, I shudder to see[113] thee approach my couch!—Blood trickles from thy garments; "snakes writhe around thy brows:" thy hand holds the well-known fatal dagger, and plunges it still reeking in my breast!—Then do I shriek in agony; then do I start distracted from thy arms!—Oh! how I hate thee, Sleep!—Friend of Virtue, oh! how I dread thy coming!*

(*Exit with Saib*)

HASS.[114] (*Alone.*)—Yes, thou art sweet, Vengeance!—"Oh! how it joys "me when the white man suffers!"[115]—Yet weak are his pangs, compared to those I felt when torn from thy shores, O native Africa![116]—from thy bosom, my faithful Samba!—Ah! dost thou still exist, my wife?—"Has "sorrow for my loss traced thy smooth brow with wrinkles!"—My boy too, whom on that morning when the man-hunters seized me, I left sleeping on thy bosom, say, Lives he yet?—"Does he ever speak of me?—Does "he ask, 'Mother, describe to me my father; show me how the warrior "looked?' "**—Ha! has my bosom still room for thoughts so tender? Hence with them! Vengeance must possess it all!—"Oh! when I forget "my wrongs, may I forget myself!—When I forbear to hate these Chris-"tians, God of my fathers! mayst thou hate me!"—Ha! Whence that light? A man moves this way with a lamp!—How cautiously he steals along!—He must be watched. This friendly column will shield me from his regards. Silence! He comes. (*Retires.*)

*Kenric enters softly with a Lamp.*

KENR. All is hushed!—The Castle seems buried in sleep.—Now then to Angela!

(*Exit.*)

HASS. (*Advancing.*)—It was Kenric!—Still he moves onwards—Now he stops—'Tis at the door of Angela's chamber!—He unlocks it!—He enters!—Away then to the Earl; Christian, soon shall we meet again!

(*Exit*)

---

*This scene will doubtless have reminded the Reader of *Clarence's Dream, Richard's Dream,* &c.: But it bears a much closer resemblance to the *Dream of Francis* in *Schiller's Robbers,* which, in my opinion, is surpassed by no vision ever related upon the Stage. Were I asked to produce an instance of the terrific and sublime, I should name the Parricide's confession—"*Ich kannte den Mann!*" (Lewis's note) Lewis refers to *Richard III* (I, iv; V, iii) and *The Robbers* (V, i); the German phrase means, "I knew that man," and it comes in Frantz's dream when he recognizes the father he has killed.

**I suspect this idea to be the property of some other person, but what other person I know not. It is much at the service of any one who may think it worth claiming. (Lewis's note) 113. The Larpent version has "trembling I see." 114. In the Larpent version, this speech is marked for deletion, presumably by the examiner. 115. The Larpent version has "He suffers." 116. The Larpent version has "Senegal."

SCENE II   *Angela's Apartment.*

*Angela stands by the Window, which is open, and through which the Moon is seen.*

ANGELA. Will it never arrive, this tedious lingering hour? Sure an age must have elapsed since the Friar left me, and still[117] the bell strikes not one!—"Percy, does thy impatience equal mine? Dost thou too count the "moments which divide us?—Dost thou too chide the slowness of Time's "pinions, which moved so swiftly when we strayed together on the Chev- "iot Hills?—Methinks I see him now, as he paces the Conway's margin: If "a leaf falls, if a bird flutters, he flies towards it, for he thinks 'tis the "foot-step of Angela: Then, with slow steps and bending head, disap- "pointed he regains the fisher's cottage. Perhaps, at this moment, his eyes "like mine are fixed on yonder planet; perhaps, this sweet wind which "plays on my cheek, is freighted with the sighs of my Lover.—Oh! sigh "no more, my Percy!—Soon shall I repose in safety on your bosom; soon "again see the moon shed her silver light on Cheviot, and hear its green "hills repeat the carol of your mellow horn!"[118]

SONG

How slow the lingering moments wear!
  Ye hours, in pity speed your flight,
Till Cheviot's hills so fresh and fair
  Again shall meet my longing sight!
Oh! then what rapture 'twill afford
  Once more those scenes beloved to see,
Where Percy's heart first told its Lord,
  He loved the Lass of low degree!

No founding titles graced my name,
  No bounteous kinsmen swelled my dower;
But Percy sought no high-born Dame,
  But Percy sought not wealth or power.
He sought a fond, a faithful heart,
  He found the heart he sought in me;
He saw her pure and free from art,
  And loved the Lass of low degree.*

---

117. The Larpent version has "yet." 118. The Larpent version has "Oh! how my heart longs to see the Moon shed once more her silver light on Cheviot, and hear its green hills repeat the carol of Percy's horn."
*Owing to the great exertions which her character demanded, Mrs. Jordan omitted this Song. (Lewis's note)
The Larpent version includes a different song:

"The Castle seems to be still already:—Would the Friar had named an "earlier hour!—By this I might have been safe in the fisher's cot-"tage."[119]—Hark!—Surely I heard—Some one unlocks the door!—Oh! should it be the Earl!—"Should he not retire ere the Monk arrives!"— The door opens!—How!—Kenric here!—Speak—What would you? *Enter Kenric.*

KENR. Softly, Lady! [Speak softly]—If over-heard, I am lost, and your fate is connected with mine—(*Placing his lamp on the table.*)

ANG. What means this mystery?—This midnight visit—

KENR. [It] is the visit of a Friend, of a Penitent!—Lady, I must away from the Castle:—The keys are in my possession:—I will make you the com- panion of my flight, and deliver you safe into the hands of Percy.—But, ere we depart—(*Kneeling.*)—Oh! tell me, Lady, will you plead for me with one, who to me alone owes sixteen years of hard captivity?

ANG. Rise, Kenric—I understand you not.—Of what captive do you speak?

KENR. Of one, "who by me has been most injured"—who to you will be most dear!—Listen, Lady, to my strange narration.—"I was brought up "with Osmond"[120]—"was" the partner of his pleasures—the confident of his cares. The latter sprang solely from his elder brother, whose birth- right he coveted, whose superiority he envied. Yet his aversion burst not forth, till Evelina Neville, rejecting his hand, bestowed hers with her heart on Reginald.—Then did Osmond's passion over-leap all bounds. He resolved to assassinate[121] his brother "when returning form the Scot- "tish wars", carry off the Lady, and make himself master of her person by force.—This scheme he imparted to me: he flattered, threatened, prom- ised, and I yielded to his seduction!

> Oh, sad was my bosom, by force, when removed
> From all those who loved me, from all whom I loved;
> With heart near to breaking, despair in my look,
> The groves, where my Childhood was passed, I forsook,
> And said, while I sighed that my pleasures were o'er,
> —'Adieu, ye dear Scenes, I must see ye no more!'
>
> But vain were the fears, which my Bosom dismay'd;
> His purple wings flying, Love flies to my aid:
> He soothes me, he cheers me, he loosens my chains
> And he bids me return to my lov'd native plains.
> Then be hush'd my fond heart for thy Sorrows are o'er,
> And Pleasure shall soon be thy inmate once more!

119. The Larpent version has "I must not expect the Friar till one." 120. The Larpent ver- sion has "I was Osmond's friend." 121. The Larpent version has "murder."

ANG. Wretched man!

KENR. Condemn me not unheard. 'Tis true, that [with a Band of hired [ruffians] I followed Osmond to the scene of slaughter, but no blood that day imbrued my hand. It was the Earl whose sword struck Reginald to the ground: it was the Earl whose dagger was raised to complete his crime, when Evelina threw herself upon her husband's body, and received the weapon in her own.

ANG. Dreadful! Dreadful!

KENR. "His hopes disappointed by this accident," Osmond's wrath [now] became madness. He gave the word for slaughter, and Reginald's few attendants were butchered on the spot. Scarce could my prayers and arguments save from his wrath his infant niece, whose throat was already gored by his poniard. Angela,[122] yours still wears that mark.

ANG. Mine?—Almighty powers!

KENR. "Lady, 'tis true." I concealed in Allan's cottage the heiress of Conway: "There were you doomed to languish in obscurity, till, alarmed by "the report of his spies that Percy loved you, and dreading your meeting "with so powerful a supporter, Osmond decreed your death a second "time. With this intention he sought your retreat; but when in you he be- "held Evelina's living image, he changed his bloody purpose. He caused "me to reclaim you from Allan, and resolved, by making you his wife, to "give himself a lawful claim to these possessions."[123]

ANG. The monster! "Now then I know, when he pressed my hand, why "still my blood ran cold! 'Twas nature, that revolted at the fratricide's "touch: 'Twas my mother's spirit, that whispered, 'Love not my mur- "derer!' " Oh! Good good Kenric! And you knelt to me for pardon? You, to whom I owe my life! "You, to whom—"

KENR. Hold! oh! hold!—Lady, how little do I deserve your thanks!—Oh! listen! "listen!"—I was the last to quit the bloody spot: Sadly was I retiring, when a faint groan struck my ear. I sprang from my horse; I placed my hand on Reginald's heart; it beat beneath the pressure!

*Here Osmond appears at the door, motions to Saib, &c. to retire, and advances himself unobserved.*

ANG. It beat! It beat! Cruel, and your dagger—

KENR. Oh! that would have been mercy! No, Lady, "I preserved his life "to rob him of liberty." It struck me,[124] how strong would be my hold over Osmond, while his brother was in my power; and this "reflection" determined me to preserve him. Having plunged the other bodies in "the"

122. The Larpent version has "Lady." 123. The Larpent version has "—where you remained till Osmond resolved by making you his wife to give himself a lawful claim to these possessions." 124. The Larpent version has "I felt."

Conway's flood, I placed the bleeding Earl's on my horse before me,[125] and conveyed him still insensible to a retreat, to all except myself a secret. "There" I "tended his wounds carefully, and" succeeded in preserving his life.—Lady, Reginald still exists.—

*Here Osmond with a furious look draws his dagger, and motions to stab Kenric. A moment's reflection makes him stay his hand, and he returns the weapon into the sheath.*

ANG. Still exists, say you? My father still exists?

KENR. He does, "if a life so wretched can be termed existence." While his swoon lasted, I chained him to his dungeon wall; and no sooner were his wounds healed, than I entered his prison no more. "Through a wicket[126] "in his dungeon-door I supplied him with food; and when in plaintive "terms he sued to me for mercy, hasty I fled, nor gave an answer." Lady, near sixteen years have passed, since an human voice struck the ear of Reginald!

ANG. Alas! alas!

KENR. But the hour of his release draws near: "I discovered this night "that Osmond seeks my life, and resolved to throw myself on your mercy. "Then tell me, Lady, will you plead for me with your father? Think you, "he can forgive the author of his sufferings?

"ANG. Kenric, you have been guilty, cruel—But restore to me my father; "aid us to escape; and all shall be forgiven, all forgot.

KENR. "Then" follow me in silence: I will guide you to Reginald's dungeon: This key unlocks the Castle gates; and ere the cock crows, safe in the arms of Percy—

*Here his eye falls upon Osmond, who has advanced between him and Angela. She shrieks, and sinks into a chair.*

Horror!—The Earl!—Undone for ever!

OSM. Miscreant!—Within there!

*Enter Saib, Hassan, Muley, and Alaric.*

OSM. Hence with that traitor! confine him in the western tower!

ANG. (*Starting wildly from her seat.*) Yet speak, once more, Kenric!—Where is my Father?—What place conceals him?

"OSM. Let him not speak!—Away with him!

"*Kenric is forced off by the Africans.*"[127]

OSM. (*Paces the stage with a furious air, while Angela eyes him with terror: at length he stops, and addresses her.*) Nay, stifle not your curses! Why should

---

125. The Larpent version has "the bleeding Earl before me on the horse." 126. An opening in a door, like a grilled or grated window, through which items can be passed. 127. The Larpent version substitutes a stage direction: "*Kenric endeavouring to Speak is prevented by the Africans who bear him off.*"

your lips be silent when your eye speaks?— Is there not written on every feature 'Vengeance on the assassin! Justice on my mother's murderer?'— But mark me, Angela! Compared to that which soon must be thine, these titles are sweet and lovely. Know'st thou the word parricide, Angela? Know'st thou their pangs who shed the blood of a parent?—Those pangs must be thine to-morrow. This long-concealed captive, this new-found father—

ANG. Your brother, Osmond? Your brother?—Surely you cannot—will not—

OSM. Still doubt you, that I both can, and will?—Remember Kenric's tale!—Remember, though the first blow failed, the second will strike deeper!—But from whom must Reginald receive that second?—"Not "from his rival brother!" not from his inveterate foe!—From his daughter, his unfeeling daughter! 'Tis she, who, refusing me her hand, will place a dagger in mine; 'tis she, whose voice declaring that she hates me, will bid me plunge that dagger in her father's heart!

"ANG. Man! man! drive me not mad!

"OSM. (*Pointing to Reginald's portrait.*) Look upon this picture! Mark, "what a noble form! How sweet, how commanding the expression of his "full dark eye!—Then fancy that he lies in some damp solitary dungeon, "writhing in death's agonies, his limbs distorted, his eye-strings breaking, "his soul burthened with crimes from which no priest has absolved him, "his last words curses on his unnatural child, who could have saved him, "but who would not!

"ANG. Horrible! horrible!

OSM. "Yet if you still reject my offers, thus must it be. Tortures shall "compel Kenric to reveal what dungeon conceals your father; and ere to- "morrow dawns shall Angela lie a bride in my arms, or Reginald a corse at "my feet. Nay, spare entreaties!—Why should I heed your sorrows?—You "have gazed unmoved upon mine!—Why should I be softened by your "tears?—Mine never were dried by your pity!—Cold and inflexible have "you been to *my* despair, so will I be to yours. Speak then, is Percy's love "or your father's life most dear to you?—Does the false mistress or the "unnatural child sound most grating in your ears!"[128]—Must Reginald die, or will Angela be mine?

ANG. Thine?—"She will perish first!"[129]

OSM. You have pronounced his sentence, and his blood be on your head!—Farewell!

128. The Larpent version has "Name then your choice." 129. The Larpent version has "Never!"

ANG. (*Detaining him, and throwing herself on her knees.*) "Hold! hold!—
"Oh!—go not, go not yet!—Wretch that I am, where shall I fly for suc-
"cour?—Mercy, Osmond!"—Oh! mercy, mercy!—Behold me [stretched]
at your feet, "see me bathe them with my tears!" Look with pity on a
creature "whom your cruelty has bowed to the earth," whose heart you
have almost broken, whose brain you have almost turned!—Mercy, Osmond!—Oh! mercy! mercy!

OSM. Lovely, "lovely" suppliant!—And why not profit by the present
moment? Why owe to cold consent what force may this instant give
me?—It shall be so, and thus—

*Attempting to clasp her in his arms, she starts from the ground suddenly, and
draws her dagger with a distracted look.*

ANG. Away!—Approach me not!—Dare not to touch me, or this poniard—

OSM. Foolish girl!—Let me but say the word, and thou art disarmed that
moment.

ANG. But not by thee, Osmond! Oh! never by thee!—Hadst thou the
force of fabled giants vainly wouldst thou strive to wrest this dagger from
my hand.

OSM. Let this convince you how easily—(*Attempting to seize it, his eye rests
upon the hilt, and he starts back with horror.*) By hell,[130] the very poniard
which—

ANG. (*In an exulting tone.*) Ha! hast thou found me, villain?—Villain, dost
thou know this weapon? Know'st thou whose blood incrusts the point?
Murderer, it flowed from the bosom of my mother!

OSM. Within there!—Help!—

*Hassan and Alaric enter.*

Oh! God in heaven!

*He falls senseless into their arms, and they convey him from the chamber: the door
is locked after them.*

ANG. (*Alone.*) He faints!—Long may the villain wear thy chains, Oblivion! Long be it ere he wakes to commit new crimes! "My father in Os-
"mond's power?—Oh! 'tis a dreadful thought!—But no, it must not, shall
"not be!—I will to Osmond—will promise to be his—will sacrifice my
"love, my happiness, my peace of mind—every thing but my father!—
"yet, to bid an assassin to rest upon my bosom, to press that hand in mine
"which pierced the heart of my parent—Oh! it were monstrous!—(*Kneel-
"ing before Evelina's portrait.*) Mother! Blessed Mother! If indeed thy spirit
"still lingers amidst these scenes of sorrow, look on my despair with pity!
"fly to my aid! oh! fly, and save my father!—"

130. The Larpent version has "Almighty God!"

*"She remains for some moments prostrate on the ground in silent sorrow." The Castle-bell tolls the hour: she raises herself and counts the quarters after which it strikes 'one!'*

Hark! the bell tolls!—'Tis the time which the Monk appointed. "He will "not tarry: But I must not follow him!—I will not fly and abandon my "father!—yet may not my flight preserve him? Yes, yes, I will away to "Percy: By the same passage which favours my escape, his vassals may "easily surprise the Castle, may seize Osmond ere he effects his "crime,"[131] and to-morrow may see Reginald restored to freedom, to his domains, and to his daughter!—Oh! then sweet indeed will be my feelings!—Then only can my heart know joy, when it throbs against a father's!—Ha! what was that!—Methought the sound of music floated by me! It seemed as some one had struck the guitar!—I must have been deceived—it was but fancy.

*A plaintive voice sings within, accompanied by a guitar.*

> 'Lullaby!—Lullaby!—Hush thee, my dear,
> Thy father is coming, and soon will be here!'

ANG. [Great] Heavens! The very words which Alice—The door too!—It moves! it opens!—Guard me, good Angels!

*The folding-doors unclose, and the Oratory is seen illuminated. In its centre stands a tall female figure, her white and flowing garments spotted with blood; her veil is thrown back, and discovers a pale and melancholy countenance; her eyes are lifted upwards, her arms extended towards heaven, and a large wound appears upon her bosom. Angela sinks upon her knees, with her eyes riveted upon the figure, which for some moments remains motionless. At length the Spectre advances slowly, to a soft and plaintive strain; she stops opposite to Reginald's picture, and gazes upon it in silence. She then turns, approaches Angela, seems to invoke a blessing upon her, points to the picture and retires to the Oratory. The music ceases.[132] Angela rises with a wild look, and follows the Vision, extending her arms towards it.*

ANG. [Stop,] stay, lovely spirit!—Oh! stay yet one moment!

*The Spectre waves her hand, as bidding her farewell. Instantly the organ's swell is heard; a full chorus of female voices chaunt 'Jubilate'[133] a blaze of light flashes through the Oratory, and the folding doors close with a loud noise.*

ANG. Oh! [God of] Heaven protect me!—(*She falls motionless on the floor.*)

### END OF ACT IV

131. The Larpent version has "Oh! may he not tarry, let me implore Percy's assistance." 132. Boaden, in his life of Kemble (2:206), tells us that the music here is "Jomelli's *Chaconne*, in his celebrated overture in three flats." 133. The Larpent version has "Hallelujah," but it is crossed out and an "X" is placed in the margin, presumably marking a cut by the examiner. We again see the concern about the use of religious language on stage.

# ACT V

SCENE I  *A View of Conway Castle by Moon-Light.*

*Enter Percy and Motley.*

MOTL. "In truth," my Lord, you venture too near the Castle. Should you fall into Osmond's power a second time, your next jump may be into a better world.

PERCY. Oh! there is no danger, Motley. My followers are not far off, and will join me at a moment's warning; then fear not for me.

MOTL. With all my heart, but permit me to fear for myself. We are now within bow-shot of the Castle. The archers may think proper to amuse us with a proof of their skill; and were I to feel an arrow quivering in my gizzard, probably I should be much more surprised than pleased. Good my Lord, let us back to the fisherman's[134] hut.

PERCY. Your advice may be wise, Gilbert, but I cannot follow it. Angela's escape may be discovered—she may be pursued, and in need of my assistance. "Then counsel not my retiring; my fears of losing Angela are "too strong, the flame which burns in my bosom too ardent!

"MOTL. I'm sure no flame burning in your bosom can give you so much "pain as an arrow would give me sticking in mine; and as to your fears of "losing the Lady, I'd bet mine of losing my life against any fears of Chris- "tendom!

"PERCY. How, Gilbert? Have you not promised to stand by me to the "last? Did you not say you could die in my service with pleasure?

"MOTL. Very true.—But, Lord! if a man was always taken at his word, "the world would soon be turned upside down. When a polite gentleman "begs you to consider his house as your own, and assures you that all he "has is at your disposal, he'd be in a terrible scrape if you began knocking "down his walls, or requested the loan of his wife or daughters!—No, no, "Sir!—When I said that I should die in your service with pleasure, I in- "tended to live in it many long years; since, to tell you the truth, from a "child I had always a particular dislike to dying, and I think that with "every hour the prejudice grows stronger.—Good my Lord, let us be "gone. Ere long I doubt not—"

PERCY. Hark! Did I not hear—"No! She comes not!—Heavens, should "the Friar's plot have failed!

"MOTL. Failed, and a Priest and a Petticoat concerned in it?—Oh! no; a "plot composed of such good ingredients cannot but succeed.—Ugh!

---

134. The Larpent version has "Edric's."

"Would I were again seated by the Fisher's hearth!—The wind blows
"cruel sharp and bitter!

"PERCY. For shame, Gilbert!—Am I not equally exposed to its severity?

"MOTL. Oh! The flame in your bosom keeps you warm; and in a cold
"night love wraps one up better than a blanket.* But that not being my
"situation, the present object of my desires is a blazing wood-fire, and
"Venus would look to me less lovely than a smoking sack-posset!—Oh!
"when I was in love, I managed matters much better: I always paid my
"addresses by the fire-side, and contrived to urge my soft suit just at
"dinner-time. Then how I filled my fair-one's ears with fine speeches,
"while she filled my trencher with roast-beef!—Then what figures and
"tropes came out of my mouth, and what dainties and tid-bits went in!—
" 'Twould have done your heart good to hear me talk, and see me eat—
"and you'd have found it no easy matter to decide, whether I had most
"wit or appetite.

"PERCY. And who was the object of this voracious passion?

"MOTL. A person well calculated to charm both my heart and my stom-
"ach: It was a Lady of great merit, who did your Father the honour to
"superintend his culinary concerns. I was scarce fifteen, when she kin-
"dled a flame in my heart, while lighting the kitchen fire, and from that
"moment I thought on nothing but her. My mornings were passed in
"composing poems on her beauty, my evenings in reciting them in her
"ear; for Nature had equally denied the fair creature and myself the fac-
"ulty of reading and writing.

"PERCY. You were successful, I hope?

"MOTL. Why, at length, my Lord, a Pindaric Ode[135] upon her grace in
"frying pancakes melted her heart. She consented to be mine—when, oh!
"cruel Fortune! taking one night a drop too much—poor dear creature!
"she never got the better of it!—I wept her loss, and composed an
"Elegy[136] upon it, which has been thought, by many persons of great
"judgment, not totally destitute of taste and sublimity. It began thus—

> "Baked be the pies to coals!—Burn, roast-meat, burn!
> "Boil o'er, ye pots!—Ye spits, forget to turn!
> "Cindrelia's death—

PERCY. "Peace! peace!—" See you nothing near yonder tower?

*Sancho makes nearly the same observation upon sleep. (Lewis's note)
135.  Pindar (ca. 522–422 B.C.), a Greek lyric poet, known for his triumphal and celebratory odes; the Pindaric ode is characterized by irregularity in number of feet and by the
arbitrary deployment of rhyme.  136.  A poem of lamentation for the dead such as Shelley's
*Adonais*.

MOTL. Yes, certainly.—Two persons advance towards us—Yet they cannot be our friends, for I see neither the Lady's petticoat nor the Monk's paunch!

PERCY. Still they approach, though slowly—One leans on his companion, and seems to move with pain.—Let us retire and observe them.

MOTL. Away, Sir—I'm at your heels.—

*They draw back.*

*Enter Saib conducting Kenric.*

SAIB. Nay, yet hold up a while!—Now we are near the "Fisher's" cottage.

KENR. Good Saib, I needs must stop!—Enfeebled by Osmond's tortures, my limbs refuse to bear me further!—Here lay me down: Then fly to Percy, guide him to the dungeon, and, ere 'tis too late, bid him save the Father of Angela!

PERCY. (*To Motley.*)—Hark! Did you hear?

SAIB. Yet, to leave you thus alone!—

KENR. Oh! heed not me!—Think, that on these few moments depends our safety, Angela's freedom, Reginald's life!—You have the master-key!—Fly then—oh! fly to Percy!

PERCY. (*Starting forward.*)—Said he not Reginald?—Speak again, stranger!—What of Reginald?

SAIB. Ha! Look up, Kenric!—'Tis Percy's-self!

PERCY AND MOTLEY. How!—Kenric?

KENR. (*Sinking at Percy's feet.*) Yes, the guilty, the penitent Kenric!—Oh! surely 'twas Heaven sent you hither!—Know, Earl Percy, that Reginald lives, that Angela is his daughter!

PERCY. Amazement!—And is this known to Osmond?

KENR. Two hours have scarcely passed since he surprised the secret.—Tortures compelled me to avow where Reginald was hidden, and he now is in his brother's power.—Fly then to his aid!—Alas! "perhaps at this "moment his destruction is completed!"—Perhaps even now Osmond's dagger—

PERCY. Within there!—Allan!—Harold!—Quick, Gilbert, sound your horn!—

*Motley sounds it.*

*Enter Allan, Edric, Harold, and Soldiers.*

PERCY. Friends, may I depend on your support?

HAR. While we breathe, all will stand by you!

SOLDIERS. All!—All!

PERCY. Follow me then!—Away!

KENR. Yet stay one moment!—Percy, to this grateful friend have I confided a master-key, which will instantly admit you to the Castle, and have

described to him the retreat of Reginald!—Be he your guide, and hasten—Oh! that pang!—[I can no more] (*He faints; Allan and Edric support
him*.)

PERCY. Look to him!—He sinks!

[MOTL. 'Tis nothing but a swoon.]

PERCY. Bear him to your hut, Edric, and there tend his hurts—(*To Saib*.)
Now on, good fellow, and swiftly!—Osmond, despair!—I come!

*Exit, with Saib, Motley, Harold, and Soldiers on one side, while Allan and Edric
convey away Kenric still fainting on the other.*


SCENE II   *A Vaulted Chamber.*

*Enter Father Philip, with a Basket on his Arm and a torch, conducting Angela.*

F. PHIL. Thanks to St. Francis, we have as yet passed unobserved!—
Surely, of all travelling companions, Fear is the least agreeable: I couldn't
be more fatigued, had I run twenty miles without stopping!

ANG. Why this delay?—Good Father, let us proceed.

F. PHIL. Ere I can go further, Lady, I must needs stop[137] to take breath
and refresh my spirits with a taste of this cordial—(*Taking a bottle from the
basket*.)

ANG. Oh! not now!—Think that Osmond may discover me, and mar
your kind intentions.—This room, you say, conceals the private door:—
Pr'ythee, unclose it!—Let us from hence!—Wait till we are safe under
Percy's protection, and then drink as you list.—But not now, Father!—In
pity, not now!

F. PHIL. Well, well, be calm, Daughter!—Oh! these women! these wom-
en!—They mind no one's comfort but their own!—Now, where is the
door?

ANG. How tedious seems every moment which I pass within these hated
walls!—Ha! Yonder comes a light!

F. PHIL. So, so—I've found it at last—(*Touching a spring, a secret door flies
open*.)

ANG. It moves this way!—By all my fears, 'tis Osmond!—In, Father,
in!—Away, for Heaven's sake—

(*Exeunt, closing the door after them*)[138]

137. The Larpent version has "In faith, Lady, I must needs stop." 138. The Larpent ver-
sion handles this differently, as Lewis indicates in his note at the end of the published play:
ANG. In, Father, in!—
F. PHIL. (*In the doorway.*) Blessed St. Francis! the Door is so narrow! Oh, Daughter!—
Daughter! Undone—Undone!

*Enter Osmond and Hassan with a Torch.*

OSM. (*After a pause of gloomy meditation.*) Is all still within the Castle?

HASS. As the silence of the grave.

OSM. Where are your fellows?

HASS. Saib guards the traitor Kenric: Muley and Alaric are buried in sleep.

OSM. Their hands have been stained with[139] blood, and yet can they sleep?—Call your companions hither.—

*Hassan offers to leave the torch.*

—Away with the light! Its beams are hateful!

(*Exit Hassan*)

OSM. (*Alone.*) Yes! this is the place. "If Kenric said true," for sixteen years have the vaults beneath me rang with my brother's groans.—I dread to unclose the door!—How shall I sustain the beams of his eye when they rest on Evelina's murderer?—"How will his proud heart swell with rage "at meeting his usurping brother!—Ah! the beams of his eye must long "since have been quenched in tears!—The pride of his heart must by this "be subdued by suffering!—Great have been those sufferings—in truth "so great, that even my hatred bends before them.—Yet for that hatred "had I not cause?—At Tournaments, 'twas on Reginald that each bright "eye was bent; at Court, 'twas to Reginald that each noble proffered "friendship." Evelina too!"—Ha! at that name my expiring hate revives!—Reginald! Reginald! for thee was I sacrificed!—Oh! when it strikes a second blow, my poniard shall stab surer!

*Enter Hassan, Muley, and Alaric, with Torches.*

THE AFRICANS. (*Together.*) My Lord! My Lord!

OSM. Now, why this haste?

HASS. I tremble to inform you, that Saib has fled the Castle.—A masterkey, which he found upon Kenric, and of which he kept possession, has enabled him to escape.

OSM. Saib too gone?—All are false! All forsake me!

HASS. Yet more, my Lord; he has made his prisoner the companion of his flight.

OSM. (*Starting.*) How? Kenric escaped?

ALARIC. 'Tis but too certain; doubtless he has fled to Percy.

---

ANG. What alarms you? Why move you not?

F. PHIL. I stick! Daughter, I stick! I can neither get one way nor t'other! The Earl too is coming! I hear his steps! Oh! for the love of heaven, Lady, give me a push behind! Oh! Heav'n be thanked!—

ANG. Away! Away!—

(*Exeunt closing the Door*)

139. The Larpent version has "in."

OSM. To Percy!—Ha! Then I must be speedy: my fate hangs on a thread! Friends, I have ever found ye faithful; mark me now!—(*Opening the private door.*) Of these two passages, the left conducts to a long chain of dungeons: In one of these my brother still languishes. Once already have you seen him bleeding beneath my sword—but he yet exists.—My fortune, my love, nay my life, are at stake!—Need I say more?—
*Each half-unsheathes his sword.*
—That gesture speaks me understood. On then before, I follow you.—
*The Africans pass through the private door: Osmond is advancing toward it, when he suddenly starts back.*
—Ha! Why roll these seas of blood before me? Whose mangled corse do they bear to my feet?—Fratricide?—Oh! 'tis a dreadful name!—Yet how preserve myself and Reginald?—It cannot be! We must not breathe the same atmosphere.—Fate, thy hand urges me!—Fate, thy voice prompts me!—Thou hast spoken—I obey.—
(*He follows the Africans; the door is closed after him.*)

SCENE III   *A gloomy subterraneous Dungeon, wide and lofty: The upper part of it has in several places fallen in, and left large chasms. On one side are various passages leading to other Caverns: On the other is an Iron Door with steps leading to it, and a Wicket in the middle. Reginald, pale and emaciated, in coarse garments, his hair hanging wildly about his face, and a chain bound round his body, lies sleeping upon a bed of straw. A lamp, a small basket, and a pitcher, are placed near him. After a few moments he awakes, and extends his arms.*

REG.   My child! My Evelina!—Oh! fly me not, lovely forms!—They are gone, and once more I live to misery.—Thou wert kind to me, Sleep!— Even now, methought, "I sat in my Castle-hall:—" A maid, lovely as the Queen of Fairies, hung on my knee, and hailed me by that sweet name, 'Father!'—"Yes, I was happy!—Yet frown not on me therefore, Dark- "ness!—I am thine again, my gloomy bride!—Be not incensed, Despair, "that I left thee for a moment; I have passed with thee sixteen years!— "Ah! how many have I still to pass?—Yet fly not my bosom quite, sweet "Hope!—Still speak to me of liberty, of light!—Whisper, that once more "I shall see the morn break—that again shall my fevered lips drink the "pure gale of evening!"—God, thou know'st that I have borne my suffer- ings meekly; I have wept for myself, but never cursed my foes; I have sorrowed for thy anger, but never murmured at thy will.—"Patient have I "been—Oh! then reward me!"—Let me once again[140] press my daughter in my arms!—Let me, for one instant, feel again that I clasp to my heart

140. The Larpent version has "Let me then once."

a being who loves me!—Speed thou to heaven, prayer of a captive!—(*He sinks upon a stone, with his hands, clasped, and his eyes bent stedfastly upon the flame of the lamp.*)

*Anglela and Father Philip are seen through the chasms above, passing along slowly.*

ANG. Be cautious, Father!—Feel you not how the ground trembles beneath us?

F. PHIL. Perfectly well; and would give my best breviary to find myself once more on terra-firma. But the outlet cannot be far off: Let us proceed.

ANG. Look down upon us, blessed Angels!—Aid us!—[And] protect us!

F. PHIL Amen, fair daughter!—And now away.          (*Exeunt*)

REG. (*After a pause.*) " 'Tis that door which divides me from happiness.
"How often against that door have I knelt and prayed, and ever knelt and
"prayed in vain!—Fearful, lest my complaints should move him from his
"purpose, my gaoler listens not, replies not:—Hasty through yon wicket
"he gives my food, then flies as if this dungeon held a serpent.—Oh! then
"how my heart swells with bitterness, when the sound of his retiring
"steps is heard no more, when through yon lofty chasm I catch no longer
"the gleam of his departing torch!"—How wastes my lamp?—The hour
of Kenric's visit must long be past, and still he comes not.—How, if
death's hand hath struck him suddenly?—My existence unknown [—per-
[ishing with hunger]—Away from my fancy, dreadful idea!—(*Rising, and
taking the lamp.*)—The breaking of my chain permits me to wander at
large through the wide precincts of my prison. Haply the late storm,
whose pealing thunders were heard e'en in this abyss, may have rent some
friendly chasm:—Haply some nook yet unexplored—Ah! no, no, no!—
My hopes are vain, my search will be fruitless. Despair in these dungeons
reigns despotic; she mocks my complaints, rejects my prayers, and, when
I sue for freedom, bids me seek it in my grave!—Death! Oh! Death! how
welcome wilt thou be to me!          (*Exit*)

*The noise is heard of an heavy bar falling, the door opens.*

*Enter Father Philip and Angela.*

"F. PHIL. How's this? A door?

"ANG. It was barred on the outside.

"F. PHIL. That we'll forgive, as it wasn't bolted on the in. But I don't
"recollect—Surely I've not—

"ANG. What's the matter?"

F. PHIL. By my faith, daughter, I suspect that I've missed my way.

ANG. Heaven forbid!

F. PHIL. Nay, if 'tis so, I sha'n't be the first man who of two ways has
preferred the wrong.

ANG. Provoking! And did I not tell you to chuse the right-hand passage?

F. PHIL. Truly, did you; and that was the very thing which made me chuse the left. Whenever I'm in doubt myself, I generally ask a woman's advice. When she's of one way of thinking, I've always found that reason's on the other. In this instance, perhaps, I have been mistaken: But wait here for one moment, and the fact shall be ascertained.[141] "But, perhaps, "you fear being alone in the dark?

"ANG. I fear nothing, except Osmond.

"F. PHIL. Nay, I've no more inclination to fall into his clutches again, "than yourself. What would be the consequence? You would be married, "I should be hung! Now, daughter, you may think that I've a very bad "taste; but as I'm a Christian, I'd rather be married fifty years, than hung "for one little half-hour. (*Exit*)"

ANG. How thick and infectious is the air of this cavern! Yet perhaps for sixteen years has my poor father breathed none purer. Hark! Steps are quick advancing! The Friar comes, but why in such confusion?

*Re-enter Father Philip running.*

F. PHIL. Help! Help! It follows me!

ANG. (*Detaining him.*) What alarms you? Speak!

F. PHIL. ['Tis] his ghost! ['Tis] his ghost!—[Murder! Fire! Water!] Let me go!—let me go!—"let me go!" (*Struggling to escape from Angela, he falls, and extinguishes the torch; then hastily rises, and rushes up the stair-case, throwing the door after him.*)

ANG. (*Alone.*) Father! Father! Stay, for heaven's sake!—He's gone, I cannot find the door!—Hark!—'Twas the clank of chains!—A light too!—It comes yet nearer!—Save me, ye powers!—What dreadful form!—'Tis here!—I faint with terror!—(*Sinks almost lifeless against the dungeon's side.*)

*Re-enter Reginald with a lamp.*

"REG. He is gone! Emaciated and stiff from long disuse, scarce can I "draw my limbs along, and I strive in vain to overtake the fugitive.

"ANG. (*Recovering herself.*) Still is it there, that fearful vision!"

REG. (*Placing his lamp upon a pile of stones.*) ['Tis fruitless to follow him.] Why did Kenric enter my prison? Haply, when he heard not my groans at the dungeon door, he thought that my woes were relieved by death. Oh! when will that thought be verified?

ANG. How sunk his eye!—How wildly hangs his matted hair on his pale and furrowed brow!—Oh! those are the furrows of anguish, not of age.

REG. I have oft wiped away tears, but never caused them to flow;—oft have I lightened the prisoner's chains, but never increased their burthen:—Yet I am doomed to chains and tears!

141. The Larpent version has Father Philip "*placing his basket on the ground*" and exiting at this point.

ANG. Each sound of his hollow plaintive voice strikes to my heart. Dared I accost him—Yet perhaps a maniac—No matter; he suffers, and the accents of pity will flow sweetly in his ears!

REG. Thou art dead, and at rest, my wife!—"Safe in yon skies, no "thought of me molests thy quiet." Yet sure "I wrong thee!" At the hour of death thy spirit shall stand beside me, shall close mine eyes gently, and murmur, 'Die, Reginald, and be at peace!'

ANG. Hark! Heard I not—Pardon, good stranger—

REG. (*Starting wildly from his seat.*) 'Tis she! She comes for me! Is the hour at hand, fair vision? Spirit of Evelina, lead on, I follow thee!

(*He extends his arms toward her, staggers a few paces forwards, then sinks exhausted on the ground.*)

ANG. He faints!—perhaps expires!—Still, still!—See, he revives![142]

REG. 'Tis gone! Once more the sport of my bewildered brain—(*Starting up.*) Powers of bliss! Look, where it moves again!—Oh! say, what art thou? If Evelina, speak, oh! speak!

ANG. Ha! Named he not Evelina? That look!—This dungeon too!—The emotions which his voice—It is, it must be!—Father! Oh! Father! Father!—(*Falling upon his bosom.*)

REG. Said you?—Meant you?—My daughter—my infant, whom I left— Oh! yes, it must be true! My heart, which springs towards you, acknowledges my child!—(*Embracing her.*)

"ANG. And is it thus I find you? Burthened with chains, no warmth, no "air, no comfort!

REG. "Think of it no more, my dearest!" But say, how gained you entrance? Has Osmond—

ANG. Oh! that name recalls my terrors!—Alas! you see in me a fugitive from his violence! "Guided by a friendly Monk, whom your approach has "frightened from me, I was endeavouring to escape: We missed our way, "and chance guided us to this dungeon." But this is not a time for explanation. Answer me! Know you the subterraneous passages belonging to this Castle?

REG. Whose entrance is without the walls? I do.

ANG. Then we may yet be saved! Father, we must fly this moment. Percy, the pride of our English youth, waits for me at the Conway's side. Come then, oh! come!—Stay not one moment longer.—

*As she approaches the door, lights appear above.*

REG. Look! look, my child! The beams of distant torches flash through the gloom!

142. The Larpent version has "He faints!—perhaps expires! Oh! how shall I—(*Raises him upon her knee.*) See, see! he revives!"

"ANG. Ha! Yet, perhaps, ashamed of his desertion, 'tis but the Monk,
"who returns to seek me.

"REG.  Grant, Heaven, that it may prove so!"

OSM. (*Above.*) Hassan, guard you the door.—Follow me, friends.—
*The lights disappear.*

ANG. Osmond's voice? Undone! Undone! Oh! my father! he comes to
seek you, perhaps to—Oh! 'tis a word too dreadful for a daughter's lips!

REG.  If he seeks none but me, I am happy—But should your steps have
been traced, my child—Hark! they come! The gloom of yonder cavern
may awhile conceal you: Fly to it: Hide yourself: "Stir not, I charge you."

ANG. What, leave you? Oh! no, no!

REG.  Dearest, I entreat, I conjure you, fly! Fear not for me!—"Hark!
"they are at the door! Speed to the cavern! Speak not, move not: if pos-
"sible, breathe not!"

ANG. Father! Oh! Father!

REG.  Farewel! perhaps for ever!—

*He forces Angela into the cavern, then returns hastily, and throws himself on the
bed of straw.*

—Now then to hear my doom!

*Enter Osmond, followed by Muley and Alaric with torches.*

OSM. The door unbarred?—Softly, my fears were false!—"Lo! where
"stretched on the ground, straw his couch, a stone his pillow, he tastes
"that repose which flies from my bed of down!—" Wake, Reginald, and
arise!

REG.  You here, Osmond?—What brings you to this scene of sorrow?—
Alas! hope flies while I gaze upon your frowning eye!—Have I read its
language aright, Osmond?

OSM.  Aright, if you have read my hatred. "Reginald, I bring you
"truth!—What other present could you expect from me?—Have you not
"been ever a *thorn* in my path, a speck in my sight?—Was not 'Submit to
"your elder brother,' the galling lesson for ever sounded in my ears? And
"when I praised some favourite spot of these domains, some high-browed
"hill, or blooming valley, was not my father's answer still, 'That will be
"your elder brother's?' Yes, the first thought which struck my brain was,
" 'I am a younger son!'—The first passion which tortured my heart was
"hate to him that made me one!"

REG.  Have I deserved that hate? You often injured me, but as often I
forgave [you]. You were ever my foe, but I never forgot you were my
brother.

"OSM. Hypocrite!

"REG. Was I one when my weapon struck the fierce Scot to the ground, "whose sword already glittered above your head? Was I one when, as "embarrassed by your armour you sank beneath the Severn's waves, I "sprang into the flood, I seized, I saved you?—Twice have I preserved "your life!—Oh! let it not be for my own destruction!—See, my brother, "the once proud Reginald lies at your feet, for his pride has been humbled "by suffering!—Hear him adjure you by her ashes, within whose bosom "we both have lain, not to stain your hands with the blood of your "brother!"

OSM. (*Aside.*) He melts me in my own despite!

REG. The fountains of my eyes have been long dried up: I have no tears that can soften, no eloquence that can persuade; but Heaven[143] has lightnings that can blast!—Then, spare me, Osmond!—Kenric has told me that my daughter lives!—Restore me to her arms; permit us in obscurity to pass our days together!—Then shall my last sigh implore upon your head Heaven's forgiveness, and Evelina's.

OSM. It shall be so.—Rise, Reginald, and hear me!—You mention'd even now your daughter.—Know, she is in my power; know also, that I love her!

REG. How?

OSM. She rejects my offers.—Your authority can oblige her to accept them.—Swear to use it, and this instant will I lead you to her arms.

"REG. Osmond, she is your niece!

OSM. "I have influence at Rome—That obstacle will be none to me.— "What is your answer?—You hesitate!"—Say, will you give the demanded oath?

REG. I cannot desemble; Osmond, I never will.*

OSM. How?—Reflect that your life—

REG. Would be valueless, if purchased by my daughter's tears—would be loathsome, if embittered by my daughter's misery. Osmond I will not take the oath.

OSM. (*Almost choked with passion.*)—'Tis enough!—(*To the Africans.*)— "You know your duty!"—Drag him to yonder cavern!—Let me not see him die!

REG. (*Holding by a fragment of the wall, from which the Africans strive to force him.*)—Brother,[144] for pity's sake! for your soul's happiness!

*This is the third time that Osmond has asked the same question, and the poor man always receives the same answer. (Lewis's note)

143. The Larpent version has "God." 144. The Larpent version has "Osmond."

OSM. Obey me, slaves!—Away!

*Angela rushes in wildly.*

ANG. Hold off!—hurt him not!—He is my father![145]

OSM. Angela here?

REG. Daughter, what means—

ANG. (*Embracing him.*) You shall live, Father!—I will sacrifice all to preserve you!—Here is my hand, Osmond!—" 'Tis yours; but spare my fa-"ther! my father!

"OSM. (*Transported.*)—Lovely Angela!—

"REG. How, rash girl!—What would you do?

"OSM. Reginald, reflect—

"REG. Your uncle!—Your mother's murderer!—Remember!

ANG. "Your life is in danger; I must forget all else.—Osmond, release "my father, and solemnly I swear—"[146]

REG. Hold, girl, and first hear me!—(*Kneeling.*)—God of Nature,[147] to Thee I call!—If e'er on Osmond's bosom a child of mine rests—if e'er she calls him husband who pierced her hapless mother's heart, that moment shall a wound,[148] by my own hand inflicted—

ANG. Hold!—Oh! hold!—End not your oath!

OSM. I burn with rage!

REG. Swear never to be Osmond's!

ANG. I swear!—

REG. Be repaid by this embrace!

OSM. Be it your last!—Tear them asunder!

"ANG. Away!—Away!—I will not leave him.

OSM. "Part them, I say!"—Ha! what noise?

*Enter Hassan, hastily.*

HASS. My Lord, all is lost!—Percy has stormed the Castle, and speeds this way!

OSM. Confusion!—Then I must be sudden.—"Aid me, Hassan!—

"*Hassan and Osmond force Angela from her father, who suddenly disengages him-*"self *from Muley and Alaric.*

"REG. Friends so near?—Villains! at least you shall buy my life "dearly!—(*Suddenly seizing Hassan's sword.*)

"OSM. (*Employed with Hassan in retaining Angela, while Reginald defends him-*"self *against Muley and Alaric.*)—Down with him!—Wrest the sword from "him!—

---

145. The Larpent version has "Hold off! touch him not! Father! Oh, Father!" 146. The Larpent version has for this cut " 'Tis yours; my father, I solemnly swear—." 147. The Larpent version has "God of justice." 148. The Larpent version has "heart, at her death-hour, shall my curse sit heavy on her soul—and a wound."

"*Alaric is wounded, and falls; Muley gives back; at the same time, Osmond's*
"*party appears above, pursued by Percy's.*
"—Hark!—They come!—Dastardly villains!—Nay, then, my own hand
"must—"

*Drawing his sword, he rushes upon Reginald, who is disarmed, and beaten upon his
knees; when at the same moment that Osmond lifts his arm to stab him, Evelina's
ghost throws herself between them: Osmond starts back, and drops his sword.*

Horror!—What form is this?

ANG. Die!

*Disengaging herself from Hassan, she springs suddenly forwards, and plunges her
dagger into Osmond's bosom, who falls with a loud groan, and faints. The ghost
vanishes in a flash of fire, and a loud clap of thunder is heard; Angela and Reginald
rush into each other's arms.*

ANG. Father, thou art mine again!

*Enter Percy, Motley, Saib, Harold, &c. pursuing Osmond's party. All stop on
seeing him bleeding upon the ground.*

PERCY. Hold, my brave friends!—See where lies the object of our search!

ANG. Percy!—Dear Percy!

PERCY. (*Flying to her.*)—Dearest Angela!

ANG. My friend, my guardian angel!—Come, Percy, come! embrace my
father!—"Father, embrace the protector of your child!"

PERCY. Do I then behold Earl Reginald?

REG. (*Embracing him.*)—The same, brave Percy!—Welcome to my
heart!—Live ever next it!

ANG. Oh, moment that o'erpays my sufferings!—And yet—Percy, that
wretched man—He perished by my hand!

SAIB. Hark, he sighs!—There is life still in him!

ANG. Life?—Then save him! save him!—Bear him to his chamber!—
Look to his wound!—Heal it, if possible!—At least gain him time to repent his crime and errors!—

*Osmond is conveyed away:—Servants enter with torches, and the stage becomes
light.*

PERCY. Though ill-deserved by his guilt, your generous pity still is amiable.—But say, fair Angela, what have I to hope?—Is my love "approved
"by your noble father?—Will he—"

REG. Percy, this is no time to talk of love.—Let me hasten to my expiring
brother, and soften with forgiveness the pangs of death!

PERCY. And can you forget your sufferings?

REG. Ah! youth, has he had none?—Oh! in his stately chambers, far
greater must have been his pangs than mine in this gloomy dungeon; for
what gave *me* comfort was his terror—what gave *me* hope, was his despair.

I knew that I was guiltless—knew that, though I suffer'd in this world,
my lot would be happy in that to come!

> And, Oh thou wretch! whom hopeless woes oppress,
> Whose day no joys, whose night no slumbers bless!
> When pale Despair alarms thy phrensied eye,
> Screams in thine ear, and bids thee Heaven deny,
> Court thou Religion! Strive thy faith to save!
> Bend thy fixed glance on bliss beyond the grave!
> Hush guilty murmurs! Banish dark mistrust!
> Think there's a Power above! nor doubt that Power is just!'[149]

### EPILOGUE
#### Spoken by Mrs. Jordan

> Osmond by this arrived at Charon's ferry,[150]
> My honour saved, and dad alive and merry,
> Hither I come the public doom to know,
> But come not uncompell'd—the more's my woe!
> Even now, (oh! pity, friends, my hard mishap!)
> My shoulder felt a Bow-Street runner's tap,[151]
> Who, while I shook with fear in every limb,
> Thus spoke, with accent stern and visage grim—
>   'Mistress!' quoth he, 'to me it given in trust is,
> 'To bring you straight before our larned Justice;
> 'For know, 'tis said, to-night, the whole town o'er,
> 'You've killed one Osmond, alias Barrymore.'
>   'The fellow's mad!' 'twas thus amaz'd I spoke;
> 'Lord! Sir, I murdered Osmond for a joke
> 'This dagger, free from blood, will make it certain,
> 'He died but till the prompter dropped the curtain;
> 'And now, well pleased to quit this scene of riot,
> 'The man's gone home to sup in peace and quiet!'
>   Finding that all I said was said in vain,
> And Townshend[152] still his first design maintain,
> I thought 'twere best to fly for shelter here,
> And beg my generous friends to interfere.

149. As Lewis indicates in his end note, the line was changed from "And think there is a God! That God is just." 150. Charon was the ferryman of the dead in classical myth. 151. The Bow Street Runners were the first regular police force in London, under the chief magistrate at Bow Street, near Covent Garden. 152. Apparently the name of the Bow Street runner.

But though the awkward nature of my case
May spread some slight confusion o'er my face,
No terrors awe my bosom, I'll assure ye;
Just is my cause, and English is my jury!
Besides, it must appear, on explanation,
How very ticklish was my situation,
And all perforce, his crimes when I relate,
Must own that Osmond well deserved his fate.
He heeded not papa's pathetic pleading;
He stabbed mama—which was extreme ill-breeding;
And at his feet for mercy when *I* sued,
The odious wretch, I vow, was downright rude.
Twice his bold hands my person dared to touch!
Twice in one day!—'Twas really once too much!
And therefore justly filled with virtuous ire,
To save my honour, and protect my sire,
I drew my knife, and in his bosom struck it;
He fell, you clapped—and then he kicked the bucket!
    So perish still the wretch, whose soul can know
Selfish delight, while causing other's woe;
Who blasts that joy, the sweetest God has given,
And makes an hell, where love would make an heaven!
Forbear, thou lawless libertine! nor seek
Forc'd favours on that pale averted cheek:
If thy warm kisses cost bright eyes one tear,
Kisses from loveliest lips are bought too dear—
Unless those lips with thine keep playful measure,
And that sweet tear should be a tear of pleasure!
    Now as for Osmond—at that villains's name
I feel reviving wrath my soul inflame!
And shall one short and sudden pang suffice
To clear so base a fault, so gross a vice?
No! To your bar, dear friends, for aid I fly!
Bid Osmond live again, again to die;
Nightly with plaudits laud his breath recall,
Nightly beneath my dagger see him fall,
Give him a thousand lives!—and let *me* take them all.

## TO THE READER

Many erroneous assertions have been made respecting this Drama; some, that the language was originally extremely licentious; others, that the sentiments were violently democratic; and others again, that if Mr. Sheridan[153] had not advised me to content myself with a single Spectre, I meant to have exhibited a whole regiment of Ghosts. To disprove these reports I have deviated from the usual mode of publishing Plays, as performed, and have printed mine almost verbatim, as originally written. Whether it merited the above accusations, the reader has now had an opportunity of judging for himself. I must just mention that the last line of the Piece is altered, and that in the Second Scene of the Fifth Act, *The Friar* was made to stick in the door-way, whereas he now makes his exit without difficulty.

Other charges, however, have been brought against me on better grounds, and I must request the reader's patience while I say a few words respecting them. To originality of character I make no pretence. Persecuted heroines and conscience-stung villains certainly have made their courtesies and bows to a British audience long before the appearance of "*The Castle Spectre*;" the *Friar* and *Alice* are copies, but very faint ones, from *Juliet's Nurse*, and Sheridan's *Father Paul*,[154] and *Percy* is a mighty prettybehaved young gentleman with no character at all. I shall not so readily give up my claim to novelty, when I mention my misanthropic *Negro*: He has been compared to *Zanga*; but Young's Hero differs widely from what I meant in *Hassan*.[155] *Zanga's* hatred is confined to one object; to destroy the happiness of that object is his sole aim, and his vengeance is no sooner accomplished, than he repents its gratification. *Hassan* is a man of violent passions, and warm feelings, whose bosom is filled with the milk of human kindness, but that milk is soured by despair; whose nature was susceptible of the tenderest affections, but who feels that all the chains of his affections are broken for ever. He has lost every thing, even hope; he has no single object against which he can direct his vengeance, and he directs it at large against mankind. He hates all the world, hates even himself; for he feels that in that world there is no one that loves him

> "Lorsque l'on peut souffrir, sure que ses douleurs
> "D'aucun mortel ne sont jamais couler les pleurs,
> "On se desinteresse à la fin de soi-même;
> "On cesse de s'aimer, si quelqu'on ne nous aime!"[156]

153. Richard Brinsley Sheridan (1751–1816), playwright, politician, and manager of Drury Lane. 154. Father Paul appears in Sheridan's *The Duenna* (Covent Garden, 1775). 155. Zanga appears in Edward Young's *Revenge* (Drury Lane, 1721). 156. Lewis offers a rough translation in the preceding sentence; a fuller version might be, "When one suffers, certain that for these sorrows no one's tears will ever flow, one finally loses interest even in oneself; we cease to love ourselves, if no one loves us."

But though Hassan's heart is changed by disappointment and misfortune, that heart once was feeling and kind; nor could he hate with such inveteracy, if he had not loved with extreme affection. In my opinion this character is not *Zanga's*; but this I must leave to the public decision. I may, however, boldly, and without vanity, assert, that *Motley* is quite new to the Stage. In other plays the Fool has always been a sharp knave, quick in repartee, and full of whim, fancy, and entertainment; whereas *my* Fool (but I own I did not mean to make him so) is a dull, flat, good sort of plain matter of fact fellow, as in the course of the performance Mr. Bannister discovered to his great sorrow.

That *Osmond* is attended by *Negroes* is an anachronism, I allow; but from the great applause which Mr. Dowton constantly received in *Hassan* (a character he played extremely well), I am inclined to think that the audience was not greatly offended at the impropriety. For my own part, I by no means repent the introduction of my *Africans*: I thought it would give a pleasing variety to the characters and dresses, if I made my servants black; and could I have produced the same effect by making my heroine blue, blue I should have made her.

In the *Friar's* defence, when he most ungallantly leaves *Angela* in the cavern to shift for herself, I can only plead the necessity of the case. Stay where he was he could not; go he must at any rate; I trundled him off in the best way that I could; and, for the sake of the public, I heartily wish that way had been better. With regard to his not meeting *Osmond* in his flight, a little imagination will soon conquer that difficulty. It may be supposed, that as he lost his way in coming, he lost it again in going; or, that he concealed himself till *the Earl* had passed him; or, that he tumbled down and broke his neck; or, that he . . . . did any thing else you like better. I leave this matter entirely to the reader's fancy.

Against *my Spectre* many objections have been urged: one of them I think rather curious. She ought not to appear, because the belief in Ghosts no longer exists! In my opinion, that is the very reason she *may* be produced without danger; for there is now no fear of increasing the influence of superstition, or strengthening the prejudices of the weak-minded. I confess I cannot see any reason why Apparitions may not be as well permitted to stalk in a tragedy, as Fairies be suffered to fly in a pantomime, or Heathen Gods and Goddesses to cut capers in a grand ballet; and I should rather imagine that *Oberon* and *Bacchus* now find as little credit to the full as the *Cock-lane Ghost*, or the Spectre of *Mrs. Veal*.[157]

157. The Cock-lane Ghost was supposed to make mysterious noises at No. 33 Cock Lane, Smithfield; it was in fact a hoax perpetrated by William Parsons and his family. Samuel

Never was any poor soul so ill-used as *Evelina's*, previous to her presenting herself before the audience. The Friends to whom I read my Drama, the Managers to whom I presented it, the Actors who were to perform in it—all combined to persecute my *Spectre*, and requested me to confine my Ghost to the Green-Room. Aware that without her my catastrophe would closely resemble that of the *Grecian Daughter*,[158] I persisted in retaining her. The event justified my obstinacy: *The Spectre* was as well treated before the curtain as she had been ill-used behind it; and as she continues to make her appearance nightly with increased applause, I think myself under great obligations both to her and her representative.

But though I am conscious that it is very imperfect, I shall not so far offend my own feelings, or insult the judgment of the public, which has given it a very favourable reception, as to say that I think my Play very bad. Had such been my opinion, instead of producing it on the stage, or committing it to the press, I should have put it behind the fire, or, throwing it into the *Thames*, make a present of it to the British *Scombri*.[159] Still its success on the stage (great enough to content even an author) does not prevent my being very doubtful as to its reception in the closet, when divested of its beautiful music, splendid scenery, and, above all, of the acting, excellent throughout. Without detracting from the merits of the other performers (to all of whom I think myself much indebted for their respective exertions), I must here be permitted to return particular thanks to Mrs. Jordan, whose manner of sustaining her character exceeded my most sanguine hopes, and in whose hands my heroine acquired an importance for which she was entirely indebted to the talents of the actress.

---

Johnson was involved in the investigation. Defoe wrote the "True Relation of the Apparition of one Mrs. Veal" in 1706. Oberon appears as the king of the fairies in *A Midsummer Night's Dream* and Bacchus is the Greek god of wine and fertility. 158. *The Grecian Daughter* (Drury Lane, 1772) was written by Arthur Murphy. 159. Fish.

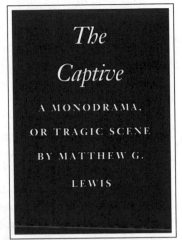

The
Captive

A MONODRAMA,
OR TRAGIC SCENE
BY MATTHEW G.
LEWIS

Lewis's *The Captive*, a monodrama consisting of a single scene, was acted at Covent Garden on 22 March 1803. Mrs. Litchfield performed the part of the captive; the music was provided by Thomas Busby. Every account of the performance stresses its horrifying impact. The *Biographia Dramatica* reports that "the author had included in this single scene all the horrors of a madhouse; imprisonment, chains, starvation, fear, madness, &c.; and many ladies were thrown into fits by the forcible and affecting manner of the actress" (II, 81). Lewis himself wrote to his mother that "It proved much too terrible for representation, and two people went into hysterics during the performance, & two more after the curtain dropped" (23 March 1803; in Peck, 221). Lewis withdrew the piece and never published it as a separate play; but he did include it in his *Poems*, and Peck tells us that it was a popular recitation piece.

There are three texts for *The Captive*. The Larpent version (LA 1374), entitled "Lines intended to be spoken in The Captive A Mono-Drama" (to which the Covent Garden playbill adds "or Tragic Scene"), provides only the words spoken. The version Lewis printed in *Poems* (London: D. N. Shury, 1812; pp. 89–92), where it is called "A Scene in a Private Mad-House," differs slightly from the Larpent version; it too lacks stage directions. The version in *The Life and Correspondence of M. G. Lewis*, by Margaret Cornwell Baron-Wilson, 2 vols. (London: Henry Colburn, 1839), pp. 236–41, again differs slightly, but it does provide stage directions. For the text of the play, I have used the version in *Poems*; the stage directions come from *Life and Correspondence*. Variants are indicated in the notes. Information on Lewis can be found in the headnote to *The Castle Spectre*.

## THE CAPTIVE

*The scene represents a dungeon, in which is a grated door, guarded by strong bars and chains. In the upper part is an open gallery, leading to the cells above.*

*Slow and melancholy music. The Captive is discovered in the attitude of hopeless grief:—she is in chains;—her eyes are fixed, with a vacant stare, and her hands are folded.*

*After a pause, the Gaoler is seen passing through the upper gallery with a lamp: he appears at the grate, and opens the door. The noise of the bars falling rouses the Captive. She looks round eagerly; but on seeing the Gaoler enter, she waves her hand mournfully, and relapses into her former stupor.*

*The Gaoler replenishes a jug with water, and places a loaf of bread by her side. He then prepares to leave the dungeon, when the Captive seems to resolve on making an attempt to excite his compassion: she rises from her bed of straw, clasps his hand, and sinks at his feet. The music ceases, and she speaks.*

> Stay, Gaoler, stay, and hear my woe!
>   She is not mad who kneels to thee,
> For what I'm now too well I know,
>   And what I was, and what should be.
> I'll rave no more in proud despair;
>   My language shall be mild,[1] though sad:
> But yet I'll firmly, truly swear,
>   I am not mad! *(Then kissing his hand.)* I am not mad!

*He offers to leave her; she detains him, and continues, in a tone of eager persuasion,*

> My tyrant husband forged the tale,
>   Which chains me in this dreary cell:[2]
> My fate unknown my Friends bewail—
>   Oh! Gaoler, haste that fate to tell!
> Oh! haste my Father's heart to cheer:
>   His heart at once 'twill grieve and glad
> To know, though kept a Captive here,
>   I am not mad! I am not mad![3]

*Harsh music, while the Gaoler, with a look of contempt and disbelief, forces his hand from her grasp, and leaves her. The bars are heard replacing.*

---

1. The Larpent and *Memoirs* versions have "calm." 2. The Larpent version has "A tyrant husband forged the tale / And chained me in this dreary Cell." 3. The Larpent and *Memoirs* versions have "I am not mad! not mad! not mad!"

He smiles in scorn, and turns the key![4]
  He quits the grate! I knelt in vain!—
His glimmering Lamp still . . . still I see!—[5]

*Music expressing the light growing fainter,[6] as the Gaoler retires through the gallery, and the Captive watches his departure with eager looks.*
  'Tis gone[7]. . . . and all is gloom again!

*She shivers, and wraps her garment more closely round her.*

Cold, bitter cold!—no warmth!—no light!—
  Life, all thy comforts once I had;
Yet here I'm chain'd this freezing night,
  *(Eagerly,)* Although not mad! No, [no, no,] no! not mad!

*A few bars of melancholy music, which she interrupts, by exclaiming suddenly,*

'Tis sure some dream! some vision vain!—
  *(Proudly.)* What? *I*, the child of rank and wealth,
Am *I* the wretch who clanks this chain,
  Bereft of freedom, friends and health?
Ah! While I dwell on blessings fled,
  Which never more my heart must glad,
How aches my heart! how burns my head!—[8]

*Interrupting herself hastily, and pressing her hands forcibly against her forehead.*

But 'tis not mad!—no! 'Tis not mad!

*She remains fixed in this attitude, with a look of fear, till the music, changing, expresses that some tender, melancholy reflection has passed her mind.*

[My child!—My child!]
Hast thou, my Child, forgot ere this[9]

4. The Larpent and *Memoirs* versions have "He turns the key!" 5. The Larpent and *Memoirs* versions have "Still—still, his glimmering lamp I see." 6. This stage direction gives us some idea of the demands made upon the composers for both monodramas and melodramas, in this case upon Dr. Thomas Busby (1755–1838) whose efforts for Lewis's play were praised by the *Monthly Mirror* of 15 April 1803: "Dr. Busby's music was admirably adapted to the action and character of the subject, and displayed great depth of science, and knowledge of effect." 7. The Larpent and *Memoirs* versions have " 'Tis lost!" 8. The Larpent and *Memoirs* versions have a slightly different version of this passage: " 'Tis sure a dream?—some fancy vain! / I—I, the child of rank and wealth! / Am I the wretch who clanks this chain, / Deprived of freedom, friends, and health? / Oh! while I count those blessings fled, / Which never more my hours must glad, / How aches my heart!—how burns my head!—" 9. The Larpent and *Memoirs* versions have "Ah! hast thou not forgot by this."

A mother's face, a mother's tongue?[10]
She'll ne'er forget your parting kiss,
  (*With a smile.*) Nor round her neck how fast you clung:
Nor how you with me[11] you sued to stay,
  Nor how that suit your Sire forbad;
(*With agony.*) Nor how. . . . (*With a look of terror.*) I'll drive such
                thoughts away;

*In a hollow hurried voice.*

They'll make me mad! They'll make me mad!

*A pause—she then proceeds with a melancholy smile,*

His rosy lips, how sweet They smiled!
  His mild blue eyes, how bright They shone!
None ever bore a lovelier child!—[12]

*With a sudden burst of passionate grief, approaching to frenzy.*

And art Thou now for ever gone,
And must I never see thee more,
  My pretty, pretty, pretty Lad!
(*With energy.*) I *will* be free! (*Endeavouring to force the grate.*)
                Unbar the[13] door!
I am not mad! I am not mad!

*She falls, exhausted, against the grate, by the bars of which she supports herself. She is roused from her stupor by loud shrieks, rattling of chains, &c.*

Oh! Hark!—what mean those yells and cries?[14]

*The noise grows louder.*

His chain some furious madman breaks!—

*The Madman is seen to rush along the gallery with a blazing firebrand in his hand.*

10. The Larpent and *Memoirs* versions have "Thy mother's" twice. The various versions have differing pronouns throughout this and other passages. Lewis seems to be playing with the movement from first to third person as an indication of the Captive's madness, as she now views her position objectively or abstractly, now identifies herself with her fate, now knows who and what she is, now feels alienated from herself. 11. The Larpent and *Memoirs* versions have "with her." 12. The Larpent and *Memoirs* versions have "Was never born a lovelier child." 13. The Larpent and *Memoirs* versions have "this." 14. The Larpent and *Memoirs* versions have "Hark! hark!—What mean those yells—those cries!"

He comes!—I see his glaring eyes!—

*The madman appears at the grate, which he endeavors to force, while she shrinks in an agony of terror.*

Now, now my dungeon-grate He shakes!—[15]
Help, help!

*Scared by her cries, the madman quits the grate.*[16]
*The madman again appears above, is seized by his keepers, with torches; and after some resistance, is dragged away.*

He's gone!—
Oh! fearful woe,
Such screams to hear, such sights to see!
My brain, my brain!—I know, I know,
I *am* not mad. . . . but soon *shall* be!
Yes! Soon!—For Lo yon!. . . . while I speak. . . .
Mark, how yon Daemon's[17] eye-balls glare!—
He sees me!—Now with dreadful shriek
He whirls a serpent[18] high in air!—
Horror!—The Reptile strikes his tooth
Deep in my heart so crush'd and sad!—
Aye,[19] laugh, ye Fiends!—I feel the truth!
Your task is done![20]—*(With a loud shriek.)* I'm mad! mad![21]
[My Child!—My Child!—][22]

*She dashes herself in frenzy upon the ground. The two Brothers cross the gallery, dragging the Gaoler; then a Servant appears with a torch, conducting the Father, who is supported by his Youngest Daughter. They are followed by Servants with torches, part of whom remain in the gallery. The Brothers appear at the grate, which they force the Gaoler to open; they enter, and on seeing the Captive, one is struck with sorrow, while the other expresses violent anger against the Gaoler, who*

15. The *Memoirs* version has "dungeon bars"; the Larpent version has "he breaks."
16. Every account of the performance of the play notes the horrifying effect it had, with women fainting and the entire house in an uproar. The *Monthly Mirror* (15 April 1803) identifies this particular moment as the most shocking, claiming that "The effect was too strong for the feelings of the audience. Two ladies fell into hysterics, the house was thrown into confusion . . . ." 17. The *Memoirs* version has "Mark yonder demon's," Larpent "Mark yonder Damon's." 18. The Larpent and *Memoirs* versions have "scorpion." 19. The Larpent version has "Yes." 20. The Larpent and *Memoirs* versions have " 'Tis done! 'tis done!" 21. The version in *Poems* ends here. 22. This line is in the Larpent version, which lacks all stage directions and which thus ends here; this may merely be her final recognition of her child embedded in the stage directions in the *Memoirs* version.

*endeavours to excuse himself; the Father and Sister enter, and approach the Captive, offering to raise her, when she starts up suddenly, and eyes them with a look of terror; they endeavour to make themselves known to her, but in vain; she shuns them, with fear and adversion, and taking some straw, begins to twine it into a crown, when her eyes falling on the Gaoler, she shrieks in terror, and hides her face; the Gaoler is ordered to retire, and obeys; the Father again endeavours to awaken her attention, but in vain. He covers his face with his handkerchief, which the Captive draws away with a look of surprise. Their hopes are excited, and they watch her with eagerness. She wipes the old man's eyes with her hair, which she afterwards touches, and finding it wet with tears, bursts into a delirious laugh, resumes her crown of straw, and after working at it eagerly for a moment, suddenly drops it, and remains motionless with a vacant stare. The Father, &c., express their despair of her recovery—the music ceases. An Old Servant enters, leading her Child, who advances with a careless look; but on seeing his mother, breaks from the servant, runs to her, and clasps her hand. She looks at him with a vacant stare, then, with an expression of excessive joy, exclaims "My child!" sinks on her knees, and clasps him to her bosom. The Father, &c., raise their hands to heaven in gratitude for the return of her reason, and the curtain falls slowly to solemn music.*

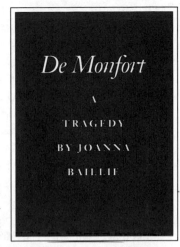

*De Monfort*

A

TRAGEDY

BY JOANNA

BAILLIE

Baillie (1762–1851) was the most respected playwright of her day. The daughter of Dorothea Hunter Baillie and the Reverend James Baillie, she was born on 11 September 1762, together with a dead twin sister. She attended a Glasgow boarding school with her sister Agnes (born 1760), where she excelled in music, drawing, mathematics, and argumentation. In 1776, her father was made professor of divinity at Glasgow, but he died two years later. When Dr. William Hunter, Dorothea's brother and a famous anatomist died, Joanna's brother Matthew (born 1761) took over his London practice, and the family moved with him. When Matthew married in 1791, the mother and two sisters moved to Hampstead, where they lived out their lives. Joanna lived to be eighty-eight, her older sister living to one hundred.

Baillie's dramatic work began with the first volume of *A Series of Plays: in which it is attempted to delineate the stronger passions of the mind—each passion being the subject of a tragedy and a comedy* (known as the *Plays on the Passions;* London, 1798), which included *De Monfort.* Two more volumes of the *Plays on the Passions* followed (1802, 1812), as did thirteen plays not in the series. *De Monfort* opened at Drury Lane on 29 April 1800 and continued for eight nights; it was revived for five nights in 1821 by Edmund Kean, again at Drury Lane. Four of her other plays were also performed, but none was a success.

A volume of *Fugitive Verses* appeared in 1790, *Metrical Legends of Exalted Characters* in 1821, and *A Collection of Poems, Chiefly Manuscript, and From Living Authors* in 1823. Her *A View of the General Tenour of the New Testament* was published in 1831, and she compiled in 1851 *The Dramatic and Poetical Works of Joanna Baillie, complete in one volume,* a work of over 800 pages that she called her "great monster book." Her writing earned her the respect of many literary figures, such as Samuel Rogers, Henry MacKenzie, and most importantly, Sir Walter Scott, with whom she became close friends. She was also admired by John Philip Kemble and Sarah Siddons, who acted together in *De Monfort*. Most interestingly, she was part of wide-ranging circle of women writers that included Lucy Aikin, Anna Laetitia Barbauld, and Mary Berry.

In preparing my text, I have drawn upon three versions of the play, though there are a number of other editions (with some changes) and a variety of acting versions as well. The versions I have consulted are: the first edition of the first volume of *Plays on the Passions* (London: T. Cadell, Jun. & W. Davies, 1798), the 1800 Larpent version (LA 1287) which was reworked by John Philip Kemble according to contemporary sources, and a manuscript version in the hand of Thomas Campbell prepared for Sarah Siddons (Huntington MS 32693), dated 29 March 1802, with some marginal comments by Siddons. My text is that of the first edition, with cuts made for the Larpent performance version being indicated by double quotation marks and material added in the Larpent version marked by square brackets. Variants are indicated in the notes, with changes in character and place names being noted only once. There are more and larger alterations to the performance version of this play than to the others in this collection. In a few places, I have drawn upon the Campbell/Siddons text to clarify matters. In particular, Act III, scene v seems to have been altered several times. In the printed version, De Monfort and Rezenvelt fight, and De Monfort is disarmed; he is humiliated. In the Larpent version, Rezenvelt does not even appear in the scene; De Monfort's disgrace is avoided. However, Dutton, in his *Dramatic Censor* (1801), compares the performance to the published play and notes that in Kemble and Siddon's version Rezenvelt and De Monfort do meet but do not fight. A version matching Dutton's description of the stage performance can be found in the Campbell/Siddons manuscript.

On Baillie and *De Monfort*, see Margaret S. Carhart, *The Life and Work of Joanna Baillie* (New Haven, 1923); Bertrand Evans, *Gothic Drama from Walpole to Shelley* (Berkeley, 1947); and Marlon B. Ross, *Contours of Masculine Desire* (Oxford, 1989).

DRAMATIS PERSONAE
Drury Lane, 29 April 1800

| | |
|---|---|
| De Monfort[1] | Mr. Kemble |
| Rezenvelt | Mr. Talbot |
| Count Freberg, Friend to De Monfort | |
| and Rezenvelt[2] | Mr. Barrymore |

1. In the Larpent version, listed as Matthias, Marquis De Monfort. 2. In the Larpent version, listed as Count Albert.

| | |
|---|---|
| Manuel, Servant to De Monfort | Mr. Powell |
| Jerome, De Monfort's old landlord | Mr. Dowton |
| Grimbald, an artful knave[3] | Mr. Caulfield |
| Bremer, Servant to De Monfort[4] | . . . . . .[8] |
| Jacques, Servant to De Monfort[4] | . . . . . .[8] |
| Louis, Servant to De Monfort[4] | . . . . . .[8] |
| Berg, Servant to De Monfort[4] | . . . . . .[8] |
| Bernard, a Monk | . . . . . .[8] |
| Count Waterlan[4] | . . . . . .[8] |
| Ambrose—Monks[4] | . . . . . .[8] |
| Francis[4] | . . . . . .[8] |
| Peter[4] | . . . . . .[8] |
| Jane De Monfort, sister to De Monfort | Mrs. Siddons |
| Countess Freberg, Wife to Freberg[5] | Miss Heard |
| Theresa, Servant to the Countess[6] | Miss Tidswell |
| Abbess[7] | Mrs. Crouch |
| Agatha, a nun[7] | . . . . . .[8] |

Scene, a Town in Germany
The Music of the Third Act composed by Shaw and of the Second
and Fourth Acts by Kelly. The Scenes designed by Greenwood, Jr.
and Capon

## PROLOGUE[9]
### Spoken by Mrs. Powell

Too long has fancy led her fairy Dance,
Thro' all the various mazes of Romance;
On Classic ground her motley standard rear'd
While honest nature blush'd, and disappear'd—
    O, shame!—why borrow from a foreign store?
As if the Rich should pilfer from the poor.—
We who have forc'd th' astonished world to yield,
Led by immortal Shakespeare to the Field;—

3. In the Larpent version and subsequent editions, listed as Conrad. 4. For these servants, monks, etc., the first edition merely adds "Monks, Gentlemen, Officers, Page, &c. &c." 5. In the Larpent version, listed as the wife to Albert. 6. In the Larpent version, listed as Katherine; the playbill identifies Miss Tidswell as playing the part of a maid, presumably Theresa. 7. For the Abbess, Nuns, etc., the first edition merely adds "Abbess, Nuns, and a Lay Sister, Ladies, &c." 8. The playbill lists Cory, Pack, Holland, Archer, Maddocks, Clarke, Sparks, Trueman, Surmont, Fisher, Chippendeale and Rider without assigning them parts. 9. From the Larpent manuscript. John Payne Collier indicates the prologue was written by the Hon. Francis North, the author of *The Kentish Barons*.

Whose Sires have felt all tender Otway's woe,
Have glow'd with Dryden, and have wept with Rowe.—
And we, their sons, now dull and senseless grown,
When all the realm of Comedy's our own?
Congreve and Vanbrugh boast eternal Fame,
And living authors, we forbear to name.—[10]
    Should you approve, on this auspicious Day
The British Drama reassumes her sway.
    Ye Men, be candid to a Virgin Muse,—
To move you more,—Perhaps a Woman Sues:[11]
Let her Dramatic Saplin[12] 'scape your Rage,
And Spare this tender Scyon[13] of the Stage—
Support the infant Tree, ye pitying fair
Protect its blossoms from the blighting air,—
So may its leaves move gently with your sighs,
The Branches flourish water'd by your Eyes.—


## ACT I

SCENE I   *Jerome's House. A large old fashioned Chamber.*

JER. (*Speaking without.*) This way good masters.
*Enter Jerome, bearing a light, and followed by Manuel, and Servants[14]
carrying luggage.*

                               Rest your burdens here.
This spacious room will please the Marquis best.[15]

10. Thomas Otway (1652–1685) was best known for *Venice Preserved* (1682), the most popular tragedy in the repertoire after Shakespeare. John Dryden (1631–1700), the major poet of his day (made Poet Laureate in 1668), wrote such heroic dramas as *The Conquest of Granada* (2 parts, 1670, 1671) and the blank verse tragedy *All for Love* (1677). Nicholas Rowe (1674–1718) was best known for his domestic historical tragedy, *The Tragedy of Jane Shore* (1714). William Congreve (1670–1729) wrote *Love for Love* (1695) and *The Way of the World* (1700); John Vanbrugh (1664–1726), who was also an architect, wrote *The Relapse* (1696) and *The Provoked Wife* (1697). The living author probably most likely to come to mind here would have been Richard Brinsley Sheridan (1751–1816), author of *The Rivals* (1775), *The School for Scandal* (1777), and the enormously popular adaptation from Kotzebue, *Pizarro* (1799); he was also the manager of Drury Lane. 11. The *Morning Post* of 30 April 1800 states in its review of *De Monfort* that "The Prologue announces it indirectly from a female pen, but it has been adapted to the stage by Mr. Kemble." There had been debate about the sex of *De Monfort*'s author since its publication in 1798. 12. For "sapling." 13. For "scion." 14. The Larpent version identifies the servants as Bremer and Jacques; their names will be used below when the Larpent version adds material. 15. The Larpent version has "This room I know will please De Monfort best."

*(Exit Servants)*

He takes me unawares; but ill prepar'd:
If he had sent, e'en tho' a hasty notice,
I had been glad.
*Bremer and Jacques bring in more luggage.*
MAN.　　　　　Be not disturb'd, good Jerome;
Thy house is in most admirable order;
And they who travel o'cold winter nights
Think homeliest quarters good.
JER. He is not far behind?[16]
MAN.　　　　　　　A little way.
*(To the servants.)* Go you and wait below till he arrives.

*(Exit Bremer and Jacques)*

JER. *(Shaking Manuel by the hand.)* Indeed, my friend, I'm glad to see
　　you here,[17]
Yet marvel wherefore.
MAN. I marvel wherefore, too, my honest Jerome:
But here we are, pri'thee be kind to us.
JER. Most heartily I will, I love your master:
"He is a quiet and a lib'ral man:"
A better inmate never cross'd my door.
MAN. Ah! but he is not now the man he was.
"Lib'ral he will, God grant he may be quiet."
JER. What has befallen him?
MAN.　　　　　　I cannot tell thee:
But faith, there is no living with him now.
JER. And yet, methinks, if I remember well,
You were about to quit his service, Manuel,[18]
When last he left this house. You grumbled then.
MAN. I've been upon the eve of leaving him
These ten long years; for many times is he
So difficult, capricious, and distrustful,
He galls my nature[19]—yet, I know not how,
A secret kindness binds me to him still.
JER. Some, who offend from a suspicious nature,
Will afterwards such fair confession make

16. The Larpent version has "How far is he behind?" 17. The Larpent version has "Well,
I am glad to see you here in Augsburg." 18. The Larpent version has "And yet, friend
Manuel, I recollect / You were about to quit De Monfort's service." 19. The Larpent ver-
sion has "I scarce can bear it."

As turns e'en the offence into a favour.[20]
MAN. Yes, some indeed do so: so will not he;
He'd rather die than such confession make.
JER. Ay, thou art right, for now I call to mind
That once he wrong'd me with unjust suspicion,
When first he came to lodge beneath my roof;
And when it so fell out that I was proved
Most guiltless of the fault, I truly thought
He would have made profession of regret;
But silent, haughty, and ungraciously
He bore himself as one offended still.
Yet shortly after, when unwittingly
I did him some slight service, o' the sudden[21]
He overpower'd me with his grateful thanks;
And would not be restrain'd from pressing on me
A noble recompense. I understood
His o'erstrain'd gratitude and bounty well,
And took it as he meant.
MAN.                         'Tis often thus.
I would have left him many years ago,
But that with all his faults there sometimes come
Such bursts of natural goodness from his heart,
As might engage a harder churl than I
To serve him still.—And then his sister too,
A noble dame, who should have been a queen:
"The meanest of her hinds,[22] at her command,
"Had fought like lions for her, and the poor,
"E'en o'er their bread of poverty had bless'd her—"
She would have griev'd if I had left my Lord.
JER. Comes she along with him?
MAN. No, [she was on a visit at some distance
[And] he departed all unknown to her,
Meaning to keep conceal'd his secret route;
But well I knew it would afflict her much,
And therefore left a little nameless billet,

20. The Larpent version has "As turns the injury into a favour." 21. The Larpent version
has "And when it afterwards was prov'd that I / Was guiltless of the fault, I thought your
Lord / Would have made some profession of regret; / But no;—in silence, haughty and un-
gracious / He bore himself as one offended still, / Yet shortly after, when it was my chance /
 To do him some slight service, o' the sudden." 22. A hind is a servant, usually a
farmhand.

Which after our departure, as I guess,
Would fall into her hands, and tell her all.[23]
What could I do? O 'tis a noble lady!
JER. All this is strange—something disturbs his mind—
Belike he is in love.
MAN.            No, Jerome, no.
Once on a time I serv'd a noble master,
Whose youth was blasted with untoward love,
And he with hope and fear and jealousy
For ever toss'd, led an unquiet life:[24]
Yet, when unruffled by the passing fit,
His pale wan face such gentle sadness wore
As mov'd a kindly heart to pity him;[25]
But Monfort, even in his calmest hour,
Still bears that gloomy sternness in his eye
Which sullenly repels all sympathy.
O no! good Jerome, no, it is not love.
*Noise without.*
JER. Hear I not horses trampling at the gate? (*Listening.*)
He is arriv'd—stay thou—I had forgot—
A plague upon't! my head is so confus'd—
I will return i'the instant to receive him.                    (*Exit hastily*)
*A great bustle without. Exit Manuel with lights, and returns again lighting
in De Monfort, as if just alighted from his journey, four servants follow-
ing him.*[26]
MAN. Your ancient host, my lord, receives you gladly,
And your apartment will be soon prepar'd.[27]
DE MON. 'Tis well.
"MAN. Where shall I place the chest you gave in charge?
"So please you, say my lord.
"DE MON. (*Throwing himself into a chair.*) Where-e'er thou wilt."
MAN. I would not move that luggage till you came. (*Pointing to certain
    things.*)
DE MON. Move what thou wilt, and trouble me no more.

23. The Larpent version has "But as I knew it would afflict her much / I wrote a note un-
sign'd with any name, / Which I contriv'd should fall into hands / When she set out from
home, and tell her all." 24. The Larpent version has "And he 'tis true, still toss'd with hope
and fear, / And Jealousy, led an unquiet life." 25. The Larpent version has "As mov'd one's
very heart to pity him." 26. The Campbell/Siddons version lists the servants as Louis,
Berg, Jacques and Bremer. 27. The Larpent version has "Your host, old Jerome, will be
proud to see you: / He is preparing your apartment, Sir."

*Manuel, with the assistance of other Servants, sets about putting the things in order, and De Monfort remains sitting in a thoughtful posture.*[28]

*Enter Jerome, bearing wine, &c. on a salver. As he approaches De Monfort, Manuel pulls him by the sleeve.*

MAN. (*Aside to Jerome.*) No, do not now;[29] he will not be disturb'd.

JER. What not to bid him welcome to my house,
And offer some refreshment?

MAN.                              No, good Jerome.
Softly, a little while: I pri'thee do.

*Jerome walks softly on tip-toes, till he gets near De Monfort, behind backs, then peeping on one side to see his face.*

JER. (*Aside to Manuel.*) Ah, Manuel, what an alter'd man is here!
His eyes are hollow, and his cheeks are pale—
[Methinks, he is ten years older than he was.—]
He left this house [last spring] a comely gentleman.

DE MON. Who whispers there?

MAN.                              'Tis your old landlord, sir.

JER. I joy to see you here—I crave your pardon—
I fear I do intrude.—[30]

DE MON. No, my kind host, I am oblig'd to thee.[31]

"JER. How fares it with your honour?"

"DE MON.                              Well enough."

JER. Here is a little of the fav'rite wine
That you were wont to praise. Pray honour me. (*Fills a glass.*)

DE MON. (*After drinking.*) I thank you, Jerome, 'tis delicious.

"JER. Ay, my dear wife did ever make it so."

DE MON. And how does she?[32]

JER.                              Alas, my lord! she's dead.

DE MON. Well, then she is at rest.[33]

JER.                              How well, my lord?

DE MON. Is she not with the dead, the quiet dead,
Where all is peace. Not e'en the impious wretch,
Who tears the coffin from its earthy vault,
And strews the mould'ring ashes to the wind
Can break their rest.

28. The Larpent version has the servants "carry away the luggage"; the Campbell/Siddons version indicates the servants are Louis and Berg. 29. The Larpent version has "No, no,—not now." 30. The Larpent version has "If I intrude, my Lord—." 31. The Larpent version has "No, no, good Jerome, I am oblig'd to you." 32. The Larpent version makes the cut and has "and / How does your wife?" 33. The Larpent version reads more clearly: "Then all is well with her."

JER. Woe's me! I thought you would have griev'd for her.
She was a kindly soul! Before she died,
When pining sickness bent her cheerless head,
She set my house in order—
And but the morning ere she breath'd her last,
Bade me preserve some flaskets[34] of this wine,
That should the Lord De Monfort come again
His cup might sparkle still.
*De Monfort walks across the stage, and wipes his eyes.*
"Indeed I fear I have distres'd you, sir:"
I surely thought you would be griev'd for her.[35]
DE MON. (*Taking Jerome's hand.*) I am, my friend. How long has she
 been dead?
JER. Two sad long years.[36]
DE MON.                    Would she were living still!
I was too troublesome, too heedless of her.[37]
"JER. O no! she lov'd to serve you.
"*Loud knocking without.*
"DE MON. What fool comes here, at such untimely hours,
"To make this cursed noise. (*To Manuel.*) Go to the gate. (*Exit Manuel*)
"All sober citizens are gone to bed;
"It is some drunkards on their nightly rounds,
"Who mean it but in sport.
"JER. I hear unusual voices—here they come.
"*Re-enter Manuel, shewing in Count Freberg and his Lady.*
"FREB. (*Running to embrace De Monfort.*) My dearest Monfort! most
 "unlook'd-for pleasure.
"Do I indeed embrace thee here again?
"I saw thy servant standing by the gate,
"His face recall'd, and learnt the joyful tidings.
"Welcome, thrice welcome here!
"DE MON. I thank thee, Freberg, for this friendly visit,
"And this fair Lady too. (*Bowing to the Lady.*)
"LADY.                    I fear, my Lord,
"We do intrude at an untimely hour:

34. Small flasks. 35. The Larpent version substitutes, "I thought your honour would be
griev'd for her." 36. The Larpent version has "Six months and more." 37. The Larpent
version has "for her." The Larpent version cuts from here to the beginning of Scene ii which
is merged into this scene. The following transition is added: "DE MON. And she is dead?— /
Good Jerome, leave me, and prepare my chamber. (*Exit Jerome*)." He then addresses Manuel
with his opening speech from I, ii.

"But now returning from a midnight mask,

"My husband did insist that we should enter.

"FREB. No, say not so; no hour untimely call,

"Which doth bring together long absent friends.

"Dear Monfort, wherefore has thou play'd so sly,

"To come upon us thus all suddenly?

"DE MON. O! many varied thoughts do cross our brain,

"Which touch the will, but leave the memory trackless;

"And yet a strange compounded motive make

"Wherefore a man should bend his evening walk

"To th' east or west, the forest or the field.

"Is it not often so?

"FREB. I ask no more, happy to see you here

"From any motive. There is one behind,

"Whose presence would have been a double bliss:

"Ah! how is she? The noble Jane de Monfort.

"DE MON. (*Confused.*) She is—I have—I have left my sister well.

"LADY. (*To Freberg.*) My Freberg, you are heedless of respect:

"You surely meant to say the Lady Jane.

"FREB. Respect! No, Madam; Princess, Empress, Queen,

"Could not denote a creature so exalted

"As this plain native appellation doth,

"The noble Jane de Monfort.

"LADY. (*Turning from him displeased to Monfort.*) You are fatigued, my

   "Lord; you want repose;

"Say, should we not retire?

"FREB.                          Ha! is it so?

"My friend, your face is pale, have you been ill?

"DE MON. No, Freberg, no; I think I have been well.

"FREB. (*Shaking his hand.*) I fear thou hast not, Monfort—Let it pass.

"We'll re-establish thee: we'll banish pain.

"I will collect some rare, some cheerful friends,

"And we shall spend together glorious hours,

"That gods might envy. Little time so spent

"Doth far outvalue all our life beside.

"This is indeed our life, our waking life,

"The rest dull breathing sleep.

"DE MON. Thus, it is true, from the sad years of life

"We sometimes do short hours, yea minutes strike,

"Keen, blissful, bright, never to be forgotten;

"Which thro' the dreary gloom of time o'erpast

"Shine like fair sunny spots on a wild waste.
"But few they are, as few the heaven-fir'd souls
"Whose magick power creates them. Bless'd art thou,
"If in the ample circle of thy friends
"Thou canst but boast a few.
"FREB. Judge for thyself: in truth I do not boast.
"There is amongst my friends, my later friends,
"A most accomplish'd stranger. New to Amberg,
"But just arriv'd; and will ere long depart.
"I met him in Franconia[38] two years since.
"He is so full of pleasant anecdote,
"So rich, so gay, so poignant in his wit,
"Time vanishes before him as he speaks,
"And ruddy morning thro' the lattice peeps
"Ere night seems well begun.
"DE MON.                     How is he call'd?
"FREB. I will surprise thee with a welcome face:
"I will not tell thee now.
"LADY. (*To De Monfort.*) I have, my Lord, a small request to make,
"And must not be denied. I too may boast
"Of some good friends, and beauteous country-women:
"To-morrow night I open wide my doors
"To all the fair and gay; beneath my roof
"Musick, and dance, and revelry shall reign.
"I pray you come and grace it with your presence.
"DE MON. You honour me too much to be denied.
"LADY. I thank you, Sir; and in return for this,
"We shall withdraw, and leave you to repose.
"FREB. Must it be so? Good night—sweet sleep to thee. (*To De
  "Monfort.*)
"DE MON. (*To Freberg.*) Good night. (*To Lady.*) Good-night, fair Lady.
"LADY.                     Farewell!
                              "(*Exeunt Freberg and Lady*)
"DE MON. (*To Jerome.*) I thought Count Freberg had been now in
  "France.
"JER. He meant to go, as I have been inform'd.
"DE MON. Well, well, prepare my bed; I will to rest.
                              "(*Exit Jerome*)
"DE MON. (*Alone.*) I know not how it is, my heart stands back,

38. Franconia is a region in Western Germany in Bavaria. Amberg is a city near Nuremberg.

"And meets not this man's love.—Friends! rarest friends!
"Rather than share his undiscerning praise
"With every table wit, and book-form'd sage,
"And paltry poet puling to the moon,
"I'd court from him proscription; yea abuse,
"And think it proud distinction.                    (*Exit*)"


"SCENE II   *A Small Apartment in Jerome's House: a table and breakfast set out.*

"*Enter De Monfort, followed by Manuel, and sets himself down by the table, with*
"*a cheerful face.*"

DE MON. Manuel, this morning's sun shines pleasantly:
These old apartments too are light and cheerful.
Our landlord's kindness has reviv'd me much;
He serves as though he lov'd me. This pure air
Braces the listless nerves, and warms the blood:
I feel in freedom here. (*Filling a cup of coffee, and drinking.*)
MAN.                    Ah! sure, my Lord,
No air is purer than the air at home.
DE MON. Here can I wander with assured steps,
Nor dread, at every winding of the path,
Lest an abhorred serpent cross my way,
And move—(*Stopping short.*)
MAN. What says your honour?
There are no serpents in our pleasant fields.
DE MON. Think'st thou there are no serpents in the world
But those who slide[39] along the grassy sod,
And sting the luckless foot that presses them?
There are who in the path of social life
Do bask their spotted skins in Fortune's sun,
And sting the soul—Ay, till its healthful frame
Is chang'd to secret, fest'ring, sore disease,
So deadly is the wound.
MAN. Heaven guard your honour from such horrid skathe:[40]
They are but rare, I hope?
DE MON. (*Shaking his head.*) We mark the hollow eye, the wasted frame,
The gait disturb'd of wealthy honour'd men,
But do not know the cause.

39. The Larpent version has "But such as glide along." 40. For "scathe," a hurt or
damage.

"MAN. 'Tis very true. God keep you well, my Lord!

"DE MON. I thank thee, Manuel, I am very well.

"I shall be gay too, by the setting sun.

"I go to revel it with sprightly dames,

"And drive the night away. (*Filling another cup, and drinking.*)

"MAN. I should be glad to see your honour gay.

"DE MON. And thou too shalt be gay. There, honest Manuel,

"Put these broad pieces in they leathern purse,

"And take at night a cheerful jovial glass.

"Here is one too, for Bremer; he loves wine;

"And one for Jacques: be joyful all together."

*Enter Servant.*[41]

SER. My Lord, I met e'en now, a short way off,

Your countryman the Marquis Rezenvelt.[42]

DE MON. (*Starting from his seat, and letting the cup fall from his hand.*)
   Who, say'st thou?

SER.                Marquis Rezenvelt, an' please you.

"DE MON. Thou ly'st—it is not so—it is impossible.

"SER. I saw him with these eyes, plain as yourself."

DE MON. Fool! 'tis some passing stranger thou hast seen,

And with a hideous likeness been deceiv'd.

SER. [Indeed, my lord, the Marquis spoke to me;]

No other stranger could deceive my sight.[43]

DE MON. (*Dashing his clenched hand violently upon the table, and overturning
   every thing.*) Heaven blast thy sight! it lights on nothing good.

"SER. I surely thought no harm to look upon him.

"DE MON. What, dost thou still insist? Him must it be?

"Does it so please thee well?"

*Servant endeavours to speak.*

                    Hold thy damn'd tongue.

By heaven I'll kill thee.[44] (*Going furiously up to him.*)

MAN. (*In a soothing voice.*) "Nay harm him not, my Lord; he speaks the
   "truth;

"I've met his groom, who told me certainly

"His Lord is here."[45] I should have told you so,

But thought, perhaps, it might displease your honour.

41. The Larpent version identifies him as Bremer. 42. The Larpent version has "My lord, the Marquis Rezenvelt, e'en now passing the door—" 43. The Larpent version has "It was no stranger that deceiv'd my sight." 44. The Larpent version has "or I will choke thee, villain." 45. The Larpent version substitutes "He speaks the truth, my lord; I met his Groom, / Who told me that the Marquis Rezenvelt / Is surely here."

DE MON. (*Becoming all at once calm, and turning sternly to Manuel.*) And
   how dar'st thou to think it would displease me?
What is't to me who leaves or enters Amberg?[46]
But it displeases me, yea ev'n to frenzy,
That every idle fool must hither come
"To break my leisure with the paltry tidings"
Of all the cursed things he stares upon.[47]
*Servant attempts to speak—De Monfort stamps with his foot.*
Take thine ill-favour'd visage from my sight,
And speak of it no more.[48]                    (*Exit Servant*)
And go thou too; I choose to be alone.         (*Exit Manuel*)
"*De Monfort goes to the door by which they went out; opens it, and looks.*
"But is he gone indeed? Yes, he is gone.
"*Goes to the opposite door, opens it, and looks: then gives loose to all the fury of*
"*gesture, and walks up and down in great agitation.*"
It is too much: by heaven it is too much!
He haunts me—stings me—like a devil haunts—
He'll make a raving maniack of me—Villain!
The air wherein thou draw'st thy fulsome breath
Is poison to me—Oceans shall divide! (*Pauses.*)
But no; thou think'st I fear thee, cursed reptile![49]
"And hast a pleasure in the damned thought."
Though my heart's blood should curdle at thy sight,
I'll stay and face thee still.[50]
*Knocking at the chamber door.*
                   Ha! Who knocks there?[51]
"FREB. (*Without.*) It is thy friend, De Monfort.
"DE MON. (*Opening the door.*) Enter, then.
"*Enter Freberg.*
"FREB. (*Taking his hand kindly.*) How art thou now? How has thou past
   "the night?

46. The Larpent version has Augsburg, which would move the play south, nearer to
Munich. 47. The Larpent version has "With all the odious sights he stares upon."
48. The Larpent version has "Hence from my sight and speak of it no more." 49. The
Larpent version has "he thinks I fear him,—cursed reptile!" 50. The Larpent version has
"his sight" and "face him still." 51. In the Larpent version, this is the first time Freberg
(there called Albert) appears. He is introduced when Manuel answers from without: "MAN.
Your friend, my Lord, Count Albert. DE MON. Show him in.— / So he has learn'd that I'm
arriv'd already. / I thought that Albert had been now in Italy. (*Enter Manuel conducting Albert
and Exit*)." The Larpent version then returns to the cut material from Freberg's first visit,
offering a slightly altered version (the Countess is not present) through De Monfort's statement that "I have left my sister well." A transition is then provided back to the present
scene, with the Count saying, "You seem disturb'd."

"Has kindly sleep refresh'd thee?

"DE MON. Yes, I have lost an hour or two in sleep,

"And so should be refresh'd.

"FREB.                              And art thou not?

"Thy looks speak not of rest. Thou art disturb'd."

DE MON. No, somewhat ruffled from a foolish cause,

Which soon will pass away. [—Count Rezenvelt!—]

FREB. (*Shaking his head.*) Ah no, De Monfort! something in thy face

Tells me another tale.[52] "Then wrong me not:

"If any secret grief distracts thy soul,

"Here am I all devoted to thy love;

"Open thy heart to me. What troubles thee?

"DE MON. I have no grief: distress me not, my friend.

"FREB. Nay, do not call me so. Wert thou my friend,

"Would'st thou not open all thine inmost soul,

"And bid me share its every consciousness?

"DE MON. Freberg, thou know'st not man; not nature's man,

"But only him who, in smooth studied works

"Of polish'd sages, shines deceitfully

"In all the splendid foppery of virtue.

"That man was never born whose secret soul

"With all its motley treasure of dark thoughts,

"Foul fantasies, vain musings, and wild dreams,

"Was ever open'd to another's scan.

"Away, away! it is delusion all.

"FREB. Well, be reserved then: perhaps I'm wrong.

"DE MON. How goes the hour?

"FREB. 'Tis early: a long day is still before us,

"Let us enjoy it. Come along with me;"

I'll introduce you to my pleasant friend.[53]

"DE MON. Your pleasant friend?

"FREB.                              Yes, he of whom I spake.

"(*Taking his hand.*) There is no good I would not share with thee,

"And this man's company, to minds like thine,

---

52. The Larpent version has "Ah, no, Matthias; something in your Face / Tells me another Tale." It then returns to the scene of Freberg's earlier visit to include the exchange on De Monfort's health and Freberg also tells De Monfort that "This night my wife doth open wide our doors / To all the fair and gay; beneath our roof Musick and dance, and revelry shall reign; / I pray you, come, and grace it with your presence." Freberg then describes Rezenvelt; we return to the present scene with the offer to introduce him. 53. The Larpent version rejoins the first edition here, but introduces the name of Rezenvelt through a single speech by Albert/Freberg: "I'll introduce you to my pleasant friend. / But 'tis most like he's no stranger to you.— / He is your townsman, noble Rezenvelt."

"Is the best banquet-feast I could bestow.
"But I will speak in mystery no more,
"It is thy townsman, noble Renzenvelt."
[DE MON. Rezenvelt!]
*De Monfort pulls his hand hastily from Freberg and shrinks back.*
FREB. Ha! What is this? Art thou pain-stricken, Monfort?
"Nay, on my life, thou rather seem'st offended:"
Does it displease thee that I call him friend?
DE MON. No, all men are thy friends.
FREB. No, say not all men. But thou art offended.
"I see it well. I thought to do thee pleasure."
But if his presence is not welcome here,[54]
He shall not join our company to-day.
DE MON. What dost thou mean to say? What is't to me
Whether I meet with such a thing as Rezenvelt
To-day, to-morrow, every day, or never.
FREB. In truth, I thought you had been well with him.
He prais'd you much.
DE MON. I thank him for his praise—"Come, let us move:
"This chamber is confin'd and airless grown."
[REZ. (*Without.*) 'Tis well, 'tis well,—
[Give my respects, and say, I wait upon him.]
DE MON. (*Starting.*) I hear a stranger's voice!
FREB.                    'Tis Rezenvelt.
Let him be told we are gone abroad.
DE MON. (*Proudly.*) No; let him enter. Who waits there? Ho! Manuel![55]
*Enter Manuel.*
What stranger speaks below?
MAN.                    The Marquis Rezenvelt.
I have not told him that you are within.
DE MON. (*Angrily.*) And wherefore did'st thou not? Let him ascend.

                                   (*Exit Manuel*)

*A long pause. De Monfort walking up and down with a quick pace. Enter
Rezenvelt, and runs freely up to De Monfort.*
REZ. (*To De Monfort.*) My noble Marquis, welcome.
DE MON.                                   Sir, I thank you.
REZ. (*To Freberg.*) My gentle friend, well met.[56] Abroad so early?
FREB. "It is indeed an early hour for me."

---

54. The Larpent version has "Nay, if his presence is not welcome to thee." 55. The Larpent version has "No; let him enter.—Manuel!—Who waits?" 56. The Larpent version has
"And you, my friend, well met."

How sits thy last night's revel on thy spirits?

REZ. O, light as ever. On my way to you
E'en now I learnt De Monfort was arriv'd,
And turn'd my steps aside; so here I am. (*Bowing gaily to De Monfort.*)

DE MON. I thank you, Sir; you do me too much honour. (*Proudly.*)

REZ. Nay, say not so; not too much honour, Marquis,
Unless, indeed, 'tis more than pleases you.

DE MON. (*Confused.*) Having no previous notice of your coming,
I look'd not for it.

REZ. Ay, true indeed; when I approach you next,
I'll send a herald to proclaim my coming,
And make my bow to you by sound of trumpet.

DE MON. (*To Freberg. Turning haughtily from Rezenvelt with affected
indifference.*) How does your cheerful friend, that good old man?

FREB. My cheerful friend? I know not whom you mean.

"DE MON. Count Waterlan.

"FREB.                    I know not one so named."[57]

DE MON. (*Very confused.*) O[58] pardon me—it was at Bâle I knew him.

FREB. You have not yet enquired for honest Reisdale.
I met him as I came, and mention'd you.
He seemed amaz'd; and fain he would have learnt
What cause procur'd us so much happiness.
He question'd hard, and hardly would believe
I could not satisfy his strong desire.

REZ. And know you not what brings De Monfort here?[59]

FREB. Truly, I do not.

REZ.                    O! 'tis love of me.
I have but two short days in Amberg been,[60]
And here with postman's[61] speed he follows me,
Finding his home so dull and tiresome grown.

FREB. (*To De Monfort.*) Is Rezenvelt so sadly miss'd with you?
Your town so chang'd?

DE MON.               Not altogether so:
Some witlings and jest-mongers still remain
For fools to laugh at.

REZ. But he laughs not, and therefore he is wise.
He ever frowns on them with sullen brow

---

57. He does know him, however, in Act III, scene i. 58. The Larpent version has "True." 59. The Larpent version has "hither." 60. The Larpent version has five days and substitutes Augsberg for Amberg. 61. The Larpent version has "footman's speed"; "running footmen" ran alongside slow-moving coach horses.

Contemptuous; therefore he is very wise.
Nay, daily frets his most refined soul
With their poor folly, to its inmost core;
Therefore he is most eminently wise.
FREB. Fy, Rezenvelt![62] You are too early gay;
Such spirits rise but with the ev'ning glass.
They suit not placid morn.
*To De Monfort, who after walking impatiently up and down, comes close to his ear, and lays hold of his arm.*

                    What would you, Monfort?[63]
DE MON. Nothing—Yet, what is't o'clock?
No, no—I had forgot—'tis early still. (*Turns away again.*)
FREB. (*To Rezenvelt.*) Waltser informs me that you have agreed
To read his verse o'er, and tell the truth.
It is a dangerous task.
REZ.              Yet I'll be honest:
I can but lose his favour and a feast.
*Whilst they speak, De Monfort walks up and down impatiently and irresolute; at last, pulls the bell violently.*
*Enter Servant.*[64]
DE MON. (*To Servant.*) What dost thou want?—
SER.                    I thought your honour
   had rung.
DE MON. I have forgot—Stay; are my horses saddled?
SER. I thought, my Lord, you would not ride to-day,[65]
After so long a journey.
DE MON. (*Impatiently.*) Well—'tis good.
Begone!—I want thee not.                    (*Exit Servant*)
REZ. (*Smiling significantly.*) I humbly crave your pardon, gentle
   Marquis.
It grieves me that I cannot stay with you,
And make my visit of a friendly length.
I trust your goodness will excuse me now;
Another time I shall be less unkind.
(*To Freberg.*) Will you not go with me?
FREB. Excuse me, Monfort,[66] I'll return again.
                    (*Exeunt Rezenvelt and Freberg*)

---

62. The Larpent version has "A Truce, Rezenvelt!" 63. The Larpent version gives this speech to Rezenvelt. 64. The Larpent version indicates it is Manuel who enters. 65. The Larpent version substitutes "What, will you ride to day, again, my lord." 66. The Larpent version has "Your leave, De Monfort."

DE MON. (*Alone, tossing his arms distractedly.*) Hell hath no greater
   torment for th'accurs'd
Than this man's presence gives—
Abhorred fiend! he hath a pleasure too,
A damned pleasure in the pain he gives!
"Oh! the side glance of that detested eye!"
That conscious smile! that full insulting lip!
It touches every nerve: "it makes me mad.
"What, does it please thee? Dost thou woo my hate?
"Hate shalt thou have! determin'd, deadly hate,
"Which shall awake no smile." Malignant[67] villain!
The venom[68] of thy mind is rank and devilish,
And thin the film that hides it.
"Thy hateful visage ever spoke thy worth:
"I loath'd thee when a boy."
That [men][69] should be besotted with him thus!
And Freberg likewise so bewitched is,
That like a hireling flatt'rer, at his heels
He meanly paces, off'ring brutish praise,
O! I could curse him too.                          (*Exit*)


## ACT II


SCENE I  *A very splendid apartment in Count Freberg's house, fancifully
decorated. A wide folding door opened, shews another magnificent room lighted
up to receive company. Enter through the folding doors the Count and Countess,
richly dressed.*

FREB. (*Looking around.*) In truth, I like those decorations well:
They suit those lofty walls. And here, my love,
The gay profusion of a woman's fancy
Is well display'd. Noble simplicity
Becomes us less on such a night as this
Than gaudy show.
"LADY. Is it not noble, then? (*He shakes his head.*) I thought it so,
"And as I know you love simplicity,

---

67. The Larpent version has "Detested." 68. The Larpent version has "malice." 69. The
first edition has a blank ("——") here; later editions provide "men." The Larpent version
closes this speech somewhat differently: "That all the world should be besotted thus! / Like
hireling flatt'rers lackeying at his heels / With brutish praise!—O, I could curse them too!"

"I did intend it should be simple too.
FREB. "Be satisfy'd, I pray; we want to-night
"A cheerful banquet-house, and not a temple.
"How runs the hour?"[70]
LADY. It is not late, but soon we shall be rous'd
With the loud entry of our frolick guests.
*Enter a Page, richly dressed.*
PAGE. Madam, there is a Lady in your hall,[71]
Who begs to be admitted to your presence.
LADY. Is it not one of our invited friends?
PAGE. No, far unlike to them; it is a stranger.
LADY. How looks her countenance?
PAGE. So queenly, so commanding, and so noble,
I shrunk at first in awe; but when she smil'd,
For "so" she did to see me thus abash'd,
Methought I could have compass'd sea and land
To do her bidding.
"LADY.            Is she young or old?
"PAGE. Neither, if right I guess, but she is fair;
"For time hath laid his hand so gently on her,
"As he too had been aw'd."
LADY.                    The foolish stripling![72]
She has bewitch'd thee, [Boy.] "Is she large in stature?
"PAGE. So stately and so graceful is her form,
"I thought at first her stature was gigantick,
"But on a near approach I found, in truth,
"She scarcely does surpass the middle size."
LADY. What is her garb?
PAGE. I cannot well describe the fashion of it.
She is not deck'd in any gallant trim,
But seems to me clad in the usual weeds,
Of high habitual state; for as she moves
Wide flows her robe in many a waving fold,
As I have seen unfurled banners play
With the soft breese.
LADY.                Thine eyes deceive thee, boy,
It is an apparition thou hast seen.

---

70. The Larpent version bridges the cut with "But say,—how runs the hour?" 71. The Larpent verson has "a Lady waits within." 72. The Larpent version has "Do you hear the stripling?"

FREB. (*Starting from his seat, where he has been sitting during the converstion between the Lady and the Page.*) It is an apparition he has seen.
Or it is Jane de Monfort.                                    (*Exit, hastily*)
LADY. (*Displeased.*) "No; such description surely suits not her."
Did she enquire for me?
PAGE. She ask'd to see the lady of Count Freberg.
LADY. Perhaps it is not she—"I fear it is—"
Ha! here they come.[73] "He has but guess'd too well."
*Enter Freberg, leading in Jane de Monfort.*[74]
"FREB. (*Presenting her to Lady.*) Here, madam, welcome a most worthy "guest."
LADY. Madam, a thousand welcomes. Pardon me;
I could not guess who honour'd me so far;
I should not else have waited coldly here.
JANE. I thank you for this welcome, gentle Countess,
But take those kind excuses back again;
I am a bold intruder on this hour,
And am entitled to no ceremony.
I came in quest of a dear truant friend,[75]
But Freberg has inform'd me—
(*To Freberg.*) And he is well you say?
FREB.                                    Yes, well, but joyless.
JANE. It is the usual temper of his mind:[76]
It opens not, but with the thrilling touch
Of some strong heart-string o'the sudden press'd.
FREB. It may be so, I've known him otherwise.
He is suspicious grown.
JANE. Not so, Count Freberg, Monfort is too noble.
Say rather, that he is a man in grief,
Wearing at times a strange and scowling eye;
And thou, less generous than beseems a friend,
Hast thought too hardly of him.
FREB. (*Bowing with great respect.*) So will I say,
I'll own nor word, nor will, that can offend you.
LADY. De Monfort is engag'd to grace our feast,
Ere long you'll see him here.
JANE. I thank you truly, but this homely dress
Suits not the splendour of such scenes as these.

---

73. The Larpent version has "Ha! here she comes." 74. The Larpent version indicates that the Page exits here. 75. The Larpent version has "Brother." 76. The Larpent version has "tenor of his soul."

FREB. (*Pointing to her dress.*) Such artless and majestick elegance,
So exquisitely just, so nobly simple,
Will make the gorgeous blush.
[LADY. Indeed! so struck?]
JANE. (*Smiling.*) Nay, nay, be more consistent, courteous knight,
And do not praise a plain and simple guise
With such profusion of unsimple words.
I cannot join your company to-night.
LADY. Not stay to see your brother?
JANE. Therefore it is I would not, gentle hostess.
Here he will find all that can woo the heart
To joy and sweet forgetfulness of pain;
The sight of me would wake his feeling mind
To other thoughts. I am no doting mistress,
No fond distracted wife, who must forthwith
Rush to his arms and weep. I am his sister:
The eldest daughter of his father's house:
Calm and unwearied is my love for him;
And having found him, patiently I'll wait,
Nor greet him in the hour of social joy,
To dash his mirth with tears.—
The night wears on; permit me to withdraw.
FREB. Nay, do not, do not injure us so far!
Disguise thyself, and join our friendly train.
JANE. You wear not masks to-night?
LADY. We wear not masks, but you may be conceal'd
Behind the double foldings of a veil.
JANE. (*After pausing to consider.*) In truth, I feel a little so inclin'd.
Methinks unknown, I e'en might speak to him,
And gently prove the temper of his mind:
But for the means I must become your debtor. (*To Lady.*)
LADY. Who waits?
*Enter her Woman.* [77]

    Attend this lady to my wardrobe,
And do what she commands you.

         (*Exeunt Jane and Waiting-woman*)
FREB. (*Looking after Jane, as she goes out, with admiration.*) Oh! what a
 soul she bears! see how she steps!
Nought but the native dignity of worth

77. The Larpent version gives the woman's name as Katherine.

E'er taught the moving form such noble grace.
LADY. Such lofty mien, and high assumed gait
I've seen ere now, and men have call'd it pride.
FREB. No, 'faith! thou never did'st, but oft indeed[78]
The paltry imitation thou hast seen.
"(*Looking at her.*) How hang those trappings on thy motly[79] gown?
"They seem like garlands on a May-day queen,
"Which hinds have dress'd in sport.
"LADY. I'll doff it, then, since it displeases you.
"FREB. (*Softening.*) No, no, thou art lovely still in every garb.
"But see the guests assemble."[80]
*Enter groups of well dressed people, who pay their compliments to Freberg and his Lady; and followed by her pass into the inner apartment, where more company appear assembling, as if by another entry.*
FREB. (*Who remains on the front of the stage, with a friend or two.*)
How loud the hum of this gay meeting croud![81]
'Tis like a bee-swarm in the noonday sun.
"Musick will quell the sound. Who waits without?
"Musick strike up."
*A grand piece of musick is playing, and when it ceases, enter from the inner apartment Rezenvelt, with several gentlemen, all richly dressed.*[82]
FREB. (*To those just entered.*) What lively gallants quit the field so soon?
Are there no beauties in that moving crowd
To fix your fancy?[83]
REZ. Ay, marry, arc there! men of ev'ry mind
May in that moving croud[84] some fair one find,
To suit their taste, tho' whimsical and strange,
As ever fancy own'd.
"Beauty of every cast and shade is there,
"From the perfection of a faultless form,
"Down to the common, brown, unnoted maid,
"Who looks but pretty in her Sunday gown."
1ST GENT. There is, indeed, a gay variety.[85]

---

78. The Larpent version substitutes "too" for "but." The interjection "'faith" means "in faith, good faith." 79. For "motley," composed of many differing, even incongruous colors and parts; the dress of jesters is motley. 80. The Larpent version has "Hark! hark—the guests are entering. (*Musick.*)" 81. The Larpent version has "How gay the buzz of this assembling crowd!" 82. The Larpent version indicates that there is a dance. 83. The Larpent version has "What, my gallants, what quit the field so soon? / Are there no beauties then in all the crowd / To fix your fancy?" 84. The Larpent version has "motley group." 85. The Larpent version has Freberg/Albert make this speech.

REZ. And if the liberality of nature
Suffices not, there's store of grafted charms
Blending in one the sweets of many plants
"So obstinately, strangely opposite,
"As would have well defy'd all other art
"But female cultivation. Aged youth,
"With borrow'd locks in rosy chaplets bound
"Cloaths her dim eye, parch'd lip, and skinny cheek,
"In most unlovely softness.
"And youthful age, with fat round trackless face,
"The down-cast look of contemplation deep,
"Most pensively assumes.
"Is it not even so?" The native prude,
With forced laugh,[86] and merriment uncouth,
Plays off the wild coquet's successful charms
With most unskilful pains; and the coquet,
In temporary crust of cold reserve,
Fixes her studied looks upon the ground
Forbiddingly demure.

FREB. Fy! thou art too severe.

REZ.                              Say, rather, gentle.
I' faith! the very dwarfs attempt to charm
With lofty airs of puny majesty,
Whilst potent damsels, of a portly make,
Totter like nurselings, and demand the aid
Of gentle sympathy.
From all those diverse modes of dire assault,
He owns a heart of hardest adamant,
Who shall escape to-night.[87]

FREB. (*To De Monfort, who has entered during Rezenvelt's speech, and heard the greatest part of it.*) "Ha, ha, ha, ha!"
How pleasantly he gives his wit the rein,
Yet guides its wild career!

*De Monfort is silent.*

REZ. (*Smiling archly.*) What, think you,[88] Freberg, the same powerful spell
Of transformation reigns o'er all to-night?

---

86. The Larpent version has "laugh suborn'd." 87. The Larpent version has "Of gentle sympathy. He owns a heart / Of hardest adamant, who shall escape / From all their varied arts of dire assault." 88. The Larpent version has "think'st thou."

Or that[89] De Monfort is a woman turn'd,
So widely from his native self to swerve,
As grace my gai'ty with a smile of his?
DE MON. Nay, think not, Rezenvelt, there is no smile
I can bestow on thee. There is a smile,
A smile of nature too, which I can spare,
And yet, perhaps, thou wilt not thank me for it. (*Smiles contemptuously.*)
REZ. Not thank thee! It were surely most ungrateful
No thanks to pay for nobly giving me[90]
What, well we see, has cost thee so much pain.
For nature hath her smiles, of birth more painful
Than bitt'rest execrations.
FREB. "These idle words will lead us to disquiet:
"Forbear, forbear, my friends." Go, Rezenvelt,
Accept the challenge of those lovely dames,
Who thro' the portal come with bolder steps
To claim your notice.[91]
*Enter a group of Ladies from the other apartment. Rezenvelt shrugs up his shoulders, as if unwilling to go.*
1ST GENT.[92] (*To Rezenvelt.*) Behold in sable veil a lady comes,
Whose noble air doth challenge fancy's skill
To suit it with a countenance as goodly. (*Pointing to Jane De Monfort,*
  *who now enters in a thick black veil.*)
REZ. Yes, this way lies attraction. (*To Freberg.*) With permission,
(*Going up to Jane.*) Fair lady, tho' within that envious shroud
Your beauty deigns not to enlighten us,
We bid you welcome, and our beauties here
Will welcome you the more for such concealment.
With the permission of our noble host—[93] (*Taking her hand, and leading
  her to the front of the stage.*)
JANE. (*To Freberg.*) Pardon me this presumption, courteous sir:
I thus appear, (*Pointing to her veil.*) not careless of respect
Unto the gen'rous lady of the feast.
Beneath this veil no beauty shrouded is,

89. The Larpent version has "Think'st thou." 90. The Larpent version has "To pay no thanks for nobly giving me." 91. The Larpent version has "Rezenvelt / Go meet the challenge of those lovely dames, / Who thro' the portal come with hurrying steps / To claim your notice." The first edition has the incorrect "comes." 92. In the Larpent version, Rezenvelt gives this speech. 93. The Larpent version has "Here lies attraction,—Lady, with your leave;— / Tho' veil'd behind that shroud of envious night, / Your beauty deign not to enlighten us, / We bid you welcome.— / With the permission of our noble host,—."

That, now, or pain, or pleasure can bestow.
Within the friendly cover of its shade
I only wish unknown, again to see
One who, alas! is heedless of my pain.
DE MON. Yes, it is ever thus. "Undo that veil,
"And give they count'nance to the cheerful light."
Men now all soft, and female beauty scorn,
And mock the gentle cares which aim to please.
It is most damnable! undo thy veil,
And think of him no more.
JANE. I know it well, even to a proverb grown,
Is lovers' faith, and I had borne such slight:
But he who has, alas! forsaken me⁹⁴
Was the companion of my early days,
My cradle's mate, mine infant play-fellow.
Within our op'ning minds with riper years
The love of praise and gen'rous virtue sprung:
Thro' varied life our pride, our joys, were one;
At the same tale we wept: he is my brother.
DE MON. And he forsook thee?—No, I dare not curse him:
My heart upbraids me with a crime like his.
JANE. Ah! do not thus distress a feeling heart.
All sisters are not to the soul entwin'd
With equal bands; thine has not watch'd for thee,
Weep'd for thee, cheer'd thee, shar'd thy weal and woe,
As I have done for him.
DE MON. (Eagerly.) Ha! has she not?
By heaven! the sum of all thy kindly deeds
Were but as chaff pois'd against the massy gold,
Compar'd to that which I do owe her love.
O pardon me! I mean not to offend—
I am too warm—But she of whom I speak
Is the dear sister of my earliest love;
In noble virtuous worth to none a second:
And tho' behind those sable folds were hid
As fair a face as ever woman own'd,
Still would I say she is as fair as thee.
How oft amidst the beauty-blazing throng,
I've proudly to th'inquiring stranger told

94. The Larpent version has "such slight I could have borne: / But he, by whom I am forsaken, Sir."

Her name and lineage! yet within her house,
The virgin mother of an orphan race
Her dying parents left, this noble[95] woman
Did, like a Roman matron, proudly[96] sit,
"Despising all the blandishments of love;"
Whilst many a youth his hopeless love conceal'd,
Or, humbly distant, woo'd her like a queen.
Forgive, I pray you! O forgive this boasting!
In faith! I mean you no discourtesy.

JANE. (*Off her guard, in a soft natural tone of voice.*) Oh no! nor do me
    any.

DE MON. What voice speaks now? Withdraw, withdraw this shade!
For if thy face bear semblance to thy voice,
I'll fall and worship thee. Pray! pray undo!

*Puts forth his hand eagerly to snatch away the veil, whilst she shrinks back, and
Rezenvelt steps between to prevent him.*

REZ. Stand off: no hand shall lift this sacred veil.

DE MON. What, dost thou think De Monfort fall'n so low,
That there may live a man beneath heav'n's roof
Who dares to say he shall not?

REZ. He lives who dares to say—

JANE. (*Throwing back her veil, very much alarmed, and rushing between
    them.*) Forbear, forbear!

*Rezenvelt, very much struck, steps back respectfully, and makes her a very low
bow. De Monfort stands for a while motionless, gazing upon her, till she, looking
expressively to him, extends her arms, and he, rushing into them, bursts into tears.
Freberg seems very much pleased. The company then gather about them, and the
Scene closes.*[97]

---

95. The Larpent version has "lovely." 96. The Larpent version has "nobly." 97. The
Larpent version closes the scene differently after De Monfort rushes into his sister's
arms:

DE MON. My sister!

JANE.         O, my dearest brother!

ALB/FREB.                         Pray,
Retire awhile; and privately indulge
These kind emotions:—I will have it so.         (*Exit Jane and De Monfort*)
Nay, friends, this must not interrupt our mirth.—
Come, let us hear that song you promis'd us.—
    SONG. *As the song ends, enter the Page and bows to the Countess.*
ALB/FREB. My friends, we have made some trifling preparation;—
Come, lead the way;—it waits:—we follow you.
    *MUSICK.*             (*Exeunt Page—Countess—Rezenvelt the Guests and Albert*)

LARPENT SCENE II[98]   *A Street.*

*Enter Conrad.*

CON. What frantick Demon has possess'd the Spirits
Of all this City? Revels, Donnings, Masques,
In every street, and turning night to day!—
The Melancholy Monfort has not chosen
This scene for his retreat, I fear; and yet
I track him at the foot.

*Enter Bremer bearing a torch.*

A word, good friend.
BREM. Let it be short then, friend; for I am in haste.
CON. And short withal yourself.—Can you inform
A stranger here in Augsburg, whether Matthias,
The Noble Lord De Monfort, may be found
Within these walls.
BREM. De Monfort is in Augsburg.—
What is your business with him?
CON. Softly there.—
Good night—I have my errand—you are in haste.
BREM. So close!—This fellow looks suspiciously.—
Well, I may bar your passage to him yet.—
Good night!—                                      (*Exit Bremer*)
CON. And if thou dost, I think thou'lt deal
With some more cunning conjurer than thyself.—
Now to look out for a lodging for the night.—
If he's above ground, I am resolv'd I'll see him:—
No common thwart shall make me lose my pains.    (*Exit Conrad*)


SCENE II[99]   *De Monfort's apartments.*

*Enter De Monfort, with a disordered air, and his hand pressed upon his forehead, followed by Jane.*

DE MON. No more, my sister, urge me not again:
"My secret troubles cannot be revealed."
From all participation of its thoughts
My heart recoils: I pray thee be contented.
JANE. What, must I, like a distant humble friend,

98. This scene appears in the Larpent version, not the first edition; Conrad is Grimbald in the printed version. 99. In the Larpent version, this is Act II, scene iii.

Observe thy restless eye, and gait disturb'd,
In timid silence, whilst with yearning heart
I turn aside to weep? O no! De Monfort!
A nobler task thy noble mind will give;
Thy true intrusted friend I still shall be.
DE MON. Ah, Jane, forbear! I cannot e'en to thee.
"JANE. Then fy upon it! fy upon it, Monfort!
"There was a time when e'en with murder stain'd,
"Had it been possible that such dire deed
"Could e'er have been the crime of one so piteous,
"Thou would'st have told it me.
DE MON. "So would I now—but ask of this no more."
All other trouble but the one I feel
I had disclos'd to thee. I pray thee spare me.
It is the secret weakness of my nature.
JANE. Then secret let it be; I urge no farther.
"The eldest of our valiant father's hopes,
"So sadly orphan'd, side by side we stood,
"Like two young trees, whose boughs, in early strength,
"Screen the weak saplings of the rising grove,
"And brave the storm together—"
I have so long, as if by nature's right,
Thy bosom's inmate and adviser been,
I thought thro' life I should have so remain'd,
Nor ever known a change. Forgive me, Monfort,
A humbler station will I take by thee:
The close attendant of thy wand'ring steps;
"The cheerer of this home, by strangers sought;"
The soother of those griefs I must not know,
This is mine office now: I ask no more.
DE MON. Oh Jane! thou dost constrain me with thy love!
Would I could tell it thee!
JANE. Thou shalt not tell me. Nay, I'll stop mine ears,
Nor from the yearnings of affection wring
What shrinks from utt'rance. Let it pass, my brother.
I'll stay by thee; I'll cheer thee, comfort thee:
Pursue with thee the study of some art,
Or nobler science, that compels the mind
To steady thought progressive, driving forth
All floating, wild, unhappy fantasies;
Till thou, with brow unclouded, smil'st again,

Like one who from dark visions of the night,
"When th' active soul within its lifeless cell
"Holds its own world, with dreadful fancy press'd
"Of some dire, terrible, or murd'rous deed,"
Wakes to the dawning morn, and blesses heaven.
DE MON. It will not pass away; 'twill haunt me still.
JANE. Ah! say not so, for I will haunt thee too;
And be to it so close an adversary,[100]
That, tho' I wrestle darkling with the fiend,
I shall o'er come it.
DE MON.            Thou most gen'rous woman!
Why do I treat thee thus? It should not be—
And yet I cannot—O that cursed villain!
He will not let me be the man I would.
JANE. What say'st thou, Monfort? Oh! what words are these?
They have awak'd my soul to dreadful thoughts.
I do beseech thee speak!
*He shakes his head and turns from her; she following him.*
By the affection thou didst ever bear me,
By the dear mem'ry of our infant days;
By kindred living ties, ay, and by those
Who sleep i' the tomb, and cannot call to thee,
I do conjure thee speak.
*He waves her off with his hand, and covers his face with the other, still turning
from her.*
                    Ha! wilt thou not?
(*Assuming dignity.*) Then, if affection, most unwearied love,
Tried early, long, and never wanting found,
O'er gen'rous man hath more authority,[101]
More rightful power than crown and sceptre give,
I do command thee.
*He throws himself into a chair greatly agitated.*
De Monfort, do not thus resist my love.
Here I entreat thee on my bended knees. (*Kneeling.*)
Alas! my brother!
*De Monfort starts up, and, catching her in his arms, raises her up, then placing her
in the chair, kneels at her feet.*
DE MON. Thus let him kneel who should the abased be,[102]

---

100. The Larpent version has "And be so close an adversary to it." 101. The Larpent version has "Hath more authority o'er generous man." 102. The Larpent version has "No,—let me kneel, who should indeed be humbled.—"

"And at thine honour'd feet confession make."
I'll tell thee all—but oh! thou wilt despise me.
For in my breast a raging passion burns,
"To which thy soul no sympathy will own."
A passion which hath made my nightly couch
A place of torment; "and the light of day,
"With the gay intercourse of social man,
"Feel like th'oppressive airless pestilence.
"O" Jane! thou wilt despise me.
JANE.                                        "Say not so:"
I never can despise thee, gentle brother.
A lover's jealousy and hopeless pangs
No kindly heart contemns.
DE MON.                    A lover, say'st thou?
No, it is hate! black, lasting, deadly hate; (*Starts up from his knees.*)
Which thus hath driv'n me forth from kindred peace,
From social pleasure, from my native home,
To be a sullen wand'rer on the earth,
Avoiding all men, cursing and accurs'd.
JANE. De Monfort, this is fiend-like, frightful, terrible!
What being, by th' Almighty Father form'd,
Of flesh and blood, created even as thou,
Could in thy breast such horrid tempest wake,
Who art thyself his fellow?[103]
Unknit thy brows, and spread those wrath-clench'd hands:
Some sprite accurst within thy bosom mates
To work thy ruin. Strive with it, my brother!
Strive bravely with it; drive it from thy breast:
'Tis the degrader of a noble heart;
Curse it, and bid it part.
DE MON. It will not part. (*His hand on his breast.*) I've lodged it here too
    long.
With my first cares I felt its rankling touch,
I loath'd him when a boy.
JANE. Who did'st thou say?
DE MON.                          Oh! that detested Rezenvelt!
E'en in our early sports, like two young whelps
Of hostile breed, instinctively reverse,[104]
Each 'gainst the other pitch'd his ready pledge,

---

103. The Larpent version reorders these lines: "Could in thy breast, who art thyself his fellow, / Such horrid tempests wake?—" 104. The Larpent version has "averse."

And frown'd defiance. As we onward pass'd
From youth to man's estate, his narrow art,
And envious gibing[105] malice, poorly veil'd
In the affected carelessness of mirth,
Still more detestable and odious grew.
There is no living being on this earth
Who can conceive the malice of his soul,
"With all his gay and damned merriment,"
To those, by fortune or by merit place'd
Above his paltry self. "When, low in fortune,
"He look'd upon the state of prosp'rous men,
"As nightly birds, rous'd from their murky holes,
"Do scowl and chatter at the light of day,
"I could endure it; even as we bear
"Th'impotent bit of some half-trodden worm,
"I could endure it. But when honours came,
"And wealth and new-got titles fed his pride;
"Whilst flatt'ring knaves did trumpet forth his praise,
"And grov'ling idiots grinn'd applauses on him;
"Oh! then I could no longer suffer it!"
It drove me frantick.[106]—"What! what would I give!"
What would I give to crush the bloated toad,
So rankly do I loath him!
JANE. And would thy hatred crush the very man
Who gave to thee that life he might have ta'en?
That life which thou so rashly did'st expose
To aim at his! Oh! this is horrible!
DE MON. Ha! thou hast heard it, then? From all the world,
But most of all from thee, I thought it hid.[107]
JANE. I heard a secret whisper, and resolv'd
Upon the instant to return to thee.
Did'st thou receive my letter?
DE MON. I did! I did! 'twas that which drove me hither.
I could not bear to meet thine eye again.
JANE. Alas! that, tempted[108] by a sister's tears,
I ever left thy[109] house! these few past months,
These absent months, have brought us all this woe.

105. Taunting. The Larpent version has "galling." 106. The Larpent version has "It drives me mad." 107. The Larpent version has "Ha! thou hast heard it, then? / From thee, of all the world, I wish'd it hid." 108. The Larpent version has "vanquish'd." 109. The Larpent version has "our."

Had I remain'd with thee it had not been.
And yet, methinks, it should not move you thus.
You dar'd him to the field; both bravely fought;
He more adroit[110] disarm'd you; courteously
Return'd the forfeit sword, which, so return'd,
You did refuse to use against him more;
And then, as says report, you parted friends.[111]
DE MON. When he disarm'd this curs'd, this worthless hand
Of its most worthless weapon, he but spar'd
From dev'lish pride, which now derives a bliss
In seeing me thus fetter'd, sham'd, subjected
With the vile favour of his poor forbearance;
Whilst he securely sits with gibing brow
And basely bates me, like a muzzled cur
Who cannot turn again.—
Until that day, till that accursed day,
I knew not half the torment of this hell,
Which burns within my breast. Heaven's lightning blast him!
"JANE. O this is horrible! Forbear, forbear!
"Lest heaven's vengeance light upon thy head,
"For this most impious wish.
"DE MON.                              Then let it light.
"Torments more fell than I have felt already
"It cannot send. To be annihilated;
"What all men shrink from; to be dust, be nothing,
"Were bliss to me, compar'd to what I am."
JANE. Oh! would'st thou kill me with these dreadful[112] words?
DE MON. (*Raising his arms to heaven.*) Let me but once upon his ruin
   look,
Then close mine eyes for ever!
*Jane, in great distress, staggers back, and supports herself upon the side scene. De Monfort, alarm'd, runs up to her with a soften'd voice.*
Ha! how is this? "thou'rt ill; thou'rt very pale."
What have I done to thee? "Alas, alas!
"I meant not to distress thee.—O my sister!
"JANE. (*Shaking her head.*) I cannot speak to thee.
DE MON.                              "I have kill'd thee.
"Turn, turn thee not away! look on me still!"

110. The Larpent version has "expert." 111. The Larpent version has "Return'd the forfeit sword, which thus return'd, / You greatly scorn'd to use against him more; / And so, as I have heard, you parted friends." 112. The Larpent version has "impious."

Oh! droop not thus, my life, my pride, my sister!
Look on me yet again.
JANE.                    Thou too, De Monfort,
In better days, wert wont to be my pride.
"DE MON. I am a wretch, most wretched in myself,
"And still more wretched in the pain I give.
"O curse that villain! that detested villain!
"He hath spread mis'ry o'er my fated life:
"He will undo us all."
JANE. I've held my warfare through a troubled world,
And borne with steady mind my share of ill;
For then the helpmate of my toil wert thou.¹¹³
But now the wane of life comes darkly on,
And hideous passion tears thee from my heart,
Blasting thy worth.—I cannot strive with this.
DE MON. (*Affectionately.*) What shall I do?¹¹⁴
"JANE.                              Call up thy noble spirit,
"Rouse all the gen'rous energy of virtue;
"And with the strength of heaven-endued man,
"Repel the hideous foe. Be great; be valiant.
"O, if thou coul'st! E'en shrouded as thou art
"In all the sad infirmities of nature,
"What a most noble creature would'st thou be!
"DE MON. Ay, if I could: alas! alas! I cannot."
JANE. Thou can'st, thou may'st, thou wilt.
We shall not part till I have turn'd thy soul.
*Enter Manuel.*
"DE MON. Ha! some one enters. Wherefore com'st thou here?
"MAN. Count Freberg waits your leisure.
"DE MON. (*Angrily.*) Be gone, be gone.—I cannot see him now."¹¹⁵
                                          (*Exit Manuel*)

JANE. Come to my closet;¹¹⁶ free from all intrusion,
I'll school thee there; and thou again shalt be
My willing pupil, and my gen'rous friend;
The noble Monfort I have lov'd so long,

---

113. The Larpent version has "For thou wast then the helpmate of my toil." 114. The Lar-
pent version has "Nor can I strive with this [predestin'd <?>; crossed out] resistant [?]
Hate." The Campbell/Siddons version has "enrooted" for the uncertain word. 115. The
Larpent version has this exchange: "MAN. Count Albert and his Lady sent to hope,— DE
MON. Begone!—I am well:— / I cannot hear their cold enquiries now.—" 116. The Lar-
pent version has "chamber."

And must not, will not lose.

"DE MON. Do as thou wilt; I will not grieve thee more.    *(Exeunt)*"[117]


SCENE III[118]   *Count Freberg's house.*

*Enter the Countess, followed by the Page, and speaking as she enters.*

LADY. Take this and this. (*Giving two packets.*) And tell my gentle
    friend,[119]
I hope to see her[120] ere the day be done.
PAGE. Is there no message for the Lady Jane?
LADY. No, foolish boy, that would too far extend
Your morning's route, and keep you absent long.
PAGE. O no, dear Madam! I'll the swifter run.
The summer's light'ning moves not as I'll move,
If you will send me to the Lady Jane.
LADY. No, not so slow, I ween.[121] The summer's light'ning!
Thou art a lad of taste and letters grown:
Would'st poetry admire, and ape thy master.
"Go, go; my little spaniels are unkempt;
"My cards unwritten, and my china broke:"
Thou art too learned for a lady's page.
Did I not bid thee call Theresa[122] here?
PAGE. Madam, she comes.
*Enter Theresa, carrying a robe over her arm.*
LADY. (*To Theresa.*) What has employ'd you all this dreary while?
I've waited long.
THER.          Madam, the robe is finish'd.
LADY. Well, let me see it.
*Theresa spreads out the robe.*
(*Impatiently to the Page.*) Boy, hast thou ne'er a hand to lift that fold?
See where it hangs.
*Page takes the other side of the robe, and spreads it out to its full extent before her,*
*whilst she sits down and looks at it with much dissatisfaction.*

117. The Larpent version concludes with lines cut earlier in the scene, with De Monfort's
question, "What shall I do?" and Jane's response. Within Jane's speech, "heaven-endued
man" is changed to "man endued from Heav'n" and a line ("Be thy former self.—") is added
after "be valiant." 118. In the Larpent version, this is moved to Act III, scene ii. In the
1851 version, this scene is Act III, scene i, but it is cut through the exit of the
Page. 119. The Larpent version has "And tell them—Do you hear?—" 120. The Larpent
version has "them." 121. The Larpent version has "so slow, young Sir"; "To ween" is "to
suppose." 122. The Larpent version has "my woman," and there she is called Katherine.

THER. Does not my lady like this easy form?

LADY. That sleeve is all awry.

THER.                                    Your pardon, madam;
'Tis but the empty fold that shades it thus.
"I took the pattern from a graceful shape;"
The Lady Jane De Monfort wears it so.

LADY. Yes, yes, I see 'tis thus with all of you.
What'er she wears is elegance and grace,
"Whilst ev'ry ornament of mine, forsooth,
"Must hang like trappings on a May-day queen."
(*Angrily to the Page, who is smiling to himself.*) Youngster be gone.
Why do you loiter here.                                    (*Exit Page*)
"THER. What would you, madam, chuse to wear to-night?
"One of your newest robes?

"LADY.                        I hate them all.

"THER. Surely, that purple scarf became you well,
"With all those wreaths of richly hanging flowers.
"Did I not overhear them say, last night,
"As from the crouded ball-room ladies past,
"How gay and handsome, in her costly dress,
"The Countess Freberg look'd.

"LADY.                        Didst thou o'erhear it?

"THER. I did, and more than this.

"LADY. Well, all are not so greatly prejudic'd;
"All do not think me like a May-day queen,
"Which peasants deck in sport.

"THER.                        And who said this?

"LADY. (*Putting her handkerchief to her eyes.*) E'en my good lord, Theresa.

"THER. He said it but in jest. He loves you well.

LADY. "I know as well as thee he loves me well;
"But what of that?"[123] he takes no pride in me.
Elsewhere his praise and admiration go,
And Jane De Monfort is not mortal woman.

THER. The wond'rous character this lady bears
For worth and excellence; from early youth
The friend and mother of her younger sisters
"Now greatly married, as I have been told,
"From her most prudent care," may well excuse
The admiration of so good a man

---

123. The Larpent version adds "And Albert too—" as a transition.

As my good master is. And then, dear madam,
I must confess, when I myself did hear
How she was come thro' the rough winter's storm,
To seek and comfort an unhappy brother,
My heart beat kindly to her.
LADY. Ay, ay, there is a charm in this I find:
But wherefore may she not have come as well,
Through wintry storms to seek a lover too?[124]
THER. No, madam, no, I could not think of this.
LADY. That would reduce her in your eyes, mayhap,
To woman's level.—Now I see my vengeance!
I'll tell it round that she is hither come,[125]
Under pretence of finding out De Monfort,
To meet with Rezenvelt. When Freberg hears it
'Twill help, I ween,[126] to break this magick charm.
THER. And say what is not, madam?
LADY. How can'st[127] thou know that I shall say what is not?
'Tis like enough I shall but speak the truth.
THER. Ah no! there is—
LADY.                     Well, hold thy foolish tongue.
Carry that robe into my chamber, do:[128]
I'll try it there myself.                              (*Exeunt*)


## ACT III


SCENE I[129]   *De Monfort discovered sitting by a table reading. After a little time he lays down his book, and continues in a thoughtful posture. Enter to him Jane De Monfort.*

JANE. [He seems more calm this morning—] Thanks, gentle
    brother.—(*Pointing to the book.*)
Thy willing mind has been right well employ'd.
Did not thy heart warm at the fair display
Of peace and concord and forgiving love?
DE MON. I know resentment may to love be turn'd;

124. The Larpent version has "Ay, ay, there lies the potent charm, I find.— / But wherefore may she not as well have come / Through wintry storms to seek a lover here?"
125. The Larpent version has "That would perhaps reduce her in your eyes / To woman's level—I believe 'tis so: / And I have told it round that she is come." 126. The Larpent version has "trust." 127. The Larpent version has "dost." 128. The Larpent version has "go." 129. This is Act III, scene ii in the 1851 version.

"Tho' keen and lasting, into love as strong:"
And[130] fiercest rivals in th' ensanguin'd field
Have cast their brandish'd weapons to the ground,
Joining their mailed breasts in close embrace,
With gen'rous impulse fir'd. I know right well
The darkest, fellest wrongs have been forgiven
Seventy times o'er from blessed heavenly love:
I've heard of things like these; I've heard and wept.[131]
But what is this to me?
JANE.                    All, all, my brother!
It bids thee too that noble precept learn,
To love thine enemy.
DE MON. Th' uplifted stroke that would a wretch destroy[132]
Gorg'd with my richest spoil, stain'd with my blood,
I would arrest and cry, hold! hold! have mercy:
But when the man most adverse to my nature;
"Who e'en from childhood hath, with rude malevolence,
"Withheld the fair respect all paid beside,
"Turning my very praise into derision;"
Who galls and presses me where'er I go,
Would claim the gen'rous feelings of my heart,[133]
Nature herself doth lift her voice aloud,
And cries, it is impossible.
JANE. (*Shaking her head.*)—Ah Monfort, Monfort!
DE MON. I can forgive th' envenom'd reptile's sting,
But hate his loathsome self.
JANE. And canst thou do no more for love of heaven?
DE MON. Alas![134] I cannot now so school my mind
As holy men have taught, nor search it truly:
But this, my Jane, I'll do for love of thee;
And more it is than crowns could win me to,
Or any power but thine. I'll see the man.
"Th' indignant risings of abhorrent nature;
"The stern contraction of my scowling brows,
"That, like the plant, whose closing leaves do shrink
"At hostile touch, still knit at his approach;
"The crooked curving lip, by instinct taught,

130. The Larpent version has "That." 131. The Larpent version has "like these; and wept at them." 132. The Larpent version has "The stroke uplifted to destroy the wretch." 133. The Larpent version has "When he would claim the yieldings of my heart." 134. The Larpent version has "Sister."

"In imitation of disgustful things,
"To pout and swell, I strictly will repress;
"And meet him with a tamed countenance,
"E'en as a townsman, who would live at peace,"[135]
And pay him the respect his station claims.
I'll crave his pardon too for all offence
My dark and wayward temper may have done;
Nay more, I will confess myself his debtor
For the forebearance I have curs'd so oft.
Life spar'd by him, more horrid than the grave
With all its dark corruption! This I'll do.
Will it suffice thee?[136] More than this I cannot.
JANE. No more than this do I require of thee
In outward act, tho' in thy heart, my friend,[137]
I hop'd a better[138] change, and still will hope.
I told thee Freberg had propos'd a meeting.[139]
DE MON. [Ha!] "I know it well."
JANE.                    And Rezenvelt consents
He meets you here; so far he shews respect.
DE MON. Well, let it be; the sooner past the better.
JANE. I'm glad to hear you say so, for, in truth,
He has propos'd it for an early hour.
'Tis almost near his time; I came to tell you.
DE MON. What, comes he here so soon? "shame on his speed!"
It is not decent thus to rush upon me.
He loves the secret pleasure he will feel
To see me thus subdued.
JANE. O say not so! he comes with heart sincere.
DE MON. Could we not meet elsewhere? "from home—i' the fields,
"Where other men"—must I alone receive him?
"Where is your agent, Freberg, and his friends,
"That I must meet him here? (*Walks up and down very much disturbed.*)"
Now did'st thou say?—how goes the hour?—e'en now!
I would some other friend were first arriv'd.
JANE. See, to thy wish comes Freberg and his dame.[140]
DE MON. "His lady too! why comes he not alone?"

135. The Larpent version has "I will repress the risings of my Soul." 136. The Larpent version has "Will this content thee." 137. The Larpent version has "my brother." 138. The Larpent version has "stricter." 139. The Larpent version has "Count Albert has propos'd a meeting.—" 140. The Larpent version has "See, to thy wish thy friend Count Albert comes."

Must all the world stare upon our meeting?[141]
*Enter Count Freberg "and his Countess."*[142]
FREB. A happy morrow to my noble marquis
And his most noble sister.

JANE.                                    Gen'rous Freberg,
Your face, methinks, forbodes a happy morn
Open and cheerful. What of Rezenvelt?
FREB. I left him at his home, prepar'd to follow:
He'll soon appear.[143] "(*To De Monfort.*) And now, my worthy friend,
"Give me your hand; this happy change delights me.
*"De Monfort gives him his hand coldly, and they walk to the bottom of the stage*
*"together, in earnest discourse, whilst Jane and the Countess remain in the front.*
"LADY. My dearest madam, will you pardon me?
"I know Count Freberg's bus'ness with De Monfort,
"And had a strong desire to visit you,
"So much I wish the honour of your friendship.
"For he retains no secret from mine ear.
"JANE. (*Archly.*) Knowing your prudence.—You are welcome, madam,
"So shall Count Freberg's lady ever be.
*"De Monfort and Freberg returning towards the front of the stage, still engaged*
*"in discourse.*
FREB. "He is indeed a man, within whose breast,
"Firm rectitude and honour hold their seat,
"Tho' unadorned with that dignity
"Which were their fittest garb. Now, on my life!"
I know no truer heart than Rezenvelt.
DE MON. Well, Freberg, well, there needs not all this pains
To garnish out his worth; let it suffice.
I am resolv'd I will respect the man,
As his fair station and repute demand.
"Methinks I see not at your jolly feasts
"The youthful knight, who sung so pleasantly.
FREB. "A pleasant circumstance detains him hence;
"Pleasant to those who love high gen'rous deeds
"Above the middle pitch of common minds;
"And, tho' I have been sworn to secrecy,

141. The Larpent version has "So,—all the world must stare upon our meeting!" 142. In the Larpent version, the Countess does not appear in this scene. 143. The Larpent version has "be here." The following exchange between the women is cut in the Larpent version. It joins the two speeches by the Count with "Believe me, worthy friend, / I cannot say how much this change delights me."

"Yet must I tell it thee."[144]
This knight is near a kin to Rezenvelt
To whom an old relation, short while dead,
Bequeath'd a good estate, some leagues distant.[145]
But Rezenvelt, now rich in fortune's store,
Disdain'd the sordid love of further gain,
And gen'rously the rich bequest resign'd
To this young man, blood of the same degree
To the deceas'd, and low in fortune's gifts,
Who is from hence to take possession of it.[146]
Was it not nobly done?

DE MON.                    'Twas right, and honourable.
This morning is oppressive, warm, and heavy:
There hangs a foggy closeness in the air;
Dost thou not feel it?[147]

FREB.[148] O no! to think upon a gen'rous deed
Expands my soul, and makes me lightly breathe.

DE MON. Who gives the feast to-night?[149] His name escapes me.
You say I am invited.

FREB.                    Old Count Waterlan.
In honour of your townsman's gen'rous gift[150]
He spreads the board.

DE MON. He is too old to revel with the gay.

FRED. But not too old is he to honour virtue.[151]
I shall partake of it with open soul;
For, on my honest faith, of living men
I know not one, for talents, honour, worth,
That I should rank superiour to Rezenvelt.

"DE MON. How virtuous he hath been in three short days!

"FREB. Nay, longer, Marquis, but my friendship rests
"Upon the good report of other men;
"And that has told me much."

---

144. The Larpent version handles this exchange differently: "DE MON. Albert, I saw not at your house, I think / The youthful knight, who sung so pleasantly. ALB. A pleasant circumstance has ta'en him from us,— / And brings us Rezenvelt so hastily. DE MON. I had not heard that he had left Vienna." 145. The Larpent version has "a fair estate, in Saxony." 146. The Larpent version has "And he is gone to take possession of it." 147. The Larpent version has this question addressed to Jane. 148. The Larpent version gives this speech to Jane. 149. The Larpent version has "to-day." 150. The Larpent version has "In honour of this gift of Rezenvelt's." 151. The Larpent version has Jane say, "But not too old to honour virtue, brother." The Count gives the rest of the speech.

DE MON. (*Aside, going some steps hastily from Freberg, and rending his cloak with agitation as he goes.*) Would he were come! By heaven I would he were!

This fool besets me so.

"*Suddenly correcting himself, and joining the Ladies, who have retired to the bot-*
"*tom of the stage, he speaks to Countess Freberg with affected cheerfulness.*

"The sprightly dames of Amberg rise by times

"Untarnish'd with the vigils of the night.

"LADY. Praise us not rashly, 'tis not always so.

"DE MON. He does not rashly praise who praises you;

"For he were dull indeed—(*Stopping short, as if he heard something.*)

"LADY.                                                     How dull indeed?

DE MON. "I should have said—It has escap'd me now." (*Listening again, as if he heard something.*)

JANE. (*To De Monfort.*) What, hear you ought?

DE MON. (*Hastily.*)                         'Tis nothing.

"LADY. (*To De Monfort.*) Nay, do not let me lose it so, my lord.

"Some fair one has bewitch'd your memory,

"And robs me of the half-form'd compliment.

"JANE. Half-utter'd praise is to the curious mind,

"As to the eye half-veiled beauty is,

"More precious than the whole. Pray pardon him.

"Some one approaches. (*Listening.*)"

FREB. No, no, it is a servant who ascends;

He will not come so soon.[152]

DE MON. (*Off his guard.*) 'Tis Rezenvelt: I heard his well-known foot!

"From the first stair-case, mounting step by step."

FREB. How quick an ear thou hast for distant sound!

I heard him not.

*De Monfort looks embarrassed, and is silent.*

*Enter Rezenvelt.*

*De Monfort, recovering himself, goes up to receive Rezenvelt, who meets him with a cheerful countenance.*

DE MON. (*To Rezenvelt.*) I am, my lord, beholden to you greatly.

This ready visit makes me much your debtor.

REZ. Then may such debts between us, noble marquis,

Be oft incurr'd, and often paid again.

(*To Jane.*) Madam, I am devoted to your service,

And ev'ry wish of yours commands my will.

152. The Larpent version has "No; or, perhaps; he will not come so soon.—"

"(*To Countess.*) Lady, good morning. (*To Freberg.*) Well, my gentle
   friend,"
You see I have not linger'd long behind.
FREB. No, thou art sooner than I look'd for thee.
REZ. A willing heart adds feather to the heel,
And makes the clown a winged mercury.
DE MON. Then let me say, that with a grateful mind
I do receive these tokens of good will;
And must regret that, in my wayward moods,
I have too oft forgot the due regard
Your rank and talents claim.
REZ.                No, no, De Monfort,
You have but rightly curb'd a wanton spirit,
Which makes me too, neglectful of respect.
Let us be friends, and think of this no more.
FREB.[153] Ay, let it rest with the departed shades
Of things which are no more; whilst lovely concord,
Follow'd by friendship sweet, and first esteem,
Your future days enrich. "O heavenly friendship!
"Thou dost exalt the sluggish souls of men,
"By thee conjoin'd, to great and glorious deeds;
"As two dark clouds, when mix'd in middle air,
"The vivid lightning's flash, and roar sublime."
Talk not of what is past, but future love.
DE MON. (*With dignity.*) No, Freberg, no, it must not. (*To Rezenvelt.*)
   No, my lord.
I will not offer you an hand of concord
And poorly hide the motives which constrain me.
I would that, not alone these present friends,[154]
But ev'ry soul in Amberg were assembled,
That I, before them all, might here declare
I owe my spared[155] life to your forbearance.
(*Holding out his hand.*) Take this from one who boasts no feeling
   warmth,
But never will deceive.
*Jane smiles upon De Monfort with great approbation, and Rezenvelt runs up to
him with open arms.*
REZ. Away with hands! I'll have thee to my breast.

153. The Larpent version has the first four lines spoken by Jane and the final line spoken by
the Count. 154. The Larpent version has "not alone these present now." 155. The Larpent version has "forfeit."

Thou art, upon my faith, a noble spirit![156]

DE MON. (*Shrinking back from him.*) Nay, if you please, I am not so
  prepar'd—

My nature is of temp'rature too cold—

I pray you pardon me. (*Jane's countenance changes.*)

But take this[157] hand, the token of respect;

"The token of a will inclin'd to concord;"

The token of a mind that bears within

A sense impressive of the debt it owes you;

And cursed be its power, unnerv'd its strength,

If e'er again it shall be lifted up

To do you any harm.

REZ. Well, be it so, De Monfort, I'm contented;

I'll take thy hand since I can have no more.

(*Carelessly.*) I take of worthy men whate'er they give.

Their heart I gladly take; if not, their hand:

If that too is withheld, a courteous word,[158]

"Or the civility of placid looks;"

And, if e'en these are too great favours deem'd,[159]

'Faith, I can set me down contentedly

With plain and homely greeting, or, God[160] save ye!

DE MON. (*Aside, starting away from him some paces.*) By the[161] good light,
  he makes a jest of it!

*Jane appears greatly distressed, and Freberg endeavours to cheer her.*

FREB. (*To Jane.*) Cheer up, my noble friend; all will go well;

For friendship is no plant of hasty growth.

"Tho' planted in esteem's deep-fixed soil,"

The gradual culture of kind intercourse

Must bring it to perfection.

"(*To the Countess.*) My love, the morning, now, is far advanced;

"Our friends elsewhere expect us; take your leave."[162]

"LADY. (*To Jane.*) Farewell! dear madam, till the ev'ning hour.

"FREB. (*To De Monfort.*) Good day, De Monfort. (*To Jane.*) Most
  devoutly yours.

REZ. "(*To Freberg.*) Go not too fast, for I will follow you.

"(*Exeunt Freberg and his Lady*)"

---

156. The Larpent version reverses these two lines. 157. The Larpent version has "my."
158. The Larpent version has "a passing nod." 159. The Larpent version has "And if e'en
this be deem'd too great a favour." 160. The Larpent version has "heaven." 161. The Larpent version has "this." 162. The Larpent version has "Marquis, come; / The evening is
advancing fast upon us; / Our friends elsewhere expect us:—Take your leave."

(*To Jane.*) The Lady Jane is yet a stranger here:
She might, perhaps, in the purlieus of Amberg
Find somewhat worth her notice.

JANE. I thank you, Marquis, I am much engaged;
I go not out to-day.

REZ. Then fare ye well! I see I cannot now
Be the proud man who shall escort you forth,
And shew to all the world my proudest boast,
The notice and respect of Jane De Monfort.

DE MON. (*Aside, impatiently.*) He says farewell, and goes not!

JANE. (*To Rezenvelt.*) You do me honour.

REZ. (*To Jane.*) Madam, adieu! Good morning, noble marquis.     (*Exit*)
*Jane and De Monfort look expressively to one another, without speaking, and then
Exeunt, severally.*


SCENE II[163]     *A splendid Banquetting Room. De Monfort, Rezenvelt, Freberg,
Master of the House,*[164] *and Guests, are discovered sitting at table, with wine,
&c. before them. Servants waiting.*

SONG.—A GLEE
Pleasant is the mantling bowl,
And the song of merry soul;
And the red lamps' cheery light,
And the goblet glancing bright;
Whilst many a cheerful face,[165] around,
Listens to the jovial sound.
Social spirits, join with me;
Bless the God of jollity.

FREB. (*To De Monfort, who rises to go away.*) Thou wilt not leave us,
    Monfort? wherefore so?

DE MON. (*Aside to Freberg.*) I pray thee take no notice of me now.
Mine ears are stunned[166] with these noisy fools;
Let me escape.                                        (*Exit, hastily*)

MAST. What, is De Monfort gone?

FREB.                         Time presses him.

REZ. It seem'd to sit right heavily upon him,

163. In the Larpent version, this is Act III, scene iii. In 1851, where it is Act IV, scene i,
it is cut until the point that Rezenvelt and Albert/Freberg are alone. 164. The Larpent version identifies him as Count Waterlan. 165. The Larpent version has "guest." 166. The
Larpent version has "My brain's distracted."

We must confess.

MAST. (*To Freberg*.) How is your friend? he wears a noble mien,
But most averse, methinks, from social pleasure.
Is this his nature?

FREB.　　　　　No, I've seen him cheerful,
And at the board, with soul-enliven'd face,
Push the gay goblet round.—But it wears late.[167]
We shall seem topers[168] more than social friends,
"If the returning sun surprise us here.
"(*To Master*.) Good rest, my gen'rous host; we will retire.
"You wrestle with your age most manfully,
"But brave it not too far. Retire to sleep."[169]

MAST. "I will, my friend, but do you still remain,
"With noble Rezenvelt, and all my guests.
"Ye have not fourscore years upon your head;
"Do not depart so soon. God save you all!"[170]
　　　　　　　　"(*Exit Master, leaning upon a Servant*)

"FREB. (*To the Guests*.) Shall we resume?

"GUESTS.　　　　　　　The night is too far spent.

"FREB. Well then, good rest to you.

"REZ. (*To Guests*.)　　　　　Good rest, my friends."
　　　　　　　(*Exeunt all but Freberg and Rezenvelt*)

FREB. Alas! my Rezenvelt!
"I vainly hop'd the hand of gentle peace,
"From this day's reconciliation sprung,
"Those rude unseemly jarrings had subdu'd:"[171]
But I have mark'd, e'en at the social board,
Such looks, such words, such tones, such untold things,
Too plainly told, 'twixt you and Monfort pass,
That I must now despair.
Yet who could think, two minds so much refin'd,[172]
So near in excellence, should be remov'd,
So far remov'd, in gen'rous sympathy.

167. The Larpent version has "But, if we sit, . . . ." 168. Heavy drinkers or drunks. 169. The Larpent version has "'Tis time for all of us to bid farewell / Adieu, my gen'rous host,—we must retire." 170. The Larpent version has this speech: "Is't even so?—Why, fare you well!—Our feast / Hath been but broken; but another time / We'll piece it.—Friends, good day, and thanks, to all." At this point everyone exits except Rezenvelt and Albert/Freberg. 171. The Larpent has "I hop'd from this day's reconciliation / These rude unseemly jarrings would have ceas'd." 172. The Larpent version has "Such looks, such words, twixt you and Monfort pass. / Such untold things, too plainly told, that I / Must now despair. Yet who could think two minds."

REZ. Ay, far remov'd indeed.
FREB. And yet, methought, he made a noble effort,
And with a manly plainness bravely told
The galling debt he owes to your forbearance.
REZ. 'Faith! so he did, and so did I receive[173] it;
When, with spread arms, and heart e'en mov'd to tears,
I frankly proffer'd him a friend's embrace:
And, I declare, had he as such receiv'd it,
I from that very moment had forborne
All opposition,[174] pride-provoking jest,
Contemning carelessness, and all offence;
"And had caress'd him as a worthy heart,
"From native weakness such indulgence claiming:"
But since he proudly thinks that cold respect,
The formal tokens of his lordly favour,
So precious are, that I would sue for them
As fair distinction in the world's eye,
Forgetting former wrongs, I spurn it all;
And but that I do bear the noble woman,[175]
His worthy, his incomparable sister,
Such fix'd profound regard, I would expose "him;"
And "as a mighty bull, in senseless rage,
"Rous'd at the baiter's will, with wretched rage
"Of ire-provoking scarlet, chaffs and bellows,
"I'd" make him at small cost of paltry wit,
With all his deep and manly faculties,
The scorn and laugh[176] of fools.
FREB. For heaven's sake, my friend; restrain your wrath;
For what has Monfort done of wrong to you,
Or you to him, bating[177] one foolish quarrel,
Which you confess from slight occasion rose,
That in your breasts such dark resentment dwells,
So fix'd, so hopeless?
REZ. O! from our youth he has distinguish'd me
With ev'ry mark of hatred and disgust.
For e'en in boyish sports I still oppos'd

173. The Larpent version has "accept." 174. The Larpent version has "From opposition." 175. The Larpent has "And formal tokens of his lordly favour, / So precious are, that I, / Forgetting former wrongs, would sue them / As fair distinction in the eyes of men, / I spurn them all: And, but I do bear that noble woman." 176. The Larpent version has "jest." 177. Omitting, excepting (*obs.*).

His proud pretensions to pre-eminence;
Nor would I to his ripen'd greatness give
That fulsome adulation of[178] applause
A senseless croud bestow'd. Tho' poor in fortune,
I still would smile at vain-assuming wealth:
But when unlook'd-for fate on me bestow'd
Riches and splendour equal to his own,
"Tho' I, in truth, despise such poor distinction,"
Feeling inclin'd to be at peace with him,
And with all men beside, I curb'd my spirit,
And sought to soothe him. Then, with spiteful rage,
From small offence he rear'd a quarrel with me,
And dar'd me to the field. The rest you know.
In short, I still have been th' opposing rock,[179]
O'er which the stream of his o'erflowing pride
Hath foam'd and bellow'd.[180] See'st thou how it is?

FREB. Too well I see, and warn thee to beware.
Such streams have oft, by swelling floods surcharg'd,[181]
Borne down with sudden and impetuous force
The yet unshaken stone of opposition,
Which had for ages stopp'd their flowing course.
I pray thee, friend, beware.

REZ. Thou canst not mean—he will not murder me?

FREB. What a proud heart, with such dark passion toss'd,
May, in the anguish of its thoughts, conceive,
I will not dare to say.

REZ.                    Ha, ha! thou know'st him not.
Full often have I mark'd it[182] in his youth,
And could have "almost" lov'd him for the [human] weakness;
He's form'd with such antipathy, by nature,
To all infliction of corporeal pain,
To wounding life, e'en to the sight of blood,
He cannot if he would.[183]

FREB.                    Then fy upon thee!
"It is not gen'rous" to provoke him thus.

178. The Larpent version has "and." 179. The Larpent version has "th' impedi-
ment." 180. The Larpent version has "fretted." 181. The Larpent version has "Such
streams, by swelling floods surcharg'd, have oft." 182. The Larpent version has "him."
  183. The Larpent version has "His nature's form'd, however proud and haughty, / So piti-
ful, with such antipathy / To all infliction of corporeal pain / With such abhorrence of the
sight of blood, / I think he would not kill the fly that bit him."

But let us part; we'll talk of this again.
Something[184] approaches.—We are here too long.
REZ. "Well, then, to-morrow I'll attend your call.
"Here lies my way. Good night."[185]                                    (*Exit*)
*Enter Grimbald.*
GRIM. [Ay, that's my man—now fortune be my speed!—]
Forgive, I pray, my lord, a stranger's boldness.
"I have presum'd to wait your leisure here,
"Though at so late an hour."[186]
FREB.                                    But who art thou?[187]
GRIM. My name is Grimbald, sir,
A humble suitor to your honour's goodness,
Who is the more embolden'd to presume,
In that the noble Marquis of De Monfort
Is so much fam'd for good and gen'rous deeds.
FREB. You are mistaken, I am not the man.
GRIM. "Then, pardon me; I thought I could not err.
"That mien so dignified, that piercing eye
"Assur'd me it was he."[188]
FREB. My name is not De Monfort, courteous stranger;[189]
But, if you have a favour to request,
I may, perhaps, with him befriend your suit.[190]
GRIM. I thank your honour, but I have a friend
Who will commend me to De Monfort's favour:
The Marquis Rezenvelt has known me long,[191]
Who, says report, will soon become his brother.
FREB. If thou would'st seek thy ruin from De Monfort,
The name of Rezenvelt employ, and prosper;
But, if ought good, use any name but his.
"GRIM. How may this be?
"FREB.                                    I cannot now explain.
"Early to-morrow call upon Count Freberg;
"So am I call'd, each burgher knows my house,

---

184. The Larpent version has "Some one." 185. The Larpent version has "To-morrow I will call on you; To-night / I sleep again at Waldec's Country House.— / Farewell!—" The scene then closes, and the rest of this scene appears as Act III, scene iv. 186. The Larpent version has "My pressing wants presume—." In the Larpent (and 1851) version, Grimbald is named Conrad. 187. The Larpent version has "Who art thou, friend?" 188. The Larpent version has "Pardon me, Sir; I thought you had been he." 189. The Larpent version has "honest friend." 190. The Larpent version has "I may, perhaps, befriend your suit with him." 191. The Larpent version has "I'm not unknown to Marquis Rezenvelt."

"And there instruct me how to do you service.

"Good-night."[192]                                                          (*Exit*)

GRIM. (*Alone.*) Well, this mistake may be of service to me;

"And yet my bus'ness I will not unfold

"To this mild, ready, promise-making courtier;

"I've been by such too oft deceiv'd already:

"But" if such violent enmity exists

Between De Monfort and this Rezenvelt,

He'll prove my advocate by opposition.

For, if[193] De Monfort would reject my suit,

Being the man whom Rezenvelt esteems,

Being the man he hates, a cord as strong,

Will he not favour me? "I'll think of this."[194]                          (*Exit*)


SCENE III[195]   *A lower Apartment in Jerome's House, with a wide folding glass door, looking into a garden, where the trees and shrubs are brown and leafless.*

*Enter De Monfort with his arms crossed, with a thoughtful frowning aspect, and paces slowly across the stage, Jerome following behind him with a timid step. De Monfort hearing him, turns suddenly about.*

DE MON. (*Angrily.*) "Who follows me to this sequester'd room?"[196]

JER. I have presum'd, my lord. 'Tis somewhat late;[197]

I am inform'd you eat[198] at home to-night;

Here is a list of all the dainty fare

My busy search has found; please to peruse it.

DE MON. Leave me: begone! Put hemlock in thy soup,

Or deadly night-shade, or rank hellebore,

And I will mess upon it.

JER.                          Heaven forbid!

Your honour's life is all too precious, sure—

DE MON. (*Sternly.*) Did I not say begone?

---

192. The Larpent version has this exchange: "CON/GRIM. Where may De Monfort lodge, good Sir? ALB/FREB. E'en here,— / At yonder Burgher's, at the whiten'd porch.— / Early tomorrow call upon count Albert; / My house is by the Fountain in the Square, / And there instruct me how to do you service. / Good day." 193. The Larpent version has "as." 194. The Larpent version closes with its version of lines cut earlier: "—I'll not unfold / My business to this promise-making courtier; / I've been by such too oft deceiv'd already:— / I'll seek De Monfort's self upon the instant." 195. This is Act III, scene v in the Larpent version, Act IV, scene ii in the 1851 version. 196. The Larpent version has "Who's there?—What, must I never be alone?" 197. The Larpent version has "growing late." 198. The Larpent version has "sup."

JER. Pardon, my lord, I'm old, and oft forget.                    (*Exit*)

DE MON. (*Looking after him, as if his heart smote him.*) "Why will they
   thus mistime their foolish zeal,

"That I must be so stern?

"O! that I were upon some desert coast!

"Where howling tempests and the lashing tide

"Would stun me into deep and senseless quiet;

"As the storm-beaten trav'ller droops his head,

"In heavy, dull, lethargick weariness,

"And, midst the roar of jarring elements,

"Sleeps to awake no more.

"What am I grown? All things are hateful to me."

*Enter Manuel.*

(*Stamping with his foot.*) Who bids thee break upon my privacy?

MAN. Nay, good, my lord! I heard you speak aloud,

"And dreamt not, surely, that you were alone."

DE MON. What, dost thou watch, and pin thine ear to holes,

To catch those exclamations of the soul,

Which heaven alone should hear? Who hir'd thee, pray?

Who basely hir'd thee for a task like this?

MAN. My lord, I cannot hold. For fifteen years,

Long-troubled years, I have your servant[199] been,

Nor hath the proudest lord in all the realm,

With firmer, with more honourable faith

His sov'reign serv'd, than I have served you;

But, if my honesty is doubted now,

Let him who is more faithful take my place,

And serve you better.

DE MON. "Well, be it as thou wilt. Away with thee.

"Thy loud-mouth'd boasting is no rule for me

"To judge thy merit by."[200]

*Enter Jerome hastily, and pulls Manuel away.*

JER. Come, Manuel, come away; thou art not wise.

"The stranger must depart and come again,

"For now his honour will not be disturb'd."[201]

(*Exit Manuel sulkily*)

DE MON. A stranger said'st thou. (*Drops his handkerchief.*)

199. The Larpent version has "follower." 200. The Larpent version uses lines cut earlier:
"Why will you thus mistime your foolish zeal, / That I must seem so stern! (*Drops his
handkerchief.*)" 201. The Larpent version does not have Manuel exit but say, "I see my master will not be disturb'd— / The Stranger must depart and come again."

JER. I did, good sir,[202] but he shall go away;
You shall not be disturb'd. (*Stooping to lift the handkerchief.*)
                    You have dropp'd somewhat.
DE MON. (*Preventing him.*) Nay, do not stoop, my friend! I pray thee
    not!
Thou art too old to stoop.—
I am much indebted to thee.—Take this ring—
I love thee better than I seem to do.
I pray thee do it—thank me not.—What stranger?
JER.[203] A man who does most earnestly entreat
To see your honour, but I know him not.
DE MON. Then let him enter.[204]

                                                    (*Exit Jerome*)

*A pause. Enter Grimbald.*
DE MON. You are the stranger who would speak with me?
GRIM. I am so far unfortunate, my lord,[205]
That, though my fortune on your favour hangs,
I am to you a stranger.
DE MON. How may this be? What can I do for you?
GRIM. Since thus your lordship does so frankly ask,
The tiresome preface of apology
I will forbear, and tell my tale at once.—
In plodding drudgery I've spent my youth,
A careful penman in another's office;
And now, my master and employer dead,
They seek to set a stripling o'er my head,
And leave me on to drudge, e'en to old age,
Because I have no friend to take my part.
"It is an office in your native town,
"For I am come from thence, and I am told
"You can procure it for me."[206] Thus, my lord,
From the repute of goodness which you bear,
I have presum'd to beg.
DE MON. [Pshaw!] They have befool'd thee with a false report.

202. The Larpent version has "my lord"; it gives Manuel this line. 203. The Larpent version gives this speech to Manuel. 204. The Larpent version has "Well" for "Then." Manuel and Jerome exit here, and Monfort speaks the lines (beginning "O! that I were upon some desert coast") that were cut above, changing "droops his head" to "bows his head." 205. The Larpent version has "I am so far unhappy, good my Lord." 206. The Larpent version has "It is a position in one of your dependencies, / Where I am native, and I am assur'd / By your kind influence with the magistrates / You can command it for me."

GRIM. Alas! I see it is vain to plead.
Your mind is pre-possess'd against a wretch,
Who has, unfortunately for his weal,
Offended the revengeful Rezenvelt.
DE MON. What dost thou say?
GRIM. What I, perhaps, had better leave unsaid.
Who will believe my wrongs if I complain?
I am a stranger, Rezenvelt my foe,
Who will believe my wrongs?
DE MON. (*Eagerly catching him by the coat.*) I will believe them!
Though they were base as basest, vilest deeds,
In ancient record told, I would believe them.
Let not the smallest atom of unworthiness
That he has put upon thee be conceal'd.
Speak boldly, tell it all; for, by the light!
I'll be thy friend, I'll be thy warmest friend,
If he has done thee wrong.
GRIM. Nay, pardon me, it were not well advis'd,
If I should speak so freely of the man,[207]
Who will so soon your nearest kinsman be.
DE MON. What canst thou mean "by this"?
GRIM.                                    That Marquis Rezenvelt
Has pledg'd his faith unto your noble sister,
And soon will be the husband of her choice.
So, I am told, and so the world believes.[208]
DE MON. 'Tis false! 'tis basely false!
What wretch could drop from his envenom'd tongue
A tale so damn'd?—"It chokes my breath—"
(*Stamping with his foot.*) What wretch did tell to thee?[209]
GRIM. Nay, every one with whom I have convers'd
Has held the same discourse. I judge it not.[210]
But you, my lord, who with the lady dwell,
You best can tell what her deportment speaks;
"Whether her conduct and unguarded words
"Belie such rumour."
*De Monfort pauses, staggers backwards, and sinks into a chair; then starting
up hastily.*

207. The Larpent version has "Nay, my good Lord, it will not speed my cause, / To speak
so freely even of the foe." 208. The Larpent version has "as" for "so" twice in this line.
209. The Larpent version has "What liar told thee so?" 210. The Larpent version has "Nay,
all with whom I have convers'd in Augsburg / Have held the same discourse. I know it not."

DE MON. Where am I now? 'midst all the cursed thoughts
That on my soul like stinging scorpions prey'd,
This never came before—Oh, if it be!
The thought will drive me mad.—Was it for this
She urged her warm request on bended knee?
Alas! I wept, and thought of sister's love,
No damned love like this.
Fell devil! 'tis hell itself has lent thee aid
To work such sorcery! (*Pauses.*) I'll not believe it.
I must have proof clear as the noon-day sun
For such foul charge as this! Who waits without![211]
*Paces up and down furiously agitated.*
GRIM. (*Aside.*) What have I done? I've carried this too far.
I've rous'd a fierce ungovernable madman.[212]
*Enter Jerome.*
DE MON. (*In a loud angry voice.*) Where did she go, "at such an early
   hour,"
And with such slight attendance?
JER. Of whom inquires your honour?
DE MON. Why, of your lady. Said I not my sister?
JER. "The Lady Jane," your sister?
DE MON. (*In a faultering voice.*) Yes, I did call her so.[213]
JER. In truth, I cannot tell you where she went.
E'en now, from the short-beechen walk hard-by,[214]
I saw her through the garden-gate return.
The Marquis Rezenvelt, and Freberg's Countess
Are in her company. This way they come,[215]
"As being nearer to the back apartments;"
But I shall stop them, if it be your will,
And bid them enter here.
DE MON. No, stop them not. I will remain unseen,
And mark them as they pass. Draw back a little.[216]
*Grimbald seems alarm'd, and steals off unnoticed. De Monfort grasps Jerome
tightly by the hand, and drawing back with him two or three steps, not to be seen
from the garden, waits in silence with his eyes fixed on the glass-door.*

211. The Larpent version has "No damned love like this,—'Tis hell itself / Has lent him
aid to work such sorcery.— / I'll not believe it:—no, I will have proof / Clear as the noon-
day sun—who waits without?" 212. The Larpent version has "What change is this? I've
overshot my aim:— / My plans are destin'd never to succeed." 213. The Larpent version
has "Yes, I think I call'd her so." 214. The Larpent version has "But from the beechen walk
hard by, e'en now." 215. The Larpent version has "Yonder they walk." 216. The Larpent
version has "Do you begone"; Jerome and Conrad exit.

DE MON. I hear their footsteps on the grating sand.
"How like the croaking of a carrion bird,
"That hateful voice sounds to the distant ear!
"And now she speaks—her voice sounds cheerly too—
"O curse their mirth!—
"Now, now, they come, keep closer still! keep steady! (*Taking hold of Jerome with both hands.*)
"JER. My lord, you tremble much.
"DE MON.                                  What, do I shake?
"JER. You do, in truth, and your teeth chatter too.
"DE MON. See! see they come! he strutting by her side."
*Jane, Rezenvelt, and Countess Freberg appear through the glass-door, pursuing their way up a short walk leading to the other wing of the house.*
See, how he turns his odious face to her's!
Utt'ring with confidence some nauseous jest.
And she endures it too—Oh! this looks vilely!
Ha! mark that courteous motion of his arm—
What does he mean?—He dares not take her hand!
(*Pauses and looks eagerly.*) By heaven and hell he does!
"*Letting go of his hold of Jerome, he throws out his hands vehemently, and thereby*
"*pushes him against the scene.*
"JER. Oh! I am stunn'd! my head is crack'd in twain:
"Your honour does forget how old I am.
"DE MON. Well, well, the wall is harder than I wist.
"Begone! and whine within.
                         "(*Exit Jerome, with a sad rueful countenance*)"
DE MON. (*Comes forward to the front of the stage, and makes a long pause, expressive of great agony of mind.*)
It must be so; each passing circumstance;
Her hasty journey here; her keen distress
Whene'er my soul's abhorrence I express'd;
Ay, and that damned reconciliation,
With tears extorted from me: Oh, too well!
All, all too well bespeak the shameful tale.
I should have thought of heav'n and hell conjoin'd,
The morning star mix'd with infernal fire,
Ere I had thought of this—[217]
"Hell's blackest magick, in the midnight hour,
"With horrid spells and incantation dire,
"Such combination opposite, unseemly,

217. The Larpent version has "Ere I had doubted this."

"Of fair and loathsome, excellent and base,
"Did ne'er produce.—But every thing is possible,
"So as it may my misery enhance!"
Oh! I did love her with such pride of soul!
When other men, in gayest pursuit of love,
Each beauty follow'd, by her side I stay'd;
Far prouder of a brother's station there,
Than all the favours favour'd lovers boast.
"We quarrel'd once, and when I could no more
"The alter'd coldness of her eye endure,
"I slipp'd o' tip-toe to her chamber door;
"And when she ask'd who gently knock'd—Oh! oh!"
Who could have thought of this?
*Throws himself into a chair, covers his face with his hand, and bursts into tears.*
*After some time he starts up from his seat furiously.*
Hell's direst torment seize th'infernal villain!
"Detested of my soul! I will have vengeance!
"I'll crush thy swelling pride—I'll still thy vaunting—
"I'll do a deed of blood—Why shrink I thus?"
If, by some spell or magick sympathy,
Piercing the lifeless figure on that wall²¹⁸
Could pierce his bosom too, would I not cast it?²¹⁹ (*Throwing a dagger*
  *against the wall.*)
"Shall groans and blood affright me? No, I'll do it.
"Tho' gasping life beneath my pressure heav'd,
"And my soul shudder'd at the horrid brink,
"I would not flinch.—Fy, this recoiling nature!
"O that his sever'd limbs were strew'd in air,
"So as I saw him not!
"*Enter Rezenvelt behind, from the glass door. De Monfort turns round, and on*
"*seeing him starts back, then drawing his sword, rushes furiously upon him.*
"Detested robber; now all forms are over:
"Now open villany, now open hate!
"Defend thy life.
"REZ.          De Monfort, thou art mad.
"DE MON. Speak not, but draw. Now for thy hated life!
"*They fight: Rezenvelt parries his thrusts with great skill, and at last disarms*
"*him.*
"Then take my life, black fiend, for hell assists thee.

218. The Larpent version has "Piercing that lifeless figure on the wall." 219. The Larpent
version has "thus would I cast it."

"REZ. No, Monfort, but I'll take away your sword.
"Not as a mark of disrespect to you,
"But for your safety. By to-morrow's eve
"I'll call on you myself and give it back;
"And then, if I am charg'd with any wrong,
"I'll justify myself. Farewell, strange man!                    (*Exit*)
"*De Monfort stands for some time quite motionless, like one stupified.*" Enter to him
a *Servant:*[220] *he starts.*

220. The Larpent version identifies him as Manuel not Jacques. The long cut suggests the
difficulties Baillie and her interpreters had with this scene. The original duel and disarming
of De Monfort could diminish him in our eyes. The Larpent text thus cuts Rezenvelt from
the scene entirely. However, descriptions of the performance suggest that in fact neither the
Larpent or printed versions were performed. Here is the text from the much-edited Camp-
bell/Siddons manuscript which matches the descriptions; this version has a confrontation
between the two men, but De Monfort is not defeated because no duel takes place:

*Jane & the Countess take leave of Rezenvelt at the Glass door—he is passing thro the room. De Monfort
starts up.*
DE MON. Who passes there? By heaven & hell 'tis he!—
Detested fiend quick to thy safest guard
Defend thy life.—
REZ. De Monfort! art thou mad?—
DE MON. Speak not but draw.
REZ. Draw! and beneath this roof?
What! in your sister's presence?
DE MON. Sister! Villain,
Thou hast bewitch'd her heart with spells & charms:—
Short shall thy triumph be: all forms are over;
'Tis open hatred, open vengeance now.
REZ. Yet for your Sister
Were I so bless'd to merit her regard,
I should not wait an angry brother's leave
To make my triumph lasting as his hate;—
Sir, for your challenge my resolve is final
Ne'er accept it:—but this very morn you
Vow'd never to lift that hand against me.—
I'll not be guilty of your perjuries.—
Find out some free, some untried adversary;
If this rash fit should hold you, you again
May be a trifling life in debt to *him*,
Again acknowledge and again forget.                    (*Exit*)
DE MON. Baffled! upbraided! menaced!—hold my brain
The Infernal Villain!
Where is she—Where's my sister
Jane, why, Jane,—
If by some power of magic sympathy

[SER. My Lord,—]

DE MON. Ha! who art thou?

SER.                    'Tis I, an' please your honour.

"DE MON. (*Staring wildly at him.*) Who art thou?"

SER. Your servant Jacques.

DE MON.                    Indeed I know thee not.[221]

Leave me, and when [yon] Rezenvelt is gone,

Return and let me know.

SER.                    He's gone already, sir.

DE MON. How, gone so soon?

SER.                    Yes, as his servant told me,

He was in haste to go, for night comes on,

And at the ev'ning hour he must take horse,

To visit some old friend whose lonely mansion[222]

Stands a short mile beyond the "farther" wood;

And, as he loves to wander thro' those[223] wilds,

Whilst yet the early moon may light his way,

He sends his horses round the usual road,

And crosses it alone.

I would not walk thro' those wild dens alone

For all his wealth. For there, as I have heard,

Foul murders have been done, and ravens scream;

And things unearthly, stalking thro' the night,

Have scar'd the lonely trav'ller from his wits.

*De Monfort stands fixed in thought.*

I've ta'en your mare, an' please you, from her field,[224]

And wait your farther orders.[225][—He heeds me not.—]

*De Monfort heeds him not.*

Her[226] hoofs are sound, and where the saddle gall'd

Begins to mend.[227] What further must be done?

*De Monfort still heeds him not.*

"His honour heeds me not. Why should I stay?"

DE MON. (*Eagerly, as he is going.*) He goes alone saidst thou?

---

Piercing that lifeless figure on the wall

Could pierce his heartstrings too, thus would I—

*Enter Manuel as De Monfort draws his sword.*

221. The Larpent version has "I knew thee not.—" 222. The Larpent version has "To visit old Count Waldec—he whose house." 223. The Larpent version has "the." 224. The Larpent version has "They have brought back the horse you rode, my Lord." 225. The Larpent version has "further will." 226. The Larpent version has "His." 227. The Larpent version has "Will shortly mend."

SER. His servant told me so.

DE MON.                          And at what hour?

SER. He 'parts from Amberg by the fall of eve.
Save you, my lord? how chang'd your count'nance is!
Are you not well?

DE MON.          Yes, I am well: begone!
And wait my orders by the city wall:
I'll that way bend, and speak to thee again.          (*Exit Servant*)

*De Monfort walks rapidly two or three times across the stage; then seizes his dagger
from the wall; looks steadfastly at its point, and Exit, hastily.*


# ACT IV


SCENE I[228]   *Moon-light. A wild path in a wood, shaded with trees. Enter De
Monfort, with a strong expression of disquiet, mixed with fear, upon his face, looking behind him, and bending his ear to the ground, as if he listened to something.*

DE MON. How hollow groans the earth beneath my tread!
Is there an echo here? Methinks it sounds
As tho' some heavy footstep follow'd me.
"I will advance no farther.
"Deep settled shadows rest across the path,
"And thickly-tangled boughs o'er hang this spot.
"O that a tenfold gloom did cover it!
"That 'midst the murky darkness I might strike;
"As in the wild confusion of a dream,
"Things horrid, bloody, terrible, do pass,
"As tho' they pass'd not; nor impress the mind
"With the fix'd clearness of reality."
*An owl is heard screaming near him.*
(*Starting.*) What sound is that? (*Listens, and the owl cries again.*) It is the
     screech-owl's cry.
Foul bird of night! what spirit guides thee here?
Art thou instinctive drawn to scenes of horrour?
"I've heard of this. (*Pauses and listens.*)"
How[229] those fall'n leaves so rustle on the path,
With whisp'ring noise, as tho' the earth around me
Did utter secret things![230]

228. This is Act IV, scene iii in the 1851 version. 229. The Larpent version has "And."
230. The Larpent version adds "I've heard of this," cut above.

The distant river, too, bears to mine ear
A dismal wailing. O mysterious night!
Thou art not silent; many tongues hast thou.
A distant gath'ring blast sounds thro' the wood,
And dark clouds fleetly hasten o'er the sky.²³¹
O! that a storm would rise, a raging storm;
Amidst the roar of warring elements
I'd lift my hand and strike: but this pale light,
The calm distinctness of each stilly thing,
Is terrible. (*Starting.*) [But hark—] Footsteps are near—
He comes, he comes! I'll watch him farther on—
I cannot do it here.                                              (*Exit*)
*Enter Rezenvelt, and continues his way slowly across the stage, but just as he is
going off the owl screams, he stops and listens, and the owl screams again.*
REZ. Ha! does the night-bird greet me on my way?
How much his hooting is in harmony
With such a scene as this! I like it well.
Oft when a boy, at the still twilight hour,
I've leant my back against some knotted oak,²³²
And loudly mimick'd him, till to my call
He answer would return, and thro' the gloom
"We friendly converse held.
"Between me and the star-bespangl'd sky
"Those aged oaks their crossing branches wave,
"And thro' them looks the pale and placid moon.
"How like a crocodile, or winged snake,
"Yon sailing cloud bears on its dusky length!
"And now transformed by the passing wind,
"Methinks it seems a flying Pegasus.
"Ay, but a shapeless band of blacker hue
"Come swiftly after.—
"A hollow murm'ring wind comes thro' the trees;"²³³
I hear it from afar; this bodes a storm.
I must not linger here—
*A bell heard at some distance.*

231. The Larpent version has "Thou hast many tongues! / A distant hurrying blast whirrs
thro' the wood, / And dark clouds fleetly scud athwart the sky." 232. The Larpent version
has "I've lean'd my back against some ragged bough." 233. The Larpent version has "We
friendly converse held.—More rev'rend Oaks / Stretch out their arms across the night /
Obscuring all the road;—but the white moon / Chequers the shade, and guides me on my
way.— / A hollow wind comes murmuring thro' the trees."

What bell is this?
It sends[234] a solemn sound upon the breeze.
Now, to a fearful superstitious mind,
In such a scene, 'twould like a death-knell come:
For me it tells but of a shelter near,
And so I bid it welcome.                                    (*Exit*)

SCENE II[235]   *The inside of a Convent Chapel, of old Gothick architecture, almost dark; two torches only are seen at a distance, burning over a new-made grave. The noise of loud wind, beating upon the windows and roof, is heard. Enter two Monks.*[236]

1ST MONK. The storm increases: hark how dismally
It howls along the cloisters.[237] How goes time?
2D MONK. It is the hour: I hear them near at hand;
And when the solemn requiem has been sung[238]
For the departed sister, we'll retire.
Yet, should this tempest still more violent grow,[239]
We'll beg a friendly shelter till the morn.
1ST MONK. See, the procession enters: let us join.
*The organ strikes up a solemn prelude. Enter a procession of Nuns, with the Abbess, bearing torches. After compassing the grave twice, and remaining there some time, whilst the organ plays a grand dirge, they advance to the front of the stage.*

SONG, BY THE NUNS
Departed soul, whose poor remains
This hallow'd lowly grave contains;
Whose passing storm of life is o'er,
Whose pains and sorrows are no more!
"Bless'd be thou with the bless'd above!
"Where all is joy, and purity, and love.

"Let him, in might and mercy dread,
"Lord of the living and the dead;
"In whom the stars of heav'n rejoice,
"To whom the ocean lifts his voice,

234. The Larpent version has "swings." 235. This is Act V, scene i in the 1851 version. 236. In the Larpent version, they are identified as Francis and Peter. 237. The Larpent version has "The storm comes on apace:—how dismally / It roars along the cloisters." 238. The Larpent version has "Soon as the holy requiem has been sung"; beginning here, all of the rest of the lines up to the entry of the nuns are given to Francis, the first monk. 239. The Larpent version has "Yet should the tempest grow more violent."

"Thy spirit purified to glory raise,
"To sing with holy saints his everlasting praise.

"Departed soul, who in this earthly scene
"Hast our lowly sister been."
Swift be thy way to where the blessed dwell!
Until we meet thee there, farewell! farewell!

*Enter a Lay Sister,*[240] *with a wild terrified look, her hair and dress all scattered, and rushes forward amongst them.*

ABB. Why com'st thou here, with such disorder'd looks,
To break upon our sad solemnity?
SIST. Oh! I did hear,[241] thro' the receding blast,
Such horrid cries! it[242] made my blood run chill.
ABB. 'Tis but the varied voices of the storm,[243]
Which many times will sound like distant screams:
It has deceiv'd thee.
SIST. O no, for twice it call'd, so loudly call'd,[244]
With horrid strength, beyond the pitch of nature.
"And murder! murder! was the dreadful cry."
A third time it return'd with feeble strength,
But o'the sudden ceas'd, as tho' the words
Were rudely smother'd in the grasped throat;[245]
"And all was still again, save the wild blast
"Which at a distance growl'd—
"Oh! it will never from my mind depart!
"That dreadful cry all i'the instant still'd,
"For then, so near, some horrid deed was done,
"And none to rescue."[246]
ABB. Where didst thou hear it?
SIST.                             "In the higher cells,
"As now a window, open'd by the storm,
"I did attempt to close."[247]
1ST MONK. I wish our brother Bernard were arriv'd;

240. The Larpent version identifies her as Agatha. 241. The Larpent version has "I have heard." 242. The Larpent version has "they." 243. The Larpent version has "It is the varied howling of the storm." 244. The Larpent version has "groan'd, most sadly groan'd." 245. The Larpent version has "A third time it return'd with feebler sound, / And o' the sudden ceas'd, as tho' some words / Were rudely smother'd in the gasping throat." 246. The Larpent version has "Some fearful murder surely has been done." 247. The Larpent version has "From your cell,—but now,— / Closing a casement shatter'd by the storm."

"He is upon his way."[248]

ABB. [249] Be not alarm'd; it still may be deception.

'Tis meet we finish our solemnity,

Nor shew neglect unto the honour'd dead.

*Gives a sign, and the organ plays again: just as it ceases a loud knocking is heard without.*

ABB. Ha! who may this be? hush! [It is the sound

    [Of one in haste.—]

*"Knocking heard again.*

"2ND MONK. It is the knock of one in furious haste.

"Hush, hush, What footsteps come? Ha! brother Bernard."

*Enter Bernard bearing a lantern.*

"1ST MONK. See, what a look he wears of stiffen'd fear!

"Where hast thou been, good brother?

"BERN. I've seen a horrid sight!

"ALL. (*Gathering round him and speaking at once.*) What hast thou

    seen?"[250]

BERN. "As on I hasten'd, bearing thus my light,"

Across the path, not fifty paces off,

I saw a murther'd corse stretch'd on its back,

Smear'd with new blood, as tho' but freshly slain.[251]

"ABB. A man or woman?

"BERN.             A man, a man!"

ABB. Did'st thou examine it within its breast

There yet is lodg'd some small remains of life?

Was it quite dead?[252]

BERN.         "Nought in the grave is deader.

"I look'd but once, yet life did never lodge

"In any form so laid.—

"A chilly horrour seiz'd me, and I fled."[253]

"1ST MONK. And does the face seem all unknown to thee?

"BERN. The face! I would not on the face have look'd

---

248. The Larpent version has the Abbess say, "I would the holy brotherhood were arrived." 249. The Larpent version has the Friar say, "Be not alarm'd; it still may be delusion. / 'Tis meet we finish our solemnity, / Nor shew neglect to this departed Saint." 250. For this exchange, the Larpent version has: FRIAR. What means that look of haste and fear, good Brother? / Where hast thou been? BERN. Good heaven protect us all!— / I've seen a dismal sight! ABB. It is too true!—" 251. The Larpent version has "Across the path, not fifty paces hence, / I found a murder'd corse stretch'd on his back, / Streaming with blood, as tho' but newly slain." 252. The Larpent version has "Alas, alas!—perhaps within his breast / There yet are lodg'd some small remains of life? / Say, was it dead?—art sure of it?" 253. The Larpent version has "For ever."

"For e'en a kingdom's wealth, for all the world.
"O no! the bloody neck, the bloody neck! (*Shaking his head, and
    shuddering with horrour.*)"
*Loud knocking heard without.*
SIST. Good mercy! who comes next?
BERN.                            Not far behind
I left our brother Thomas on the road;
But then he did repent him as he went,
And threaten'd to return.
2D MONK.              See, here he comes.[254]
*Enter brother Thomas, with a wild terrified look.*
"1ST MONK. How wild he looks!"
BERN. (*Going up to him eagerly.*) What, hast thou seen it too?[255]
THOM. Yes, yes![256] it glar'd upon me as it pass'd.
BERN. What glar'd upon thee?[257]
"ALL. (*Gathering round Thomas and speaking at once.*) O! what hast thou
    seen?"
THOM. As, striving with the blast, I onward came,
Turning my feeble lantern from the wind,
Its light upon a dreadful visage gleam'd,
Which paus'd, and look'd upon me as it pass'd.
But such a look, such a wildness of despair,
Such horrour-strain'd features never yet
Did earthly visage show. I shrunk and shudder'd.
If damned spirits may to earth return
I've seen it.[258]
"BERN.      Was there blood upon it?"
"THOM. Nay, as it pass'd, I did not see its form;
"Nought but the horrid face."
BERN. It is the murderer. [—We must follow him;
    [Our duty so ordains.—Brothers let's go.—
    [We will return—Till then good heaven be with you.]
"1ST MONK.                        What way went it?

254. For this exchange, the Larpent version has "ABB. Have mercy! who comes here? BERN.
Not far behind / I quitted my companion on the road / Who call'd upon a message from the
Abbott / At the next monastery. FRIAR. 'Tis Ambrose comes." Thomas is called Ambrose.
255. The Larpent version has "What, Ambrose, hast thou seen this fearful sight?"
256. The Larpent version has "Too sure." 257. The Larpent version has "Pass'd—glar'd
upon thee?" 258. The Larpent version rearranges this speech, opening with "If damned
spirits may to earth return, / I've surely seen it:—as I onward came . . . ." It follows the
rest of the speech except it has "Features so strain'd with horror never yet / Did human visage show."

"THOM. I durst not look till I had pass'd it far,
"Then turning round, upon the rising bank,
"I saw, between me and the paly sky,
"A dusky form, tossing and agitated.
"I stopp'd to mark it, but, in truth, I found
"'Twas but a sapling bending to the wind,
"And so I onward hied, and look'd no more.
"IST MONK. But we must look to't; we must follow it:
"Our duty so commands. (*To 2d Monk.*) Will you go, brother?
"(*To Bernard.*) And you, good Bernard?
"BERN.                                  If I needs must go.
"IST MONK. Come, we must all go."
ABB.[259]                          Heaven be with you, then!

                                         (*Exeunt Monks*)

SIST. Amen, amen! Good heaven be with us all!
O what a dreadful night!
ABB. Daughters retire; peace to the peaceful dead!
Our solemn ceremony now is finish'd.
*The organ plays.*                                 (*Exeunt*)


LARPENT SCENE III[260]   *A cloister in the Convent.*

*The Abbess and all the nuns pass in silence across the Stage.—The Organ heard all the while at a distance.*


SCENE III[261]   *A large room in the Convent, very dark. Enter the Abbess, Lay Sister*[262] *bearing a light, and several Nuns. Sister sets down the light on a table at the bottom of the stage, so that the room is still very gloomy.*

ABB. They have been longer absent than I thought;
I fear he has escap'd them.[263]
IST NUN.                          Heaven forbid!
SIST. No, no, found out foul murder ever is,[264]

259. The Larpent version closes the scene with a speech by the Abbess, using much of the following language: "Amen, Amen good Heaven be with us all! / Peace to the peaceful dead!—Retire, my daughters; / We have fulfill'd her pious obsequies." 260. This scene appears only in the Larpent version. 261. This is Act IV, scene iv in the Larpent version; Act V, scene ii in the 1851 version. 262. In the Larpent version, identified as Agatha. 263. The Larpent version has "I would they were return'd in safety back!— / Their search for him will be in vain." 264. The Larpent version has "No, no;— / Foul murder ever is found out, good mother."

And the foul murd'rer too.

"2D NUN. The good Saint Francis will direct their search;

"The blood so near his holy convent shed

"For threefold vengeance calls."

*A noise without.*

ABB. I hear a noise within the inner court,

They are return'd; (*Listening.*) and Bernard's voice I hear:

"They are return'd."

"SIST.                    Why do I tremble so?

"It is not I who ought to tremble thus.

"2D NUN. I hear them at the door."

BERN. (*Without.*) Open the door, I pray thee, brother Thomas;[265]

I cannot now unhand the prisoner.

ALL. (*Speak together, shrinking back from the door, and staring upon one
    another.*) [Then] he is with them.

*A folding door at the bottom of the stage is opened, and enter Bernard, Thomas,
and the other two Monks, carrying lanterns in their hands, and bringing in De
Monfort. They are likewise followed by other Monks. As they lead forward De
Monfort the light is turned away, so that he is seen obscurely; but when they come
to the front of the stage they all turn the light side of their lanterns on him at once,
and his face is seen in all the strengthened horrour of despair, with his hands and
cloaths bloody.*

ABB. AND NUNS. (*Speak at once, and starting back.*) Holy saints be with
    us.[266]

BERN. (*To Abbess.*) Behold the man of blood!

ABB. Of misery too; I cannot look upon him.

BERN. "(*To Nuns.*) Nay, holy sisters, turn not thus away."

(*To Abbess.*) Speak to him, if, perchance, he will regard you:[267]

For from his mouth we have no utt'rance heard,

Save one deep and smother'd exclamation,

When first we seiz'd him.

ABB. (*To De Monfort.*) Most miserable man, how art thou thus?

(*Pauses.*) Thy tongue is silent, but those bloody hands

Do witness horrid things. What is thy name?

DE MON. (*Roused; looks steadfastly at the Abbess for some time, then speaking
    in a short hurried voice.*) I have no name.

ABB. (*To Bernard.*) Do it thyself: I'll speak to him no more.

265. The Larpent version has "father Ambrose." 266. The Larpent version has the Abbess alone say, "Holy saints defend us!" 267. The Larpent version has "Speak to him, he,
perchance, will answer you."

"sist. O holy saints! that this should be the man,
"Who did against his fellow lift the stroke,
"Whilst he so loudly call'd.—
"Still in mine ear it sounds: O murder! murder!
"de mon. (*Starting.*) He calls again!
"sist. No, he did call, but now his voice is still'd.
" 'Tis past.
"de mon. (*In great anguish.*) 'Tis past!
"sist. Yes it is past, art thou not he who did it?"
*De Monfort utters a deep groan, and is supported from falling by the Monks. A noise is heard without.*
abb. What noise is this of heavy lumb'ring steps,[268]
Like men who with a[269] weighty burden come?
bern. [We met some of our order on our way:]
It is the body: I have orders given
That here it should be laid.[270]
*Enter Men bearing the body of Rezenvelt, covered with a white cloth, and set it down in the middle of the room: they then uncover it. De Monfort stands fixed and motionless with horrour, only that a sudden shivering seems to pass over him when they uncover the corps. The Abbess and Nuns shrink back and retire to some distance; all the rest fixing their eyes steadfastly upon De Monfort. A long pause.*
bern. (*To De Monfort.*) See'st thou that "lifeless" corps, "those bloody wounds,"
See how[271] he lies, who but so shortly since
A living creature was, with all the powers
Of sense, and motion, and humanity?
Oh! what a heart had he who did this deed!
"1st monk. (*Looking at the body.*) How hard those teeth against the lips are press'd,
"As tho' he struggled still!
"2d monk. The hands, too, clench'd: the last efforts of nature."
*De Monfort still stands motionless. Brother Thomas then goes to the body, and raising up the head a little, turns it towards De Monfort.*
thom. Know'st thou this ghastly face?
de mon. (*Putting up his hands before his face in violent perturbation.*)
Oh do not! do not! veil it from my sight!
Put me to any agony but this!
thom. Ha! dost thou then confess the dreadful deed?

---

268. The Larpent version has "What sound is this of heavy-falling steps?" 269. The Larpent version has "some." 270. The Larpent version has "I have given command / That they should lay it here." 271. The Larpent version has "Look where."

"Hast thou against the laws of awful heav'n

"Such horrid murder done? What fiend could tempt thee? (*Pauses and looks steadfastly at De Monfort.*)

"DE MON. I hear thy words but do not hear their sense—

"Hast thou not cover'd it?"

"BERN. (*To Thomas.*) Forbear, my brother, for thou see'st right well

"He is not in a state to answer thee.

"Let us retire and leave him for a while.

"These windows are with iron grated o'er;

"He cannot 'scape, and other duty calls.

"THOM. Then let it be.

"BERN. (*To Monks, &c.*) Come, let us all depart."[272]

*Exeunt Abbess and Nuns, followed by the Monks. One Monk*[273] *lingering a little behind.*

DE MON. All gone! (*Perceiving the Monk.*) O stay thou here!

MONK.                                          It must not be.

DE MON. I'll give thee gold; I'll make thee rich in gold,

If thou wilt stay e'en but a little while.[274]

MONK. I must not, must not stay.

"DE MON.                      I do conjure thee!

"MONK. I dare not stay with thee. (*Going.*)"

DE MON.                      And wilt thou go?

(*Catching hold of him eagerly.*) "O! throw thy cloak upon this grizly form!

"The unclos'd eyes do stare upon me still."

O do not leave me thus!             (*Monk covers the body, and Exit*)

DE MON. (*Alone, looking at the covered body, but at a distance.*)

Alone with thee! but thou art nothing now.

'Tis done, 'tis number'd with the things o'erpast,

Would! would it were to come!

"What fated end, what darkly gath'ring cloud

"Will close on all this horrour!

"O that dire madness would unloose my thoughts,

"And fill my mind with wildest fantasies,

"Dark, restless, terrible! ought, ought but this!

"(*Pauses and shudders.*) How with convulsive life he heav'd beneath me,

"E'en with the death's wound gor'd. O horrid, horrid!

272. The Larpent version has a single speech for these cut lines: "Nay, forbear;—thou see'st / He is not in a state to answer thee. / Let us retire and leave him for a while. / Time may compose him,—Go, my daughters, go.—" 273. In the Larpent version, it is Bernard. 274. The Larpent version has "e'en but a moment with me."

"Methinks I feel him still.—What sound is that?"[275]

I heard a smother'd groan.—It is impossible! (*Looking steadfastly at the body.*)

It moves! it moves! the cloth doth heave and swell.

It moves "again."—I cannot suffer this—

"Whate'er it be I will uncover it."[276]

(*Runs to the corps and tears off the cloth in despair.*) All still beneath.

Nought is there here but fix'd and grizly death.

How sternly fixed! Oh! those glazed eyes!

They look me still.[277] (*Shrinks back with horrour.*)

Come, madness! come unto me senseless death!

I cannot suffer this! Here, rocky wall,

Scatter these brains, or dull them.[278] (*Runs furiously, and, dashing his head against the wall, falls upon the floor.*)

*Enter two Monks, hastily.*[279]

1ST MONK. See; wretched man, he hath destroy'd himself.

2ND MONK. He does but faint. Let us remove him hence.

1ST MONK. We did not well to leave him here alone.

2ND MONK. Come, let us bear him to the open air.

(*Exeunt, bearing out De Monfort*)

## ACT V

SCENE I[280]  *Before the gates of the Convent. Enter Jane De Monfort, Freberg and Manuel. As they are proceeding towards the gate, Jane stops short and shrinks back.*

FREB. Ha! wherefore? has a sudden illness seiz'd thee?

JANE. No, no, my friend.—And yet I am very faint—

I dread to enter here!

MAN.                  "Ay! so I thought:

"For, when between the trees, that abbey tower

"First shew'd its top, I saw your count'nance change.

"But breathe a little here;" I'll go before,

---

275. The Larpent version has "What, what is that?" 276. The Larpent version has "Then thus—" 277. The Larpent version has "How sternly fixed those eyes!—those glassy eyes!— / They stare upon me still." 278. The Larpent version has "and let me die at once!" 279. The Larpent version has Bernard and Ambrose enter; Ambrose speaks the same first line, then Bernard closes the scene: "Let us remove him hence:—he does but faint.— / We did not well to leave him here alone. / We'll move the body to the sacristy.— / Come, let us bear him to the open air." 280. In the 1851 version, this is Act V, scene iii.

And make enquiry at the nearest gate.[281]

FREB. "Do so, good Manuel."

*Manuel goes and knocks at the gate.*

Courage, dear madam: all may yet be well.

Rezenvelt's servant, frighten'd with the storm,

And seeing that his master join'd him not,

As by appointment, at the forest's edge,

Might be alarm'd, and give too ready ear

To an unfounded rumour.

He saw it not; he came not here himself.

JANE. (*Looking eagerly to the gate, where Manuel talks with the Porter.*) Ha!
see, he talks with some one earnestly.

And see'st thou not that motion of his hands?

He stands like one who hears a horrid tale.

Almighty God![282]

*Manuel goes into the convent.*

        "He comes not back; he enters."

FREB. Bear up, my noble friend.

JANE. I will, I will! But this suspence is dreadful.

*A long pause. Manuel re-enters from the convent, and comes forward slowly, with a sad countenance.*

[He comes, he comes.—O Albert, Albert!—There,—]

Is this the pace of one who bears good tidings?

O God![283] his face doth tell the horrid fact;

There is nought doubtful here.

FREB.                     How is it Manuel?

MAN. I've seen him through a crevice in his door:[284]

It is indeed my master. (*Bursting into tears.*)

*Jane faints, and is supported by Freberg.—Enter Abbess and several Nuns from the convent, who gather about her, and apply remedies. She recovers.*

1ST NUN. The life returns again.[285]

"2ND NUN.                Yes, she revives."

ABB. (*To Freberg.*) Let me entreat "this noble lady's leave"

To lead her in. She seems in great distress:

We would with holy kindness soothe her woe,

And do by her the deeds of christian love.

FREB. Madam, your goodness has my grateful thanks.

               (*Exeunt, supporting Jane into the Convent*)

---

281. The Larpent version has "at the convent gate." 282. The Larpent version has the milder "Almighty powers." 283. The Larpent version has "O heaven!" 284. The Larpent version has "through the grating of his door." 285. In the Larpent version, this becomes part of the Abbess's speech.

SCENE II[286] *De Monfort is discovered sitting in a thoughtful posture. He remains so for some time. His face afterwards begins to appear agitated, like one whose mind is harrowed with the severest thoughts; then, starting from his seat, he clasps his hands together, and holds them up to heaven.*

DE MON. O that I had ne'er known the light of day![287]
"That filmy darkness on mine eyes had hung,
"And clos'd me out from the fair face of nature!"
O that my mind, in mental darkness pent,
Had no perception, no distinction known,
Of fair or foul, perfection nor defect;
Nor thought conceiv'd[288] of proud pre-eminence!
"O that it had! O that I had been form'd
"An idiot from the birth! a senseless changeling,
"Who eats his glutton's meal with greedy haste,
"Nor knows the hand who feeds him.—"
(*Pauses; then, in a calmer, sorrowful voice.*) What am I now? how ends the
    day of life?
For end it must; and terrible this gloom,[289]
The[290] storm of horrours that surround its close.
This little term of nature's agony
Will soon be o'er, and what is past is past:
But shall I then, on the dark lap of earth
Lay me to rest, in still unconsciousness,
"Like senseless clod that doth no pressure feel
"From wearing foot of daily passenger;
"Like steeped rock o'er which the breaking waves
"Bellow and foam unheard?" O would I could!
*Enter Manuel, who springs forward to his master, but is checked upon perceiving
De Monfort draw back and look sternly at him.*
MAN. My lord, my master! O my dearest master!
*De Monfort still looks at him without speaking.*
Nay, do not thus regard me; good my lord!
Speak to me: am I not your faithful Manuel?
DE MON. (*In a hasty broken voice.*) Art thou alone?
MAN. No, sir, the lady Jane is on her way;
She is not far behind.
DE MON. (*Tossing his arm over his head in agony.*) This is too much! All I
    can bear but this!

286. In the 1851 version, this is Act V, scene iv. 287. The Larpent version has "O, that I
ne'er had seen the light of day!" 288. The Larpent version has "Nor any thought."
289. The Larpent version has "the storm." 290. The Larpent version has "This."

It must not be.—Run and prevent her coming.
Say, he who is detain'd a pris'ner here
Is one to her unknown. I now am nothing.
I am a man, of holy claims bereft;
Out from the pale of social kindred cast;[291]
Nameless and horrible.—
Tell her De Monfort far from hence is gone
Into a desolate, and distant land,
Ne'er to return again. Fly, tell her this;
For we must meet no more.

*Enter Jane De Monfort, bursting into the chamber, and followed by Freberg, Abbess, and several Nuns.*

JANE. We must! we must! My brother, O my brother!

*De Monfort turns away his head and hides his face with his arm. Jane stops short, and, making a great effort, turns to Freberg, and the others who followed her; and with an air of dignity stretches out her hand, beckoning them to retire. All retire but Freberg, who seems to hesitate.*

And thou too, Freberg: call it not unkind.

           *(Exit Freberg, Jane and De Monfort only remain)*
           My hapless Monfort!

*De Monfort turns round and looks sorrowfully upon her; she opens her arms to him, and he, rushing into them, hides his face upon her breast and weeps.*

Ay, give thy sorrow vent: here may'st thou weep.

DE MON. (*In broken accents.*) Oh! this, my sister, makes me feel again
The kindness of affection.
My mind has in a dreadful storm been tost;
Horrid and dark.—I thought to weep no more.—
I've done a deed—But I am human still.

JANE. I know thy suff'rings: leave thy sorrow free;
Thou art with one who never did upbraid;
Who mourns, who loves thee still.

DE MON. Ah! say'st thou so? no, no; it should not be.
(*Shrinking from her.*) I am a foul and bloody murderer,
For such embrace unmeet. "O leave me! leave me!
"Disgrace and public shame abide me now;
"And all, alas! who do my kindred own
"The direful portion share."—Away, away!
Shall a disgrac'd and publick criminal
Degrade thy name, and claim affinity

291. The Larpent version has "Cast from the pale of kindred charities."

To noble worth like thine?—I have no name—
I am nothing, now, not e'en to thee; depart.
*She takes his hand, and grasping it firmly, speaks with a determined voice.*
JANE. De Monfort, hand in hand we have enjoy'd
The playful term of infancy together;
And in the rougher path of ripen'd years
We've been each other's stay. Dark lowers our fate,
And terrible the storm that gathers over us;
But nothing, till that latest agony
Which severs thee from nature, shall unloose
This fix'd and sacred hold. In thy dark prisonhouse;
In the terrifick face of armed law;
Yea, on the scaffold, if it needs must be,
I never will forsake thee.
DE MON. (*Looking at her with admiration.*) Heav'n bless thy gen'rous
    soul, my noble Jane.
I thought to sink beneath this load of ill,
Depress'd with infamy and open shame;
"I thought to sink in abject wretchedness."
But for thy sake I'll rouse my manhood up,
And meet it bravely; no unseemly weakness,
"I feel my rising strength," shall blot my end,
To cloth thy cheek with shame.[292]
JANE. Yes, thou art noble still.
DE MON. With thee I am; who were not so with thee?
But, ah, my sister! short will be the term:
Death's stroke will come, and in that state beyond,
Where things unutterable wait the soul,
"New from its earthly tenement discharg'd,"
We shall be sever'd far.
For as the spotless purity of virtue
Is from the murd'rer's guilt, far shall we be.[293]
This is the gulf "of dread uncertainty"
From which the[294] soul recoils.
JANE. The God who made thee is a God of mercy;
Think upon this.[295]

292. The Larpent version has "Shall blot my end, to give thy cheek a blush." 293. The
Larpent version has "we shall be sever'd." 294. The Larpent version has "my." 295. In
the Larpent version, this speech is crossed out, as is a rewrite. The final version reads, "The
power who made us is exceeding good." The religious language apparently again caused
difficulties.

"DE MON. (*Shaking his head.*) No, no! this blood! this blood!
"JANE. Yes, e'en the sin of blood may be forgiv'n,
"When humble penitence hath once aton'd.
DE MON. (*Eagerly.*) "What, after terms of lengthen'd misery,
"Imprison'd anguish of tormented spirits,
"Shall I again, a renovated soul,
"Into the blessed family of the good
"Admittance have? Think'st thou that this may be?
"Speak if thou canst:" O speak me comfort here![296]
"For dreadful fancies, like an armed host,
"Have push'd me to despair. It is most horrible—"
O speak of hope! if any hope there be.[297]
*Jane is silent and looks sorrowfully upon him; then clasping her hands, and turning*
*her eyes to heaven, seems to mutter a prayer.*
DE MON. Ha! dost thou pray for me? Heav'n hear thy prayer!
I fain would kneel[298]—Alas I dare not do it.
JANE. Not so; all by th' Almighty Father form'd
May in their deepest mis'ry call on him.[299]
Come kneel with me, my brother.
*She kneels and prays to herself; he kneels by her, and clasps his hands fervently, but*
*speaks not. A noise of chains clanking is heard without, and they both rise.*
DE MON. Hear'st thou that noise? They come to interrupt us.
JANE. (*Moving towards a side door.*) Then let us enter here.
DE MON. (*Catching hold of her with a look of horrour.*) Not there—not
   there—the corps—the bloody corps.[300]
JANE. What, lies he there?—Unhappy Rezenvelt!
DE MON. A sudden thought has come across my mind;[301]
How came it not before? Unhappy Rezenvelt!
Say'st thou but this?
JANE. What should I say? he was an honest man;
[Spite of the levities which misbecame him:]
I still have thought him such, as such lament him.[302]
*De Monfort utters a deep groan.*[303]

---

296. The Larpent version has "O thou speak'st comfortably!" 297. The Larpent version
has "Tell me of hope,—if there be a hope for me." 298. The Larpent version has "And I
will kneel!" 299. The Larpent version has "Do it; our Father has commanded it / In deepest misery to call on him." The religious language again seems to be the problem: "we are
commanded by our God" is crossed out. 300. The Larpent version has "Not there—not
there, my sister,—pray not there!—" 301. The Larpent version has "Ha—thou hast wak'd
my brain to such a thought—" 302. The Larpent version has "I still have thought of him
such, and I am sorry for him." 303. The Larpent version provides the moan: "O! O! O!"

What means this heavy groan?

"DE MON.                   It hath a meaning."

*Enter Abbess and Monks,*[304] *with two Officers of justice carrying fetters in their hands to put upon De Monfort.*

JANE. (*Starting.*) What men are these?

1ST OFF. Lady, we are the servants of the law,[305]

And bear with us a power, which doth constrain[306]

To bind with fetters this our prisoner. (*Pointing to De Monfort.*)

JANE. A stranger uncondemn'd? this cannot be.

1ST OFF. As yet, indeed, he is by law unjudg'd,

But is so far condemn'd by circumstance,

"That law, or custom sacred held as law,

"Doth fully warrant us,"[307] and it must be.

JANE. Nay, say not so; he has no power to escape:

Distress hath bound him with a heavy chain;

There is no need of yours.

1ST OFF. We must perform our office.

JANE. O! do not offer this indignity!

1ST OFF. Is it indignity in sacred[308] law

To bind a murderer? (*To 2d Officer.*) Come, do thy work.

JANE. Harsh are thy words, and stern thy harden'd brow;

Dark[309] is thine eye; but all some pity have

Unto the last extreme of misery.

I do beseech thee! if thou art a man—(*Kneeling to him.*)

*De Monfort roused at this, runs up to Jane, and raises her hastily from the ground; then stretches himself up proudly.*

DE MON. (*To Jane.*) Stand thou erect in native dignity;

And bend to none on earth the suppliant knee.

Though cloth'd in power imperial. To my heart

It gives feller gripe than many irons.

(*Holding out his hands.*) Here, officers of law, bind on those[310] shackles,

"And if they are too light bring heavier chains.

"Add iron to iron, load, crush me to the ground;

"Nay, heap ten thousand weight upon my breast,

"For that were best of all."

304. The Larpent version has Bernard, Ambrose, Peter and Francis enter with the two officers. 305. The Larpent version has "the officers of justice." 306. The Larpent version has "doth command us." 307. The Larpent version has "That we are warranted." 308. The Larpent version has "equal." In the previous line the first edition has "after" in place of the the Larpent's "offer." 309. The Larpent version has "fierce." 310. The Larpent version has "your."

*A long pause, whilst they put irons upon him. After they are on, Jane looks at him sorrowfully, and lets her head sink on her breast. De Monfort stretches out his hands, looks at them, and then at Jane; crosses them over his breast, and endeavours to suppress his feelings.*

1ST OFF. (*To De Monfort.*) I[311] have it, too, in charge to move you hence,

Into another chamber, more secure.

DE MON. Well, I am ready, sir.

*Approaching Jane, whom the Abbess is endeavouring to comfort, but to no purpose.*

Ah! wherefore thus! most honour'd and most dear?

Shrink not at the accoutrements of ill,

Daring the thing itself. (*Endeavouring to look cheerful.*)

Wilt thou permit me with gyved[312] hand?

*She gives him her hand, which he raises to his lips.*

This was my proudest office.

(*Exeunt, De Monfort leading out Jane*)


SCENE III[313]   *A long narrow gallery in the convent, with the doors of the cells on each side. The stage darkened. A Nun is discovered at a distance listening. Enter another Nun at the front of the stage, and starts back.*

1ST NUN. Ha! who is this not yet retir'd to rest?

My sister, is it you? (*To the other who advances.*)

2D NUN. Returning from the sister Nina's cell,

311. The Larpent version has "We." 312. Fettered. 313. This is Act V, scene v in the 1851 version, though there the scene is handled differently. It is also quite different in Larpent:

*Enter Ambrose.*

AMB. I cannot bear to look upon this sight:
And yet he brav'd it with a manly spirit,
And led with shackled hand his sister forth,
Like one resolv'd to bear misfortune nobly.—
*Enter Agatha.*
That such a man should do this deed!—How now?—
AGA. Returning from the Mother Abbess's cell,
Passing the door where the poor pris'ner's laid,
The sound of one who struggl'd with his fate
Struck on me as I went; such piteous groans!
*Enter Bernard.*
AMB. How is it, Father, with your penitent?
BERN. Full many a bed of death, in painful charity,
With all its pangs and horror I have seen,
But never ought like this.
AMB. He's dying then?

Passing yon door where the poor pris'ner lies,
The sound of one who struggl'd with despair
Struck on me as I went: I stopp'd and listen'd;
O God! such piteous groans!
1ST NUN. Yes, since the ev'ning sun it hath been so.
The voice of mis'ry oft hath reach'd mine ear,
E'en in the cell above.
2D NUN.                    How is it thus?
Methought he brav'd it with a manly spirit,
And led, with shackl'd hands, his sister forth,
Like one resolv'd to bear misfortune boldly.
1ST NUN. Yes, with heroick courage, for a while
He seem'd inspir'd; but, soon depress'd again,
Remorse and dark despair o'erwhelm'd his soul,
And so he hath remain'd.
*Enter Father Bernard, advancing from the further end of the gallery, bearing a crucifix.*
1ST NUN. How goes it, father, with your penitent?
We've heard his heavy groans.
BERN. Retire, my daughters; many a bed of death,
With all its pangs and horrour I have seen,
But never ought like this.

---

BERN. Yes, death is dealing with him.
The violent contrition of his heart,
And strong suppression of the shame he labour'd with,
Have burst some stream of life within his breast.—
Heav'n grant his pangs be short!
AGA. How does his sister?
BERN. I could not bear to stay,—I left her with him:—
She sits and bears his head upon her lap;
And like a heaven-inspired angel speaks
The word of comfort to his troubled soul:
Then does she wipe the cold drops from his brow,
With such a look of tender wretchedness
It wrings the heart to see her.
*A Bell tolls.*
AMB. Ha! that sound!—
BERN. It is the knell of death:—his pains are past;
The wretched struggler hath his warfare clos'd.
May heaven have mercy on him!
*Bell tolls again.*
Retire my daughter; let us all retire
For scenes like this to meditation call.                    (*Exeunt bell tolling*)

2D NUN. He's dying, then?

BERN.                    Yes, death is dealing with him.
From violent agitation of the mind,
Some stream of life within his breast has burst;
For many times, within a little space,
The ruddy-tide has rush'd into his mouth.
God, grant his pains be short!

1ST NUN.                         Amen, amen!

2D NUN. How does the lady?

BERN. She sits and bears his head upon her lap;
And like a heaven-inspir'd angel, speaks
The word of comfort to his troubled soul:
Then does she wipe the cold drops from his brow,
With such a look of tender wretchedness,
It wrings the heart to see her.

1ST NUN. Ha! hear ye nothing?

2D NUN. (*Alarmed.*)         Yes, I heard a noise.

1ST NUN. And see'st thou nothing? (*Creeping closer to her sister.*)

BERN.                         'Tis a nun in white.

*Enter Lay Sister in her night cloaths, advancing from the dark end of the gallery.*

(*To Sister.*) Wherefore, my daughter, hast thou left thy cell?
It is not meet at this untimely hour.

SIST. I cannot rest. I hear such dismal sounds,
Such wailings in the air, such shrilly shrieks,
As though the cry of murder rose again
From the deep gloom of night. I cannot rest:
I pray you let me stay with you, good sisters!
*Bell tolls.*

NUNS. (*Starting.*) What bell is that?

BERN.                          It is the bell of death.
A holy sister was upon the watch
To give notice.
              *Bell tolls again.*
                         Hark, another knell!
The wretched struggler hath his warfare clos'd;
May heaven have mercy on him.
*Bell tolls again.*
Retire, my daughters; let us all retire,
For scenes like this to meditation call.          (*Exeunt, bell tolling again*)

SCENE IV[314]    *A hall or large room in the convent. The bodies of De Monfort and Rezenvelt are discovered laid out upon a low table or platform, covered with black. Freberg, Bernard, Abbess, Monks, and Nun attending.*

ABB. (*To Freberg.*) Here must they lie, my lord, until we know
Respecting this the order of the law.[315]
FREB. "And you have wisely done, my rev'rend mother.
"*Goes to the table, and looks at the bodies, but without uncovering them.*
"Unhappy men! ye, both in nature rich,
"With talents and with virtues were endu'd.
"Ye should have lov'd, yet deadly rancour came,
"And in the prime and manhood of your days
"Ye sleep in horrid death." O direful hate!
What shame and wretchedness his portion is
Who, for a secret inmate, harbours thee!
And who shall call him blameless who excites,
Ungen'rously excites, with careless scorn,
Such baleful passion in a brother's breast,
Whom heav'n commands to love. Low are ye laid:
Still all contention now.—Low are ye laid.
I lov'd you both, and mourn your hapless fall.
ABB. They were your friends, my lord?
FREB. I lov'd them both. How does the Lady Jane?
ABB. "She bears misfortune with intrepid soul."
I never saw in woman bow'd with grief
Such moving dignity,
FREB.                    "Ay, still the same."
I've known her long; of worth most excellent;
But, in the day of woe, she ever rose
Upon the mind with added majesty,
"As the dark mountain more sublimely tow'rs
"Mantled in clouds and storm."
*Enter Manuel and Jerome.*[316]
MAN. (*Pointing.*) Here, my good Jerome,[317] there's a piteous sight.
JER. A piteous sight! yet I will look upon him:
I'll see his face in death. Alas, alas![318]

314. In the 1851 version, this is Act V, scene vi. 315. The Larpent version has "The order of the law respecting them." 316. In the Larpent version, Bernard, Ambrose, and Agatha also enter here. 317. The Lampert version has "honest Jerome." 318. The Larpent version has "Ah! what a change!—"

I've seen him move a noble gentleman;
And when the vexing passion undisturb'd,
He look'd most graciously.
*"Lifts up in mistake the cloth from the body of Rezenvelt, and starts back with*
*"horrour.*
"Oh! this was bloody work! Oh! oh! oh, oh!
"That human hands could do it! (*Drops the cloth again.*)
"MAN. That is the murder'd corps; here lies De Monfort. (*Going to*
  uncover the other body.*)
"JER. (*Turning away his head.*) No, no! I cannot look upon him now.
"MAN. Didst thou not come to see him?
"JER. Fy! cover him—inter him in the dark—
"Let no one look upon him.
"BERN. (*To Jerome.*) Well dost thou show the abhorrence nature feels
"For deeds of blood, and I commend thee well.
"In the most ruthless heart compassion wakes
"For one who, from the hand of fellow man,
"Hath felt such cruelty.
"(*Uncovering the body of Rezenvelt.*) This is the murder'd corse.
"(*Uncovering the body of De Monfort.*) But see, I pray!
"Here lies the murderer. What think'st thou here?
"Look on those features, thou hast seen them oft,
"With the last dreadful conflict of despair,
"So fix'd in horrid strength.
"See those knit brows, those hollow sunken eyes;
"The sharpen'd nose, with nostrils all distent,
"That writhed mouth, where yet the teeth appear,
"In agony, to gnash the nether lip.
"Think'st thou, less painful than the murd'rer's knife
"Was such a death as this?
"Ay, and how changed too those matted locks!
"JER. Merciful heaven! his hair is grisly grown,
"Chang'd to white age, what was, but two days since,
"Black as the raven's plume. How may this be?
"BERN. Such change, from violent conflict of the mind,
"Will sometimes come.
JER.                    "Alas, alas! most wretched!"[319]
Thou wert too good to do a cruel deed,
And so it kill'd thee.[320] Thou hast suffer'd for it.

319. The Larpent version has "Ah me!—Ah me!—" 320. The Larpent version has "And
it has kill'd thee."

"God rest thy soul! I needs must touch thy hand,
"And bid thee long farewell." (*Laying his hand on De Monfort.*)
BERN. Draw back, draw back! see where the lady comes.
*Enter Jane De Monfort. Freberg, who has been for sometime retired by himself to
the bottom of the stage, now steps forward to lead her in, but checks himself on
seeing the fixed sorrow of her countenance, and draws back respectfully. Jane ad-
vances to the table, and looks attentively at the covered bodies. Manuel points out
the body of De Monfort, and she gives a gentle inclination of the head, to signify
that she understands him. She then bends tenderly over it, without speaking.*
MAN. (*To Jane, as she raises her head.*) Oh, madam! my good lord.
JANE. Well says thy love, my good and faithful Manuel;
But we must mourn in silence.
MAN. Alas! the times that I have follow'd him!
JANE. Forbear, my faithful Manuel. For this love
Thou hast my grateful thanks; and here's my hand:
Thou has lov'd him, and I'll remember thee;
Where'r I am; in whate'er spot of earth
I linger out the remnant of my days,
I'll remember thee.
MAN. Nay, "by the living God!" where'er you are,
There will I be. I'll prove a trusty servant:
"I'll follow you, e'en to the world's end.
"My master's gone, and"[321] I, indeed, am mean,
Yet will I show the strength of nobler men,
Should any dare upon your honour'd worth
To put the slightest wrong.[322] Leave you, dear lady!
Kill me, but say not this! (*Throwing himself at her feet.*)
JANE. (*Raising him.*) Well, then! be thou my servant, and my friend.[323]
Art thou, good Jerome, too, in kindness come?
I see thou art. How goes it with thine age?
JER. "Ah, madam! woe and weakness dwell with age:
"Would I could serve you with a young man's strength!
"I'd spend my life for you."[324]
JANE.                          Thanks, worthy Jerome.
O! who hath said,[325] the wretched have no friends.
FREB. In every sensible and gen'rous breast

321. The Larpent version has "Your brother was a noble master to me,— / He is gone from
you." 322. The Larpent version has "Should any dare to put the slightest wrong / Upon
your honour'd worth." 323. The Larpent version has Jerome enter here. 324. The Larpent version has "I cannot speak to you." 325. The Larpent version has "My worthy Jerome. / O! who shall say."

Affliction finds a friend; but unto thee,
Thou most exalted and most honourable,
The heart "in warmest adoration bows,
"And even a worship pays."
JANE. Nay, Freberg, Freberg! grieve me not, my friend.
He to whose ear my praise most welcome was,
Hears it no more; and, oh our piteous lot!
What tongue will talk of him? Alas, alas!
"This more than all will bow me to the earth;"
I feel my misery here.
The voice of praise was wont to name us both:
I had no greater pride.
*Covers her face with her hands, and bursts into tears. Here they all hang about her;*
*Freberg supporting her tenderly; Manuel embracing her knees, and old Jerome*
*catching hold of her robe affectionately. Bernard, Abbess, Monks, and Nuns, like-*
*wise, gather round her, with looks of sympathy. Enter Two Officers of law.*
1ST OFF.                    Where is the prisoner?
Into our hands he straight must be consign'd.[326]
BERN. He is not subject now to human laws;
The prison that awaits him is the grave.
1ST OFF. Ha! sayst thou so?[327] there is foul play in this.
MAN.[328] (*To Officer.*) Hold thy unrighteous tongue, or hie thee hence,
Nor, in the presence of this honour'd dame
Utter the slightest meaning of reproach.
1ST OFF. "I am an officer on duty call'd,
"And have authority to say, how died?"[329]
*Here Jane shakes off the weakness of grief, and repressing Manuel,[330] who is about*
*to reply to the Officer, steps forward with dignity.*
JANE. Tell them by whose authority you come,
He died that death which best becomes a man
Who is with keenest sense of conscious ill
And deep remorse assail'd, a wounded spirit.
A death that kills the noble and the brave,
And only them. He had no other wound.
"1ST OFF. And shall I trust to this.
"JANE.                    Do as you wilt:
"To one who can suspect my simple word
"I have no more reply. Fulfill thy office."

326. The Larpent version has "He straight must be consign'd into our hands." 327. The Larpent version has "What dost thou say?" 328. The Larpent version gives this speech to Albert/Freberg. 329. The Larpent version has "My lord, we do but execute our duty, / And have authority to search the truth." 330. In the Larpent version, it is Albert.

1ST OFF. No, lady, I believe your honour'd word,
And will no farther search.[331]
JANE. I thank your courtesy; thanks, thanks to all!
My rev'rend mother, and ye honour'd[332] maids;
Ye holy men; and you, my faithful friends,
The blessing of the afflicted rest with you;
And he, who to the wretched is most piteous,
Will recompense you.—Freberg, thou[333] art good,
Remove the body of the friend you lov'd,
'Tis Rezenvelt I mean. Take thou[334] this charge:
'Tis meet that, with his noble ancestors
He lie entomb'd in honourable state.[335]
And now, I have a sad request to make,
Nor will these holy sisters scorn my boon;
That I, within these sacred cloister walls
May raise a humble, nameless tomb to him,
Who, but for one dark passion, one dire deed,
Had claim'd a record of as noble worth,
As e'er enrich'd the sculptur'd pedestal.                    (*Exeunt*)


## EPILOGUE[336]

Ere yet affection's Tears have ceas'd to flow
I come to cherish, not forget my woe.
No kindred heart will bid me check the tear;
A Sister's love may claim protection here.
Dire is the passion that our Scenes unfold
And foreign to each heart of British Mould
For Briton's sons their generous code maintain

*Note.*—The last three lines of the last speech are not intended to give the reader a true character of *De Monfort*, whom I have endeavoured to represent throughout the play as, notwithstanding his other good qualities, proud, suspicious, and susceptible of envy, but only to express the partial sentiments of an affectionate sister, naturally more inclined to praise him from the misfortune into which he had fallen. [Baillie's note]
331. The Larpent version has "Lady, I trust me to your honoured word / And ask your gracious pardon." The officers then exit. 332. The Larpent version has "gentle." 333. The Larpent version has "you." 334. The Larpent version has "you." 335. The Larpent version has "sort." 336. From the Larpent manuscript. John Payne Collier tells us the epilogue was written by the Duchess of Devonshire. It was spoken by Mrs. Siddons. The *Dramatic Censor* (II, 134) tells us that on Saturday, April 3, 1800, the epilogue was omitted: "Mrs. Siddons fatigued herself so much with her exertions . . . that she was unable to speak the *Epilogue*. An apology was accordingly made for its omission, and very favourably received by a drowsy audience, who were happy to find the Tragedy had reached its conclusion."

Prompt to defend & slow in giving pain.
Warm in the Battle, yet the contest o'er
They deem to [337] vanquish'd to be foes no more.
Sure with compassion then this night they'll view
De Monfort's fate, its ruthless court[338] pursue;
And mourn a nature once by honour grac'd
By one foul deed's attrocious guilt defac'd.

    To court your smiles & win your hop'd applause
Ah! let me proudly boast my Sex's cause.
A Female Muse triumphant has design'd
A paragon indeed of woman kind!
Has in this fair majestic portrait wove
Commanding Wisdom, & devoted Love
And bade e'en strength & tenderness agree
In maiden meditation—fancy free.

    Yet, tho' she fail'd a Brother to controul
And soothe the frantic troubles of his Soul,
Still be the Lesson of to-night imprest
To wake the judgement & to calm the breast,
To check by strong example's potent spell
And each advance of subtle passion quell.

    E'en in these happier times where restless rage
Nor dark revenge, no fatal conflicts wage,
Where mild reflection heals the transient strife
And smoothly flows the tranquil course of life:—
Yet may our Muse with timely voice impart
Some wholesome Lesson to the erring heart,
May check full vengeance for a past offence
And from the suff'ring mind remove suspence.

    Thus turn not heedless from the Scene tho' pass'd
Nor view in vain destructive passion's blast,
But cherish ties, for which 'tis life to live;
Enjoy the good your love & kindness give;
Banish from Friendship each offending fear,
And from confiding Love the doubtful tear.

    Such the bright picture which the contrast shews,
Such the reverse of hatred's deadly woes.
Thus let us bid the scene's dread horror cease
And hail the blessing of domestic peace.

337. For "the"? 338. for "course"?

Bertram; or,
The Castle of
St. Aldobrand

A TRAGEDY

IN FIVE ACTS

BY CHARLES

ROBERT MATURIN

Maturin (1780–1824) is known today for his wonderful Gothic novel, *Melmoth the Wanderer* (1820). During his lifetime, however, he was much better known as the author of *Bertram*, which opened at the Theatre Royal, Drury Lane on 9 May 1816 to become the most successful new tragedy of its day.

The son of William and Fidelia Maturin and one of six children, Charles Robert Maturin was born on 25 September 1780. He graduated from Trinity College, Dublin in 1800 with honors in classics and in rhetoric and poetry. He was ordained in 1803 and appointed to a county curacy at Longhrea in 1804; after a year he was given the curacy of St. Peters in Dublin, which he held until his death. Also in 1803, he married into an ecclesiastical family, taking as his wife the beautiful Henrietta Kingsberry. His literary work was not looked upon favorably by his religious superiors, and thus he advanced no further in the church. Despite some literary success, his large family and extravagant habits reduced him to poverty; he died, feeling defeated, on 30 October 1824.

Maturin had two plays other than *Bertram* produced but neither succeeded: *Manuel* opened at Drury Lane on 8 March 1817, and *Fredolfo* was offered at Covent Garden on 12 May 1819. In addition to *Melmoth*, his novels include *The Family of Montorio* (under the name Dennis Jasper Murphy, 1807), *Women; or Pour et Contre* (1818), and the *Albigenses* (1818).

There are three important texts of *Bertram*: the manuscript version Maturin sent as a present to Scott, which is held in the Abbotsford library; the Larpent copy (LA 1922); and the first edition published in London by John Murray, 1816. There were seven (perhaps eight) editions in 1816 alone, and the play was included in such acting collections as *Cumberland's British Drama* and *Dick's Standard Plays*, so there is considerable evidence about performance versions. My text is that of the first edition. Material not in the Larpent version (and thus cut in performance) is marked by double quotation marks; the printed version also indicates some performance cuts, so these are also marked with double quotation marks and signaled in a note. Material in the Larpent text and not in the first edition is marked by square brackets. Variants can be found in the notes, as can some significant additions from the Abbotsford manuscript. The so-called Dark Knight scenes, cut from the play at the urging of Scott and George Lamb but preserved in the manuscript, are provided in an appendix, along with a synopsis of the original fifth act.

Criticism of *Bertram* must begin with Chapter 23 of Coleridge's *Biographia Literaria. The Correspondence of Sir Walter Scott and Charles Robert Maturin*, ed. Fannie E. Ratchford and William H. McCarthy, Jr. (Austin, 1937) provides information on the alterations to the play. Useful books on Maturin include: Nilo Idman, *Charles Robert Maturin: His Life and Works* (London, 1923); Robert Lougy, *Charles Robert Maturin* (Lewisburg, PA, 1975); and Dale Kramer, *Charles Robert Maturin* (New York, 1973). On *Bertram*, see: Joseph W. Donohue, Jr., *Dramatic Character in the English Romantic Age* (Princeton, 1970); Henry W. Hinck, *Three Studies on Charles Robert Maturin* (New York, 1980); Alethea Hayter, "Coleridge, Maturin's *Bertram*, and Drury Lane" in *New Approaches to Coleridge*, ed. Donald Sultana (London, 1981), pp. 17–37; and Cox, *In The Shadows of Romance: Romantic Tragic Drama in Germany, England, and France* (Athens, OH, 1987).

To Walter Scott
The *Scottsman*
The *only* Friend of the *Irish* Author
This play is by his permission most gratefully dedicated[1]

PREFACE[2]

In the Absence of the Author of this Tragedy the Editor cannot print this edition, which the curiosity of the Public has necessarily rendered a hasty one, without acknowledging in the Author's name, the claims which the Performers and Managers of Drury Lane Theatre have upon his attention.

To those who have witnessed the exertion of Mr. Kean's talents in the finest characters of the Drama, it is unnecessary to say, he in this Tragedy had opportunities, of which the Public rapturously testified how well he knew to avail himself.

It were to neglect a positive duty not to pay here a tribute to the performance of the part of Imogine by a Young Lady,[3] who will find it a

1. From the Abbotsford manuscript. As the publisher's preface makes clear, the first edition went into print while Maturin was unavailable, so he could not supply a dedication or author's preface. 2. From the first edition, published by Murray, 1816. 3. Imogine was played by Miss Somerville.

noble, perhaps an arduous task, to realize all the expectations which her successful debut has excited.

To Mr. Holland, Mr. Pope, Miss Boyce, and the other Gentlemen and Ladies who performed it, as well as to Mr. T. Cooke the Composer of some very effecative Music introduced into the Play, the Author's thanks are eminently due.

## PREFACE[4]

In this my first dramatic attempt, I have *attempted* to do, what few dramatists have hitherto done,—I have looked as much as possible to dramatic speech, and as little, as possible to mere practical writing, or dramatic speech-making—The best plays I think have failed from their writers overlooking the marked distinction between the play of the closet, and the play of the stage—whatever admits the senses among its judges, must in some measure consult the senses—it is absurd to deride processions, music etc—they make a very sorry figure in Marginal directions, but a very good one on the Stage.

I have adopted obsolete language, not only because it is the language of the Fra[5] of the play, but because it may be called the Sacred language of the English Drama—the language of Shakespeare, and of those writers with whom Lamb's "Specimens"[6] have made us familiar, and the language of a modern dramatist (Miss Bailey)[7] scarce inferiour to any of them—

When I presume to name my own unknown name with those in the last sentence I may well deprecate my own presumption, I may say of myself—

δς καὶ θνητὸς ἐὼν ἔπεθ ἵπποις ἀθανάτοισι.[8]

Should this play succeed, it will be the first prosperous event in a life of almost unmingled misery, should it fail that misery can scarce admit of aggravation.[9]

DRAMATIS PERSONAE.
Drury Lane, 9 May 1816

| St. Aldobrand | Mr. Pope |
| Bertram | Mr. Kean |

4. From the Abbottsford manuscript; never published. 5. The Prior of St. Anselm. 6. Charles Lamb's *Specimens of English Dramatic Poets Who Lived About the Time of Shakespeare* (1808). 7. Joanna Baillie, whose *De Monfort* is included in this volume. 8. He quotes the *Iliad*, Book 16, line 154: "He, mortal as he was, ran beside the immortal horses" (Lattimore's translation; Chicago, 1961). 9. This last paragraph is cancelled in the manuscript.

| | |
|---|---|
| Prior of St. Anselm | Mr. Holland |
| 1st Monk[10] | Mr. Powell |
| 2d Monk | Mr. R. Phillips |
| 3d Monk | Mr. Barnard |
| 1st Robber | Mr. Kent |
| 2d Robber | Mr. Cooke |
| Hugo | Mr. Carr |
| Pietro | Mr. Coveney |
| Page | Miss Carr |
| Child of Aldobrand | Miss J. Carr |
| Imogine, Wife to Aldobrand | A Young Lady[11] |
| Clotilda, Her attendant | Miss Boyce |
| Teresa | Miss Cooke |

Knights, Monks, Soldiers, Banditti, &c. &c.
[Scene. Sicily—about the Eleventh Century]


## PROLOGUE
### Written by J. Hobhouse, Esq.[12]
### Spoken by Mr. Rae

Taught by your judgment, by your favour led,
The grateful Stage restored her mighty dead.
But not, when wits of ages past revive,
Should living genius therefore cease to thrive.
No! the same liberal zeal that fondly tries
To save the Poet, though the mortal dies,
Impartial welcomes each illustrious birth,
And, justly crowns contemporary worth.


This night a Bard, who yet, alas! has known
Of conscious merit but the pangs alone;
Through dark misfortune's gloom condemned to cope
With baffled effort and with blighted hope,

10. The Larpent manuscript names the monks: Father Hilary, Father Bernardo, and Father Antonio. 11. Miss Somerville. 12. J. Hobhouse is John Cam Hobhouse (1786–1869), Byron's friend from Cambridge, traveling companion, and "groomsman." He was elected to Parliament in 1820 as a Reform candidate from Westminster; the Secretary of War in Earl Grey's ministry (1832), he was created Baron Broughton de Gyfford in 1851. Maturin had hoped for a prologue by Byron himself.

Still dares to think one friendly voice shall cheer
His sinking soul, and thinks to hail it—*here!*
Fanned by the breath of praise, his spark of fame
Still, still may glow, and burst into a flame.


Nor yet let British candour mock the toil
That rear'd the laurel on our sister soil;[13]
That soil to Fancy's gay luxuriance kind,
That soil which teems with each aspiring mind,
Rich in the fruits of glory's ripening sun—
Nurse of the brave—the land of WELLINGTON.[14]


Here, too, this night—another candidate,[15]
Aspires to please; and trembles for her fate;—
And, as the flower whose ever-constant gaze
Turns to her sun and wooes the genial blaze,
To those kind eyes our blushing suppliant bends,
And courts the light that beams from smiling friends;
Oh! calm the conflict of her hopes and fears,
Nor stain her cheek with more than mimic tears.


Since, then, alike each bold adventurer sues
The vot'ry, and the handmaid of the Muse,
Think that the same neglect—the same regard,
Must sink, or save, the actress, and the bard.


# ACT I

SCENE I   *Night, a Gallery in a Convent, a large Gothic window in the extremity, through which lightning is seen flashing.*

*Two Monks enter in terror.*

1ST MONK. Heaven for its mercy!—what a night is here—
Oh! didst thou hear that peal?
2D MONK. The dead must hear it.—

13. As the second edition makes clear, the reference in this verse paragraph is to Ireland: "That rear'd the laurel on Hibernia's soil"; Hobhouse made many such minor alterations to the prologue for the second edition. 14. Arthur Wellesley, 1st Duke of Wellington (1769–1852). 15. Miss Somerville.

*A pause—thunder.*
Speak! speak, and let me hear a human voice.
1ST MONK. While the dark terror hurtled distantly,
Lapt[16] in the skirts of the advancing clouds,
I cower'd with head full low upon my pallet,
And deem'd that I might sleep—till[17] the strong light
Did, clear as noon day, show each object round me.
Relic, and rosary, and crucifix,
Did rock and quiver in the bickering glare—
Then forth I rush'd in agony of fear.
2D MONK. Among the tombed tenants of the cloister
I walked and told my beads,
But, by the momently[18] gleams of sheeted blue,
Did the pale marbles glare so sternly on me,
I almost deem'd they lived, and fled in horror.
1ST MONK. There is much comfort in a holy man
In such an hour as this. *(Knocking at a door.)*
Ho, wake thee, prior.
2D MONK. Oh! come forth, holy prior, and pray for us.
*Enter the Prior.*
PRIOR. All peace be with you!—'tis a fearful hour.
1ST MONK. Hath memory a parallel to this?
2D MONK. How hast thou fared in this most awful time?
PRIOR. As one whom fear did not make pitiless:
I bowed me at the cross for those whose heads
Are naked to the visiting blasts of Heav'n
In this its hour of wrath—
For the lone traveller on the hill of storms,
For the tossed shipman on the perilous deep;
Till the last peal that thundered o'er mine head
Did force a cry of—mercy for myself.
"1ST MONK. *(Eagerly.)* Think'st thou these rock-based
    turrets will abide?
"2D MONK. Think'st thou they will not topple o'er our heads?
"PRIOR. The hand of Him who rules the storm is o'er us."
1ST MONK. Oh, holy prior, this is no earthly storm.
The strife of fiends is on the battling clouds,
The glare of hell is in these sulphurous lightnings,—

16. "Lapped," wrapped up, disguised.  17. The Larpent version has "But."  18. Moment by moment.

This is no earthly storm.[19]

PRIOR. Peace, peace—thou rash and unadvised man;
Oh! add not to this night of nature's horrors
The darker shadowing of thy wicked fears.
The hand of Heaven,[20] not man, is dealing with us,
And thoughts like thine do make it deal thus sternly.
*Enter a Monk pale and breathless.*
PRIOR. Speak, thou has something seen.

3D MONK.                             A fearful sight.

PRIOR. What hast thou seen?

3D MONK.                             A piteous, fearful sight—
A noble vessel labouring with the storm
Hath struck upon the rocks beneath our walls,
And by the quivering gleams of livid blue
Her deck is crowded with despairing souls,
And in the hollow pauses of the storm[21]
We heard their perishing cries—

PRIOR. Now haste ye forth,
Haste all—

3D MONK. It cannot be, it is too late;
For many a fathom doth the beetling rock
Rise o'er the breaker's surge that dashes o'er them,—
No help of human hand can reach them there—
One hour will hush their cries—and by the morn
Thou wilt behold the ruin—wreck and corse
Float on the weltering wave.

PRIOR.                             Almighty power,[22]
Can nought be done? All things are possible—
Wave high your torches on each crag and cliff—
Let many lights blaze on our battlements—
Shout to them in the pauses of the storm,
And tell them there is hope—
And let our deep-toned bell its loudest peal
Send cheerly o'er the deep—
'Twill be a comfort to the wretched souls

---

19. The Abbotsford manuscript has here the first reference to the "Dark Knight": "The dark Knight of the forest hath done this / Dealing with damned sprites in midnight airs." 20. The Abbotsford manuscript has "God"; the fact that such a reference is already eliminated in the licensing manuscript sent to Larpent is an indication that the theaters tailored their texts to what they knew to be the concerns and demands of the censor. 21. The Larpent version has "blast." 22. The Abbotsford manuscript has "Almighty God."

In their extremity—all things are possible;
Fresh hope may give them strength, and strength deliverance—
I'll hie me forth with you.
3D MONK.                    Wilt thou go forth—
Hardly the vigorous step of daring youth
May hold its footing on those wave-washed crags:
And how wilt thou abide?
1ST MONK.                    'Tis tempting Heaven.—
PRIOR. To succour man, not tempt my God, I go;
He will protect his servant.                    *(Exeunt)*


SCENE II    *The Rocks—The Sea—A Storm—The Convent illuminated in the
back ground—The Bell tolls at intervals—A groupe of Monks on the rocks with
torches—A vessel in distress in the offing.*

*Enter the Prior and Monks below.*
PRIOR. *(Clasping his hands.)* Holy St. Anselm[23]—what a sight is here!
1ST MONK. Pray for their souls—their earthly part is doomed—
PRIOR. Oh! that a prayer could hush the elements!—
Hold, I do espy a hope, a blessed hope—
That wave hath heaved her from the rock she struck on.
Lo, every arm on board is plied for safety—
Now, all the saints to speed.—
1ST MONK. No saint doth hear.
Lo, the recoiling surge drives fiercely o'er her—
In, holy prior, or ere their drowning shriek
Do rive[24] the sense; in, in, and tell thy beads—
PRIOR. I will not in, while to that hopeless wreck
One arm doth cling: while o'er the roaring waste
One voice be raised for help—I will not hence.
MONKS. *(Above.)* She sinks—she sinks—Oh hour of woe and horror!
*The vessel sinks—The Prior falls into the arms of the Monks.*
                    *The scene shuts.*


SCENE III    *The gallery.*

*Enter the 1st Monk and the Prior.*
1ST MONK. Now rest you, holy prior, you are much moved—
PRIOR. *(Not heeding him.)*—All, all did perish—

23. St. Anselm (1033–1109), Archbishop of Canterbury (1093), author of such works as
*Cur Deus Homo*, and monastic reformer. 24. Rend, shatter, tear apart.

1ST MONK. Change those drenched weeds—
PRIOR. I wist[25] not of them—every soul did perish—
*Enter third Monk hastily.*
3D MONK. No, there was one did battle with the storm
With careless, desperate force; full many times
His life was won and lost, as though he recked not—
No hand did aid him, and he aided none—
Alone he breasted the broad wave, alone
That man was saved—
PRIOR. Where is he? lead him hither.
*The Stranger is led in by Monks.*
PRIOR. Raise to St. Anselm, thou redeemed soul,
Raise high thy living voice in prayer and praise;
For wondrous hath his mercy been to thee—
2D MONK. He hath not spoken yet—
STRAN.                               Who are those round me?
Where am I?
PRIOR. On the shore of Sicily—
The convent of St. Anselm this is called—
Near is the castle of Lord Aldobrand—
A name far known, if, as thy speech imports,
Thou'rt of Italian birth—
*At the name of Aldobrand, the Stranger makes an effort to break from the Monks,*
    *but falls through weakness.*
Tell us thy name, "sad man—"
STRAN. A man of woe—
PRIOR. What is thy woe, that Christian love may heal it—
Hast thou upon the pitiless water lost
Brother, or sire, or son? did she thou lovest
Sink in thy straining sight!—
Or have the hoardings of thy worldly thrift
Been lost with yonder wreck?—
*To these questions the Stranger gives signs of dissent.*
Why dost thou then despond?
STRAN.                               Because I live—
PRIOR. Look not so wild—can we do aught for thee?
STRAN. Yes, plunge me in the waves from which ye snatched me;
"So will the sin be on your souls, not mine—"
PRIOR. I'll question not with him—his brain is wrecked—
For ever in the pauses of his speech

25. Know.

His lips doth work with inward mutterings,
And his fixed eye is rivetted fearfully
On something that no other sight can spy,
Food and rest will restore him—lead him in—
STRAN. *(Dashing off the monks as they approach.)*
Off—ye are men—there's poison in your torch,—*(Sinking back.)*
But I must yield, for this hath left me strengthless.

*(Exeunt)*


SCENE IV[26]   *A hall in the Castle of Aldobrand.*

*Enter Pietro and Teresa meeting.*
PIET. Hah! Teresa waking! was ever such a tempest?
TERES. The lady Imogine would watch all night.—
And I have tended on her. What roused thee?
PIET. Would you could tell me what would give me sleep in such a night.
I know of but one remedy for fear and wakefulness; that is a flaggon of
wine. I hope the thunder would have waked old Hugo to open the cellar
door for me.[27]
TERES. He hath left his bed. E'en now I passed him
Measuring the banquet-hall with restless steps
And moody fretful gestures. He approaches.
*Enter Hugo.*
PIET. Hugo, well met. Does e'en thy age bear memory of so terrible a
storm?
HUG. They have been frequent lately.
PIET. They are ever so in Sicily.
HUG. So it is said. But storms when I was young
Would still pass o'er like Nature's fitful fevers
And render'd all more wholesome. Now their rage
Sent thus unseasonable and profitless
Speaks like the threats of Heaven.
TERES. Heaven grant its wrath visit not my kind Lady!
HUG. Heaven grant, Teresa,
She may be still as happy in these halls,
As when she tripp'd the green a rural maid

26. This scene is not in the Abbotsford manuscript. In a letter to Maturin, 5 February
1816, George Lamb indicated that he had inserted this scene, along with the scene in which
the robbers sing their glee (II, ii). 27. Pietro speaks the play's only prose (by Lamb not
Maturin?). This follows the convention of giving the servants prose to speak rather than the
verse of the noble characters.

"And caroll'd light of heart"—ere her good father's ruin;
Or our Lord saw and loved her!
PIET. See, if Madam Clotilda be not roused.
TERES. I'm glad, for she's our lady's loved companion
And most esteemed attendant.[28]
*Enter Clotilda.*
CLOT. Is the Lady Imogine risen?[29]
TERES. She hath not rested through the night,
Long ere the storm arose, her restless gestures
Forbade all hope to see her bless'd with sleep.
CLOT. Since her lord's absence it is ever thus.
But soon he will return to his loved home,
And the gay knights and noble wassailers
Banish her lonely melancholy.
*Horn heard without.*
MONK. *(Without.)* What, ho.
HUG. There's some one at the gate.
My fears presage unwelcome messengers
At such untimely hours.
CLOT. Attend the summons, Hugo.
I seek the Lady Imogine. If 'tis aught
Concerns her or our Lord, follow me thither.

*(Exeunt)*


SCENE V    *A Gothic apartment. Imogine discovered sitting at a table, looking at a picture.*

IMO. Yes,
The limner's[30] art may trace the absent feature,
And give the eye of distant weeping faith
To view the form of its idolatry;
But oh! the scenes 'mid which they met and parted—
The thoughts, the recollections sweet and bitter—
Th' Elysian dreams of lovers, when they loved—
Who shall restore them?
"Less lovely are the fugitive clouds of eve,
"And not more vanishing"—if thou couldst speak,
Dumb witness of the secret soul of Imogine,

28. The Larpent version has "And chosen attendant." 29. The Larpent version has "Is your Lady risen?" 30. A limner is a portrait painter.

Thou might'st acquit the faith of womankind—
Since thou wast on my midnight pillow laid
Friend hath forsaken friend—the brotherly tie
Been lightly loosed—the parted coldly met—
Yea, mothers have with desperate hands wrought harm
To little lives from their own bosoms lent.
But woman still hath loved—if that indeed
Woman e'er loved like me.
*Enter Clotilda.*
CLOT. The storm seems hushed—wilt thou to rest, lady?
IMO. I feel no lack of rest—
CLOT.                    Then let us stay—
And watch the last peal murmuring on the blast.
I will sit by the while, so thou wilt tell
Some pleasant story to beguile the time.
IMO. I am not in the mood.
CLOT. I pray thee, tell me of some shadowy thing
Crossing the traveller on his path of fear
On such a night as this—
Or shipwrecked seaman clinging to a crag
From which some band of darkness pushes him.[31]
IMO. Thou simple maid—
Thus to enslave thy heart to foolish fears.
CLOT. Far less I deem of peril in such,
Than in those tales women most love to list to,
The tales of love—for they are all untrue.[32]
IMO. Lightly thou say'st that woman's love is false,
The thought is falser far—
For some of them are true as martyrs' legends,
As full of suffering faith, of burning love,
Of high devotion—worthier heaven than earth—
Oh, I do know a tale.
CLOT.                    Of knight or lady?
IMO. Of one who loved—she was of humble birth
Yet dared to love a proud and noble youth.
His sovereign's smile was on him—glory blazed

31. The Abbotsford manuscript adds lines on the Dark Knight: "Or wilt thou tell some wild and thrilling legend / Of the dark Knight who in forest dwells. / I've heard strange tales of him—" 32. The Abbotsford manuscript adds lines with an intriguing reference to vampires: "Yet do they bear in them a wicked charm / That sweetly stirs the blood it turns to fire / As the light fanning of the vampire's wing / Lulls the protracted slumber into death—."

Around his path—yet did he smile on her—
Oh then, what visions were that blessed one's!
His sovereign's frown came next—
Then bowed the banners on his crested walls
Torn by the enemies' hand from their proud height,
Where twice two hundred years they mocked the storm.
The stranger's step profaned his desolate halls,
An exiled outcast, houseless, nameless, abject,
He fled for life, and scarce by flight did save it.
No hoary beadsman bid his parting step
God speed—no faithful vassal followed him;
For fear had withered every heart but hers,
Who amid shame and ruin lov'd him better.

CLOT. Did she partake his lot?

IMO.                        She burned to do it,
But 'twas forbidden.

CLOT.                  How proved she then her love?

IMO. Was it not love to pine her youth away?
In her lone bower she sat all day to hearken
For tales of him, and—soon came tales of woe.
High glory lost he recked not what was saved—
With desperate men in desperate ways he dealt—
A change came o'er his nature and his heart
Till she that bore him had recoiled from him,
Nor know the alien visage of her child.
Yet still she loved, yea, still loved hopeless on.

CLOT. Hapless lady! what hath befallen her?

IMO. Full many a miserable year hath past—
She knows him as one dead, or worse than dead;
And many a change her varied life hath known,
But her heart none.
In the lone hour of tempest and of terror
Her soul was on the dark hill's side with Bertram,
Yea, when the launched bolt did sear her sense
Her soul's deep prisons were breathed for him.
Was this not love? yea, thus doth woman love.

CLOT. I would I had beheld their happier hours,
Has thou e'er seen the dame? I pray thee, paint her.

IMO. They said her cheek of youth was beautiful
Till withering sorrow blanched the bright rose there—
And have heard men swear her form was fair;

But grief did lay his icy finger on it,
And chilled it to a cold and joyless statue.
"Methought she carolled blithely in her youth,
"As the couched nestling trills his vesper lay,
"But song and smile, beauty and melody,
"And" youth and happiness are gone from her.
Perchance—even as she is—*he* would not scorn "her"
If he could know her—for, for him she's changed;
She is much altered—but her heart—her heart.
CLOT. I would I might behold that wretched lady,
In all her sad and waning loveliness.
IMO. Thou would'st not deem her wretched—outward eyes
Would hail her happy.
They've decked her form in purple and in pall.
When she goes forth, the thronging vassals kneel,
And bending pages bear her footcloth well—
No eye beholds that lady in her bower,
That is her hour of joy, for then she weeps,
Nor does her husband hear.
CLOT.                              Sayest thou her husband?—
How could she wed, "she who did love so well?
IMO. "How could she wed!" what could I do but wed—
"Hast seen the sinking fortunes of thy house—
"Hast felt the gripe of bitter shameful want—"
Hast seen a father on the cold cold earth,
Has read his eye of silent agony,
That asked relief, but would not look reproach
Upon his child unkind—
I would have wed disease, deformity,
Yea, griped Death's grisly form to 'scape from it—
And yet some sorcery was wrought on me,
For earlier things do seem as yesterday,
But, I've no recollection of the hour
They gave my hand to Aldobrand.
CLOT.                              Blessed saints—
And was it thou indeed?
IMO.                    I am that wretch—
The wife of a most noble, honored lord—
The mother of a babe whose smiles do stab me—
"But *thou* art Bertram's still, and Bertram's ever! *(Striking her heart.)*"
CLOT. Hath time no power upon thy hopeless love?

IMO. Yea, time hath power, and what a power I'll tell thee,
A power to change the pulses of the heart
To one dull throb of ceaseless agony,
To hush the sigh on the resigned lip
And lock it in the heart—freeze the hot tear
And bid it on the eyelid hang for ever—
Such power hath time o'er me.
CLOT.                             And has not then
A husband's kindness—
IMO.                         Mark me, Clotilda.
And mark me well; I am no desperate wretch
Who borrows an excuse from shameful passion
To make its shame more vile—
"I am a wretched, but a spotless wife,"
I've been a daughter but too dutiful—
But, oh! the writhings of a generous soul
Stabb'd by a confidence it can't return,
To whom a kind word is a blow on th' heart—
I cannot paint thy wretchedness. *(Bursts into tears.)*
CLOT.                             Nay, nay,
Dry up your tears, soon will your lord return,
Let him not see you thus by passion shaken.[33]
IMO. Oh wretched is the dame, to whom the sound
'Your lord will soon return'—no pleasure brings.
CLOT. Some step approaches—'tis St. Anselm's Monk.
IMO. Remember—now, what wouldst "thou" reverend father?
*Enter 1st Monk.*
MONK. St. Anselm's benison on you, gracious dame,
Our holy prior by me commends him to you—
The wreck that struck upon our rocks i' th' storm
Hath thrown some wretched souls[34] upon his care.
(For many have been saved since morning dawned)
Wherefore he prays the wonted hospitality
That the free noble usage of your castle
Doth grant to ship-wreck'd and distressed men—
IMO. Bear back my greetings to your holy prior—
Tell him the lady of St. Aldobrand
Holds it no sin, although her lord be absent,

33. The Larpent version has "Nay, nay. Dry up those tears / Nor let me see you thus—by passion shaken." 34. The Larpent version has "men."

To ope her gates to wave-tossed mariners—
Now Heaven forefend your narrow cells were cumbered
While these free halls stood empty—tell your prior
We hold the custom of our castle still.                    *(Exeunt)*

END OF ACT I

## ACT II

SCENE I   *An Apartment in the Convent, the Stranger lies sleeping on a couch.*
*The Prior watching him.*

PRIOR. He sleeps, if it be sleep; this starting trance
Whose feverish tossings and deep muttered groans,
Do prove the soul shares not the body's rest—*(Hanging over him.)*
How the lip works, how the bare teeth do grind—
And beaded drops course down his writhen brow—
I will awake him from this horrid trance,
This is no natural sleep—ho, wake thee, stranger—
STRAN. What, wouldst thou have, my life is in thy power—
PRIOR. Most wretched man, whose fears alone betray thee—
What art thou,—speak.
STRAN.                    Thou sayest I am a wretch—
And thou sayest true—these weeds do witness it—
These wave-worn weeds—these bare and bruised limbs,[35]
What wouldst thou more—I shrink not from the question.
I am a wretch, and proud of wretchedness,
'Tis the sole earthly thing that cleaves to me.
PRIOR. Lightly I deem of outward wretchedness,
For that hath been the lot of blessed saints—
But in their dire extreme of outward wretchedness
Full calm they slept in dungeons and in darkness—
Such hath not been thy sleep—
STRAN. Didst watch my sleep—
But thou couldst glean no secret from my ravings.—
PRIOR. Thy secrets, wretched man, I reck not of them—
But I adjure thee by the church's power[36]
(A power to search man's secret heart of sin)

35. The Larpent version has "bruised and wasted limbs." 36. The Abbotsford manuscript
again has a clearer religious reference: "But I adjure thee by the blessed saints— / Yea, I
command thee by the Churches power."

Show me thy wound of soul—
Weep'st thou, the ties of nature or of passion
Torn by the hand of Heaven—
Oh no! full well I deemed no gentler feeling
Woke the dark lightning of thy withering eye—
What fiercer spirit is it tears thee thus?
Shew me the horrid tenant of thy heart—
Or wrath, or hatred, or revenge, is there—
STRAN. *(Suddenly starting from his Couch, falling on his knees; and raising his clasped hands.)*
I would consort with mine eternal enemy,[37]
To be revenged on him.—
PRIOR. Art thou a man, or fiend, who speakest thus.
STRAN. I was a man, I know not what I am—
What others' crimes and injuries have made me.
Look on me—what am I?—*(Advancing.)*
PRIOR.               I know thee not.
STRAN. I marvel that thou say'st it—
For lowly men full oft remember those
In changed estate, whom equals have forgotten:
A passing beggar hath remembered me,
When with strange eyes my kinsmen looked on me—
I wore no sullied weeds on that proud day
When thou a barefoot monk didst bow full low
For alms, my heedless hand hath flung to thee—
Thou doest not know me.—*(Approaching him.)*
PRIOR. Mine eyes are dim with age—but many thoughts
Do stir within me at thy voice.
STRAN. List to me, monk, it is thy trade to talk,
As reverend men do use in saintly wise,
Of life's vicissitudes and vanities—
Hear one plain tale that doth surpass all saws—
Hear it from me—*Count Bertram*—aye—Count Bertram—
The darling of his liege and of his land
"The army's idol, and the council's head—"[38]
Whose smile was fortune, and whose will was law—
Doth bow him to the prior of St. Anselm
For water to refresh his parched lip,

37. The Abbotsford manuscript adds a line of demonic imagery: "Yea, clutch his fiery talon in my grasp." 38. Was this line cut because it might be taken to refer to Wellington? Napoleon?

And this hard-matted couch to fling his limbs on.—
PRIOR. Good Heaven and all its saints!—
BER. Wilt thou betray me?
PRIOR. Lives there the wretch beneath these walls to do it?
Sorrow enough hath bowed thy head already
Thou man of many woes.—
For more I fear lest thou betray thyself.
Hard by do stand the halls of Aldobrand
(Thy mortal enemy and cause of fall),
Where ancient custom doth invite each stranger
Cast on this shore to sojourn certain days,
And taste the bounty of the castle's lord—
If thou goest not, suspicion will arise
And if thou doest (all changed as thou art),
Some desperate burst of passion will betray thee
And end in mortal scathe—
What dost thou gaze on with such fixed eyes?
BER. —What sayest thou?
I dreamed I stood before Lord Aldobrand
Impenetrable to his searching eyes—
And I did feel the horrid joy men feel
Measuring the serpent's coil whose fangs have stung them;
Scanning with giddy eye the air-hung rock
From which they leapt and live by miracle;
"Following the dun skirt of the o'erpast storm
"Whose bolt did leave them prostrate—"
—To see that horrid spectre of my thoughts
In all the stern reality of life—
To mark the living lineaments of hatred,
And say, this is the man whose sight should blast me;
Yet in calm dreadful triumph still gaze on:—
It is a horrid joy.
PRIOR.            Nay, rave not thus—
Thou wilt not meet him, many a day must pass
Till from Palermo's walls he wend him homeward—
Where now he tarries with St. Anselm's knights.—
His dame doth dwell in solitary wise
Few are the followers in his lonely halls—
Why dost thou smile in that most horrid guise?—
BER. (Repeating his words.) His dame doth dwell alone—perchance his
   child—

Oh, no, no, no—it was a damned thought.
PRIOR. I do but indistinctly hear thy words,
But feel they have some fearful meaning in them—
BER. Oh, that I could but mate him in his might,
Oh, that we were on the dark wave together,
With but one plank between us and destruction,
That I might grasp him in these desperate arms,
And plunge with him amid the weltering billows—
And view him gasp for life—and—
PRIOR. Horrible—horrible—I charge thee cease—
The shrines are trembling on these sainted walls—
The stony forms will start to life and answer thee.[39]
BER. Ha, ha—I see him struggling—
I see him—ha, ha, ha *(A frantic laugh.)*
PRIOR.            Oh horrible—
Help, help—to hold him—for my strength doth fail—
*Enter 1st Monk.*
MONK. The lady of St. Aldobrand sends greeting—
PRIOR. Oh, art thou come, this is no time for greeting—
Help—bear him off—thou see'st his fearful state.

*(Exeunt bearing him off)*

SCENE II    *Hall in the castle of St. Aldobrand.*

*Enter Hugo shewing in Bertram's comrades, Clotilda following.*
HUGO. This way, friends, this way, good cheer awaits you.
SAIL. Well then, good cheer was never yet bestowed
On those who need it more.
HUGO.                To what port bound,
Did this fell storm o'ertake you?
1ST SAIL. No matter
So we find here a comfortable haven.
HUGO. Whence came you?

39. A possible echo of the Don Juan story, to which Coleridge compared *Bertram* in the *Biographia Literaria*. Bertram's next speech is longer in the Abbotsford manuscript (where this is I, v and the end of the first act): "*(Without heeding him.)*—aye, and after death / To grasp his shuddering sprite, if spirit be tangible / And hold it shuddering over the dark abyss / Where groans, and gnashing, and the torturous shriek / Tuned to the tossing of the fiery waves / Do make the vile music of despair— / Then, then to hurl him down ten thousand fathom / Aye, though I plunge with him. Ha,—ha—ha! I see him struggling / I see him—ha—ha."

1ST SAIL.                              Psha, I cannot answer fasting.

HUGO. Roughness, the proverb says, speaks honesty,
I hope the adage true.

CLOT.[40]                    Lead them in, Hugo,
They need speedy care—which is your leader?

1ST SAIL. He will be here anon—what ye would know,
Demand of him.

2D SAIL. (Advancing.) He's here.

CLOT.                              I fain would learn
Their country and their fortunes.

*Enter Bertram, with a sullen air, but scrutinizing all around.*

CLOT.                              Is that him?
His looks appal me, I dare not speak to him.

*All pause at his appearance.*

HUGO. Come, come, the feast's prepared within, this way.

                         (*Bertram passes on sullenly and exit.*)

CLOT. The grief that clothes that leader's woeworn form.
The chilling awe his ruin'd grandeur wears
Is of no common sort—I must observe him.          (*Exit Clotilda*)

SAIL. Now, comrades, we will honour our host's bounty
With jovial hearts, and gay forgetfulness
Of perils past and coming.

                         GLEE.
          We be men escaped from dangers,
          Sweet to think of o'er our bowls;—
          Wilds have ne'er known hardier rangers,
          Hall shall ne'er see blither souls.

                                             (*Exeunt*)


SCENE III[41]  *Moonlight; a terrassed rampart of the Castle; a part of the latter
is seen, the rest concealed by woods.*

*Imogine alone, she gazes at the Moon for some time, and then advances slowly.*

IMO.                              Mine own loved light,
That every soft and solemn spirit worships,
That lovers love so well—strange joy is thine,
Whose influence o'er all tides of soul hath power,

---

40. Several performance versions cut Clotilda and Bertram from the scene; the scene is not
in the Abbotsford version at all. 41. In the Abbotsford manuscript, Act II begins here.

Who lendst thy light to rapture and despair;—
The glow of hope and wan hue of sick fancy
Alike reflect thy rays: alike thou lightest
The path of meeting or of parting love—
Alike on mingling or on breaking hearts
Thou smil'st in throned beauty.—Bertram—Bertram.
How sweet it is to tell the listening night
The name beloved—it is a spell of power
To wake the buried slumberers of the heart,
Where memory lingers o'er the grave of passion
Watching its tranced sleep!—
The thoughts of other days are rushing on me,
The loved, the lost, the distant, and the dead,
Are with me now, and I will mingle with them
'Till my sense fails, and my raised heart is wrapt
In secret[42] suspension of mortality.
*Enter Clotilda.*
CLOT. Why dost thou wander by this mournful light,
Feeding sick fancy with the thought that poisons?—
IMO. I will but weep beneath the moon awhile.
Now do not chide my heart for this sad respite,
The thoughts it most doth love do visit it then,
And make it feel like heaven—
CLOT Nay, come with me, and view those storm-'scaped men
A-feasting in thy hall; 'twill cheer thy heart—
Of perils 'scaped by flood and fire they tell,
And many an antique legend wild they know
And many a lay they sing—hark, their deep voices
Come faintly on the wind.
*Noise of singing and revelry without.*[43]
IMO. Their wild and vulgar mirth doth startle me.
This clamorous wassail in a baron's hall
Ill suits the state of rescued fearful men:—
But as I passed the latticed gallery
One stood alone;—I marked him where he stood,
His face was veiled,—faintly a light fell on him;
But through soiled weeds his muffled form did shew
A wild and terrible grandeur.

42. The Larpent version has "sweet." 43. The Abbotsford manuscript provides a "chorus within castle": "We be men escaped from dangers / Sweet to think of o'er our bowls / Wilds have ne'er known hardier thoughts / Hall shall ne'er see blither souls—."

CLOT. I marked him too. He mixed not with the rest,
But o'er his wild mates held a stern controul—
Their rudest burst of riotous merriment
Beneath his dark eye's stilling energy
Was hushed to silence.
IMO. He never spoke?
CLOT. No, he did nought but sigh,
If I might judge by the high-heaving vesture
Folded so deep on his majestic breast;—
"Of sound I heard not—"
IMO. Call him hither.—
There is a mystery of woe about him
That strongly stirs the fancy.
CLOT. Wilt thou confer alone, at night, with one
Who bears such fearful form?
IMO.                               Why therefore send him—
All things of fear have lost their power o'er me—

*(Exit Clotilda)*

*Imogine appears to be debating with herself how to receive him, at length she says*
IMO. If he do bear, like me, a withered heart
I will not mock him with a sound of comfort—
*Bertram enters slowly from the end of the stage; his arms folded, his eyes fixed on the earth, she does not know him.*
IMO. A form like that hath broken on my dreams
So darkly wild, so proudly stern,
Doth it rise on me waking?
*Bertram comes to the end of the stage, and stands without looking at her.*
IMO. Stranger, I sent for thee, for that I deemed
Some wound was thine, that yon free band might chafe,—
Perchance thy worldly wealth sunk with yon wreck—
Such wound my gold can heal—the castle's almoner—
BER. The wealth of worlds were heaped on me in vain.
IMO. Oh then I read thy loss—Thy heart is sunk
In the dark waters pitiless; some dear friend,
Or brother, loved as thine own soul, lies there—
I pity thee, sad man, but can no more—
Gold I can give, but can no comfort give
For I am comfortless—
Yet if I could collect my falthering breath
Well were I meet for such sad ministry,
For grief hath left my voice no other sound—

BER. *(Striking his heart.)* No dews give freshness to this blasted soil—
IMO. Strange is thy form, but more thy words are strange—
Fearful it seems to hold this parley with thee.
Tell me thy race and country—
BER.                                    What avails it?
The wretched have no country: that dear name
Comprizes home, kind kindred, fostering friends,
Protecting laws, all that binds man to man—
But none of these are mine;—I have no country—
And for my race, the last dread trump shall wake
The sheeted relics of mine ancestry,
Ere trump of herald to the armed lists
In the bright blazon of their stainless coat,
Calls their lost child again.—
IMO.                                    I shake to hear him—
There is an awful thrilling in his voice.—
"The soul of other days come rushing in them.—"
If nor my bounty nor my tears can aid thee,
Stranger, farewell; and 'mid thy misery
Pray, when thou tell'st thy beads, for one more wretched.
BER. Stay, gentle lady, I would somewhat with thee.
*Imogine retreats terrified.*
*(Detaining her.)*—Thou shalt not go—
IMO. Shall not! Who art thou? speak—
BER. And must I speak?—
There was a voice which all the world, but thee,
Might have forgot, and been forgiven,—
IMO. My senses blaze—between the dead and living
I stand in fear—oh God!—It cannot be—
Those thick black locks—those wild and sunburn features
He looked not thus—but then that voice—
It cannot be—for he would know my name.
BER. Imogine—
*She has tottered towards him during the last speech, and when he utters her name,*
*shrieks and falls into his arms.*
                    Imogine—yes,
Thus pale, cold, dying, thus thou art most fit
To be enfolded to this desolate heart—
A blighted lily on its icy bed—
Nay, look not up, 'tis thus I would behold thee.
That pale cheek looks like truth—I'll gaze no more—

That fair, that pale, dear cheek, these helpless arms,
If I look longer they will make me human.

IMO. *(Starting from him.)* Fly, fly, the vassals of thine enemy wait
To do thee dead.

BER.          Then let them wield the thunder,
Fell is their dint, who're mailed in despair.
Let mortal might sever the grasp of Bertram.

IMO. Release me—I must break from him—he knows not—
Oh God!

BER.      Imogine—madness seizes me—
Why do I find thee in mine enemy's walls?
What dost thou in the halls of Aldobrand?
Infernal light doth shoot athwart my mind—
Swear thou art a dependent on his bounty,
That chance, or force, or sorcery, brought thee hither;
Thou canst not be—my throat is swoln with agony—
Hell hath no plague—Oh no, thou couldst not do it.

IMO. *(Kneeling.)* Mercy.

BER. Thou hast it not, or thou wouldst speak—
Speak, speak! *(With frantic violence.)*

IMO.          I am the wife of Aldobrand,—
To save a famishing father did I wed.

BER. I will not curse *her*—but the hoarded vengeance—

IMO. Aye—curse, and consummate the horrid spell,
For broken-hearted, in despairing hour
With every omen dark and dire I wedded—
Some ministering demon mocked the robed priest,
With some dark spell, not holy vow, they bound me,
Full were the rites of horror and despair.
They wanted but—the seal of Bertram's curse.

BER. *(Not heeding her.)*—Talk of her father—could a father love thee
As I have loved?—the veriest wretch on earth
Doth cherish in some corner of his heart,
Some thought that makes that heart a sanctuary
For pilgrim dreams in midnight-hour to visit,
And weep and worship there.
—And such thou wert to me—and thou art lost.
—What was a father? could a father's love
Compare with mine?—in want, and war, and peril,
Things that would thrill the hearer's blood to tell of,
My heart grew human when I thought of thee—

Imogine would have shuddered for my danger—
Imogine would have bound my leechless[44] wounds—
Imogine would have sought my nameless corse,[45]
And known it well—and she was wedded—wedded—
—Was there no name in hell's dark catalogue
To brand thee with, but mine immortal foe's?—
And did I 'scape from war, and want, and famine
To perish by the falsehood of a woman?
IMO. Oh spare me,—Bertram—oh preserve thyself—
BER. A despot's vengeance, a false country's curses,
The spurn of menials whom this hand had fed—
In my heart's steeled pride I shook them off,
As the bayed lion from his hurtless hide
Shakes his pursuers' darts—"across their path—"
One dart alone took aim, thy hand did barb it.
IMO. He did not hear my father's cry—Oh heaven—[46]
Nor food, nor fire, nor raiment, and his child
Knelt madly to the hungry walls for succour
E'er her wrought brain could bear the horrid thought
Or wed with him—or—see thy father perish.
BER. Thou tremblest lest I curse thee, tremble not—
Though thou hast made me, woman, very wretched—
Though thou hast made me—but I will not curse thee—
Hear the last prayer of Bertram's broken heart,
That heart which thou hast broken, not his foes!—
Of thy rank wishes the full scope be on thee—
May pomp and pride shout in thine addered path
Till thou shalt feel and sicken at their hollowness—
May he thou'st wed, be kind and generous to thee
Till thy wrung heart, stabb'd by his noble fondness
Writhe in detesting consciousness of falsehood—
May thy babe's smile speak daggers to that mother
Who cannot love the father of her child,
And in the bright blaze of the festal hall,
When vassals kneel, and kindred smile around thee,
May ruined Bertram's pledge hiss in thine ear—
Joy to the proud dame of St. Aldobrand—
While his cold corse doth bleach beneath her towers.
IMO. *(Detaining him.)* Stay.

44. The Larpent version has "luckless." 45. For "corpse." 46. The Abottsford manuscript
has "God."

BER. No.

IMO. Thou hast a dagger.

BER. Not for woman.—

IMO. *(Flinging herself on the ground.)* It was my prayer to die in
Bertram's presence.

But not by words[47] like these—

BER. *(Turning back.)*                —on the cold earth!

—I do forgive thee from my inmost soul—

*The Child of Imogine rushes in and clings to her.*

CHILD. Mother, [I've heard a voice! Who is this man?][48]

BER. *(Eagerly snatching up the child.)* God bless thee child—Bertram
hath kissed thy child.

*He rushes out, Clotilda enters gazing after him in terror, and goes to afford relief
to Imogine.*

*The curtain drops.*

END OF ACT II

## ACT III

SCENE I   *A wood;—the Stage darkened;—St. Aldobrand speaking to a Page behind the scenes.*[49]

ALD. Hold thou my good steed, page; the moon is down,
We've far outstript the knights, but slacker speed
Hath found a surer road—where, think'st thou, are we?

*Enter St. Aldobrand and a Page.*

Vainly I listen through the night so still
For bell that tells of holy convent near,
"Or warder's bugle from the battlement,
"Or horn of knight returning from the chase—"
All is dark, still, and lorn; where deemst thou are we?

PAGE. Oh we are nigh a fell and fearful spot,
For by the last gleams of the sunken moon
I saw the towers—

ALD.                What towers are those, boy?

PAGE. The ruined towers that 'tis said are haunted—

47. Both the Abbotsford and the Larpent versions have "wounds." 48. The printed version
has only "Mother"; perhaps Miss J. Carr could not be depended upon for more in actual
performance. 49. For the Abbotsford manuscript version of this scene (where it is II, ii),
with the Dark Knight, see the appendix to this play.

"Dimly they rose amid the doubtful gloom,
"But not one star-beam twinkled on their summits."
ALD. Then, not four leagues divide me from mine home.—
Mine home—it is a pleasant sound—there bide
My dame and child—all pleasant thoughts dwell there—
"Then, while I rest beneath this broad-armed tree,
"Or oak, or elm, in this dark night I wot not—
"It shall be thy sweet penance to rehearse
"All thou hast heard of these most fearful towers—
"The tale will sooth my sleep, nor mar my dreams—
"PAGE. Then let me couch by thee—I pray thee do—
"For ever I love 'mid frightful tales i' th' dark
"To touch the hand I tell the tale of fear to—"⁵⁰
*A bell tolls.*
ALD. Hark! 'tis the convent bell, "forego thy tale—"
The blessed thoughts of home are in that sound
That near my castle's gallant walls doth float—
*Chorus of knights heard faintly from the forest.*
ALD. What voices swell upon the midnight air?
PAGE. St. Anselm's knights.
ALD.            Yes, 'tis their pious wont,
When journeying near the sound of convent-bell
'Mid flood or fire, to raise the holy hymn
That chaunts the praise of their protecting saint—
List to the solemn harmony—
Guided by that we may rejoin their company.            *(Exeunt)*
*Chorus heard again, and continues drawing nearer till the scene changes.*


SCENE II    *The Convent. The Prior reading; Bertram views him with the attention of one who envies him, then speaks.*

BER. How many hours have passed since matin-bell?
PRIOR. I known not, till it sound again to vespers.
Time passes o'er us with a noiseless lapse:
Our hours are marked alone by prayer and study,
And know no change but by their mute succession—
BER. Yea—thus they live, if this may life be called
Where moving shadows mock the parts of men.
Prayer follows study, study yields to prayer—

---

50. This passage is also marked to be cut in the Murray edition.

Bell echoes bell, till wearied with the summons
The ear doth ache for that last welcome peal
That tolls an end to listless vacancy—
"Aye—when the red swol'n stream comes roaring down—
"Full many a glorious flower, and stately tree,
"Floats on the ruthless tide, whose unfelt sway
"Moves not the mire that stagnates at the bottom."
The storm for Bertram—and it hath been with me,
Dealt with me branch and bole, bared me to th' roots,
And where next wave bears by perished trunk
In its dread lapse, I neither known, nor reck of—
PRIOR. Thou desperate man, whom mercy woos in vain,
Although with miracles she pleads—
Forbear, I say, to taint these holy echoes
With the fell sounds of thy profane despair.—
BER. Good monk, I am beholden to your patience.
Take this from one, whose lips do mock at praise;—
Thou art a man, whose mild and reverend functions
"Might change the black creed of misanthropy,
"And" bid my better angel half return.—
But—'tis impossible—"I will not trouble thee—"
The wayward Bertram and his moody mates
Are tenants all unmeet for cloistered walls—
We will find fitter home.
PRIOR. Whither wilt thou resort?
BER.                    Is there no forest
Whose shades are dark enough to shelter us,
Or cavern rifted by the perilous lightning,
Where we must grapple with the tenanting wolf
To earn our bloody lair?—there let us bide,
Nor hear the voice of man, nor call of heaven.—
PRIOR. Wend[51] not, I charge thee, with those desperate men.
Full well I wot who are thy fearful mates—
In their stern strife with the incensed deep,
That dashed them bruised and breathless on our shores,
When their drenched hold forsook both gold and geer,
They griped their daggers with a murderer's instinct.
—I read thee for the leader of a band

51. To go off, to depart.

Whose trade is blood.—[52]

BER. Well then, thou knowest the worst—

And let the worst be known, I am their leader—

PRIOR. Mark what I reed,[53] renounce that horrid league—

Flee to the castle of St. Aldobrand,

His power may give thee safety, and his dame

May plead for thee against the law's stern purpose—

All as thou art unknown—

BER. His dame plead for me!—

When my cold corse, torn from some felon wheel,

Or dug from lightless depth of stony dungeon,

Welters in the cold gaze of pitiless strangers,

Then fling it at his gate, whose cursed stones

My living foot treads never,—yet beware

Lest the corse burst its cearments[54] stark, and curse thee—

PRIOR. Hush, hush these horrid sounds; where wilt thou bide?

Near us nor knight nor baron holds his keep,

For far and wide thy foeman's land extends.[55]

BER. The world hath ample realms beyond his power.

"There must I dwell—I seek my rugged mates—"

The frozen mountain, or the burning sand

Would be more wholesome than the fertile realm

That's lorded o'er by Aldobrand.

*(Exit Bertram)*

PRIOR. "High-hearted man, sublime even in thy guilt,

"Whose passions are thy crimes, whose angel-sin

"Is pride that rivals the star-bright apostate's.—"

Wild admiration thrills me to behold

An evil strength, so above earthly pitch—

Descending angels only could reclaim thee—

*Enter 2d Monk.*

MONK. The lady of St. Aldobrand in haste

Craves swift admittance to your sacred cell.

---

52. Such robber bands had been popular in the Gothic drama since Schiller's *Die Rauber.* Detached from the plot, the band serves here as an ideological marker, a sign of Bertram's revolt. 53. Presumably for "Rede," an obsolete word meaning "to advise or counsel." This, like "wend" above, is an example of the "obsolete language" which Maturin in his unpublished preface called for particularly in the "the language of the Fra of the play." 54. For "cerement," a waxed winding sheet. 55. For the Abbotsford manuscript version of this passage, with the Dark Knight, see the appendix to this play.

PRIOR. She is a gracious, and a pious dame,
And doth our cell much honor by her presence.
*Enter Imogine. She kneels to him.*
PRIOR. The blessings of these sainted walls be on thee.
Why art thou thus disturbed, what moves thee, daughter?
IMO. Nay, do not raise me with those reverend hands,
"Nor benison of saint greet mine approach,
"Nor shadow of holy hand stretched forth to bless me.—"
I am a wretched, soul-struck, guilty woman.
PRIOR. Thou dost amaze me; by mine holy order
I deemed no legends of our cloistered saints
Held holier records of pure sanctity
Than the clear answer of thy stainless life
To shrift's[56] most piercing search—
IMO. Oh holy prior, no matron proud and pure,
Whose dreams ne'er wandered from her wedded lord,
"Whose spoused heart was plighted with her hand,"
Kneels for thy prayer of power—I am a wretch,
Who, pale and withering with unholy love,
Lay a shrunk corse in duty's fostering arms,
And with cold smiles belied her heart's despair.
I've nursed a slumbering serpent till it stung me,
And from my heart's true guardian, hid its foulness.
PRIOR. Thou'st done an evil deed—
For sin is of the soul, and thine is tainted—
But most I blame thee, that from thy soul's guardian
Thou hiddest thy secret guilt.
IMO.                          I knew it not—
Last night, oh! last night told a dreadful secret—
The moon went down, its sinking ray shut out,
The parting form of one beloved too well.—
"The fountain of my heart dried up within me,—"
With nought that loved me, and with nought to love
I stood upon the desart earth alone—
"I stood and wondered at my desolation—"
For I had spurned at every tie for him,
"And hardly could I beg from injured hearts
"The kindness that my desperate passion scorned—"
And in that deep and utter agony,

56. Archaic word for the act of shriving or confessing.

Though then, than ever most unfit to die,
I fell upon my knees, and prayed for death.
PRIOR. "And did deserve it, wert thou meet for it—"
Art[57] thou a wife and mother, and canst speak
Of life rejected[58] by thy desperate passion—
These bursting tears, wrung hands, and burning words,
Are these the signs of penitence or passion?
Thou comest to me, for to my ear alone
May the deep secret of thy heart be told,
And fancy riot in the luscious poison—
Fond of the misery we paint so well,
Proud of the sacrifice of broken hearts,
We pour on heaven's dread ear, what man's would shrink from—
Yea, make a merit of the impious insult,
And wrest the functions of mine holy office
To the foul ministry of earthly passion.
IMO. Why came I here, I had despair at home—
Where shall the wretch resort whom Heaven forsakes?
PRIOR. Thou has forsaken Heaven.
Speed to thy castle, shut thy chamber door,
Bind fast thy soul by every solemn vow
Never to hold communion with that object—
"If still thy wishes contradict thy prayers,"
If still thy heart's responses yield no harmony
Weary thy saint with agonies of prayer;
On the cold marble quench thy burning breast;
Number with every bead a tear of soul;
Press to thy heart the cross, and bid it banish
The form that would usurp its image there—
IMO. *(Kneeling.)* One parting word—
PRIOR. No, not one parting look—
One parting thought, I charge thee on thy soul.
IMO. *(Turning away.)* He never loved.—
PRIOR. Why clingest thou to my raiment?
Thy grasp of grief is stronger on my heart—

---

57. The Larpent version has "And." 58. The Abbotsford manuscript has "unpeopled" instead of "rejected"; the Larpent version has a blank, as if the theater's copyist was unsure of what word went here. The image of "life unpeopled" when joined with Imogine's image of standing alone on the "desart earth" links her situation with that of Bertram, who in V, ii imagines himself and the corpse of Aldobrand "left alone" "The only tenants of a blasted world / Dispeopled for my punishment and changed / Into a penal orb of desolation."

"For sterner oft our words than feelings are."
*Enter 1st Monk and Page.*
MONK. Hail, holy prior, and hail thou noble dame,
With joyful heart I break upon your privacy—
St. Aldobrand before his own good gates
Doth rein his war-steed's pride; the warder's horn
Full merrily rings his peal of welcome home—
I hied me onward with the joyful tidings
To greet his happy dame.
IMO. My thanks await them—
PRIOR. Now, by my beads the news is wond'rous welcome—
Hath thy brave lord in safety reached his home—
"Raise to St. Anselm who ne'er leaves his servants.
"My rosary hath been well told for him—"
(Clear thy dimmed brow, for shame! hie to thy lord,
And shew a dame's true duty in his welcome.)
Came with thy lord the knights of good St. Anselm
Bearing the banner of their guardian saint
Safe from the infidel scathe?—[59]
PAGE.                          They come with speed—
Though lated[60] in the forest's wildering maze;
Last night their shelter was the broad brown oak—
PRIOR. High praise be given—haste, summon all our brethren;
Th' occasion, noble dame, doth call me from thee—
So Benedicite—
IMO. *(Alone.)* That word should mean—
A blessing rest on me—I am not blest—
I'm weary of this conflict of the heart—
These dying struggles of reluctant duty—
"These potent throes of wild convulsive passion."
Would I were seared in guilt, or strong in innocence—
I dare not search my heart; some iron vow
Shall bind me down in passive wretchedness,
And mock the force of my rebellious heart
To break its riveting holds—
*As she kneels, enter Bertram.*

59. St. Aldobrand and his men have presumably been on crusade. The Larpent manuscript
indicates that the play takes place "about the Eleventh Century." Pope Urban II called the
First Crusade at the Council of Clermont in 1095, so perhaps we are to imagine Aldobrand
heeding that call. However since Anselm was still alive until 1109 and thus could not yet be
a saint, there is some problem with chronology. 60. Delayed.

Ha! art thou there?—
Come kneel with me, and witness [to] the vow
I offer to renounce thee, and to die—
BER. Nay, it is meet that we renounce each other—
Have we not been a miserable pair?
Hath not our fatal passion cursed, not blessed us?—
Had we not loved, how different were our fates;
For thou hadst been a happy honoured dame,
And I had slept the sleep of those that dream not—
But life was dear, while Imogine did love.
IMO. Witness my vow—while I have breath to speak it—
BER.[61] Then make it thus—why dost thou shrink from me?
Despair hath its embrace as well as passion—
May I not hold thee in these folded[62] arms?
May I not clasp thee to this blasted[63] heart?
When the rich soil teemed with youth's generous flowers—
I felt thee sunshine—now thy rayless[64] light
Falls like the cold moon on a blasted heath
Mocking its desolation—speak thy vow—
I will not chide thee if the words should kill me—
IMO. *(Sinking into his arms.)* I cannot utter it—
BER. Have we not loved, as none have ever loved,
And must we part as none have ever parted?
I know thy lord is near; I know his towers
Must shut thee from my sight—the curfew-hour
Will send me on a far and fearful journey—
Give me one hour, nor think thou givest too much,
When grief is all the boon.—
IMO.                              One hour to *thee?*
BER. When the cold moon gleams on they castle walls,
Wilt thou not seek the spot where last we met?
That be our parting spot—Oh Imogine—
Heaven that denies the luxury of bliss
Shall yield at least the luxury of anguish,
And teach us the stern pride of wretchedness—
"Our parting hour be at the dim moonlight,

61. The Abbotsford manuscript has Bertram "clasping her in his arms." 62. Both the Abbotsford and the Larpent versions have "branded arms"; the Abbotsford text has a crossed-
out line: "May I not gaze on thee with these seared eyes—." These versions would have
linked Bertram's language to that of Imogine in her speech before his entrance. 63. The
Larpent version has "withered." 64. The Larpent version has "joyless."

"And we will make that hour of parting dearer
"Than years of happy love—what recollections—
"What rich and burning tears—in that blessed hour
"Our former hearts shall glide into our breasts,
"Mine free from care, as thine was light of sorrow—"[65]
That hour shall light my parting step of darkness—
Imogine's form did gleam on my last glance,
Imogine's breath did mix with my last sigh,
Imogine's tear doth linger on my cheek,
But ne'er must dew my grave—

IMO.                                     I am desperate
To say I'll meet thee, but I will, will meet thee;
No future hour can rend my heart like this
Save that which breaks it.—

*The Child runs in, and clings to Imogine.*

CHILD. My father is returned, and kissed and blessed me—

IMO. *(Falling on the child's neck.)* What have I done, my child; forgive
   thy mother.

BER. *(Surveying her with stern contempt.)* Woman, oh woman, and an
   urchin's kiss
Rends from thy heart thy love of many years—
Go, virtuous dame, to thy most happy lord,
And Bertram's image taint your kiss with poison.

                                                      *(Exit Bertram)*

IMO. *(Alone.)* 'Tis but the last—and I have sworn to meet him
My boy, my boy, thy image will protect me.

                    **END OF ACT III**


# ACT IV


SCENE I[66]   *A dark night under the Castle Walls;—Bertram appears in a state
of the utmost agitation;—he extends his arms towards a spot where the Moon
has disappeared.*

BER. Thou hidest away thy face, and wilt not view me,
All the bright lights of heaven are dark above me—
Beneath the black cope of this starless night
There lurks no darker soul—

---

65. This passage is marked to be cut in Murray. 66. In the Abbotsford manuscript, this is
Act III, scene i.

My fiend-like glory hath departed from me—
Bertram hath nought above the meanest losel[67]—
I should have bearded him in halls of pride—
I should have mated him in fields of death—
Not stol'n upon his secret bower of peace,
And breathed a serpent's venom on his flower.
*He looks up at the casement of the tower, at which a light appears, he gazes on it.*
—She is there—
She weeps—no husband wipes her tears away—[68]
She weeps—no babe doth cheer the guilty mother.[69]
Aldobrand—No—I never will forgive thee,
For I am sunk beneath thee—Who art thou?
*Enter two of Bertram's Band.*
1ST ROB. Why dost thou wander in the woods alone,
Leaving thy mates to play with idle hilts,
Or dream with monks o'er rosary and relic?
Give us a deed to do.
BER.                    Yes, ye are welcome,
Your spirits shall be proud—ho—hear ye, villains,
I know ye both—ye are slaves that for a ducat
Would rend the screaming infant from the breast
To plunge it in the flames;
Yea, draw your keen knives cross a father's throat,
And carve with them the bloody meal ye earned;
Villains, rejoice, your leader's crimes have purged you,
You punished guilt—I preyed on innocence—
Ye have beheld me fallen—begone—begone.
1ST ROB. Why then, Heaven's benison be with you,
Thou'lt need it if thou tarriest longer here.[70]
BER. How, slave, what fear you?
2D ROB. Fly; this broad land hath not one spot to hide thee.
Danger and death await thee in those walls.
BER. They'd fell a blasted tree—well—let it fall—

---

67. A worthless person, a scoundrel. 68. The Larpent version has "no husband wipes away her tears!" 69. This is much different from the Abbotsford manuscript, which moves to a close at this point (the entrance and exit of the robbers is moved). Bertram adds, "She kneels—no saint, thou lost one, hears thy prayer— / Bertram hath rent from thee both Earth and Heaven"; then, *"in despair,"* Bertram exclaims, "Away—away—to the Dark Knight of the forest, / To Hell from this." 70. The following exchange, which is not in the Abbotsford manuscript, seems to have been added to provide Bertram with new energy for his extreme revenge; in the manuscript, the Dark Knight provides that energy.

But though the perished trunk feel not the wound;
Woe to the smiting hand—its fall may crush him.
1ST ROB. Lord Aldobrand
Holds high commission from his sovereign liege
To hunt thy oulaw'd life through Sicily.
BER. *(Wildly.)* Who—what—
2D ROB. We mingled with the men at arms
As journeying home. Their talk was of Count Bertram,
Whose vessel had from Manfredonia's coast[71]
Been traced towards this realm.
1ST ROB. And if on earth his living form was found,
Lord Aldobrand had power to seal his doom.
Some few did pity him.
BER. *(Bursting into ferocity.)* Villain, abhorred villain.
Hath he not pushed me to extremity?
Are these wild weeds, these scarred and scathed limbs,
This wasted frame, a mark for human malice?
There have been those who from the high bark's[72] side
Have whelmed their enemy in the flashing deep;
But who hath watch'd to see his struggling hands,
To hear the sob of death?—Fool—ideot—ideot—
'Twas but e'en now, I would have knelt to him
With the prostration of a conscious villain;
I would have crouched beneath his spurning feet;
I would have felt their trampling tread, and blessed it—
For I had injured him—and mutual injury
Had freed my withered heart—Villain—I thank thee.
1ST ROB. What wilt thou do? shall we prepare for blows?
"BER. Behold me, Earth, what is the life he hunts for?
"Come to my cave, thou human hunter, come;
"For thou hast left thy prey no other lair,
"But the bleak rock, or howling[73] wilderness;
"Cheer up thy pack of fanged[74] and fleshed hounds,
"Flash all the flames of hell upon its darkness,
"Then enter if thou darest.
"Lo, there the crushed serpent coils to sting thee,

71. The gulf of Manfredonia is on the Adriatic coast of Italy; the town was named for Manfred, the son of the Emperor Frederick II of Hohenstaufen, who founded a port there in the thirteenth century—another problem for Maturin's chronology. 72. The Larpent version has "rock's." 73. The Larpent version has "lurking." 74. The Larpent version has "preyed."

"Yea, spend his life upon the mortal throe."[75]

1ST ROB. Wilt thou fly?

BER. Never—on this spot I stand
The champion of despair—this arm my brand—
This breast my panoply—and for my gage—[76]
(Oh thou hast reft from me all knightly pledge)
Take these black hairs torn from a head that hates thee—
Deep be their dye, before that pledge is ransomed—
In thine heart's blood or mine—why strivest thou with me?
*(Wild with passion.)* Lord Aldobrand, I brave thee in thy halls,
Wrecked, famished, wrung in heart, and worn in limb—
For bread of thine this lip hath never stained—
I bid thee to the conflict—aye, come on—
Coward—hast armed thy vassals?—come then all—
Follow—ye shall have work enough—Follow.

*(Exeunt)*

SCENE II[77]    *Imogine in her apartment—a lamp burning on the Table—She walks some time in great agitation and then pushes the light away.*

IMO. Away, thou glarest on me, thy light is hateful;
Whom doth the dark wind chide so hollowly?
The very stones shrink from my steps of guilt,
All lifeless things have come to life to curse me:
Oh! that a mountain's weight were cast on me;
Oh! that the wide, wild ocean heaved o'er me;
Oh! that I could into the earthy centre
Sink and be nothing.
Sense, memory, feeling, life extinct and swallowed,
With things that are not, or have never been,
Lie down and sleep the everlasting sleep—*(She sinks on the ground.)*

75. This passage is marked to be cut in Murray. 76. "Panoply," a full suit of armor; "gage," a token of defiance, particularly the glove thrown down as a challenge to combat. 77. The differences between the Abbotsford manuscript and the Larpent and Murray versions increase with this scene, which is III, ii in the manuscript; this is apparently where the major restructuring of the final acts, requested by Scott and Lamb, begins. In the Abbotsford manuscript, there is a longer exchange between Imogine and Clotilda, then Aldobrand announces he will kill Bertram, then Imogine calls Bertram to warn him, and he declares his vengeance in language used in IV, i of the Murray and Larpent versions. That is the close of Act III in the Abbotsford version; Act IV begins with the Dark Knight scene, included below in the appendix.

If I run mad, some wild word will betray me,
Nay—let me think—what am I?—no, what was I? *(A long pause.)*
I was the honoured wife of Aldobrand;
I am the scorned minion[78] of a ruffian.
*Enter Clotilda.*
IMO. Who art thou that thus comest on me in darkness?
CLOT. The taper's blaze doth make it bright as noon.
IMO. I saw thee not, till thou wert close to me.
So steal the steps of those who watch the guilty;
How darest thou gaze thus earnestly upon me;
What seest thou in my face?
CLOT.                              A mortal horror.
If aught but godless souls at parting bear
The lineaments of despair, such face is thine.
IMO. See'st thou despair alone?
Nay, mock me not, for thou hast read more deeply,
Else why that piercing look.
CLOT.                              I meant it not—
But since thy lonely walk upon the rampart—
Strange hath been thy demeanour, all thy maidens
Do speak in busy whispers of its wildness—
IMO. Oh hang me shuddering on the baseless crag,
The vampire's wing, the wild-worm's sting be on me,
But hide me, mountains, from the man I've injured.
CLOT. Whom hast thou injured?
IMO.                              Whom doth woman injure?
Another daughter dries a father's tears;
Another sister claims a brother's love;
An injured husband hath no other wife,
Save her who wrought him shame.
CLOT. I will not hear thee.
IMO. We met in madness, and in guilt we parted—
Oh! I see horror rushing to thy face—
Do not betray me, I am penitent—
Do not betray me, it will kill my lord—
Do not betray me, it will kill my boy,
My little one that loves me.
CLOT.                              Wretched woman—
Whom guilt hath flung at a poor menial's feet—

78. Primarily here a mistress or dependent; but also a darling, a favorite.

Rise, rise, how canst thou keep thy fatal secret?
Those fixt and bloodshot eyes, those wringing hands—
IMO. And were I featureless, inert, and marble—
Th' accuser *here* would speak—
CLOT. Wilt thou seek comfort from the holy prior?
IMO. When I was innocent, I sought it of him—
For if his lip of wrath refused my pardon,
My heart would have absolved me—
Now when that heart condemns me, what avails
The pardon of my earthly erring judge?
CLOT. Yet, hie from hence, upon their lady's bower
No menial dares intrude.
IMO. That seat of honour—
My guilty steps shall never violate—
What fearful sound is that?
CLOT. Alas, a feller[79] trial doth abide[80] thee;
I hear thy lord's approach.
'Madness is in thy looks, he'll know it all—
IMO. Why, I am mad with horror and remorse—
He comes, he comes in all that murderous kindness;
Oh Bertram's curse is on me.
*Enter Aldobrand. He seats himself in the front of the Stage. While Imogine walks*
   *in the back scene, so as to be concealed from him.*
ALD. How fares my dame? give me thy white hand, love.
Oh it is pleasant for a war-worn man
To couch him on the downy lap of comfort—
And on his rush-strewn floors of household peace
Hear his doffed harness ring—Take thou my helmet *(To page who*
   *goes out.)*
Well may man toil for such an hour as this.
IMO. *(Standing timidly near him.)* Yea, happier they, who on the
   bloody field
Stretch when their toil is done—
ALD.                                —What means my love?
IMO. Is there not rest among the quiet dead;
But is there surely rest in mortal dwellings?
ALD. Deep loneliness hath wrought this mood in thee,
For like a cloistered votaress, thou hast kept,
Thy damsels tell me, this long turret's bound—

---

79. Fiercer, crueler. 80. The Larpent version has "assail."

A musing walk upon the moonlight ramparts,
Or thy lute's mournful vespers all thy cheering—
Not thine to parley at the latticed casement
With wandering wooer, or—
IMO. *(Wildly.)* For mercy's sake forbear—
ALD. How farest thou?
IMO. *(Recovering.)* Well—well—a sudden pain o' th' heart.
ALD. Knowest thou the cause detained me hence so long,
And which again must call me soon away?
IMO. *(Trying to recollect herself.)* Was it not war?
ALD.         —Aye, and the worst war, love—
When our fell foes are our own countrymen.
Thou knowest the banished Bertram—why, his name
Doth blanch thy altered cheek, as if his band
With their fierce leader, were within these towers—
IMO. Mention that name no more—on with thy tale—
ALD. I need not tell thee, how his mad ambition
Strove with the crown itself for sovereignty—
The craven monarch was his subject's slave—
In that dread hour my country's guard I stood,
From the state's vitals tore the coiled serpent,
First hung him writhing up to public scorn,
Then flung him forth to ruin.
IMO. Thou need'st not tell it—
ALD. Th' apostate would be great even in his fall—[81]
On Manfredonia's wild and wooded shore
His desperate followers awed the regions round—
Late from Taranto's gulf[82] his bark was traced
Right to these shores, perchance the recent storm
Hath spared me further search, but if on earth
His living form be found—
IMO. Think'st thou be harbours here—
Go, crush thy foe—for he is mine and thine—
But tell me not when thou hast done the deed.
ALD. Why art thou thus, my Imogine, my love?
In former happier hours thy form and converse
Had, like thy lute, that gracious melancholy

---

81. The Abbotsford manuscript adds an interesting line, though it is cancelled: "He that would rule o'er angels, reigns o'er fiends." 82. The Gulf of Taranto is on Italy's Ionian coast, between Manfredonia—apparently, Bertram's base—and Sicily.

Whose most sad sweetness is in tune with joy—
Perchance I've been to thee a rugged mate—
My soldier's mood is all too lightly chafed[83]—
But when the gust hath spent its short-liv'd fury,
I bowed before thee with a child's submission,
And wooed thee with a weeping tenderness.
IMO. *(After much agitation.)* Be generous, and stab me—
ALD.                    Why is this?
I have no skill in woman's changeful moods,
Tears without grief and smiles without joy—
My days have passed away 'mid war and toil—
The grinding casque hath worn my locks of youth;
Beshrew its weight, it hath ploughed furrows there,
Where time ne'er drove its share—mine heart's sole wish
Is to sit down in peace among its inmates—
To see mine home for ever bright with smiles,
'Mid thoughts of past, and blessed hopes of future,
Glide through the vacant hours of waning life—
Then die the blessed death of aged honour,
Grasping thy hand of faith, and fixing on thee
Eyes that, though dim in death, are bright with love.
IMO. Thou never wilt—thou never wilt on me—
Ne'er erred the prophet heart that grief inspired
Though joy's illusions mock their votarist—
I'm dying, Aldobrand, a malady
Preys on my heart, that medicine cannot reach,
Invisible and cureless—look not on me
With looks of love, for then it stings me deepest—
When I am cold, when my pale sheeted corse
Sleeps the dark sleep no venomed tongue can wake
List not to evil thoughts of her whose lips
Have then no voice to plead—
Take to thine arms some honourable dame,
(Blessed will she be within thine arms of honour)
And—if he dies not on his mother's grave—
Still love my boys as if that mother lived.
ALD. Banish such gloomy dreams—
'Tis solitude that makes thee speak thus sadly—
No longer shall thou pine in lonely halls.

83. The Larpent version has "chased."

Come to thy couch, my love—
IMO. Stand off—unhand me.—

         Forgive me, oh my husband;
I have a vow—a solemn vow is on me—
And black perdition gulf[84] my perjured soul
If I ascend the bed of peace and honour
'Till that—
ALD. 'Till what?
IMO. My penance is accomplished.
ALD. Nay, Heav'n forfend I should disturb thy orisons—
The reverend prior were fittest counsellor—
Farewell!—but in the painful hour of penance
Think upon me, and spare thy tender frame.
IMO. And dost thou leave me with such stabbing kindness?
ALD. *(To Clotilda who goes out.)* Call to my page
To bring the torch and light me to my chamber—
IMO. *(With a sudden impulse falling on her knees.)*
Yet, ere thou goest, forgive me, oh my husband—
ALD. Forgive thee!—What?—
IMO.         Oh, we do all offend—
There's not a day of wedded life, if we
Count at its close the little bitter sum
Of thoughts, and words, and looks unkind and froward,
Silence that chides and woundings of the eye—
But prostrate at each other's feet, we should
Each night forgiveness ask—then what should I?—
ALD. *(Not hearing the last words.)* Why take it freely;
I well may pardon, what I ne'er have felt.
IMO. *(Following him on her knees, and kissing his hand.)*
Dost thou forgive me from thine inmost soul—
God bless thee, oh, God bless thee—
ALD. Farewell—mine eyes grow heavy, thy sad talk
Hath stolen a heaviness upon my spirits—
I will unto my solitary couch—Farewell.

                             *(Exit Aldobrand)*

IMO. There is no human heart can hide this conflict—
All dark and horrible,—Bertram must die—
But oh, within these walls, before mine eyes,
Who would have died for him, while life had value;—

84. For "engulf."

He shall not die,—Clotilda, ho, come forth—
He yet may be redeemed, though I am lost—
Let him depart, and pray for her he ruin'd,
Hah! was it fancy's work—I hear a step—
It hath the speech-like thrilling of *his* tread:
It is himself.
*Enter Bertram.*
It is a crime in me to look on thee—
But in whate'er I do there now is crime—
Yet wretched thought still struggles for thy safety—
Fly, while my lips without a crime may warn thee—
Would thou hadst never come, or sooner parted.
Oh God—he heeds me not;
Why comest thou thus, what is thy fearful business?
I know thou comest for evil, but its purport
I ask my heart in vain.
BER. Guess it, and spare me.
*A long pause, during which she gazes at him.*
Canst thou not read it in my face?
IMO. I dare not;
Mixt shades of evil thought are darkening there;
But what my fears do indistinctly guess
Would blast me to behold—*(Turns away, a pause.)*
BER. Dost thou not hear it in my very silence?
That which no voice can tell, doth tell itself.
IMO. My harassed thought hath not one point of fear,
Save that it must not think.
BER. *(Throwing his dagger on the ground.)* Speak for me,—
Shew me the chamber where thy husband lies,
The morning must not see us both alive.
IMO. *(Screaming and struggling with him.)* Ah! horror! horror! off—
    withstand me not,
I will arouse the castle, rouse the dead,
To save my husband; "villain, murderer, monster,
"Dare the bayed lioness, but fly from me.
"BER. Go, wake the castle with thy frantic cries;
"Those cries that tell my secret, blazon thine.
"Yea, pour it on thine husband's blasted ear.
"IMO. Perchance his wrath may kill me in its mercy.
"BER. No, hope not such a fate of mercy from him;
"He'll curse thee *with his pardon.*

"And would his death-fixed eye be terrible
"As its ray bent in love on her that wronged him?
"And would his dying groan affright thine ear
"Like words of peace spoke to thy guilt—in vain?
"ımo. I care not, I am reckless, let me perish.
"ber. No, thou must live amid a hissing world,
"A thing that mothers warn their daughters from,
"A thing the menials that do tend thee scorn,
"Whom when the good do name, they tell their beads,
"And when the wicked think of, they do triumph;
"Canst thou encounter this?
"ımo. I must encounter it—I have deserved it;
"Begone, or my next cry shall wake the dead.
"ber. Hear me.
"ımo.             No parley, tempter, fiend, avaunt.
"ber. *Thy son—*
*She stands stupified.*
"Go, take him trembling in thy hand of shame,
"A victim to the shrine of public scorn—
"Poor boy! his sire's worst foe might pity him,
"Albeit his mother will not—
"Banished from noble halls, and knightly converse,
"Devouring his young heart in loneliness
"With bitter thought—my mother was—a wretch."[85]
ımo. *(Falling at his feet.)* I am a wretch but who hath made me so?
I'm writhing like a worm, beneath thy spurn.
Have pity on me, I have had much wrong.
ber. My heart is as the steel within my grasp.
ımo. *(Still kneeling.)* Thou has cast me down from light,
From my high sphere of purity and peace,
Where once I walked in mine uprightness, blessed—
Do not thou cast me into utter darkness.
ber. *(Looking on her with pity for a moment.)* Thou fairest[86] flower—
Why didst thou fling thyself across my path,
My tiger spring must crush thee in its way,
But cannot pause to pity thee.
ımo.                 Thou must,

---

85. This passage is marked to be cut in Murray. This long deletion gives some idea of the drastic cuts made to plays such as *Bertram* in performance; in fact, most acting editions cut far more, particularly from Imogine's part in this scene. 86. The Larpent version has "bruised."

For I am strong in woes—I ne'er reproached thee—
I plead but with my agonies and tears—
Kind, gentle Bertram, my beloved Bertram,
For thou wert gentle once, and once beloved,
Have mercy on me—Oh thou couldst not think it—
*Looking up, and seeing no relenting in his face, she starts up wildly.*
By heaven and all its host, he shall not perish.
BER. By hell and all its host, he shall not live.
This is no transient flash of fugitive passion—
His death hath been my life for years of misery—
Which else I had not lived—
Upon that thought and not on food, I fed,
Upon that thought, and not on sleep, I rested—
I come to do the deed that must be done—
Nor thou, nor sheltering angels, could prevent me.
IMO. But man shall—miscreant—help.
BER. Thou callest in vain—
The armed vassals are far from succour—
Following St. Anselm's votarists to the convent—
My band of blood are darkening in their halls—
Wouldst have him butchered by their ruffian hands
That wait my bidding?
IMO. *(Falling on the ground.)*—Fell and horrible[87]
I'm sealed, shut down in ransomless perdition.
BER. Fear not, my vengeance will not yield its prey,
He shall fall nobly, by my hand shall fall—
But still and dark the summons of its[88] fate,
So winds the coiled serpent round his victim.
*A horn sounds without.*
Whence was that blast? those felon slaves are come—
He shall not perish by their ruffian hands.

*(Exit Bertram)*

IMO. *(Gazing round her, and slowly, recovering recollection, repeats his last
words.)*—He shall not perish—
Oh! it was all a dream—a horrid dream—[89]
He was not here—it is impossible—*(Tottering towards the door.)*
I will not be alone another moment
Lest it do come again—where, where art thou?—

87. The Larpent version has "terrible." 88. The Larpent version has "his." 89. The
Cumberland acting edition cuts from here to Aldobrand's death, which again gives an idea
of the drastic cuts made in performance.

*Enter Clotilda.*

CLOT. Didst thou not call me?—at thy voice of anguish
I hasten, though I cannot hear thy words—
IMO. Let me lean on thee, let me hold thee fast—
"Yea, strongly grasp some strong substantial thing
"To scare away foul forms[90] of things that are not—
"They have been with me in my loneliness.
"Oh, I have had such dark and horrid thoughts,
"But they are gone—we will not think of them—"[91]
CLOT. What hath been with thee?
IMO. "Something dark that hovered *(Deliriously.)*
"Upon the confines of unmingling worlds,
"In[92] dread for life—for death too sternly definite,"[93]
Something the thought doth try in vain to follow—
Through mist and twilight—
CLOT.                                  Woe is me! methought
I saw the form of Bertram as I entered—
IMO. *(Starting with sudden recollection.)* Oh God—it was no vision then,
    thou sawest him—
Give me my phrensy[94] back—one moment's thought—
'Tis done, by Heaven, 'tis done—
I will fall down before his injured feet,
I'll tell him all my shame, and all my guilt,
My wrongs shall be a weapon in his hand,
And if it fail, this tainted frame of sin
Shall fall a shield before my husband's breast—
I'll wake the castle—wake the faithful vassals
I'll—*(Going she stops suddenly.)*
I cannot be the herald of my shame,
Go thou, and tell them what I cannot utter.
CLOT. Oh, yet forgive me, through that gloomy passage
I dare not venture, lest that dark form meet me.
IMO. Nay, thou must go, 'tis I that not venture—
For, if I see him in his holy sleep
Resting so calmly on the bed I've wronged,
My heart will burst, and he must die unarmed—[95]

*(Exit Clotilda)*

90. The Larpent version has "To scare dreary foul forms." 91. This passage is marked to be cut in Murray. 92. The Larpent version has "Too." 93. This passage is marked to be cut in Murray. 94. For "frenzy." 95. Murray has "warned" instead of the Larpent version's more logical "unarmed."

IMO. *(Listening after her.)* How long she lingers—aye—he knows
  my guilt
Even from this untold summons—aye—my boy
They'll clothe thee with *my* shame.
Hush—look[96]—all's still within—an horrid stillness—
Perchance, that she, even she is bribed to aid—
Woe's me, who now can trust a menial's faith,
When that his wedded wife hath done him wrong—
*Enter Clotilda.*
CLOT. All's safe—all's well—
IMO. What meanest thou by those words?—
For sounds of comfort to my blasted ear
Do ring a death-peal—
CLOT.               Heardest thou not the horn?
IMO. I heard no horn. I only heard a voice
That meanaced murder—
CLOT.             Oh! the horn did sound—
And with it came a blessed messenger.
St. Anselm's knights within their patron's walls
Do hold a solemn feast, and o'er his shrine
They hang the holy banner of his blessing—
Full swiftly came the summons to thy lord
To join them in their solemn ceremony—
Lord Aldobrand with few attendants gone,
Though late the hour, and dark the way, ere this
Hath measured half the distance.
IMO. *(Throwing herself vehemently on her knees.)*
Thank God, thank God—Heaven bless the gallant knights!
Then he is safe until the morning's dawn.
*Enter Page.*
IMO. Speak—who are thou?
PAGE. Dost thou not know me, lady?
IMO. Well, well, I reck[97] not—wherefore art thou come?
PAGE. So fierce the mountain-stream comes roaring down,
The rivulet that bathes the convent walls
Is now a foaming flood—upon its brink
Thy lord and his small train do stand appalled—
With torch and bell from their high battlements
The monks do summon to the pass in vain;

96. The Larpent version has "hark." 97. Care, heed.

He must return to-night.

IMO. Tis false, he must not—Oh, I shall run mad—
Go thou, and watch upon the turret's height—*(To Clotilda.)*[98]
The flood must fall—the bright moon must shine forth;
Go, go and tell me so—why stayest thou here *(To page.)*
Begone, and do not heed, and do not watch me.

*(Exit Page)*

I've lost the courage of mine innocence,
And dare not have the courage of despair—
The evil strength that gave temptation danger,
Yet cannot give remorse its energy.
*Enter Clotilda.*

CLOT. The night is calm and clear, and o'er the plain
Nor arms do glimmer on my straining sight,
Nor through the stilly air, did horseman's tramp
Ring in faint echo from the hollow hill,
Though my fixed ear did list to giddiness—
Be comforted, he must have passed the stream—

IMO. Yea, I am comforted, 'tis blessed comfort—
He must have passed the stream—Oh pitying Heaven,
Accept these tears, these are not sinful tears—
Tell me again that he will not return.

CLOT. I soothly say, he must have passed the stream.
*The horn is heard without, announcing Aldobrand's return.*

CLOT. 'Tis Aldobrand, he's lost—we all are lost—*(Rushes out.)*[99]

IMO. Now Heaven have mercy on thy soul, my husband,
For man hath none—Is there no hope—no help?—
*Looking towards the door, across which the Band of Bertram march silently and
range themselves.*
None, none—his gathering band are dark around me—
I will make one last effort for their mercy—
If they be human, they will listen to me—
*Rushing towards them, they step forward and point their swords to resist her.*
Oh, there is nothing merciful in their looks;
Oh, there is nothing human in their hearts;
They are not men—Hell hath sent up its devils.
There is no hope—I'll hear his dying groan—
I'll hear his last cry for that help that comes not—

98. Clotilda must exit here, since she enters again in a few lines. 99. Murray has Clotilda
speak this line "without," while the Larpent version has her leaving first; presumably she
runs out speaking this line.

I'll hear him call upon his wife and child—
I will not hear it.—*(Stopping her ears.)*
Oh that my tightened heart had breath for prayer—
Mercy, oh mercy, Bertram.
*Another horn heard without, she starts and staggers towards the door—a noise of swords within.*
ALD. *(Within.)* Off, villain, off—
BER. Villain to thy soul—for I am Bertram.
*Aldobrand retreating before Bertram, rushes on the stage, and falls at Imogine's feet.*
ALD. Let me die at her feet, my wife, my wife—
Wilt thou not staunch the life-blood streaming from me?
Wilt thou not look at me?—Oh save[100] my boy. *(Dies.)*
*Imogine at the name of her son, rushes off;—Bertram stands over the body holding the dagger with his eyes fixed on it;—The band fill up the back.*

*The curtain drops.*

END OF ACT IV

ACT V

SCENE I[101]     *The Chapel in the Convent of St. Anselm, the shrine splendidly illuminated and decorated. The Prior rising from before the altar.*

*Enter 1st Monk.*
"MONK. How gay and glorious doth our temple seem
"Look round thee, father.
"PRIOR. I feel no joy like that the faithful feel,
"Viewing the glories of their holy place;
"An horror of great darkness is upon me,
"A fearful dread hath overwhelmed me.
"MONK. Wherefore?
"PRIOR. As at the shrine I knelt but now in prayer,
"Nor sleep, nor waking, but a horrible vision
"Fell on my tranced spirit, and I dreamed—
"On the dark mountains was the vision wrought,
"Of mist, and moonlight, mingling fitfully—
"A brinded[102] wolf did tear a struggling lion

100. The Larpent version has "spare." 101. This is also Act V, scene i in the Abbotsford manuscript. 102. Archaic form of "brindled," having obscure dark streaks or flecks on a gray or tawny ground.

"While the cowed lioness stood trembling by—
"I wist[103] not what it meant, but in mine agony,
"I prayed to be released, and as I woke
"The echoes gave me back my slumbering cries—
"MONK. 'Tis a good dream, and bodeth something good.—
"PRIOR. How sayest thou, good?
"MONK. I dreamed it on that night
"Lord Aldobrand did from his castle come,
"And blessed days of peace have followed it.—
"PRIOR. Heaven grant they may!
"MONK. Lo, where the knights approach."[104]

*Enter the Knights in solemn procession with the consecrated banner. The Prior advances to meet them.*

PRIOR. Hail! champions of the church and of the land,
The banner of our holy saint in fight
Full bravely have he borne, and scatheless back,
From unblessed weapon and from arm unholy,
Restored it to the power whose might struck for you—

*The music commences, the Knights and Monks advance in procession, the Prior bearing the banner, which he has received from the principal Knight.*

### HYMN.

Guardian of the good and brave
Their banner o'er thy shrine we wave—
Monk, who counts the midnight bead—
Knight, who spurs the battle steed,—
He, who dies 'mid clarion's swelling
He, who dies 'mid requiem's knelling—
Alike thy care, whose grace is shed
On cowled scalp and helmed head—
Thy temple of the rock and flood
For ages 'mid their wrath has stood—
Thy midnight bell, through storm and calm
Hath shed on listening ear its balm.—

*The Hymn is interrupted by 3d Monk rushing in distractedly.*
3D MONK. Forbear—forbear—
PRIOR. Why comest thou with voice of desperate fear,
Breaking upon our solemn ceremony?

---

103. Pseudo-archaic word meaning to know. 104. This passage is marked to be cut in Murray.

3D MONK. Despair is round our walls, a wailing spirit
Yea, the mixt wailings of the infernal host
Burst deaffeningly amid the shuddering blast—
No earthly lip might utterance give to such—
PRIOR. Thou'rt wild with watching, fear and loneliness,
In thy sole turret that o'erhangs the flood.
Of winds and waves, the strangely-mingled sounds
Ride heavily the night-winds hollow sweep,
Mock the sounds of human lamentation—
3D MONK. Hush, look, it comes again. *(A scream.)*
PRIOR. Defend us, heaven,[105]
'Twas horrible indeed—'tis in our walls—
Ha, through the cloister there doth something glide
That seems in truth not earthly—
*Imogine rushes in with her child, her hair dishevelled, her dress stained with blood.*
IMO. Save me—save me—
PRIOR. Save thee, from what?
IMO. From earth, and heaven, and hell,
All, all are armed, and rushing in pursuit—
*Prior, monks and knights gathering around, and speaking together.*
ALL. Who—what—what hath befallen thee? Speak.
IMO. Oh wait not here to speak, but fly to save him,
For he lies low upon the bloody ground—[106]
KNIGHT. She speaks in madness, ask the frighted boy,
Hath aught befallen his father?—
IMO. Ask him not—
He hath no father—we have murdered him—
Traitress and murderer—we have murdered him—
They'll not believe me for mine agony—
Is not his very blood upon my raiment?
Reeks not the charnel-stream of murder from me?
PRIOR AND MONKS. *(Vehemently.)* Impossible.
IMO. Aye, heaven and earth do cry, impossible,
The shuddering angels round th' eternal throne,
Vailing[107] themselves in glory, shriek impossible,
But hell doth know it true—[108]
PRIOR. *(Advancing to her solemnly.)* Spirits of madness, that possess this
    woman

---

105. The Abbotsford manuscript again has "God." 106. The Abbotsford manuscript
adds, "And there doth watch a demon for his soul—." 107. For "veiling." 108. The Larpent version has "But Fiends do know it true—."

Depart I charge you, trouble her no more,
Till she do answer to mine adjuration—
Who did the deed?
*Imogine sinks gradually from his fixed eye, till hiding her face, she falls on the*
*ground in silence.*
KNIGHT. I do believe it, horrid as it seems—
1ST MONK. I'd not believe her words, I do her silence.[109]
"PRIOR. *(Who has fallen back in horror into the arms of the monks,*
   *rushes forward.)* Oh! draw your swords, brave knights, and sheathe
   them not—
"Slack not to wield the sword of Aldobrand,
"Arise, pursue, avenge, exterminate
"With all the implements of mortal might,
"And all the thunders of the church's curse—
"*Exeunt tumultuously knights, monks, and attendants, the prior is following*
"*them, Imogine still kneeling grasps him by the robe.*"
PRIOR. *(With mixt emotion, turning on her.)* Thou art a wretch, I did so
   love and honour thee—
Thou'st broke mine aged heart—that look again—
Woman, let go thy withering hold—
IMO. I dare not—
I have no hold but upon heaven and thee.
PRIOR. "*(Tearing himself from her.)* I go, yet ere mine aged feet do
   bear me
"To the dark chase of that fell beast of blood—"
Hear thou, and—hope not—if by word or deed
Yea, by invisible thought, unuttered wish
Thou hast been ministrant to this horrid act—
With full collected force of malediction
I do pronounce upon thy soul—despair—                            *(Exit)*
IMO. *(Looking round on the chapel, after a long pause.)*
They've left me—all things leave me—all things human—
Follower and friend—last went the man of God—
The last—but yet he went—
CHILD.                      —I will not leave thee—
IMO. My son, my son, was that thy voice—
When heaven and angels, earth and earthly things
Do leave the guilty in their guiltiness—
A cherub's voice doth whisper in a child's.

109. The Larpent version has "Her words I doubted—I believe her silence."

"There is a shrine within thy little heart
"Where I will hide, nor hear the trump of doom—"
CHILD. Dear mother, take me home—
IMO.                               Thou hast no home—
She, whom thou callest mother left thee none.
We're hunted from mankind—*(Sinking down.)*
"Here will we lie in darkness down together,
"And sleep a dreamless sleep—what form is that—"
Why have they laid him there? *(Recoiling.)*
Plain in the gloomy depth he lies before me
The cold blue wound whence blood hath ceased to flow,
The stormy[110] clenching of the bared teeth—
The gory socket that the balls have burst from—
I see them all—*(Shrieking.)*
It moves—it moves—it rises—it comes on me—
'Twill break th' eternal silence of the grave—
'Twill wind me in its creaking marrowless arms.
Hold up thy hands to it, it was thy father—
Ah, it would have thee too, off—save me—off—
                              *(Rushes out with the child)*


SCENE II   *Changes to the castle.*

*Prior enters alone.*
PRIOR. His halls are desolate—the lonely walls
Echo my single tread—through the long galleries—
The hurrying knights can trace nor friend nor foe—
The murderer hath escaped—"the saints forgive me,
"I feel mine heart of weakness is come back,
"Almost I wish he had—ha, here is blood—
"Mine ebbing spirits lacked this stirring impulse—"
Ho—haste ye here—"the shedder must be near—"
*Enter the Knights, Monks, &c. supporting Clotilda.*
KNIGHT. We found this trembling maid, alone, concealed—
PRIOR. Speak—tell of Bertram—of they lord—the vassals—
CLOT. Oh, give me breath, for I am weak with fear—
Short was the bloody conflict of the night—
The few remaining[111] vassals fled in fear—
The bandits loaded with the castle's spoil—

110. The Larpent version has "stoney." 111. The Larpent version has "surviving."

Are gone—I saw them issue from the walls—
But yet I dared not venture forth, while Bertram—
ALL. Go on—go on—
CLOT. He bore the murdered body,
Alone into yon chamber *(Pointing.)*
"I heard the heavy weight trail after him—"
I heard his bloody hands make fast the door—
*There* hath he sat in dread society,
The corse and murderer are there together.
*The Knights draw their swords, and rush towards the door.*
PRIOR. *(Interposing.)* Hold, champions, hold, "this warfare is for me."
The arm of flesh were powerless on him now—
"Hark how the faltering voice of feeble age
"Shall bow him to its bidding." Ho, come forth *(Striking the door.)*
Thou man of blood, come forth, thy doom awaits thee.
*Bertram opens the door, and advances slowly, his dress is stained with blood, and he grasps the hilt of a dagger in his hands—his look is so marked and grand, that the knights, &c. make room for him, and he advances to the front of the stage untouched.*
"ALL. Who art thou?"
BER. I am the murderer—Wherefore are ye come?—
"PRIOR. —This majesty of guilt doth awe my spirit—
"Is it th' embodied fiend who tempted him
"Sublime in guilt?"[112]
BER. Marvel not at me—Wist ye whence I come?
The tomb—where dwell the dead—and I dwelt with him—
Till sense of life dissolved away within me—*(Looking round ghastily.)*
I am amazed to see ye living men,
I deemed that when I struck the final blow
Mankind expired, and we were left alone,
The corse and I were left alone together,
The only tenants of a blasted world
Dispeopled for my punishment, "and changed
"Into a penal orb of desolation."
PRIOR. Advance and bind him, are ye men and armed?
What, must this palsied hand be first on him?—
Advance, and seize him, ere his voice of blasphemy
Shall pile the roof in ruins o'er our heads—
BER. —Advance, and seize me, ye who smile at blood—

112. The Abbotsford manuscript adds "hast thou burst from Hell—."

For every drop of mine a life shall pay—
I'm naked, famished, faint, my brand is broken—
Rush, mailed champions, on the helpless Bertram—*(They sink back.)*
Now prove what fell resistance I shall make. *(Throws down the hilt of his
  dagger.)*
There—bind mine arms—if ye do list to bind them—
I came to yield—but not to be subdued—
PRIOR. Oh thou, who o'er thy stormy grandeur flingest
A struggling beam that dazzles, awes, and vanishes—
Thou, who dost blend our wonder with our curses—
Why didst thou this?
BER. He wronged me, and I slew him—
To man but thee I ne'er had said even this—
"To man but thee, I ne'er shall utter more—"[113]
Now speed ye swift from questioning to death—
*They surround him.*
One prayer, my executioners, not conquerors—
"Be most ingenious in your cruelty;"
Let rack and pincer do their full work on me—
'Twill rouse me from the dread unnatural sleep,
In which my soul hath dreamt its dreams of agony[114]—
This is my prayer, ye'll not refuse it to me—
*As they are leading him off, the Prior lays hold of him.*
PRIOR. Yet bend thy steeled sinews, bend and pray—
The corse of him thou'st murdered, lies within.
*A long pause.*
BER. I have offended Heaven, but will not mock it—
Spare me your rack and pincers, spare me words.

*(Exeunt)*

SCENE III    *A dark wood, in the back Scene a Cavern, Rocks and Precipices
above.—Imogine comes forward.*

IMO. *(Sighing heavily after a long pause.)* If I could waft away this
  low-hung mist
That darkens o'er my brow—
If I could but unbind this burning band
That tightens round my heart.

113. Bertram, who will work himself up to be a romantic Othello, seems here to echo Iago
who claims, "From this time forth I never will speak word," as he is led off to be tortured
(V, ii, 304). 114. The Larpent version has "dreams of dying."

—Or night or morning is it?
I wist not which, a dull and dismal twilight
Pervading all things, and confounding all things,
Doth hover o'er my senses and my soul. *(Comes forward shuddering.)*
The moon shines on me, but it doth not light me;
The surge[115] glides past me, but it breathes not on me.
My child, my child, where art thou; come to me—
I know thou hidest thyself for sport to mock me—
Yet come—for I am scared with loneliness—
I'll call on thee no more, lo, there he glides—
And there, and there—he flies from me—"he laughs,
"I'll sing thee songs the church-yard spirits taught me—
"I'll sit all night on the grey tombs with thee,
"So thou wilt turn to me—" he's gone—he's gone.
*Enter Clotilda, Prior and Monks surrounding.*
CLOT. She's here—she's here—and is it thus I see her?
PRIOR. All-pitying Heaven—release her from this misery.
IMO. Away, unhand me, ye are executioners—
I know your horrible errand—who hath sent you?
This is false Bertram's doing—God—oh, God,
How I did love—and how am I requited—
Well, well, accuse me of what crime you will,
I ne'er was guilty of not loving thee—
Oh, spare the torture—and I will confess—
Nay, now there heeds it not—his look's enough—
That smile hath keener edge than many daggers.
*She sinks into Clotilda's arms.*
CLOT. How could this wasted form sustain the toils—
Bearing her helpless child.
IMO. *(Starting up.)* I was a mother—'twas my child I bore—
The murderer hung upon my flying steps—
The winds with all their speed had failed to match me.
Oh! how we laughed to see the baffled fiend
Stamp on the shore, and grind his iron teeth—
While safe and far, I braved the wave triumphant,
And shook my dripping locks like trophied banner.
I was a mother then.
PRIOR.                    Where is thy child!
CLOT. *(Pointing to the cave into which she was looked.)*

115. The Larpent version has "breeze."

Oh, he lies cold within his cavern-tomb—
Why dost thou urge her with the horrid theme?
PRIOR. It was to wake one living chord o' th' heart,
And I will try—though mine own breaks at it—
Where is thy child?
IMO. *(With a frantic laugh.)* The forest fiend hath snatched him;
"He rides the night-mare[116] through the wizard woods."
PRIOR. Hopeless and dark—even the last spark extinct.
*Enter 3d Monk hastily.*
MONK. Bertram—the prisoner Bertram—
PRIOR. —Hush—thou'lt kill her—
Haste thee, Clotilda,—holy brethren, haste;
Remove her hence, aye, even to that sad shelter. *(Pointing to the cave.)*
I see the approaching torches of the guard,
"Flash their red light athwart the forest's shade—"
Bear her away—"oh my weak eye doth fail
"Amid these horrors—"
*Imogine is torn to the cave, the Prior follows. "Manet last monk—Enter a Knight.*
"KNIGHT. Where is the prior?
"MONK. In yonder cave he bides,
"And here he wills us wait, for 'tis his purpose
"Once more to parley with that wretched man:
"How fares he now?
"KNIGHT. As one whose pride of soul
"Bears him up singly in this terrible hour—
"His step is firm—his eye is fixed—
"Nor menace, nor reviling, prayers, nor curses
"Can win an answer from his closed lips—
"It pities me—for he is brave—most brave—
"MONK. Pity him not.
"KNIGHT. Hush—lo, he comes—"[117]
*A gleam of torch-light falls on the rocks, Bertram, Knights, and Monks, are seen winding down the precipices, the clank of Bertram's chains the only sound heard. They enter, Bertram is between two Monks, who bear torches.*
1ST MONK. Leave him with us, and seek the Prior, I pray you.
KNIGHT. *(Aside to Monk.)* He yet may try escape. We'll watch
    concealed.

*(Exeunt all but Bertram and the two Monks)*

---

116. The night-mare is a female monster that attacks people at night, producing a feeling of suffocation. 117. In the Larpent version, this speech is given to the monk; this passage is marked to be cut by Murray.

1ST MONK. Brief rest is here allowed thee—"murderer, pause—"
How fearful was our footing on those cliffs,
Where time had worn these steep and rocky steps—
I counted them to thee as we descended,
But thou for pride was dumb—
BER. I heard thee not—
2D MONK. Look round thee, "murderer, drear thy resting place—"[118]
This is thy latest stage—survey it well—
Lo, as I wave my dimmed torch aloft,
Yon precipice crag seems as if every tread
(Yea, echoed impulse of the passing foot)
Would loose its weight to topple o'er our heads—
Those cavities hollowed by the hand of wrath—
Those deepening gulfs, have they no horrible tenant?
Dare thine eyes scan that spectred vacancy?
BER. I do not mark the things thou tell'st me of.—
1ST MONK. Wretch, if thy fear no spectred inmate shapes—
BER. *(Starting from his trance.)* Cease, triflers, would you have *me* feel
    remorse?
Leave me alone—nor cell, nor chain, nor dungeon,
Speaks to the murderer with the voice of solitude.
1ST MONK. Thou sayest true—
In cruelty of mercy will we leave thee—                    *(Exeunt Monks)*
BER. If they would go in truth—but what avails it?
*He meditates in gloomy reflection for some minutes, and his countenance slowly
relaxes from its stern expression.*
*The Prior enters unobserved, and stands opposite him in the attitude of supplica-
tion, Bertram resumes his sternness.*
BER. Why art thou here?—There was an hovering angel
Just lighting on my heart—and thou hast scared it—
PRIOR. Yea, rather with my prayers I'll woo it back.
In very pity of thy soul I come
To weep upon that heart I cannot soften—*(A long pause.)*
Oh! thou art on the verge of awful death—
Think of the moment, when the veiling scarf
That binds thine eyes, shall shut out earth for ever—
When in thy dizzy ear, hurtles the groan
Of those who see the smiting hand upreared,
Thou canst but feel—that moment comes apace—

118. The Larpent manuscript deletes two references to Bertram as "murderer" in this
scene, apparently to protect him from attack, to solicit sympathy for him.

*Bertram smiles.*
But terrors move in thee a horrid joy,
And thou art hardened by habitual danger
Beyond the sense of aught but pride in death.
*Bertram turns away.*
Can I not move thee by one power in nature?
There have been those whom Heaven hath failed to move,
Yet moved they were by tears of kneeling age. *(Kneels.)*
I wave all pride of ghostly power o'er thee—
I lift no cross, I count no bead before thee—
By the locked agony of these withered hands,
By these white hairs, such as thy father bore,
(Whom thou could'st ne'er see prostrate in the dust)
With toil to seek thee here my limbs do fail,
Send me not broken-hearted back again—
Yield, and relent, Bertram, my son, my son *(Weeping.)*
*Looking up eagerly.*
Did not a gracious drop bedew thine eye?
"BER. Perchance a tear had fallen, hadst thou not marked it."
PRIOR. *(Rising with dignity.)* Obdurate soul—then perish in thy pride—
Hear in my voice thy parting angel speak,
Repent—and be forgiven—
*Bertram turns toward him in strong emotion, when a shriek is heard from the cavern, Bertram stands fixed in horror*
PRIOR. *(Stretching out his hands towards the cavern.)*
Plead *thou* for me—thou, whose wild voice of horror,
Has pierced the heart my prayers have failed to touch—
BER. *(Wildly.)* What voice was that—yet do not dare to tell me,
Name not her name, I charge thee.
PRIOR. Imagine—
A maniac through these shuddering woods she wanders,
But in her madness never cursed thy name.
*Bertram attempts to rush towards the cave, but stands stupified on hearing a shriek from the cavern. Imogine rushes from it in distraction, bursting from the arms of Clotilda, the Monks and Knights follow, and remain in the back ground.*
IMO. Away, away, away, no wife—no mother—
*She rushes forward till she meets Bertram, who stands in speechless horror.*
IMO. Give me my husband, give me back my child—
Nay, give me back myself—
They say I'm mad, but yet I knew thee well—
Look on me—They would bind these wasted limbs—

I ask but death—death from thy hand—*that hand can deal death well*—and yet thou wilt not give it.

BER. *(Gazing on her for a moment, then rushing to the Prior, and sinking at his feet.)*

Who hath done this? Where are the racks I hoped for?

Am I not weak? am I not humbled now?

*Grovelling at the Prior's feet, and then turning to the Knights.*

Hast thou no curse to blast—no curse for me—

Is there no hand to pierce a soldier's heart?

Is there no foot to crush a felon's neck?

IMO. *(Raising herself at the sound of his voice.)* Bertram.

*He rushes towards her, and first repeats "Imogine" feebly, as he approaches, he utters her name again passionately, but as he draws nearer and sees her look of madness and desperation, he repeats it once more in despair, and does not dare to approach her, till he perceives her falling into Clotilda's arms, and catches her in his.*

IMO. Have I deserved this of thee?—*She dies slowly with her eyes fixed on Bertram, who continues to gaze on her unconscious of her having expired.*

PRIOR. 'Tis past—remove him from the corse—

*The Knights and Monks advance, he waves them off with one hand still supporting the body.*

PRIOR. *(To the Monks.)*—Brethren, remove the corse—

BER. She is not dead—*(Starting up.)*

She must not, shall not die, till she forgives me—

Speak—speak to me—*(Kneeling to the corse.)*

(Turning to the Monks.)—Yes—she will speak anon—

*A long pause, he drops the corse.*

She speaks no more—Why do ye gaze on me—

I love her, yea, I love, in death I love her—

I killed her—but—I loved her—

What arm shall loose the grasp of love and death?

*The Knights and Monks surround, and attempt to tear him from the body, he snatches a sword from one of the Knights, who retreats in terror, as it is pointed towards him. Bertram resuming all his former previous sternness, bursts into a disdainful laugh.*

BER. Thee—against thee—oh, thou art safe—thou worm—

Bertram hath but one fatal foe on earth—

And *he is here*—*(Stabs himself.)*

PRIOR. *(Rushes forward.)* He dies, he dies.

BER. *(Struggling with the agonies of death.)*

I know thee holy Prior—I know ye, brethren

Lift up your holy hands in charity.

*With a burst of wild exultation.*
I died no felon death—
A warrior's weapon freed a warrior's soul—[119]

## EPILOGUE
### Written by the Honourable George Lamb[120]
### Spoken by Miss Kelly

Say, for our Author whose proud hopes aspire,
To sound the Tragic Bard's neglected lyre;
Say, for our novice who at once the weight,
Bears of her own and of the Poet's fate,
Oh say, what hope? 'Tis mine with doubt and fear
In this dread hour to ask your judgment here;
Yet, for my sake, before your sentence, stay,
And hear me draw one moral from the play.
   Enough for IMOGINE the tears ye gave her;
I come to say one word in BERTRAM's favour.—
BERTRAM! ye cry, a ruthless blood-stain'd rover!!
He was—but also was the truest lover:
And, faith! like cases that we daily view,
All might have prosper'd, had the fair been true.
   Man, while he loves, is never quite deprav'd,
And woman's triumph, is a lover sav'd.
The branded wretch, whose callous feelings court
Crime for his glory, and disgrace for sport;
If in his breast love claims the smallest part,
If still he values one fond female heart,
From that one seed, that ling'ring spark, may grow
Pride's noblest flow'r, and virtue's purest flow:
Let but that heart—dear female lead with care
To honour's path and cheer his progress there,
And proud, though haply, sad regret occurs
At all his guilt, think all his virtue hers.
   The fair not always view with fav'ring eyes
The very virtuous or extremely wise;
But, odd it seems, will sometimes rather take

---

119. For the Abbotsford manuscript's different close, see the appendix. 120. George Lamb (1784–1834) served on the sub-committee of management for Drury Lane (along with Byron). An amateur actor and playwright, he helped Maturin recast *Bertram* for the stage.

Want with the spendthrift, riot with the rake.
"None, howe'er vitious, find all women froward,[121]
"None—did I say? none, save the sot and coward."
The reason's plain, the good need ought to warm them
And we must love the wicked to reform them.
　　"Yet we some wives, some sweethearts, may discover,
"Almost no better than the spouse or lover;
"Nought can to peace the busy female charm,
"And if she can't do good, she must do harm—
"Can chill warm youth, yet fails to warm chill age,
"Makes sage fools, but rarely makes fools sage;
"Some women, like all men, have tastes for evil,
"And, where they should be angels, play the devil."
　　Still woman draws new power, new empire still
From every blessing and from every ill.
Vice on her bosom lulls remorseful care,
And virtue hopes congenial virtue there.
Still she most hides the strength that most subdues,
To gain each end its opposite pursues;
Lures by neglect, advances by delay,
And gains command by swearing to obey.
　　Women have pow'r too in these gallant days,
(So Authors think) of recommending plays.
The prologue proses, ere the play is known,
Rugged and dull as the male speaker's tone;
When the scene's done, and many a fault provoke's you,
Women and Epilogue come forth to coax you.
Yet dare I plead, who in this wond'rous age,
Can only speak and walk upon the stage,—
Who know nor carte, nor tierce, nor fencing odds,[122]
Nor by a rope's assistance seek the Gods![123]
Yes, I will dare; for it ye're pleased to-night
The genuine drama re-asserts its right.
　　BERTRAM in crime elate, of murder proud,
Ruthless to man, to woman's accents bow'd;
Be mov'd like him, your sterner thoughts resign
At woman's voice, and let that voice be mine!

121. "Vitious," vicious; "Froward," habitually disposed to disobedience. 122. "Carte," the game of cards; "Tierce," either a sequence of three cards of the same suit or the third of the eight defensive positions in fencing. 123. The "gods" are the holders of the cheapest seats at the top of the theater.

## APPENDIX TO *BERTRAM*

In the manuscript version of *Bertram* that Maturin sent to Scott and that is preserved in the Abbotsford library, Maturin included several speeches and scenes involving the "Dark Knight of the Forest"; he also had Bertram meet a different fate, one closer to Goethe's Faust than in the published and performance versions. As has been noted, Maturin changed the play after receiving advice from Scott, George Lamb and Byron. Many of these changes were designed to improve the pacing of the play, but the most significant revisions came in the elimination of the Dark Knight and in the alteration of the final catastrophe. I have already indicated in the notes to the play some of the places where changes were made. Below I have reproduced the three main scenes concerning the Dark Knight; and I have provided a synopsis of the last act. Scott, who had second thoughts about eliminating the Dark Knight scenes, later reproduced two of them in his review of Maturin's *Women; or Pour et Contre* (*Edinburgh Review*, June 1818); his is not an exact version, however. Below are the manuscript versions of II, ii (III, i in the published version), II, iii (III, ii in the published version), and IV, i (the published version offers a different scene, using only a few of these lines), these being the central passages concerning the Dark Knight. The close of the last act in the manuscript version is also provided to give the reader an idea of the original end of Bertram's and Imogine's lives.

## ACT II, SCENE ii.

The stage directions in the manuscript version of this scene include a "dark tower seen in the background." Aldobrand and his page enter, discussing their progress home and judging it by the turrets they have seen. Aldobrand asks, "What tower, thou foolish wight—"; the Page answers, "The turrets of the dark Knight of the forest / Dimly they rose amid the doubtful gloom / But not one star-beam twinkled on their summits." A moment later, Aldobrand teases the page about the Dark Knight:

ALD. Now hie thee hence, my page so swift of foot
Greet the dark knight from me, and say thy Lord
Threading the wild maze of his matted dell
(With good knights of Anselm's holy Banner)
Doth lack his friendly cheer, and prays him dear
For knighthood's sake, to do them courtesy—
PAGE. Oh, good my master, send me not from thee.
I'd rather rouse the grim wolf from her lair

And wring my safety from her gore-red jaws
Than knock upon the dark knight's gate for shelter—
I'd rather couch me in the dreariest pit
Where knotted adders breed, and the torn mandrake
Peals its unnatural groan in witchcraft's ear
Than sleep on down beneath the dark knight's roof—
I'd rather rush upon thy sword, Lord Baron
(That sword that never paused o'er living foe)
Than do thy fearful message—
ALD. —Art thou mad?
What means this sudden agony of fear?—
The dark knight of the forest dwells alone—
No armed vassals flock beneath his banners
No mailed champion keeps his moated towers
No warden from his battlements of pride
Sends the high challenge of his hostile clarion
To knight or traveller—what is thy fear?—
PAGE. —Oh there, they say, full oft
Foul, goblin forms glare on the battlements.
His followers fight not with sword—
Athwart the Bridge, th'unearthly champion flings
From arms unforged by man, a withering gleam
O'er the dark, shrinking wave—
ALD. —With tears like thine
Reason dost strive in vain—I have no heart
To bid thee perish in thy soul's false terrors
Because I am thy lord, and may compel thee—
(Flinging himself under a tree.) So, while I rest beneath this broad-armed
    tree
Or oak, or elm, in this dark night I wot not—
It shall be thy sweet penance to rehearse
All thou hast heard of this most powerful man—
The tale will soon sooth my sleep, not mar my dreams—
PAGE. Then let me couch by thee—I pray thee do—
For ever I love 'mid frightful tales i' th' dark
To touch the hand I tell the tale of fear to—
ALD. Go on, go on, I'll be asleep anon—
PAGE. It was a night—it might be at this season
Or somewhat later—when the brown, sere leaves
Did strew the wood path—
ALD. —Well, we will not differ
PAGE. —It was an hour—just such an hour as this—

When the stunned ear grew dizzy from the stillness
When the strained eye athwart th'unpierced gloom
Did search for forms of fear, a lated traveler
Whom chance benighted in the forest's maze
Just in the spot where now we stand, did see—
*A bell tolls.*
ALD. Hark! 'tis the convent bell, hush thy wild tale—

Here, the manuscript version and the published version again coincide.


## ACT II, SCENE iii

If St. Aldobrand does not take the Dark Knight seriously and if in II, ii
Maturin plays with his audience, things take a more frightening turn in
this scene. Bertram and the Prior are discussing what Bertram should do.
The Prior wonders, "where wilt thou bide?":

PRIOR. Near us nor knight nor baron holds his keep,
For far and wide thy foeman's land extends
Save towers that mark th'approach of human foot—
BER. Who holds those towers—
PRIOR.                                    —the dark knight of the forest—
So from his armour named and sable helm
Whose unbarred vizor mortal eye never saw—
He dwells alone; no earthly thing lives near him
Save the hoarse Raven croaking o'er his towers
And the dank weeds muffling his stagnant moat—
BER. I'll ring a summons on his barred portals
If knightly horn hang there—
Shall make them through their dark valves rock and ring.
PRIOR. Thou'rt mad to bide the quest.—Within my memory
One solitary man did venture there—
Dark thoughts dwelt with him, and he sought to vent them.
To that dark frere, we saw his tottering steps
In winter's stormy twilight seek that pass—
But days, and years are gone, and he returns not—
BER. What fate befel him there?
PRIOR. The manner of his end was never known—
BER. That man shall be my mate—Contend not with me—
Horrors to me are kindred and society.
Or man or fiend, he hath won the soul of Bertram—

                                                        *(Bertram exits)*

## ACT IV, SCENE i

*Night, a forest, Bertram wandering near a dark tower, supposed to be that of the dark knight of the forest.*

BER. Was he a man fiend?—Whate'er it was
It hath dealt wonderfully with me—
All is around his dwelling suitable;
The invisible blast to which the dark pines groan,
The unconscious tread to which the thick earth echoes,
The hidden waters rushing to their fall,
These sounds of which the causes are not seen
I love, for they are like my fate mysterious—
How tower'd his proud form through the shrouding gloom,
How spoke the eloquent silence of its motion,
How through the barred vizor did his accents
Roll their rich thunder on their[124] pausing soul!
And though his mailed hand did shun my grasp,
And though his closed morion hid his feature,
Yea all resemblance to the face of man,
I felt the hollow whisper of his welcome,
I felt those unseen eyes were fix'd on mine,
If eyes indeed were there—
Forgotten thoughts of evil, still-born mischiefs,
Foul, fertile seeds of passion and of crime,
The night-veiled thoughts of many a ghastly hour
Day may not look upon—
That wither'd in my heart's abortive core,
Rous'd their dark battle at his trumpet-peal:
So sweeps the tempest o'er the slumbering desert,
Waking its myriad hosts of burning death:
So calls the last dread peal the wandering atoms
Of bone and blood, rent flesh and dust-worn fragments,
In dire array of ghastly unity,
To bide the eternal summons—
I am not what I was since I beheld him—
I was the slave of passion's ebbing sway—
All is condensed, collected, callous now—
The groan, the burst, the fiery flash is o'er,
Down pours the dense and darkening lava-tide,

124. For "the"?

Arresting life and stilling all beneath it.
*Enter two Robbers.*
1ST ROB. Why dost thou wander in the woods alone
Leaving thy mates to play with idle hilts
Or dream with monks o'er Rosary and Relic.
Give us a deed to do—
*Bertram walks aside not hearing him.*
2D ROB. See'st thou with what a step of pride he stalks—
Thou hast the dark knight of the forest seen;
For never man, from living converse come,
Trod with such step or flash'd eye like thine.
1ST ROB. And hast thou of a truth seen the dark knight?
BER. *(Turning on him suddenly.)* Thy hand is chill'd with fear—Well!
   shivering craven,
Say I have seen him—wherefore dost thou gaze?
Long'st thou for tale of goblin-garded portal?
Of giant champion whose spell-forged mail
Crumbled to dust at sound of magic horn—
Banner of sheeted flame whose foldings shrunk
To withering weeds that o'er the battlements
Wave to the broken spell—or demon-blast
Of winded clarion whose fell summons sinks
To lonely whisper of the shuddering breeze
O'er the charm'd towers—
1ST ROB. Mock me not thus—Hast met him of a truth?—
BER. Well, fool—
1ST ROB. Why then heaven's benison be with you.
Upon this hour we part—farewell for ever.
For mortal cause I bear a mortal weapon—
But man that leagues with demons lacks not man.
BER. How slave, wouldst make thy feigned or fancied fears
A plea for treacherous mutiny—thou'rt bribed—
Hence, plead to canting monks thy well-bought service
But take its wages first from me in blood. *(Seizing him.)*
1ST ROB. Strike, for my changed soul defies thee now.
BER. If thou art fit to dye, thou'rt fit to live
And I am neither—might this deed atone—*(Releasing him.)*
Rise, hie thee from me, be a better man
Go, wend with monks, with mendicants, with slaves
Who rend from famished dogs the meal they fight for—
With aught but Bertram

And go thou with him, for my sight doth loath ye.
*Bertram alone, he pauses for a long time and seems feeling in his breast for*
*something.*
BER. When I was but a boy, in my hot mood
My mother bound about my neck a chain—
She bound it with a mother's fears, and prayed me
To think of her, when that hot mood was wakened—
And I have worn it till this very hour
And it hath been a holy talisman
And checked my hand of blood, and mood of wrath—
But in my converse with the sable man
The chain did break, and the blessed cross that hung from it
I've lost, I felt the shock upon my heart
But, is it lost—I will not look for it.

(*Exit*)


## ACT V

The first two scenes of Act V are much the same in the manuscript version as they are in the published version of the play. V, iii is a scene in
which Imogine begins to go truly insane; as the stage directions indicate,
"marks of beginning derangement are apparent in her dress and looks."
The next scene opens on "A vault below the convent, Bertram is seen
through the cavities above, led by two monks, one of whom bears a
torch—they enter through an arch—his face is fixed, pale, absent." This
is Bertram's prison. They bring the corpse of Aldobrand before him, calling it "a speechless but eloquent minister of Remorse." Bertram speaks
over the corpse:

Aye this hath power—these glazed and stiffening eyes
They have a power, beyond the glance of fire
That e'er their living orbs of hatred darted—
If thou hadst known—even thou—in days of life
To tame a heart that would not be subdued—
The hand that stabbed thee, would have fought for thee—
But thou with ruthless violence of hatred
With burning flames of malice and of fury
Didst girdle in a writhing, goaded scorpion
Till madness aimed his sting to rise and pierce thee
And henceforth art thou thus—and—I am—(*Clasps his hands*
    *over his head in agony.*)

The prior comes to him and urges him to repent. When the monks enter to tell them Imogine has disappeared, the Prior and the monks leave Bertram, who tells us he would rather die than stay with the monks; but he cannot leave without passing the dead body, which he seems unable to do.

Bertram does not appear in the final scene. We discover Imogine, weeds in her hair, and her dead child; she is insane, but insists upon her continuing love for Bertram. The Prior rushes in *"with horror in his face"* to announce that Bertram has broken from prison with a "dark form." The Prior goes to find Bertram, telling the monks, "Await me here—if in an hour I come not / Toll all your bells for a departing soul." Imogine *"rises slowly and feebly, the expression of madness is gone from her countenance"*:

IMO. A gleam of blessed light is rising in me—
Where will it lead me—
*Wanders about, till she spies the body of her child, and tearing foliage that concealed it, she throws herself on it.*
Oh thou was all I want, and now I have thee—
I'll dye a blessed death upon thy breast—
When comes the fiend to bear my soul away—
Linked with my cherub-form, his prey will mock him
But famished—murdered *by thy mother*—
*Falls with scream of dying agony on the body, the Prior rushes in with expression of supernatural horror on his face.*
CLO. *(Pointing to Imogine.)* Oh look there, look there—
*He shakes her off, the monks gather about him, he repels them, and rushing to the front of the stage, he remains for a moment on his knees in speechless terror and agony—a flash of lightning twists over the back of the scene—he rises with terrible solemnity.*
PRIOR. It is too late to pray for Bertram's soul.
*Curtain.*

Peake (1792–1847) was the son of Richard Peake, who served as the treasurer for the Theatre Royal, Drury Lane for forty years. Richard Brinsley was born 19 February 1792. He was at first articled to James Heath to become an engraver, with whom he remained from 1809 until 1817. He eventually joined his father in the theater, however. His first known play is *The Bridge that carries us safe over*, a dramatic sketch offered at the English Opera House in 1817. In his forty-odd plays, he composed farces, melodramas, burlettas, musical entertainments, and extravaganzas; he wrote for not only the English Opera House but also Covent Garden, the Adelphi, Drury Lane, and the Olympic Theatre. He also apparently composed most of Charles Mathews's "At Homes" after 1829. During the last decade of his life, he served as the treasurer of the Lyceum Theatre. He died on 4 October 1847, having seen his comedy *The Title Deeds* open at the Adelphi in June but not his drama *Gabrielli; or, The Bequeathed Heart* in November.

Peake's plays include: *Amateurs and Actors*, an operatic farce (English Opera House, 1818); *The Haunted Inn*, a melodrama (Drury Lane, 1828); *The Bottle Imp*, a melodrama (English Opera House, 1828); *Court and City*, a comedy derived from Steele and Mrs. Sheridan (Covent Garden, 1841); and *The Devil of Marseilles; or, The Spirit of Avarice* (Adelphi, 1846).

Peake's most important work is *Presumption; or, The Fate of Frankenstein*, so-called in the playbills for the English Opera House production in 1823. It opened on 28 July 1823 and had an initial run of thirty-seven performances; it continued in the repertoire until at least 1850, and sparked an imitation (Henry M. Milner's *Frankenstein; or, The Demon of Switzerland*, 1823; Milner later adapted Merle and Antony's *Le monstre et le magicien* of 1826 as *Frankenstein; or, The Man and the Monster*) and several burlesques. Mary Shelley saw and enjoyed Peake's play that in many ways determined the direction that stage and later film adaptations of her novel would follow. The play was thought by some to be impious, and it was picketed and leaflets opposing it were circulated; but the *Morning Chronicle* (26 July 1823) found a "striking moral," "the fatal consequence of that presumption which attempts to penetrate, beyond prescribed depths, into the mysteries of nature," and the *Theatrical Observer* (31 July 1823) found that "The moral here is striking. It points out that man cannot pursue objects beyond his obviously prescribed powers, without incurring the penalty of shame and regret at his audacious folly." Despite the protests, the play was an obvious success, the *Theatrical Observer* (1 August 1823) noting that "This Piece has attracted every class," and the *Morning Chronicle* (29 July 1823) finding that it has "attracted a very brilliant audience."

There is a Larpent copy of the play (LA 2359), where it is called "*Frankenstein*, A Melo-Dramatic Opera in 3 Acts." It also appeared in Dick's Standard Plays, number 431 (London, 1865?), but the only copy of that edition that I could locate is held at the Bodleian (M. Adds. 111.2.11). What we have, then, are two performance texts. I have, thus, followed the earlier Larpent text except where Dick's version clarifies spelling and punctuation. Material in Dick's but not in the Larpent version is marked with double quotation marks; material found in Larpent but not in Dick's is marked by square brackets. Variants are indicated in the notes. It should be noted that playbills for the English Opera House revival of the play in 1826 indicated that it was then offered "with an entirely new scene, conforming to the original story, representing a schooner in a violent storm in which Frankenstein and the monster are destroyed."

On the play, see: Elizabeth Nitchie, *Mary Shelley, Author of Frankenstein* (New Brunswick, 1953), appendix iv; and Steven Earl Forry's *Hideous Progenies: Dramatizations of "Frankenstein" from Mary Shelley to the Present* (Philadelphia, 1990).

## DRAMATIS PERSONAE
### English Opera House, 28 July, 1823

| | |
|---|---|
| Frankenstein | Mr. Wallack |
| Clerval (his friend, in love with Elizabeth) | Mr. Bland |
| William (brother of Frankenstein) | Master Boden |
| Fritz (servant of Frankenstein) | Mr. Keeley |
| De Lacey (a banished gentleman—blind) | Mr. Rowbotham |
| Felix De Lacey (his son) | Mr. Pearman |
| Tanskin (a gipsy) | Mr. Shield |
| Hammerpan (a tinker) | Mr. Salter |

First Gipsy[1]
A Guide (an old man)                    Mr. R. Phillips
_____[2]                         Mr. T. P. Cooke

Elizabeth (sister of Frankenstein)      Mrs. Austin
Agatha (daughter of De Lacey)           Miss L. Dance
Safie (an Arabian girl, betrothed to Felix)   Miss Povey
Madame Ninon (wife to Fritz)[3]         Mrs. T. Weippert

Gipsies, Peasants, Choristers, and Dancers (Male and Female)[4]
Scene—Geneva and its vicinity


## ACT I

SCENE I   *A Gothic Chamber in the house of Frankenstein.*

*Fritz discovered in a Gothic arm-chair, nodding asleep. During the Symphony of
the Song, he starts, rubs his eyes, and comes forward.*

AIR—FRITZ
Oh, dear me! what's the matter?
How I shake at each clatter.
  My Marrow
  They harrow.
Oh, dear me! what's the matter?
If Mouse squeaks, or cat sneezes,
"Cricket chirps, or cock wheezes,"
  Then I fret
  In cold sweat.
Every noise my nerves teazes;
Bless my heart—heaven preserve us!
I declare I'm so nervous.
  Ev'ry Knock
  Is a shock.
I declare I'm so nervous!
"I'm so nervous."

FRITZ. Oh, Fritz, Fritz, Fritz! What is it come to! you are frighten'd out
of your wits. Why did you ever leave your native village! why couldn't you

1. Listed only in the Larpent version. 2. Listed in the Larpent version as the demon, but
given no name in the Dick's version or in the playbills. 3. The Larpent version adds
"housekeeper to Elizabeth"; "mother to Elizabeth" is crossed out. 4. The Larpent version
lists "Gypseys Villagers &c.," under the male characters and "Gypseys Lasses" under the
female characters.

be happy in your native Village[5] with an innocent cow for your companion (bless its sweet breath!) instead of coming here to the City of Geneva to be hired as a servant! *(Starts.)* What's that?—nothing. And then how complimentary! Master only hired me because he thought I looked so stupid! Stupid! ha, ha, ha! "but" am I stupid though? To be sure Mr. Frankenstein is a kind man, and I should respect him, but that I thinks as how he holds converse with somebody below with a long tail, horns and hoofs, who shall be nameless. *(Starts again.)* What's that! "Oh," a gnat on my nose! Ah, anything frightens me now—I'm so nervous! I spill all my bread and milk when I feed myself at breakfast! Lauk! Lauk![6] In the country, if a dog bray'd, or a donkey bark'd ever so loud, it had no effect upon me. *(Two distinct loud knocks—Fritz jumps.)* Oh, mercy! I jump like a maggot out of cheese! How my heart beats!

CLER. *(Without.)* Fritz, Fritz!

[FRITZ. It's a human being however—]

CLER. *(Without.)* Open the door, Fritz!

FRITZ. Yes. It's only Mr. Clerval, master's friend, who is going to marry Miss Elizabeth, master's sister. *(Opens the door.)*

*Enter Clerval.*

How d'ye do, sir!

CLER. Good morrow, Fritz! Is Mr. Frankenstein to be seen?

FRITZ. I fear not, Sir, he has as usual been fumi- fumi- fumigating all night at his chemistry.[7] I have not dared to disturb him.

CLER. Mr. Frankenstein pursues his studies with too much ardour.

FRITZ. And what can be the use of it, Mr. Clerval? Work, "work," work—always at it. Now, putting a case to you. Now, when I was in the country, with my late cow (she's no more now, poor thing!) if I had sat to and milked her for a fortnight together, day and night, without stopping, do you think I should be any the better for it? I ask you as a gentleman and a scholar.

CLER. Ha, "ha," ha! Certainly not!

FRITZ. Nor my cow neither, poor creter.[8] *(Wipes his eyes.)* Excuse my crying—she's defunct, and I always whimper a little when I think on her; and my wife lives away from me, but I don't care so much for that. Oh! Mr. Clerval, between ourselves—hush! didn't you hear a noise!— between ourselves, I want to unbosom my confidence.

CLER. Well?

---

5. Dick's version has "in the country." 6. Also "lawks." A colloquial, slang version of "Lord." 7. Dick's version has Clerval supply "Fumigating"; to which Fritz replies, "Yes, sir—fumigating; thank'ee, sir—" 8. Dick's version spells it "cretur," for "creature."

FRITZ. Between ourselves—there's nobody at the door, is there?—(*Crosses to door.*)—No! well, between ourselves, Mr. Clerval, I have been so very nervous since I came to this place—

CLER. Pshaw!

FRITZ. "Nay," don't 'Pshaw!' till you've heard me out. [—My poor Mas-[ter—I know you are his friend, but he has dealings with the Gentleman [in black!

[CLER. Yes, I know—the Notary who comes to consult him on my mar-[riage contract—

FRITZ. [Notary—no—somebody deeper than that—] Oh, Mr. Clerval! I'll tell you. One night Mr. Frankenstein did indulge himself by going to bed. He was worn with fatigue and study. I had occasion to go into his chamber. He was asleep, but frightfully troubled; he groaned and ground his teeth, setting mine on edge. 'It is accomplished!' said he. *Accomplished!* I knew that had nothing to do with me, but I listened. He started up in his sleep, though his eyes were opened and dead as oysters, he cried, 'It is animated—it rises—walks!' Now, my shrewd guess, sir, is that, like Doctor Faustus,[9] my master is raising the Devil.

CLER. Fritz, you are simple; drive such impressions from your mind, you must not misconstrue your Master's words in a dream. Do you never dream?

FRITZ. (*Mournfully.*) I dream about my Cow sometimes.

CLER. Your master is a studious Chemist—nay, as I sometimes suspect, an alchemist.

FRITZ. "Eh!" Ah, I think he is. What is an alchemist Mr. Clerval?

CLER. Does he not sometimes speak of the art of making gold?

FRITZ. Lauk, sir! do you take Mr. Frankenstein for a coiner?[10]

CLER. Did you never hear him make mention of the grand elixer, which can prolong life to immortality.

FRITZ. Never in all my life!

CLER. Well go—find out if it is possible I can see him. I will not detain him.

FRITZ. Yes, sir. Oh, that laboratory! I've got two loose teeth, and I am afraid I shall loose them, for whenever I go towards that infernal place my head shakes like a dice-box. (*Goes to door.*) Oh, mercy! what's that? Two shining eyes—how they glisten! Dear, dear, why I declare it's only the cat on the stairs. Puss, puss, pussy! How you frighten'd me, you young *dog,* when you know I am so very nervous!

(*Exit Fritz*)

9. Johann Faust or Faustus of Wurttemberg who died ca. 1538 surrounded by stories of su-pernatural powers and dealings with the devil; the protagonist of Marlowe's *Tragical History of Dr. Faustus* and Goethe's *Faust.* 10. A counterfeiter.

CLER. Frankenstein, friend of my youth, how extraordinary and secret are thy pursuits! how art thou altered by study! Strange, what a hold has philosophy taken of thy mind—but thou wert always enthusiastic and of boundless ambition. But "Elizabeth—" the fair Elizabeth, his sister— what a difference in disposition! Everyone adores her. Happy Clerval, to be now the possessor of Elizabeth, who, unconscious of her beauty, stole thy heart away!

SONG—CLERVAL[11]

Ere witching love my heart possest,
　And bade my sighs the nymph pursue,
Calm as the infant's smiling rest,
　No anxious hope nor fear it knew.

But doom'd—ah! doom'd at last to mourn,
　What tumults in that heart arose!
An ocean trembling, wild, and torn
　By tempests from its deep repose.

Yet let me not the virgin blame,
　As tho' she wish'd my heart despair,
How could the maid suspect a flame,
　Who never knew that she was fair.

—But Frankenstein approaches.

*Enter Frankenstein, thoughtfully, shown in by Fritz, who exits.*
CLER. My dear friend!
FRANK. Clerval!
CLER. Frankenstein, how ill you appear—So [thin and] pale! You look as if your night-watchings had been long and uninterrupted.
FRANK. [You have guessed rightly!—] I have lately been so deeply engaged in one occupation that I have not allowed myself sufficient rest. But how left you my sister, Elizabeth?
CLER. Well, and very happy, only a little uneasy that she sees you so seldom.
FRANK. Aye, I am engaged heart and soul in the pursuit of a discovery—a grand, unheard of wonder! None but those who have experienced can conceive the enticement of science; he who looks into the book of nature, finds an inexhaustible source of novelty, of wonder, and delight. What hidden treasures are contained in her mighty volume—what strange, undreamed-of mysteries!

11. The Larpent version indicates the song was written by Dr. Walcot.

CLER. But some little respite—your health should be considered.

FRANK. *(Abstracted.)* After so much time spent in painful labour, to arrive at once[12] at the summit of my desires, would be indeed a glorious consummation of my toils.

CLER. How wild and mysterious his abstractions—he heeds me not! *(Aside.)*

FRANK. *(Apart.)* This discovery will be so vast, so overwhelming, that all the steps by which I have been progressively led will be obliterated, and I shall behold only the astonishing result.

CLER. Frankenstein!

FRANK. Ha! *(To Clerval.)* I see by your eagerness that you expect to be informed of the secret with which I am acquainted. That cannot be.

CLER. I do not wish to pry into your secrets, Frankenstein. I am no natural philosopher; my imagination is too vivid for the details of science. If I contemplate, let it be the charms of your fair sister, Elizabeth. My message hither now—I wish to fix the day for our nuptials. But we must be certain on so an important and happy an event, that we shall enjoy the society of our Frankenstein.

FRANK. Pardon me, Clerval! My first thoughts should recur to those dear friends whom I most love, and who are so deserving of my love—name the day?

CLER. On the morn after to-morrow, may I lead the charming Elizabeth to the altar?

FRANK. E'en as you will—e'en as you will! *(Aside.)* My wonderful task will be ere that completed. It will be animated! "It" will live—will think! *(Crosses in deep reflection—afterwards turns up the stage.)*

CLER. *(Apart.)* Again in reverie! this becomes alarming—surely his head is affected. I am bound in duty to counteract this madness, and discover the secret of his deep reflections.

*Frankenstein sits down—musing.*

Farewell, Frankenstein! He heeds me not—'tis in vain to claim his notice—but I will seek the cause, and, if possible, effect his cure. No time must be lost. Fritz must assist me, and this way he went.

*(Exit Clerval)*

FRANK. Every moment lost, fevers me. What time have I devoted? *(Rises.)* Had I not been heated by an almost supernatural enthusiasm, my application to this study would have been irksome, disgusting, and almost intolerable. To examine the causes of life—I have had recourse to death—I have seen how the fine form of man has been wasted and degraded—have

12. Dick's version has "at last."

beheld the corruption of death succeed to the blooming cheek of life! I have seen how the worm inherits the wonders of the eye and brain—I paused—analysing all the minutiae of causation as exemplified in the change of life from death—until from the midst of this darkness the sudden light broke in upon me! A light so brilliant and dazzling, some miracle must have produced the flash! The vital principle! The cause of life!—Like Prometheus[13] of old, have I daringly attempted the formation—the animation of a Being! To my task—away with reflection—to my task—"to my task!"                                                 (Exit)

*Enter Clerval and Fritz.*

[FRITZ. Now he's going to blow up his fire again!

[CLER. And thus you say for whole days and nights together, without re-[pose, and almost without food he has immured himself in his study.]

FRITZ. Yes—there he is—amongst otamies[14] and phials and crucibles, and retorts, and charcoal, and fire, and the Devil—for I'm sure *he's* at the bottom of it, and that makes me so nervous.

CLER. Fritz, you love your master, and are, I know, a discreet servant— but his friends and relations are all unhappy on his account. His health is rapidly sinking under the fatigue of his present labours—will you not assist to call him back to life and to his family?

FRITZ. La! I'd call out all day long, if that would do any good.

CLER. I know his mind has been devoted to obstruse and occult sciences—that his brain has been bewildered with the wild fancies of Cornelius Agrippa, Paracelsus, and Albertus Magnus—[15]

FRITZ. Oh! Mr. Clerval! how can you mention such crazy tooth-breaking names? There sounds something wicked in them.

CLER. Wicked? Psha, man! they are the renowned names of the earliest experimental philosophers. The sages who promised to the hopes of the laborious alchymist the transmutation of metals and the elixer of life.

FRITZ. "O! Ah!" indeed! Lack a daisy me!

---

13. In some classical myths, the Titan Prometheus creates man by animating clay with fire. The subtitle of Mary Shelley's novel was "The Modern Prometheus." 14. For "atomies," meaning skeletons (archaic). Dick's version has "Yes, there he goes again, amongst otamies." 15. Dick's version has " . . . Paracelsus, Albertus Magnus, and—." Henricus Cornelius Agrippa of Nettesheim (1486–1535) authored works on the occult sciences, *De Occulta Philosophia libri tres* (1529) and *De Vanitate Scientiarum* (1530). Philippus Aureolus Paracelsus (1493–1541) was born in Switzerland and wandered around Europe, particularly in Germany, as a magician, astrologer and alchemist. After receiving a chair at Basel and burning scientific works by Galen and Avicenna, he was denounced as a fake. He is considered the founder of modern chemistry. Albertus Magnus (1193–1280), from Swabia, became a Dominican friar and an important scholastic philosopher, known for his work on Aristotle. Agrippa and Paracelsus are mentioned in Mary Shelley's *Frankenstein*.

[CLER. Do you understand me!

[FRITZ. Not particularly—

[CLER. Fritz—tho' simple, you are an excellent fellow—have you any idea [what is the stange object of which your master is in search?

[FRITZ. I have my suspicions truly.

[CLER. What are they?

[FRITZ. *(Looks round.)* Hush—no—nothing but the wind—To tell you the [truth, I suspect that the grand object is—

[CLER. What?

[FRITZ. A secret—there now the murder's out.]

CLER. *(Aside.)* This fellow is more knave than fool—he wants a bribe. Now, sirrah! answer me with candour. What is it you like best in the world?

FRITZ. Milk!

CLER. Simpleton! I mean what station of Life would you covet?

FRITZ. Station?

CLER. "Yes." Would you like to be master of a cottage?

FRITZ. What, and keep a cow?—the very thing. Why, Mr. Clerval, you're a conjuror, and know my thoughts by art.[16]

CLER. Fritz, I want to discover—but you must be prudent—*(Takes out purse and gives a florin to Fritz.)* Here's an earnest of my future intentions touching the cow and cottage.

FRITZ. Bodikins! a florin![17] *(Examining money.)*

CLER. Friend Fritz, you must some time, when Mr. Frankenstein is absent from home, admit me into his study.

FRITZ. Oh, dear, I can't!—dont take your florin back again [sir]—*(Puts up money.)*—for he always locks the door. To be sure, there's a little window—on the gallery—I can see when he puffs up his fire.[18]

CLER. Well, they say the end justifies the means; and in this case I admit the maxim. You can peep through that window, and inform me minutely of what you see.

FRITZ. But what is to become of my nerves?

CLER. Remember your cottage—

FRITZ. And the Cow!

CLER. Put me in possession of the secret, and both shall be secured to you. Some one approaches.

---

16. Dick's version has "heart." 17. The Larpent version has a crown (five shillings) rather than a florin (two shillings). "Bodikins" means "a little body" and is used as an oath. 18. Dick's version reads, "To be sure, there's a little window a-top of the staircase, where I can see when he puffs up his fire."

FRITZ. Mr. Clerval, I'm your man. I'm nervous, and the devil sticks in my gizzard; but the cow will drive it out again. *(Starts.)* What's that? Oh, nothing—"oh, dear, I'm so nervous."          *(Exeunt Fritz and Clerval)*


SCENE II   *Part of the Villa Residence of Elizabeth at Belrive.—Garden Terrace—Sunset—William discovered sleeping on a garden bench—Enter Elizabeth from the house.*

### SONG—ELIZABETH

The summer sun shining on tree and on tower,
    And gilding the landscape with radiance divine,
May give joy to the heart o'er which pleasure has power,
    But eve's pensive beauties are dearer to mine.

Through trees gently sighing, the cool breeze of even
    Seems sympathy's voice to the ear of despair;
And the dew-drops (like tears shed by angels of heaven),
    Revive the frail hopes in the bosom of care.

*During this scene the stage becomes progressively dark.*
MAD. NINON. *(Within.)* William! little William!
ELIZ. Where can our little favorite have secreted himself?
*Enter Madame Ninon, from the house.*
NIN. Heaven bless Mont Blanc[19] and all the neighbouring hills! Why, where is the boy? How angry shall I be with him for staying out so late.
ELIZ. Why, Ninon, assuage your friendly wrath—yonder is William.
NIN. *(Goes to child.)* Fast asleep, I declare, the pretty boy—how like his poor mother, who is gone. La, La, I daresay my Fritz was just such another, only his hair was red. Pretty William—he was the pin basket.[20] Bless the thirteen cantons,[21] I nursed him. William—*(Kisses him.)*—a pair of gloves, Sir![22] *(William waking.)* Fie, you idle[23] urchin, sleeping so early this beautiful evening.
*William rises. All come forward.*
WILL. Indeed, dear Ninon, I know "not" how I fell asleep; but I rose with the sun, and thinking I would lie down with it, I closed my eyes, and—
NIN. Slumbered like a young dormouse?

19. In southeastern France on the Italian border, Mont Blanc is the highest of the Alps; it is the subject of a poem by Percy Shelley and is mentioned in *Frankenstein* (Chapter Ten). 20. The youngest child in a completed family.  21. The states that make up Switzerland. 22. To give a judge a pair of gloves was to tell him he should not take his seat, since ancient custom forbade judges from wearing gloves on the bench. Here, Ninon is presumably telling William to get up from the seat where he is sleeping.  23. Dick's version has "little."

ELIZ. But, William, you have not neglected your books?

WILL. Oh, no; for then I should not be such a scholar as my elder brother, Victor Frankenstein. *(Runs to end of terrace.)*[24]

ELIZ. Alas, poor Frankenstein! he studies indeed too deeply; but love—blighted love, drove him to solitude and abstruse research.

NIN. Ah, Madame, may love make you happy! Mr. Clerval was here this morning, and looked as handsome—

ELIZ. Peace, Ninon! And yet, why should I check your cheerfulness? Ninon, I have given orders to my milliner to make you a handsome new cap. When your husband, Fritz, comes from Geneva, he may call and bring it.

"NIN. Thank you, dear madam; but see—"

*Re-Enter William from terrace, and runs, crossing behind.*[25]

WILL. Oh, sister—oh, Madame Ninon! two travellers are coming up the hill—such a beautiful lady—but her guide, I think, has fallen from his horse. See—here's the lady, helping the poor man.

*Melo-Music.*[26]

*Enter Safie, supporting the Guide, from terrace.*

ELIZ. Madame, allow me to offer my assistance.

SAFIE. "Thanks"—thanks, fair Lady; it is not for myself I require rest or help, for I am young. But this aged man, my faithful follower, is completely worn with fatigue.

"ELIZ. Ninon, see him conveyed into the house. Give him your support, "and assist to welcome our guests."

NIN. *(Crossing to guide.)* Lean on me, old sir—aye, as heavy as you like; bless you my arm is strong, [tho' I am little.][27] Come, gently—gently—"there—there—"

*Ninon leads the guide into house, William following them. By this time the wing lights are turned off.*

SAFIE. I can only weep my thanks, of late I have been unused to kindness.

ELIZ. Your garb and manner denote you a stranger here—yet you are acquainted with our language, and you appear to have travelled a great distance.

SAFIE. From Leghorn,[28] a wearisome journey. How far am I distant from the Valley of the Lake?

ELIZ. But a few leagues.

SAFIE. Then to-night I probably could reach it? *(Animated.)*

24. The Larpent version has him run to a gate. 25. The Larpent version has him return "at the Gate." 26. Presumably indicating conventional music from a melodrama. 27. The Larpent version added "and ancient" and then crossed it out. 28. Leghorn is a city on the Ligurian Sea in Northwest Italy.

ELIZ. I would not advise the attempt till the morning—the sun is down now; you are distant from any inn; your horses are fatigued; permit me to offer in my house refreshment and repose.

SAFIE. No, no; "no repose" until my purpose is accomplished. Yet my poor follower needs rest; generous stranger, I gratefully accept your hospitality.

ELIZ. And be assured such comfort as Eliza Frankenstein can offer shall be freely yours.

SAFIE. You—you mention the name of Frankenstein!

ELIZ. I bear that appelation.

SAFIE. How fortunate! happy chance that brought me to your hospitable door. Know you the family of De Lacey?

ELIZ. I knew it well, but years have elapsed since I have heard of them.

SAFIE. I seek their retreat. Exiled from France, they now exist in the Valley of the Lake.

ELIZ. So near, and I not acquainted with their residence! Does the gentle Agatha De Lacey yet live?

SAFIE. Tomorrow's morn I trust will find me locked in her embrace.[29]

ELIZ. What rapturous news for my dear brother, Frankenstein—night approaches—let us in and converse further on this subject, which is of deep interest to me—hark!—the sweet nightingale is pouring forth its evening melody.[30]

DUETT—ELIZABETH AND SAFIE

Hark how it floats upon the dewy air!
Oh! what a dying, dying close was there!
'Tis harmony from yon sequester'd bower,
Sweet harmony that soothes the midnight hour!

*(Exeunt into house)*

29. Dick's version has "To-morrow's noon I trust I shall discover her." 30. Dick's version ends this scene differently, beginning with this speech:

ELIZ. What rapturous news for my dear brother, Frankenstein. Let us in and converse further on this subject, which is of deep interest to me, Night approaches.

SAFIE. On such a night was I torn from Agatha's brother. Felix, Felix! sad was the moment when you last enfolded poor Safie in your affectionate embrace.

SONG—SAFIE

Each mountain was tinged with the sun's latest beam,
Sinking red in the fathomless deep;
The pale watch lights of heaven shed their rays o'er the stream;
And nature seem'd lulled into sleep.
All was silent and hush'd over lake, lawn, and fell,
Save the whisper that breathed in the lover's farewell;
When at Fate's stern command two fond hearts doom'd to sever,
And poor Felix and Safie were parted for ever.        *(Exeunt into house)*

SCENE III   *The sleeping Apartment of Frankenstein. Dark. The Bed is within a recess between the wings, enclosed by dark green curtains. A Sword (to break) hanging. A Large French Window; between the wings a staircase leading to a Gallery across the stage, on which is the Door of the Laboratory above. A small high Lattice in centre of scene, next the Laboratory Door. A Gothic Table on stage, screwed. A Gothic Chair in centre, and Footstool. Music expressive of the rising of a storm. Enter Frankenstein, with a Lighted Lamp, which he places on the table. Distant thunder heard.*

FRANK. This "evening—this" lowering evening, will, in all probability, complete my task. Years have I laboured, and at length discovered that to which so many men of genius have in vain directed their inquiries. After days and nights of incredible labour and fatigue, I have become master of the secret of bestowing animation upon lifeless matter. With so astonishing a power in my hands, "long," long did I hesitate how to employ it. The object of my experiments lies there *(Pointing up to the laboratory.)*—a huge automaton[31] in human form. Should I succeed in animating it, Life and Death would appear to me as ideal bounds, which I shall break through and pour a torrent of light into our dark world. I have lost all soul or sensation but for this one pursuit.[32] *(Storm.)* A storm has hastily arisen!—'Tis a dreary night—the rain patters dismally against the pains—'tis a night for such a task—I'll in and attempt to infuse the spark of life.—

*Music.—Frankenstein takes up lamp, cautiously looks around him, ascends the stairs, crosses the gallery above, and exits into door of laboratory.*

*Enter Fritz, trembling, with a candle.*

FRITZ. Master isn't here—dare I peep. Only think of the reward Mr. Clerval promised me, a cow and a cottage, milk and a mansion. Master is certainly not come up yet. My candle burns all manner of colours, and spits like a roasted apple. *(Runs against the chair[33] and drops his light, which goes out.)* There, now, I'm in the dark. Oh my nerves.

*A blue flame appears at the small lattice window above, as from the laboratory.* What's that? O lauk; there he is, kicking up the devil's own flame! Oh my Cow! I'll venture up—oh my cottage! I'll climb to the window—it will be only one peep to make my fortune.

31. This passage, which owes something to Mary Shelley's novel (Chapter Four), also makes an important departure from it in calling Frankenstein's creation an "automaton." We see the movement here away from Mary Shelley's being towards the bolt-neck monster of the movie tradition. 32. The rest of this speech differs slightly in Dick's version: "I have clothed the inanimate mass, lest the chilly air should quench the spark of life newly infused. *(Thunder and heavy rain heard.)* 'Tis a dreary night, and the rain patters dismally against the panes; 'tis a night for such a task. I'll in and complete the wondrous effort." 33. A couch in the Larpent version.

*Music.—Fritz takes up footstool, he ascends the stairs, when on the gallery landing place, he stands on the footstool tiptoe to look through the small high lattice window of the laboratory, a sudden combustion is heard within. The blue flame changes to one of a reddish hue.*

FRANK. *(Within.)* It lives! it lives!

"FRITZ. *(Speaks through music.)* Oh, dear! oh, dear! oh, dear!"

*Fritz, greatly alarmed, jumps down hastily, totters tremblingly down the stairs in vast hurry; when in front of stage, having fallen flat in fright, with difficulty speaks.*

FRITZ. There's a hob—[a] hob-goblin, [and] 20 feet high![34]—[wrapp'd in [a mantle—mercy—mercy—

*[Falls down.]*

*Music.—Frankenstein rushes from the laboratory, without lamp, fastens the door in apparent dread, and hastens down the stairs, watching the entrance of the laboratory.*

FRANK. It lives! [It lives.] I saw the dull yellow eye of the creature open, it breathed hard, and a convulsive motion agitated its limbs. What a wretch have I formed, [his legs are in proportion and] I had selected his features as beautiful—"beautiful"! Ah, horror! his cadaverous skin scarcely covers the work of muscles and arteries beneath, his hair lustrous, black, and flowing—his teeth of pearly whiteness—but these luxuriances only form more horrible contrasts with the deformities of the Demon.[35]

*Music.—He listens at the foot of the staircase.*

[It is yet quiet—] What have I accomplished? the beauty of my dream has vanished! and breathless horror and disgust fill my heart. For this I have deprived myself of rest and health, "have worked my brain to madness;" and when I looked to reap my great reward, a flash breaks in upon my darkened soul, and tells me my attempt was impious, and that its fruition will be fatal to my peace for ever. *(He listens again.)* All is still! The dreadful spectre of a human form—no mortal could withstand the horror of that countenance [—a mummy endued with animation could be so hideous as the wretch I have endowed with life!]—miserable and impious being that I am! [—lost—lost] Elizabeth! brother! Agatha!—faithful[36]

---

34. Dick's version has "seven-and-twenty feet high!" It then moves Fritz's next speech here and modifies it: "Oh, my nerves; I feel as if I had just come out of strong fits, and nobody to throw cold water in my—if my legs won't lap under me, I'll just make my escape. Oh, my poor nerves! *(Exit Fritz, crawling off.)*" 35. Dick's version usually has "monster" where the Larpent version has "demon"; I have followed the Larpent text. For this description, see *Frankenstein*, Chapter Five. 36. Dick's version has "fairest."

Agatha! never more dare I look upon your virtuous faces. "Lost! lost! "lost!"

*Music—Frankenstein sinks on a chair.* [37]

[FRITZ. *(Looks up once or twice before he speaks.)* Oh my nerves; I feel as if [I had just come out of strong fits, and nobody to throw water in my [face—Master sleeps, so I'll, if my legs won't lap[38] up under me—just— [make my escape.]

*Sudden combustion heard, and smoke issues, the door of the laboratory breaks to pieces with a loud crash—red fire within.*

[FRITZ. Oh—Oh. *(Runs out hastily)*]

*Music. The Demon discovered at door entrance in smoke, which evaporates— the red flame continues visible. The Demon advances forward, breaks through the balustrade or railing of gallery immediately facing the door of laboratory, jumps on the table beneath, and from thence leaps on the stage, stands in attitude before Frankenstein, who had started up in terror; they gaze for a moment at each other.* [39]

FRANK. The demon[40] corpse to which I have given life!

*Music.—The Demon looks at Frankenstein most intently, approaches him with gestures of conciliation. Frankenstein retreats, the Demon pursuing him.* [41]

[Its unearthly ugliness renders it too horrible for human eyes!

[*The Demon approaches him.*]

Fiend! do not dare approach me[42]—avaunt, or dread the fierce vengeance of my arm [wrecked on your miserable head—]

*Music.—Frankenstein takes the sword from the nail,*[43] *points with it at the Demon, who snatches the sword, snaps it in two and throws it on stage. The Demon then seizes Frankenstein—loud thunder heard—throws him violently on the floor, ascends the staircase, opens the large window, and disappears through the casement. Frankenstein remains motionless on the ground.—Thunder and lightning until the drop falls.*

### END OF ACT I

37. The Larpent version has him sit on a chair. Dick's version has already had Fritz exit and thus combines many of these stage directions. While I have used the fuller descriptions found in Dick's version, I have placed them where they would go in Larpent's version. 38. Fold or roll up. 39. In the Larpent version, the creature "appears in the light of the Laboratory," and "he looks around cautiously, descends the staircase rapidly— surveys the apartment—crosses to Frankenstein, and lays hand upon him." 40. Dick's version has "horrid." 41. The Larpent version has the Demon retreat first, but then has him approach in the lines cut in Dick's version. Both sets of stage directions seem to be trying to balance between portraying the creature as a neutral being, forced to violence only by Frankenstein's response, and seeing him as a "monster" or "demon," ready to attack. 42. Dick's version has "dare not to approach me." 43. The Larpent version has the sword on the table.

# ACT II

SCENE I *An apartment in the House of Elizabeth, at Belrive.—Table and chairs. The hurried music from the close of the First Act to play in continuance until this scene is discovered, and Frankenstein enters, hastily, to centre of stage. Music ceases.*

FRANK. At length in my sister's house!—and safe! I have paced with quick steps, but at every turn feared to meet the wretch—my heart palpitates with the sickness of fear! [He does not pursue me—dreams that [have been my food and pleasant rest for so long a space, are now become [a hell to me—the change so rapid, the overthrow so complete—] What have I cast on the world? a creature powerful in form, of supernatural and gigantic strength, but with the mind of an infant. Oh, that I could recall my impious labour, or suddenly extinguish the spark which I have so presumptuously bestowed.—Yet that were murder—murder in its worse and most horrid form—for he is mine—my own formation. Ha! who approaches?

*Enter Elizabeth, they embrace.*

ELIZ. My dear Victor! my dear brother!

FRANK. Elizabeth! [My love, how sweet is this embrace—]

ELIZ. You [are] come to stay, I hope, until[44] our wedding is over. Clerval will be here presently. Alas! Frankenstein! your cheek is pallid—your eye has lost its wonted lustre. Oh, Victor, what are the secrets that prey upon your mind and form?—The pernicious air of your laboratory will be fatal to you.

FRANK. *(Apart.)* Fatal indeed!

ELIZ. I pray you, for my sake, cease—I understand upon one subject you have laboured incessantly.

FRANK. One subject! *(Aside.)* Am I discovered?

ELIZ. You change colour, my dear brother. I will not mention it—I—there is a wildness in your eyes for which I cannot account.

FRANK. *(Starts.)* See—see—he is there!

ELIZ. Dearest Frankenstein—what is the cause of this?

FRANK. Do not ask me. "I"—I thought I saw the dreaded spectre glide into the room.

ELIZ. Calm your mind, Victor.

FRANK. Pardon me, Elizabeth. I know not what you will think of me.

ELIZ. I have intelligence of one dear to you, and for whom, prior to your close attention to study, you had the tenderest regard.—Say, Victor, will

44. Dick's version has "till."

you not be glad to hear that I have a clue to lead you to your lost love, Agatha De Lacey!

FRANK. Agatha! dearest Agatha! her name recalls my sinking spirits—where—where is she to be found? Oh, would that I ne'er had been robbed of her! 'Twas her loss that drove me to deep and fatal experiments!

ELIZ. A traveller! a beautiful Arabian girl, was here but last night; she was seeking Felix De Lacey, the brother of Agatha, to whom she had been betrothed—she gave me the information that the family are but a short distance from 'hence—the Valley of the Lake.

FRANK. And Agatha there?—Agatha! there is yet life and hope for me—Ah no. *(Aside.)* The dreadful monster I have formed!—away with thought! Elizabeth, I will instantly seek her. Agatha's smiles shall move this heavy pressure—to the Valley of the Lake.—Farewell, sister, farewell!

*(Embraces Elizabeth, and Exit hastily)*[45]

[ELIZ. Unfortunate Frankenstein!—what can thus agitate him?—he will
[not hint the mysterious calamity to his affectionate sister—but he flies
[now to seek her who possessed his first love, and Agatha will sooth
[his mind to its former peaceful state—Ah Love! All potent Love!—If
[care or misfortune prey on my heart, I have only to think of Clerval, and
[be happy.—

[SONG—ELIZABETH
[When evening breezes mildly blow,
  [And all day's tumults cease;
[Where streams in gentle murmurs flow;
  [And all around breathes peace—
[What shall my pensive mind employ,
  [From ev'rything free?[46]
[I'll turn to life's best dearest joy,
  [And think of Love and Thee!

[When pleasure's smile no longer gleams,
  [And sorrow weighs my breast
[When hope withdraws its placid beams
  [I sink with care opprest—
[Ah whither shall my heart then turn,
  [To what sweet refuge flee?
[With passion's fire it then shall burn
  [And throb with love and thee.                    *(Exit)*]

45. Dick's version ends this scene here, with both of them exiting. 46. This is a conjecture from the Larpent version's "From ev'ry to free."

SCENE II   *A wood in the neighbourhood of Geneva. A Bush—A Gypsy's fire flaming, over which hangs a cauldron. A group of Gypsies discovered surrounding the fire in various positions. All laugh as the scene discovers them. When Tanskin, Hammerpan, with others (male and female) advance to sing the following*[47]

CHORUS

Urge the slow rising smoke,
Give the faggot a poke,
For unroof'd rovers are we;
Whilst our rags flutt'ring fly,
We the brown skin espy,
Our vellum of pedigree.
Behold each tawney face
Of our hard-faring race,
Which[48] the cold blast ne'er can feel;
See our glossy hair wave,
Hear us, loud, as we crave
But dumb only when we steal![49]

TANS. I tell you it was even so, friend Hammerpan—a giant creature with something of a human shape; but ugly and terrible to behold as you would paint the Devil.

HAM. And does this monster any mischief, or is he a pacific monster?

TANS. I never heard of any being harmed by him!

HAM. Then why are you so frightened, "Master" Tanskin? For my part, should he come across my path, let who will fly, I'll stand my ground like an anvil!

TANS. And get "well" beat like one for your pains.

"*Flute heard.*

"What sounds are those?

HAM. "(*Returning to the fire.*) Why, 'tis Felix, the son of old De Lacey. "The young fellow is much famed for his excellence upon the flute, as the "father for his piety, charities, and twanging on the harp, which, together "with the beauty of his daughter, seems to have turned the heads and won "the hearts of all the surrounding country." Now[50] my merry wanderers, our meal is smoking. I'faith, I'm in a rare relishing humour for it, so, prithee, Dame, ladle us our porridge, with a whole dead sheep in it. Fegs, it scents rarely! (*Sniffs.*)[51]

---

47. The Larpent version indicates that there is "a platform at the back." 48. Dick's version has "Whilst." 49. The Larpent version has Tanskin and Hammerpan enter after the chorus. 50. Dick's version has "But come." 51. Dick's version has "ladle us our porridge. Fegs, it scents rarely! (*Sniffs.*) Leeks, mutton porridge, with a whole dead sheep in it." "Fegs" is apparently a meaningless word used in exclamations of astonishment.

*Music.—The gipsies crowd round the fire with their bowls. The Demon rapidly crosses the platform at the back—Disappears.*[52]

1ST GYP.[53] Hilliho!—what tall bully's that? the steeple of Ingoldstadt taking a walk. See yonder, comrades!

HAM. See what?

TANS. *(Trembling.)* As I'm a living rogue, 'tis he!

HAM. One of the Devil's grenadier's, mayhap! Pooh, pooh! Old Tanskin, we all know you are a living rogue, but you won't frighten us with with your ten feet. "Come," give me a drink, I say.

*One of the gipsies gives him a wooden bowl.*

Gentlemen Gipsies, here's all your good—"ha! ha! ha!—"

*Music.—The Demon appears on an eminence of the bush, or a projecting rock.*

Help! murder! wouns! 'tis the Devil himself! away with the porridge!

*Music. Throws bowl away. Hammerpan and all the Gipsies shriek and run off. The Demon descends, pourtrays by action his sensitiveness of light and air, perceives the gipsies's fire, which excites his admiration—thrusts his hand into the flame, withdraws it hastily in pain. Takes out a lighted piece of stick, compares it with another faggot which has not been ignited. Takes the food expressive of surprise and pleasure. A flute is heard, without. The Demon, breathless with delight, eagerly listens. It ceases—he expresses disappointment. Footsteps heard and the Demon retreats behind the rock.*[54]

*Enter Agatha, followed by Felix, his flute slung at his back.*

AGA. Those sweet sounds recall happier days to my memory.—[55] In the midst of [our] poverty, how consoling it is to possess such a brother as you are. Dear, thoughtful Felix, the first little white flower that peeped out from beneath the snowy ground you brought, because you thought it would give pleasure to your poor Agatha.

FELIX. We are the children of misfortune; [Agatha—] poverty's chilling grasp nearly annihilates us. Our poor blind father, now the inmate of yon[56] cottage—he who has been blessed with prosperity to be thus reduced—the noble-minded old De Lacey. Wretched man that I am, to have been the cause of ruin to both father and sister.

---

52. In Dick's version, the creature does not yet appear. 53. In Dick's version, this speech is given to Tanskin; "*Pointing off,*" he opens the speech differently: "See there! that's he! that's the tall bully. He looks like the steeple of Ingoldstadt taking a walk." Ingoldstadt is in Bavaria, Germany, north of Munich. 54. The creature's actions enact experiences mentioned in the novel, Chapter Eleven. Dick's version does not have the business with the flute, and has the creature hide behind a bush. 55. Dick's version substitutes a longer passage for this first sentence: "Yes, my dear Felix, our father is anxious for your return. He bade me seek you, and conducted by the mellifluous sounds of your flute, the task was not one of great difficulty. Oh, Felix! how delightful is the reflection that both you and my father possess the skill of banishing for a few moments the horrors of our present misery." 56. Dick's version has "our."

AGA. Why,[57] Felix, we suffered in a virtuous cause! Poor Safie, thy beloved—

FELIX. Is, I fear, lost to me for ever. The treacherous Mahometan, her father, whose escape I aided from a dungeon in Paris (where he was confined as a State prisoner), that false father has doubtless arrived at Constantinople, and is triumphing at the fate of his wretched dupes.

AGA. Nay, Felix—

FELIX. Alas, Agatha! for aiding that escape, my family—my beloved family—are suffering exile and total confiscation of fortune.

AGA. But Safie still loves you?

FELIX. That thought is the more maddening! Safie! fairest Safie!—and she was my promised reward for liberating her faithless father—dragged away with him and forced to comply with his obdurate wishes. "Oh," she is lost "—lost" to me for ever!

[AGA. Let not hope forsake you, Felix—

FELIX. [Agatha! It requires resignation to bear our heavy woes.] The early passion of each of us has been blighted, our rigorous imprisonment and sudden banishment have driven all trace of thee from thy admirer, "young" Frankenstein.

AGA. Dear Felix, press not more wretched recollections on my mind. I consider Frankenstein lost to me for ever. In abject poverty, dare I hope that the brilliant and animated student could e'er think of the unfortunate Agatha. *(Weeps.)* Let me dry these unworthy tears and exert a woman's firmest fortitude. My soul is henceforth devoted exclusively to the service of my poor dark father. Felix, you shall behold me no longer unhappy.

### DUETT—FELIX AND AGATHA[58]

Of all the knots which Nature ties,
The secret, sacred sympathies,
That, as with viewless chains of gold,
The heart a happy prisoner hold,
None is more chaste—more bright—more pure,
Stronger, stern trials to endure;
None is more pure of earthly leaven,
More like the love of highest heaven,
Than that which binds, in bonds how blest
A daughter to a father's breast.               *(Exeunt)*

*Music.—The Demon cautiously ventures out—his mantle having been caught by the bush, he disrobes himself, leaving the mantle attached to the rock; he watches*

*Felix and Agatha with wonder and rapture, appears irresolute whether he dares to follow them; he hears the flute of Felix, stands amazed and pleased, looks around him, snatches at the empty air, and with clenched hands puts them to each ear—appears vexed at his disappointment in not possessing the sound; rushes forward afterwards, again listens, and, delighted with the sound, steals off, catching at it with his hands.*

SCENE III    *Exterior of the Cottage of Old De Lacey. On right, a hovel, with a low door, near which are two or three large logs of wood and a hatchet; a small basket with violets on a stool at the right side of the cottage door, and a stool also on the left side of the cottage, whereon De Lacey is discovered seated, leaning on his cane, a common harp at his side.—Music.*

DEL. Another day is added to the life of banished De Lacey![59] *(Rises and comes forward.)* But how will it be passed—like the preceding days—in wretched poverty, hopeless grief, and miserable darkness! *(Calls.)* Agatha! Felix! Alas! I am alone! Hark—no—I thought I heard footsteps[60]—my children come. They must not suppose me cheerless—my lute[61] is here—'tis a fair deceit on them—this lute which has so oft been damped with the tears from my sightless eyes—the sound of it is the only indication I can give that I am contented with my lot!

*Music.—De Lacey returns to his seat and plays several chords. The Demon enters, attracted by the lute, suddenly perceives De Lacey, and approaches towards him—expresses surprise by action that De Lacey does not avoid him—discovers his loss of sight, which the Demon appears to understand by placing his hand over his own eyes, and feeling his way. At the conclusion of the music on the lute—occasioned, as it were, by the Demon having placed his hand on the instrument—a short pause, and during which the Demon, having lost the sound, appears to be looking for it, when the lute music is again resumed. In the midst of the music (without ceasing) a voice is heard.*

"FELIX. *(Within.)* This way, Agatha."

*The Demon, alarmed, observes the little door of hovel, which he pushes open, signifies that he wishes for shelter, and retreats into this hovel or wood-house by the ending of the lute music by De Lacey, when Enter Felix and Agatha.*

FELIX. *(Apart to Agatha.)* Observe his countenance, beaming with benevolence and love—behold those silver hairs—and, Agatha, I—I have reduced him to this pitiable state of poverty!

59. Dick's version has "to the banished life of De Lacey." 60. Dick's version has "Hark! 'tis the flute of Felix!" 61. Dick's version has "harp"; it later has "my harp" for "this lute."

AGA. Cease, Felix—this self reproach? (*Goes to De Lacey.*[62]) We have returned, dear father. Have you wanted us?

*Agatha leads her father forward.*

DEL. No, no, Agatha! You anticipate all my wants, and perform every little office of affection with gentleness.

AGA. Is it not my duty, and am I not rewarded by your kind smiles?

DEL. Amiable girl, let thy poor father kiss thee. (*They embrace.*) Felix, my son, where are you? (*Felix comes forward, and takes his hand.*) Now I am cheerful—I am happy!—indeed I am, my children. Let me encourage you to cast off your gloom. What—a tear, Agatha!

AGA. Nay, dear sir!

DEL. 'Tis on my hand. (*Pressing her hand to his lips, which he had held in his while speaking to Felix.*)

[*The Demon appears watching them with attention and interest.*

FELIX. [(*Apart.*) At first my father's countenance was illuminated with [pleasure—but thoughtfulness and sadness have again succeeded—] (*Assuming gaiety.*) Now must I "to" labour again. Our [stock of] fuel is nearly exhausted. My time has been lately so occupied I have omitted my task in the forest.

*Music.—Felix takes up a hatchet and chops a log of wood.*

[AGA. And I, too, have been neglectful[63]—these flowers of which you [are so fond, my dear father, have wither'd—they must be replaced— [*Music—she takes them from the basket—Felix is busied cutting the wood—*]

SAFIE. (*At a distance.*) Felix!

AGA. What voice was that?

"FELIX. It cannot be—no—it was but fancy!

"*Music resumed.—Felix chops the log in continuance—at a similar break in the* "*tune the same voice heard again, nearer.*

"SAFIE. (*Without.*) Felix!

"*No music.*"

FELIX. That magic sound! Alas! no—there is no such happiness in store for me!

SAFIE. (*Without, louder.*) Felix! Felix!

*Music.—Felix drops the hatchet, rushes forward.—At the same instant Safie enters, and falls into the arms of Felix—pronouncing* "Felix."

FELIX. 'Tis she!—Safie! Beloved of my soul!—Ah! revive!

DEL. Safie, the traitor's daughter? Impossible!

AGA. 'Tis, indeed, our sweet Safie!

62. Dick's version has "her father." 63. Corrected from the Larpent version's "have been neglected."

FELIX. We never will part more! Father! father! would that you could behold her! It is my dear, lost Safie.

*Music.—Safie revives, and crosses to old De Lacey, kneels, and kisses his hand, during which the Demon appears at the little hovel, watching them, and then retires within again.*[64]

DEL. Bless you, my child! where is your father—where the treacherous friend who devoted us to ignominy?

SAFIE. *(Rises.)* I have fled from him; he would have sacrificed his daughter, loathing the idea that I should be united to one of Christian faith. [Sickening at the prospect of again returning to Asia and being immured [in a harem—ill suited to the temper of my soul now accustomed to a [nobler emulation—] I "—I" have sought the love and protection of my Felix!

FELIX. Faithful girl! Your constancy shall be crowned by eternal love and gratitude.

AGA. But Safie, you are fatigued. Come, dear girl, and on my lowly couch, seek repose.

*Music.—Safie affectionately kisses and presses De Lacey's hand, embraces Felix, crosses back to Agatha, and is led into the cottage by Agatha and Felix.*

FELIX. *(Who returns with a gun from the cottage-door.)* Father, I am wild with joy!—no longer the sad, pining Felix. The sun of prosperity again gleams on us—Safie is[65] returned! I am rich!—happy! But hold! I must procure refreshment for our guest. Our larder is not too much encumbered with provision. I'll to the village—I'll cross the forest—I'll hunt, shoot—and all in ecstasy! Farewell, father! I'll soon be back. Farewell!

[*Music.—Exit Felix.—The Demon ventures out, and looks with a kind expression [on De Lacey.*

[DEL. Good Felix! Now, by the return of Safie will his hopes be re-[warded—yet must he remain in perpetual poverty and unceasing labour. [But this instant, did he complain that our store of fuel was consumed—[unless he possessed superhuman strength his day's employment must be [doubled—where are my favorite violets?

[*Music.—De Lacey feels for the Basket which contained them—the Demon ap-[pears to comprehend his wish, and rushes off.*

[DEL. My flower basket not yet replenished.—My dear children amply [repay my former anxious care—they have toiled for my support though-[out our misfortunes—

[*Music.—The Demon re-enters cautiously and tremblingly with a handful of [flowers, which he gently places in the basket.*

---

64. In the Larpent version, the creature had already appeared, above. 65. Dick's version has "has."

[DEL. Thanks dear Agatha!—ever watchful of your poor father's com-
[fort—]

*Music.—De Lacey turns up the stage, and again seats himself on the cottage
stool.—The Demon examines log of wood, takes up hatchet, points to the wood,
intimating he understands the use of it—Agatha appearing at the window—The
Demon rushes off with the hatchet.—Music ceases.*

DEL. Agatha!

*Enter Agatha from cottage.*

AGA. Did you call, father?

DEL. Sleeps your sweet guest?

AGA. Fatigue will soon lull her to repose. I should not have left her had I
not thought I heard you call me. [Ah, father, some one has punished my
[negligence by replenishing your basket of violets.

[DEL. Did you not fill it, Agatha?

[AGA. No, dear sir.—Ah, Felix has forestalled me.]

*Exit Agatha into cottage again.*

DEL. [No person has been here since the departure of Felix.] *(De Lacey
rises and takes up the basket of flowers from the stool. Smelling the violets.)* How
delightful is the perfume!—more exquisite because I am debarred the
pleasure of beholding these sweet emblems of spring! The touch and
scent elevate my spirits! How ungrateful am I to complain! In the contemplation of thee, oh, Nature, the past will be blotted from my memory!—the present is tranquil, and the future gilded by bright rays of hope
and anticipated joy![66]

*Music.—De Lacy replaces the basket of flowers, and returns to his seat, leaning
pensively on his cane.—The Demon enters with a pile of green faggots with foliage
on his shoulders and throws them loosely on the stage.—Smiles with gratulation at
that which he has accomplished.—Approaches De Lacey, falls flat at his feet, then
kneels to him, and is about to press his hand.—De Lacey feels around him with his
cane and hand, without the knowledge of anyone being near him, and seated all the
time—then calls.*

DEL. "Agatha! Agatha!"

*Music.—The Demon instantly retreats into hovel, and Agatha enters from cottage
door.*

Agatha, child, I pray you lead me in. *(Rises from his seat and comes forward.)*

AGA. "Yes, father." Good Heavens! why, Felix could not have returned
from the forest so quickly? What a quantity of wood!

DEL. How?

66. Dick's version has "anticipations of joy!"

AGA. Here is fuel to last us for a long time. [—Surely some kind spirit [watches over us—or] how could we have been so bountifully supplied? Come, father, to the cottage—come!

*Music.—Agatha leads De Lacy into cottage, afterwards comes forward.*[67]

"—Frankenstein! vain is the endeavour to drive you from my recollection. "Each bird that sings, each note of music that I hear, reminds me of the "sweet moments of my former love!

"SONG—AGATHA

"*(Flute accompaniment, behind the scenes.)*
"In vain I view the landscapes round,
   "Or climb the highest hill;
"In vain, in vain, I listen to the sound
   "Of ev'ry murmuring rill.
"For vain is all I hear or see,
"When Victor dear is far from me.     *(Thrice.)*
"But hark, hark, hark,
"My love, my love is near,
"His well-known dulcet notes I hear.     *(Thrice.)*

"Oh, yes, my love is near,
   "I hear him in the grove;
"Soon will he be here,
   "And breathe soft vows of love.
"Oh, fly not yet, ye blissful hours,
   "Oh, fly not yet away;
"While love its soft enchanting pours,
   "Prolong, prolong your stay!     *(Thrice.)*
"Oh, yes, my love is near,
   "I hear him in the grove,
"Soon will he be here,
   "And breathe soft vows of love!

"*(Exit Agatha into cottage)*"

SCENE IV   *A Wild Forest.*

*Enter Felix, with his gun.*

FELIX. Not a shot yet—and, egad, joy has made my hand so unsteady, that were a fine pheasant to get up, I could not bring it down again. Thy

---

67. The Larpent version ends here with the following stage direction: "*Music.—Agatha leads De Lacey into the Cottage—The Demon peeps from behind the wood—creeps to window, and watches them with interest and affection.—*"

return, sweet Safie, has restored me to existence. When I thought I had lost thee for ever, I was occupied by gloomy thoughts, and neither heeded the descent of the evening star nor the golden sunrise reflected on the lake; but now my love fills my imagination, and all is enjoyment!

SONG—FELIX

Thy youthful charms, bright maid, inspire
    And grace my fav'rite theme,
Whose person kindles soft desire,
    Whose mind secures esteem.
Oh, hear me then my flame avow,
    And fill my heart[68] with joy—
A flame which taught by time to grow,
    No time can e'er destroy.
My tender suit with smiles approve,
And share the sweets of mutual love.

When autumn yields her ripen'd corn,
    Or winter, darkening, lowers,
With tenderest care I'll soothe thy morn,
    And cheer thy evening hours.
Again, when smiling spring returns,
    We'll breathe the vernal air;
And still when summer sultry burns,
    To woodland walks repair—
There seek retirement's sheltered grove,
    And share the sweets of mutual love.

*Felix retires up stage.*
*Enter Frankenstein.*

FRANK. In vain do I seek a respite from these dreadful thoughts—where'er I turn my eyes, I expect to behold the supernatural Being!—to see him spring from each woody recess—but on, on to Agatha, and repose.

FELIX. A traveller! and surely I know his air and manner. *(Comes forward.)*

FRANK. Good stranger, can you direct me to the habitation of old De Lacey?

FELIX. Better than most persons, I trust.

FRANK. How! Felix De Lacey!

FELIX. The same! the same! Frankenstein! You know, my friend[69]—'tis long since we have met.

68. Dick's version has "breast." 69. Dick's version has "your hand, my friend."

FRANK. Your strange and sudden disappearance from Paris—

FELIX. Makes as strange a story, with which I shall not now detain you.
Come to our humble cottage. [—Ah, Frankenstein, we have been as poor
[as mice, and our dwelling is not much larger than a trap—] Egad! I'm
overjoyed to see you!

FRANK. And Agatha?

FELIX. [Is queen of the Castle!—and between ourselves Frankenstein] has
still a warm corner of her heart for you. Come, we have only to cross the
wood. [—I'm in high spirits, my friend—I've this day recover'd my mis-
[tress—but that will make another strange story.—This is indeed a lucky
[day—Safie is restored—and I ramble out to kill a Pheasant, and pop
[upon a philosopher who is likely to become a brother-in-law—]

HAM. *(Without.)* Any good Christians in the neighbourhood?

FELIX. What have we here?

*Enter Hammerpan, with a long pole, tinker's utensils, fire kettle, &c.*

HAM. Real Christians! human beings! Oh, good Gentlemen, have you
seen it?

FELIX. It!—what?

HAM. Ah! that's it! As I live, I saw it an hour ago in the forest![70]

FELIX. What do you mean by *it?*

HAM. My hair stood on end like mustard and cress, and so will yours
when you see it!

FELIX. Get you gone! you are tipsy!

HAM. I wish I was. "As" I take it, you are Master Felix, of the Valley of
the Lake; we've done business "together" before now.

FELIX. I know you not!

HAM. I mended your kettle t'other day. You did me a good turn—one
good turn deserves another—I'll put you on your guard—the very devil
is abroad.

FRANK. *(Aside.)* How!

FELIX. *(Laughs.)* Ha! ha! "ha!" You romancing tinker! [—and pray how
[was his worship dressed?

HAM. [Dress'd—why it was stark undressed all but a cloak.] You may
laugh, but the other gentleman don't laugh. You may perceive *he* believes
"it". *(To Frankenstein.)* I saw it—"I" saw with *this one eye.*

FELIX. One eye!

HAM. Yes, I'm blind of the other[71]—a little boy threw a pebble at it, so[72]
I've been *stone* blind ever since, gentlemen. He was ten foot six long,

---

70. Dick's version has "As I live, an hour ago, I saw it in the forest!" 71. Dick's version has
"I've lost the other." 72. Dick's version has "and."

*(Holds his pole high up.)* with a head of black lanky locks down to his very elbows.

FRANK. 'Tis the Demon! *(Apart to himself.)*

[HAM. I lifted up my hammer to strike it but I was so tremulous that I [knock'd my own head instead.]

FRANK. What did this strange object? *(To Hammerpan.)*

HAM. It didn't speak to me, nor I to *it*. "I saw it at first in the forest "picking acorns and berries—and then," after it had dispersed our tribe, like a ferret among the rats—it took a drink at[73] our broth, and burnt its fingers in our fire.

FRANK. And what became of this creature?

HAM. I wasn't curious enough to inquire. My wife was in fits at the sight of the devil—so I was obliged to keep my "one" eye upon her.

FELIX. Your one eye has been pretty well employed. Come, come, gipsy, we'll cross the wood and see if this man mountain is to be met.

HAM. The good genius of wandering tinkers forbid!

FELIX. *(To Frankenstein.)* And now, my friend, we'll on to the cottage.

FRANK. "So, so!" *(Apart.)* I will follow ye!

*(Exeunt Felix and Hammerpan)*

So! the peasants have already been terrified by the ungainly form! Ambitious experimentalist! The consciousness of the crime I have committed eternally haunts me! "I have indeed drawn a horrible curse on my head!" He may be malignant, and delight [for its own sake] in murder and wretchedness! a whole country may execrate me as their[74] pest! Every thought that bears towards my baneful project causes my lips to quiver and [my] heart to palpitate. [But, away with these wretched reflections—] I must now to the cottage of Felix. Agatha, fairest Agatha, [fairest Ag-[atha,] instead of smiles, your lover will meet you with dark and hopeless despondency!

*(Exit Frankenstein)*

SCENE V  *Evening.—Interior of the cottage of De Lacey.—The thatched roof in sight. A wood fire.—Through an open rustic porch are visible a rivulet, and small wooden bridge—a wooden couch—Music.—De Lacey discovered seated thereon, with Agatha next him in attendance. The Demon appears through the portico, watching them, and regards Agatha with rapture.—Agatha kisses her father's hand, takes a small pail or hand bucket, and trips through the portico on to the bridge to procure water. The Demon having retreated on Agatha's approach, pursues her on the bridge. Agatha, turning suddenly perceives the Demon, screams loudly, and swoons, falling into the rivulet.[75]*

73. Dick's version has "of." 74. Dick's version has "its." 75. This scene is handled differently in Dick's version; see the end of the act for Dick's text.

DEL. Gracious Heaven—that cry of horror! Agatha!

*The Demon leaps from the bridge and rescues her.*

DEL. Gracious Heaven—that cry of Horror!—Agatha! My sweet child, where art thou?—Agatha, Agatha!

*Music.—The Demon places Agatha, insensible, on a bench near De Lacey.*

DEL. This silence—this suspense is dreadful!

*The Demon tenderly guides the hand of De Lacey and places it on Agatha.*

DEL. My child—cold, cold, and insensible!—this mystery—cruel fate—Dead?—no, no, no, her heart still beats.—Kind Heaven has saved me that pang!—Felix, Felix, where art thou? My dear daughter, for your poor father's sake revive!

*Music.—Agatha recovers.—The Demon hangs over them, with fondness. Felix and Frankenstein suddenly enter.*

FRANK. Misery! The Demon!

FELIX. What horrid monster is this?—Agatha, my father is in danger?

*The Demon retreats.*

*Music.—Felix discharges his gun and wounds the Demon, who writhes under the wound.—In desperation pulls a burning branch from the fire—rushes at them—beholds Frankenstein—in agony of feeling dashes through the portico.*

*Safie Enters to Agatha.—Hurried Music.*

### FINALE

Tell us—tell us—what form was there?
(With anxious fear enquiring)
Saw you its Eye—the hideous glare
Terrific dread inspiring!

*The Demon is seen climbing the outside of the Portico. He bursts through the thatch with burning brand.*

The fiend of Sin
With ghastly grin!
Behold the Cottage firing!

*The Demon hangs to the Rafters, setting light to the thatch and Rafters, with malignant joy—as parts of the building fall—groups of gypsies appear on the bridge, and through the burning appertures—who join in the Chorus.*

#### FULL CHORUS OF GYPSIES

Beware! Beware!
The hideous glare,
The fiend of Sin
With ghastly grin—
Behold the cottage firing.

*Felix forces his way through the flames with his father and Safie—Frankenstein rushes out with Agatha.*[76]

**END OF ACT II**

## ACT III

SCENE I    *The Garden of Elizabeth, at Belrive.—Morning. (Same as Act I, Scene ii.)*

*Enter Clerval from terrace entrance.*

CLER. What a delightful morning! It is an auspicious commencement of the day which is to make me happy in the possession of my love! Elizabeth yet sleeps, peaceful be her slumbers! [Love has awakened me—the

76. Dick's version offers this scene after Agatha falls in the rivulet:
*The Monster leaps from the bridge, and rescues her.*
DEL. *(Speaks during the melo-music.)* Gracious Heaven! *(Starting forward from the couch.)* That cry of horror! Agatha!—Despair!—My sweet child where art you? Agatha! Agatha!
*The Monster appears at the portico entrance, with Agatha insensible in his arms.—The Monster comes forward, gently places Agatha in her father's arms, tenderly guiding the hand of old De Lacey to support his daughter.—Agatha recovers, and perceiving the Monster, with a shriek, faints—the Monster hovering over them with fondness.—Felix, with his gun (loaded), suddenly enters through the open portico, and speaks whilst entering.*
FELIX. Agatha! Victor Frankenstein is here! What horrid monster is this! Agatha!—my father in danger!
*Music.—The Monster retreats, Felix following him—discharges his gun—wounds the Monster in the shoulder—who writhes under the agony of the wound from which the blood flows—would rush on Felix, who keeps the gun presented—he is deterred by fear of a repetition of the wound. Felix remaining on the defensive.—Safie, alarmed at the firing of the gun by Felix, rushes on to Agatha and De Lacey.—Enter Frankenstein through the portico. The Monster rushes up to Frankenstein, and casts himself at his feet, imploring protection.*
FRANK. Misery! the Fiend! Hence, avoid me! do not approach me—thy horrid contact would spread a pestilence throughout my veins!—hence—no, no! You shall not quit this spot—but thus—thus I destroy the wretch I have created!
*Music.—Frankenstein endeavours to stab him with his dagger, which the Monster strikes from his hand—and expresses that his kindly feeling towards the human race, have been met by abhorrence and violence; that they are all now converted into hate and vengeance.—In desperation, the Monster pulls a flaming brand from the fire, and in agony of feeling, dashes through the portico, setting fire to the whole of the portico, and the entire back of the cottage—the thatched roof and rafters.*
FELIX. Ha! Frankenstein! 'tis no time to parley—the cottage is on fire! that fierce gigantic figure of terrific aspect waves aloft his torch, as if in triumph of the deed.
*The large doors in the centre are suddenly closed from without, as if to prevent escape. A coarse yelling laugh is heard.*
FRANK. Ha! 'tis that hideous voice! Quick, quick, let us fly! his hellish malice pursues me, and but with his death or mine, will this persecution cease. Could I but place you beyond his power.

[freshness of the air, and the beauty of the scenery animate me to the [height of cheerfulness—] soft, she approaches.

*Enter Elizabeth from the house.*

Elizabeth, my love, why that look of anxiety?

ELIZ. Oh, Clerval! We have had strange occurrences since you quitted me yesternight,[77] our house is full of guests, my brother has brought here the family of De Lacey of whom you have heard me so often speak—

CLER. The family of De Lacey, the relatives of Agatha.

ELIZ. By some extraordinary mystery, which is yet unexplained to me, the cottage in which Frankenstein discovered his mistress and her family was destroyed by fire; they arrived late last night and all appear overcome with fatigue and terror; some dreadful calamity hangs about my dear brother.

CLER. How astonishing is his conduct. Alas! my sweet Elizabeth, "in the "midst of all this misery I am selfish"—I trust these singular occurrences will not postpone our marriage. Consider, our friends are invited, the church is prepared.

ELIZ. A few hours may explain all.[78] See now *(Looks towards house.)* Frankenstein approaches—observe his agitated countenance and restless step; he has not slept since his return—he has armed himself with pistols and appears continually watching.

CLER. We will retire and avoid him for the present. This way, "love."

*(Exeunt)*

*Music.—Enter Frankenstein from house.*

FRANK. How am I to avoid[79] the powerful vengeance of the monster formed by my cursed ambition. I gave him energy and strength, to crush my own guilty head! My hours pass in dread, and soon the bolt may fall which will deprive me of existence! [The diabolical act I have committed [in raising a being, recurs each moment and conscience stricken—I shud-[der to think—Agatha! Agatha! gladly would I sacrifice my own life to

---

*Felix and Frankenstein (as soon as the Monster disappears, having climbed outside of the portico) force open the doors, when flaming faggots are thrown down at the portico entrance, and falling trees on fire block up the entrance. Felix and Frankenstein place the couch longways over the fallen trees, and fiery pile of faggots at the portico entrance, and Felix forces his way through the flames with old De Lacey, and then Safie—and, lastly, Frankenstein rushes out, bearing Agatha in his arms over the couch, in the midst of which parts of the building fall. The Monster brandishing the burning brand on the bridge, laughs exultingly, on which the drop falls.—Continue the 'Presto music' until*

**END OF ACT II**

77. Dick's version has "yesterday." 78. Dick's version has "explain these mysterious transactions." 79. Dick's version has "Oh! how to avoid."

[preserve yours—] Yet the Demon[80] preserved the life of Agatha—he had some feeling of affection—[and] how were those feelings requited!—by detestation, scorn, and wounds!—his look of everlasting malice! He will watch with the wiliness of a serpent, that he may sting with its venom! There is no hope but in the destruction of the Demon.[81] *(Takes out pistol.)* I must not cease to guard and protect my friends. *(Going to the door.)* Agatha has arisen. *(Conceals pistol.)*

*Enter Agatha, a locket round her neck, from the house.*

AGA. Frankenstein, I behold you unhappy—flying to solitude—and I cannot help supposing that you might regret the renewal of our connexion.[82] [Do you not love another?

[FRANK. Agatha! Can you forgive my cold neglect? At the sight of you, [my long smothered passion bursts out anew—but I thought you lost— [receive me once again with smiles and bring me back to life and hope.

AGA. [These transports ill accord with the heavy gloom which pervades [you—] Dear Frankenstein, I still love you, and confess that in my airy dreams of futurity you have been my constant friend and companion.

FRANK. [Blessed Sounds—] Agatha, you shall be mine! I will then divulge to you the secret which disturbs—nay, distracts me.

*Music, the Harmonica.—Distant church bells.*

Those cheerful chimes announce the wedding day of Elizabeth and Clerval! [This way—Agatha—] My care-worn looks will but damp their merriment.

*(Music.—Exeunt Frankenstein and Agatha)*

*Enter Felix and Safie from house.*

FELIX. Listen, Safie, to those merry village bells; they ring a rare contrast to our last night's misery. Soon, my eastern Rose, will they chime for us; and then away with care. This kiss—*(Embracing her.)*

SAFIE. Fie, Felix! in open daylight. You will deepen the blush of your Eastern rose.

### DUET—SAFIE AND FELIX[83]

Come with me, dear, to my mountain home,
And Hymen[84] shall hallow the peaceful dome.
Leave all the world for love and for me,
And I will be all the world to thee.
Our life shall be all holiday—
Shall be all holiday.
Come o'er the dew-bespangled vale,

80. Dick's version has "Yet *he* preserved." 81. Dick's version has "but in his destruction." 82. Dick's version has "intercourse." 83. The Larpent version indicates a "duett" but does not give the text. 84. The god of marriage.

Where the violet blue and primrose pale
Peep from the verdant shade.
Come o'er the dew-bespangled vale,
Where the violet blue and primrose pale,
Where the violet blue and primrose pale
Peep from the verdant shade.
Come o'er the dew, &c., &c.

We'll fly to the shady grove,
And sign and whisper, love
Till day begins to fade,
Till day begins, &c., &c.
We'll roam, and I will woo thee, love,
Where birds sing sweetly through the grove—
Where birds sing sweetly thro' the grove
Till day begins to fade.

We'll roam, and I will woo thee, love,
Where birds sing sweetly thro' the grove—
While birds sing, &c., &c., &c.

*Music, with the Bells.—Enter Madame Ninon, leading a group of Dancing Villagers, from the terrace entrance, and Elizabeth, with Clerval, re-enter.*

NIN. Now, Madame Elizabeth—now, Mr. Clerval—we are "all" ready, and the priest is in waiting.

*Music resumed.—Elizabeth and Clerval, as also Safie and Felix, join the procession, and all the villagers dance off to music along the terrace, except Madame Ninon.*

NIN. There they go to be coupled, pretty dears! *(Calls.)* Fritz! Fritz! where is my stupid husband? I've stretched my neck out of joint looking for him. I expect him from the market at Geneva with a cargo of eatables and my new-fashioned beehive cap—all for our wedding festival "of Mr. "Frankenstein, who has brought his bride and family here in conse- "quence, as I am told, of their cottage being accidentally destroyed by fire "last night." Oh! here the fellow comes, with a basket on his back, creeping like a snail.

*Enter Fritz, from terrace entrance, with hamper at his back containing various articles, a lady's cap, and a live duck.*

FRITZ. Here I am, spousy. I've brought your list of articles.

*Ninon assists him in putting down his basket.*

There's[85] the trout, and the sugar-loaf, and the melons, and the nutmegs.

---

85. Dick's version has "Here's."

NIN. But dear Fritz, where's my new beehive [cap] you were to bring from the milliner's at Geneva?

FRITZ. Somewhere, I know. *(Looking and examining the contents of the hamper, cautiously opening the top.)* The three live ducks are lying a top of the maccaroni, squeezed up under the large Gruyere cheese.

NIN. I hope to goodness my cap is not squeezed up!

FRITZ. It's quite safe, I tell you. I put it at the very bottom of the basket.

NIN. It will be in a nice state for my head, then!

FRITZ. Lord, here's a rummaging fuss for the cap. I was[86] so nervous about it—you cautioned me so, you know. *(Still kneeling and searching the hamper.)* "Oh, dear, where is it now?" Oh, la, to be sure, spousy—here it is "at last;" la, I knew it was safe. *(He pulls the cap out, with a live duck in it.)*

NIN. *(Takes her cap from him.)* Oh, Fritz, it's spoiled! That duck has been *laying* in it.

FRITZ. Not an egg, I hope, Ninon!

NIN. Alas! see how it is rumpled. *(She takes from the cap two or three of the duck's small feathers, which fall on the stage.)*

FRITZ. *(Aside.)* "Ha!—" he! he! Cap and feathers![87]

NIN. You careless, good for-nothing dog![88]

[FRITZ. *(Aside.)* Dog and Duck!][89]

NIN. Take the basket in, you sinner! *(Having first replaced her cap in the hamper.)*

FRITZ. Oh! *(To the duck.)* You look very jolly, my fine fellow, considering you are going to be killed for dinner. Wait till the peas are ready! I never seen such a piece of *quackery* as that cap in all my life!

*Draws the basket after him into the house, and comes forward during the duet.*

NIN. My finery destroyed by that varlet! But even *that* shall not disconcert me. My sweet mistress is united to-day to the man of her heart, and in spite of my cap[90] I will be merry, and dance till [I'm so old] I can dance no longer.

DUET—NINON AND FRITZ
(Welsh air.)

NIN.          Oh! I'll hail the wedding day,
              And be the gayest of the gay,
              Till age has tripp'd my steps away.

---

86. Dick's version has "I'm." 87. "Cap and feather days" are one's childhood. 88. Dick's version has "fellow." 89. Since "dog" can refer to the male of certain animals, as in "dog-fox," this may be a version of "ducks and drakes"; "to play at ducks and drakes" is to throw away one's money carelessly to make an impression. 90. Dick's version has "my loss."

| | |
|---|---|
| FRITZ. | *(Re-entering from house.)* Away! |
| NIN. | Your manners were not taught in France. |
| FRITZ. | La, wife! when you're too old to Dance— |
| | A horse at sixty—*(Aside.)*—cannot prance—[91] |
| | Ah, nay! |
| NIN. | While pipes and tabors playing sweetly, |
| | With all my soul I'll foot it featly, |
| FRITZ.. | Yes, I guess you'll hobble neatly. |
| | Wife! |
| NIN. | Don't wife me, you saucy fellow! |
| | Sure you're tipsy— |
| FRITZ. | Only mellow. |
| | We'll all be so, for that is fun and life! |
| TOGETHER. | { Don't wife me, you saucy fellow. |
| | { I won't wife you, I'm only mellow. |
| NIN. | I ne'er was tipsy. |
| FRITZ. | You ne'er was tipsy, only mellow. |
| | Wife! |

*Fritz dances her up to the house, Ninon turns, boxes his ear, and they exeunt into house.*

*Music.—The Demon appears from terrace entrance, watching about, and retreats as Fritz re-enters from house.*

FRITZ. Oh! *(Rubbing his cheek.)* What's the use of a fine cap to her? "she's "so short," unless she stood upon a chair, in the crowd—no one would see her, or her "new-fashioned" bee-hive either.

*During the above speech, William comes from the house, behind Fritz on tiptoe, and gives Fritz a smart smack on the back, who being fearfully alarmed, cries out lustily.*

Oh, bless my soul! There now, that's just the way to make me nervous again.[92] What do you want, Master William?

WILL. I can't get a soul to speak to me in the house—some are busy—some are going[93] to be married—will you play with me, Fritz?

FRITZ. I like a game of play—it's so relaxing. When work was over I used to play with my cow.[94]

WILL. *(Throwing a ball.)* Run and fetch that ball—

91. Dick's version has "you never learnt to dance, / A horse at fifty—*(Aside.)*—cannot prance." 92. Dick's version has "Oh, dear! who's that? There now, that's the way just to make me nervous again." 93. Dick's version has "gone." 94. Dick's version has "with my cow's calf." It also handles the rest of this scene differently:
WILL. Do play with me, Fritz.

FRITZ. Lauks, my dear, that's very fatiguing.—What a way you've thrown it—right among the cauliflowers.

*Music—Goes off. Demon suddenly appears at the railing—watches the Child—Fritz returns.*

FRITZ. Here it is, Master Willy! There's your ball, William Frankenstein.

WILL. Now again.

FRITZ. La—no—you give me more trouble than your brother used in his laboratory—when he—

*William throws the ball behind the balustrade.*

I won't fetch it—you may find it yourself—

*Demon points to William—intimating that the boy must be dear to Frankenstein.*

WILL. If you are too idle to go—I'm not—

FRITZ. I shan't look—

*William goes to the balustrade.—The Demon suddenly seizes him.*

WILL. Help! help! help!

FRITZ. Ah—that won't do—that won't do, young master—I'm not to be had—

WILL. Help! help!

*Music. The Demon stops the boy's mouth—and throws him across his shoulder—Fritz turns—sees them—utters a cry of horror—the Demon rushes off.*

FRITZ. Help! help! murder—wife! wife! the devil—oh my nerves!

*(Runs off)*


SCENE II    *A Country View. Rustic Church in the distance. A large Yew Tree, spread plentifully with boughs. Music.—A Foreground with pathway behind it. The procession, as before, returning from the marriage ceremony. The corps de ballet, Villagers, preceding, dancing, followed by Felix, Safie, Clerval, and Elizabeth.*

[CONGRATULATORY SESTETTO
[*Agatha—Safie—Elizabeth—Felix—Clerval and Bass*

[Since all to beauty's rip'ning bloom
[Their cheerful homage pay,

---

*Music.—Dances backwards towards the balustrade of terrace, when the Monster, during the foregoing speeches had been watching the child, then disappearing by falling flat on his face between the balustrades of the terrace, waits the opportunity as William is tripping backwards, and suddenly seizes the child, throws him across his shoulder (à la Rolla), and rushes off, terrace entrance, to hurried music. Fritz turning round, sees them, utters a cry of horror, and speaks through the music.*
FRITZ. Help, help, murder! Wife; the devil! Oh, my nerves!
*(Exit Fritz, frightened, into house)*
The phrase "à la Rolla" refers to the character in Sheridan's adaptation of Kotzebue, *Pizarro.*

[Be not displeas'd that we presume
[To hail thy bridal day.

[But if, by Time's all conquering hand,
[Thy bloom must wear away,
[The roses of thy mind shall stand
[And never more decay.]

NIN. *(Heard without.)* Oh, mistress! Oh!

FRITZ. I couldn't help it—murder!

*Ninon and Fritz enter.*

NIN. But where did you leave him?

FRITZ. He left me—Oh dear—*(Cries.)* Murder![95]

NIN. Oh wretched fate!

ELIZ. What is the matter, good Ninon?

NIN. William, your brother William is the matter; the boy is lost. I sent him to that Fritz, that he might be out of the way.

FRITZ. Yes; and now he's out of everybody's way.

ELIZ. This is most extraordinary—a frolic of the little rogue.

FRITZ. No, no, it isn't; I saw—"my nerves!" Oh, "dear!" I saw—a great something snatch him up. *(Cries.)*[96] I—oh dear—oh dear. Oh! murder!

CLER. Here's[97] Frankenstein.

*Enter Frankenstein, with a pistol.*

ELIZ. My dear Victor, know you aught of William? The child has been missed in a most unaccountable manner.

FRANK. My brother missing!

NIN. Fritz was with him.

FRITZ. Oh, master! a great creature—[wrapped in a mantle.] oh! "oh! "oh!" [*(Cries.)* murder!]

FRANK. [*(Aside.)* No sooner has the idea crossed my imagination than I [am convinced of its truth—the horrible Demon!]][98]

CLER. Hasten, my friends, one and all—all search. Our pastime is marr'd till the boy is found.

---

95. Dick's version alters this and the next few speeches:

FRITZ. I didn't leave him, he left me. Oh, dear. *(Cries.)* Murder! My nerves!

NINON. Oh, wicked Fritz!

ELIZ. What is the matter, good Ninon?

FRITZ. She says her husband's wicked.

NINON. *(To Elizabeth.)* William, your brother William is the matter; the boy is lost, no one can find him. I sent him to that Fritz, that he might be out of the way.

96. Dick's version has him cry, "I—oh!—oh—dear! Oh, oh, oh! Murder!"  97. Dick's version has "There's."  98. Dick's version has "Oh, horror!—the demon!"

*Music.—All exeunt in consternation at different entrances, excepting Franken-stein, who appears lost in desponding reverie.—He turns; the boughs of the yew tree are pulled apart, and the Demon is discovered behind it, with William in his grasp.—Frankenstein draws a pistol, and points it—the Demon holds forth the child, when Frankenstein lowers his pistol, and kneels.—The Demon again shoul-ders the child, and rushes off within the path.—Frankenstein rises, and pursues them in despair.*

SCENE III   *An Apartment in the Villa Belrive.—A wide folding window open-ing to the Garden, closed. A table with red baize covering.*

*Enter Agatha and Ninon.*

NIN. The most unaccountable disappearance of my dear little boy, at such a moment—on such a day—when we should have been so merry!

AGA. It is indeed strange and fearful; let us hope that William will soon be discovered, and brought home. *(Aside.)* The wild phantom that fired our cottage, surely, is not concerned.

NIN. I can do nothing but think of William—that is your room, ma'am— *(Pointing to the door.)*—you will find it well furnished—with such sweet blue eyes—everything is comfortable—unhappy little boy! There's a fire[99] grate in the room—with two little dimples on each cheek! There's a cabinet in the corner—curly locks! Forgive me, ma'am; I fostered the pretty child, and I cannot get him out of my head.

AGA. Pray leave me, Ninon, and give me "the" earliest intelligence of Mr. Frankenstein's return.

NIN. All the festivities of the wedding-day destroyed, till this[100] dear un-lucky urchin is found. [Bless me the large looking glass, with the curtain [undrawn—well, it may e'en remain so—for we cannot be gay till the tru-[ant comes back.] *(Sobbing.)* The sweet little, naughty, rosy-cheek'd rogue! how I will whip him when he comes home.          *(Exit Ninon)*

*During the above the Demon is seen at the window watching, and disappears.*

AGA. Frankenstein! what a singular fatality is attached to you—with wealth and friends, doomed to be miserable!—This mystery!—I feel a heavy foreboding of mischance! a presentiment of evil pervades my mind. I may regret the day that I have again met Frankenstein[101]—I may rue the hour that I left our humble hut.          *(Exit Agatha to Room)*

*Afterwards, enter Frankenstein, reflecting—two pistols in his belt.*

FRANK. One sudden and desolating change has taken place—the fangs of remorse tear my bosom and will not forgo their hold!—pursue the

99. Dick's version has "fine." 100. Dick's version has "the." 101. Dick's version has "I may regret the day that I have given my affection to Frankenstein."

Demon![102] One might as well attempt to overtake the winds, or confine a mountain torrent. My poor Brother—I—I am thy murderer—the author of unalterable evils. [I live in momentary fear lest the monster I have cre-[ated should still commit some signal crime which by its enormity will [almost efface the recollection of the past.] There is scope for fear, so long as anything I love remains. *(Goes to door.)* Agatha! she reclines sleeping on yon sofa [—yesternight's fatigue.]

*Music.—The Demon during the above soliloquy reappears on the balcony of the window—and while Frankenstein is looking in at the door, the Demon creeps in at the window, crouching beneath the table, unseen.*

Sleep on, sweet innocence! I dare not leave you; I will stay and guard your slumber, or the remorseless Demon[103] will snatch your breath away.

*Music.—Frankenstein takes out a pistol and primes it—lays it on the table.*[104]

The wretch ev'n now may be haunting the room—let me search around.

*[Searches—The Demon eludes him—Frankenstein goes to the curtain which covers [the glass.*

*[This Drapery which covers the glass may conceal the monster.*

*[Frankenstein feels the drapery fearfully with the point of the sword—while Fran-[kenstein is thus employed—Demon creeps along the floor into Agatha's room—*

*[Frankenstein draws the curtain—Agatha's door is reflected in the glass.]*[105]

"Oh," Agatha! would that I had banished myself for ever from my native country, and wandered a friendless outcast over the earth, "rather" than I had again met you—perhaps to bring you in the grasp of my fiendish adversary—perhaps to—[106] *(A piercing scream.)*—My blood curdles! that shriek! Ah! What do I behold!

*In the large glass—Agatha appears on her knees with a veil over her head.—The Demon with his hand on her throat—she falls—the Demon disappears—after tearing a locket from Agatha's neck.*

My last, last hope! *(Rushes into room.)*

---

102. Dick's version has "wretch!" 103. Dick's version has "fiend." 104. In the Larpent version, he has pistols; in Dick's version, he keeps the pistol in his hand. 105. Dick's version drops the business with the glass:

*Music.—Frankenstein fearfully examines each avenue, advancing.—The Monster, unperceived by him, follows his footsteps, making an ineffectual attempt occasionally to gain his loaded pistol. Frankenstein leads on, looking in at door, passes behind table, when the Monster falls flat before table, still unseen by Frankenstein, who then places the loaded pistol on table, and turns to close the folding large window. While Frankenstein has his back turned, the monster snatches up the pistol, hugs it, and escapes into door. Frankenstein having closed the window comes forward.*

106. Dick's version ends the scene differently:

*Pistol-shot heard, and a piercing shriek.*

FRANK. —My blood curdles! *(Goes to door.)* Ah! what do I behold? My last, last hope! *Music.—He rushes off into door.*

*The figure of Frankenstein appears in the glass, kneeling over the body of Agatha. The Demon crosses by the window in a boat with great swiftness—exulting.*

SCENE IV *An Ante-chamber in Belrive.*

*Enter Elizabeth, hastily, meeting Ninon.—Music ceases.*

ELIZ. Whence is this fresh alarm?

NIN. I know not madam. Oh, wretched day for poor Ninon! Mr. Frankenstein is stark mad; he ran but out this instant, jumped into his boat, and rowed off rapidly.

*Enter Fritz, alarmed.*

FRITZ. Oh, "oh," oh!—I've seen it—seen it again! The great monster,[107] it got out of one of our windows and scudded off in a boat, and there's Mr. Frankenstein got another boat, and is going after the great creature like lightning.

ELIZ. Where—where are our friends?

FRITZ. Mr. Clerval and Mr. Felix have followed Mr. Frankenstein.[108]

SAFIE. *(Without.)* Help! ah, help!

*Enter Safie hastily, throws herself into the arms of Elizabeth.*

SAFIE. Ah Madam! Agatha, my sister—the gentle Agatha—I fear, is no more!

OMNES. Agatha!

ELIZ. Gracious Heaven! what horrible destiny hangs over us?

SAFIE. Stretched on the ground she lies! [a livid mark on her neck!] Ah! Elizabeth, the spark of life may yet not be extinct.

ELIZ. Hasten—hasten to the room.[109]

*Hurried Music.*

*(Exeunt hastily)*

SCENE V *Wild Border of the Lake. At the extremity of the stage, a lofty overhanging mountain of snow.*

*Music.—All the Gipsies discovered in various groups. A pistol shot is heard. The Gipsies start up alarmed. A second pistol is fired nearer. The Demon rushes on with the locket worn by Agatha, during the piece. The Gipsies scream out and fly in all directions. Hammerpan is on the point of escaping, when the Demon seizes him,*

---

107. Dick's version has "creature." 108. Dick's version has Fritz answer, "Oh, I don't know; there's Mr. Frankenstein gone after the great creature, Mr. Clerval and Mr. Felix have gone after Mr. Frankenstein, and I'm going after them all. *(Runs off.)*" 109. Dick's version has "apartment."

*and Hammerpan falls down on being dragged back. The Demon points off, to intimate that Frankenstein is approaching, throws down the locket, commands the gipsy, Hammerpan, to show it to Frankenstein—the Demon threatens him, and rushing up the mountain, climbs, and disappears. Enter Frankenstein, with two loaded pistols and a musket "unloaded."*[110] *At the same time Hammerpan rises and gets near 1st wing.*

FRANK. In vain do I pursue the wretch, in vain have I fired on him. *"(Throws his gun from him.)"* He eludes the bullet. Say, fellow, have you seen aught pass here?

HAM. The giant creature, who aroused us in the forest, rushed upon me but this instant, and pointing to the path by which you came, intimated that I should give you this. *(Presents locket to Frankenstein.)*

FRANK. 'Tis Agatha's—the murdered Agatha! Malicious fiend! it will joy you to know that my lacerated heart bleeds afresh. Revenge shall henceforth be the devouring and only passion of my soul. I have but one resource—I devote myself either in my life or death to the destruction of the Demon. Agatha! William! you shall be avenged!

HAM. See yonder *(Points.)* the monster climbs the snow.

FRANK. Then this rencontre[111] shall terminate his detested life or mine. *Music.—Frankenstein draws his pistol—rushes off at back of stage.—The gipsies return at various entrances.—At the same time, enter Felix and Clerval with pistols, and Safie, Elizabeth, and Ninon following.—The Demon appears at the base of the mountain, Frankenstein pursuing.*

CLER. Behold our friend and his mysterious enemy.

FELIX. See—Frankenstein aims his musket at him—let us follow and assist him.[112] *(Is going up stage with Clerval.)*

HAM. Hold master! if the gun is fired, it will bring down a mountain of snow [on their heads.] Many an avalanche has fallen there.

[FELIX. He fires—]

*Music.—Frankenstein discharges his musket.*[113]*—The Demon and Frankenstein meet at the very extremity of the stage.—Frankenstein fires—the avalanche falls and annihilates the Demon and Frankenstein.—A heavy fall of snow succeeds.— Loud thunder heard, and all the characters form a picture as the curtain falls.*

110. The Larpent version does not indicate that the musket is unloaded, nor does it have Frankenstein throw it down during his next speech. He thus fires it once at the end of the play to create the avalanche. In Dick's version, he has only the pistols to fire at the end. 111. Recounter, an encounter between opposing forces, a battle. 112. Dick's version has "See—Frankestein overtakes him—let us follow and assist him." 113. In Dick's version, Frankenstein fires first one, then the other pistol.

# Acknowledgments

This project would never had taken the
shape it did without the support of Texas
A&M University's Interdisciplinary Group
for Historical Literary Study. The work of
the fellows and visiting scholars of the Interdisciplinary Group has been
a continuing source of intellectual stimulation and inspiration; the community that the Interdisciplinary Group creates was vital to my work. A
few members of the Group deserve special mention: Donald Dickson
helped with the most difficult annotations; Katherine O'Brien O'Keeffe
and Larry Reynolds, the guiding spirits behind the Group, provided valuable commentary on my work; Margaret Ezell, whose own work stands as
a model of historical literary scholarship, has been a help from the initial
research until the final revisions; Robert Newman and David Anderson
have provided ideas and friendly support. Others who have made generous offerings of their time and expertise include Robert Langbaum, Frederick Burwick, Gerald Gillespie, Timothy Moore, and Pat Phillippy. I
also want to thank the staff of Ohio University Press, in particular Holly
Panich and Helen Gawthrop.

Various librarians and their staffs helped make this collection possible.
I am indebted to the following institutions for permission to quote from
manuscripts held by them and for their helpful assistance: the Henry E.
Huntington Library, San Marino, California; the Department of Special
Collections, The University Library, University of California, Los Angeles; and the Manuscripts Department of the Bodleian Library, Oxford. I
want to give particular thanks to Patricia Maxwell-Scott for allowing me
to draw on the manuscript of Maturin's *Bertram* at Abbotsford and for
making my time there a real pleasure.

I also want to offer my thanks for the financial support provided by the
Henry E. Huntington Library through a Huntington/Exxon grant and by
the College of Liberal Arts, Texas A&M and its Dean Daniel Fallon
through a Summer Research Grant.

Finally, I want to thank my wife Amy, to whom this book is dedicated
with love, and my daughters Julia and Emma, my own Gothic monsters.